Ben Abernathy	Editor, Original Series
Kristy Quinn	Assistant Editor, Original Series
Kristy Quinn	Editor
Larry Berry	Art Director
Diane Nelson	President
Dan DiDio and Jim Lee	Co-Publishers
Geoff Johns	Chief Creative Officer
John Rood	Executive Vice President–Sales, Marketing and Business Development
Patrick Caldon	Executive Vice President–Finance and Administration
Amy Genkins	Senior VP–Business and Legal Affairs
Steve Rotterdam	Senior VP–Sales and Marketing
John Cunningham	VP–Marketing
Terri Cunningham	VP–Managing Editor
Alison Gill	VP–Manufacturing
David Hyde	VP–Publicity
Hank Kanalz	VP–General Manager, WildStorm
Sue Pohja	VP–Book Trade Sales
Alysse Soll	VP–Advertising and Custom Publishing
Bob Wayne	VP–Sales
Mark Chiarello	Art Director

SUSTAINABLE
FORESTRY
INITIATIVE

Certified Chain of Custody
Promoting Sustainable
Forest Management
www.sfiprogram.org

Fiber used in this product
line meets the sourcing
requirements of the
SFI program.

www.sfiprogram.org
NSF-SFICOC-C0001801.

EX MACHINA: RING OUT THE OLD. Published by WildStorm
Productions, an imprint of DC Comics. 888 Prospect St. #240,
La Jolla, CA 92037. Cover and compilation Copyright © 2010
Brian K. Vaughan and Tony Harris. All Rights Reserved. EX
MACHINA is ™ Brian K. Vaughan and Tony Harris. Originally
published in single magazine form as EX MACHINA #40-44 ©
2009 and EX MACHINA SPECIAL #4 © 2009 Brian K. Vaughan
and Tony Harris.

DC Comics, a Warner Bros. Entertainment Company.

ISBN: 978-1-4012-2694-7

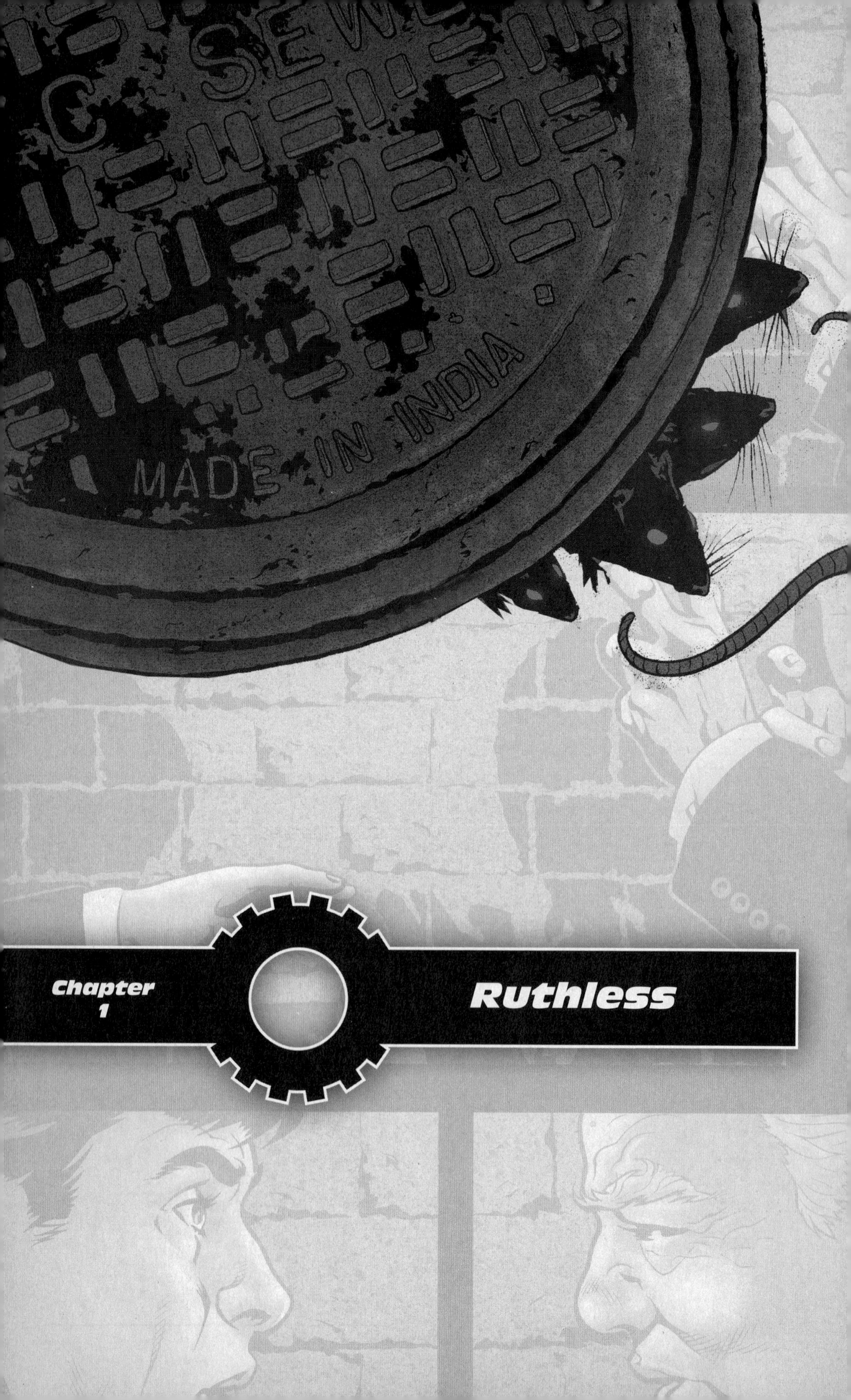
MADE IN INDIA

Chapter 1 Ruthless

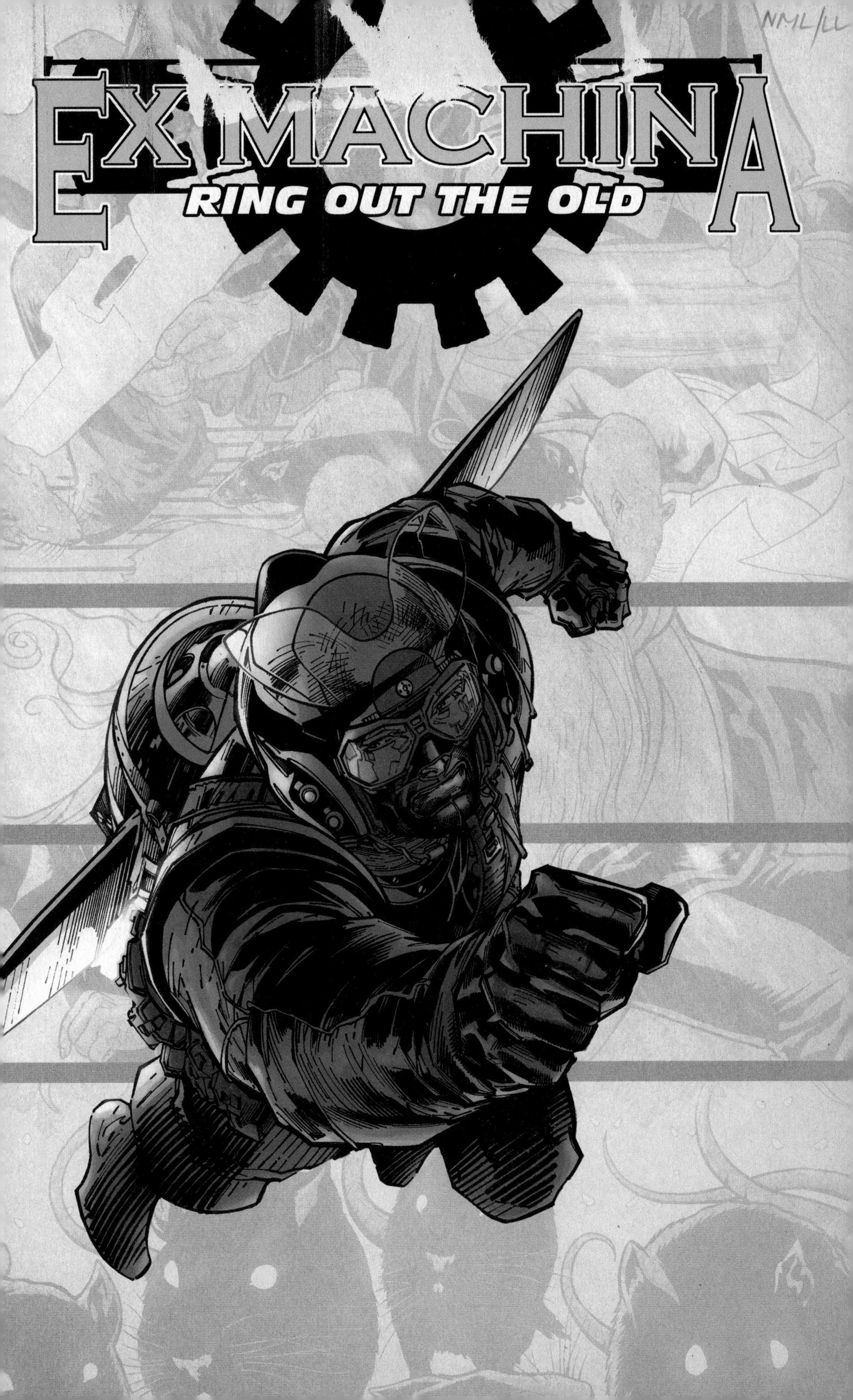
EX MACHINA
RING OUT THE OLD

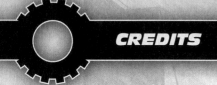

CREDITS

BRIAN K. VAUGHAN: WRITER
TONY HARRIS: PENCILS
JIM CLARK & TONY HARRIS: INKS
JOHN PAUL LEON: ART (GREEN)

THANKS TO GARTH ENNIS, JIM LEE & RICHARD FRIEND FOR THEIR CONTRIBUTIONS TO ISSUE #40

JD METTLER: COLORS
JARED K. FLETCHER: LETTERS

Ex Machina created by Vaughan and Harris
Cover by Harris & Mettler
Original series covers by Harris
Variant Cover to Green by John Paul Leon and Jonny Rench

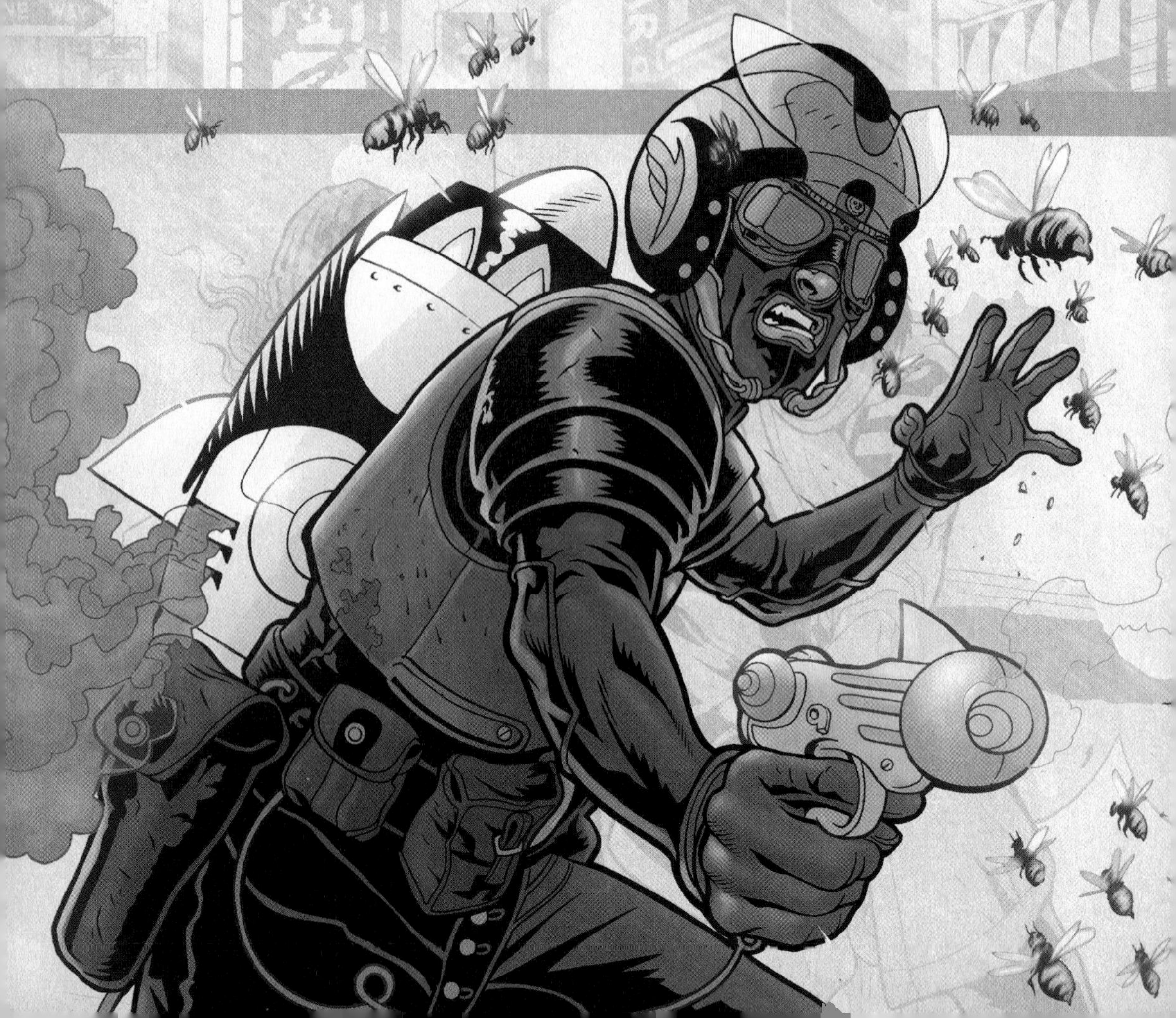

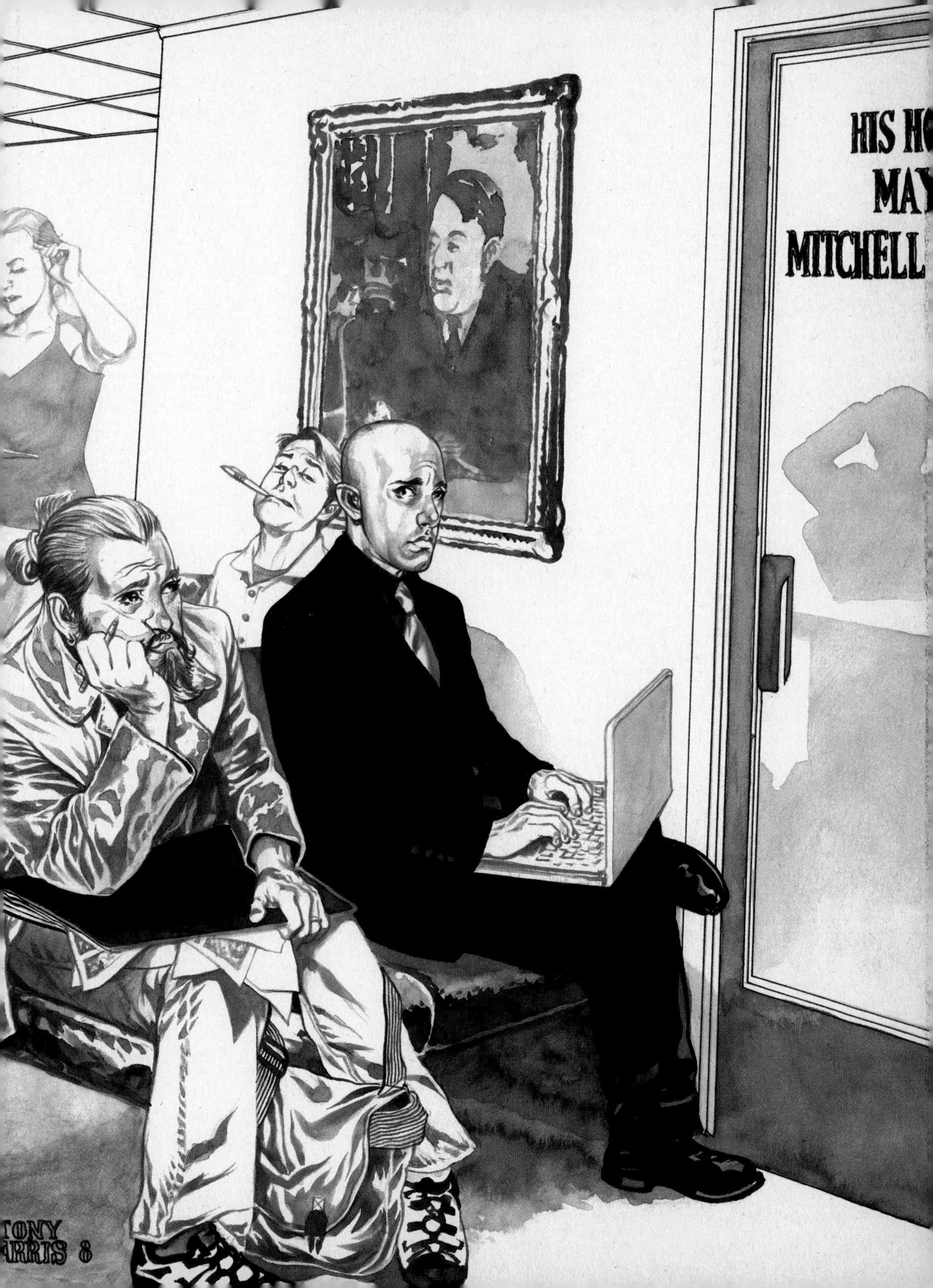
HIS HO
MAY
MITCHELL
TONY
ARRIS 8

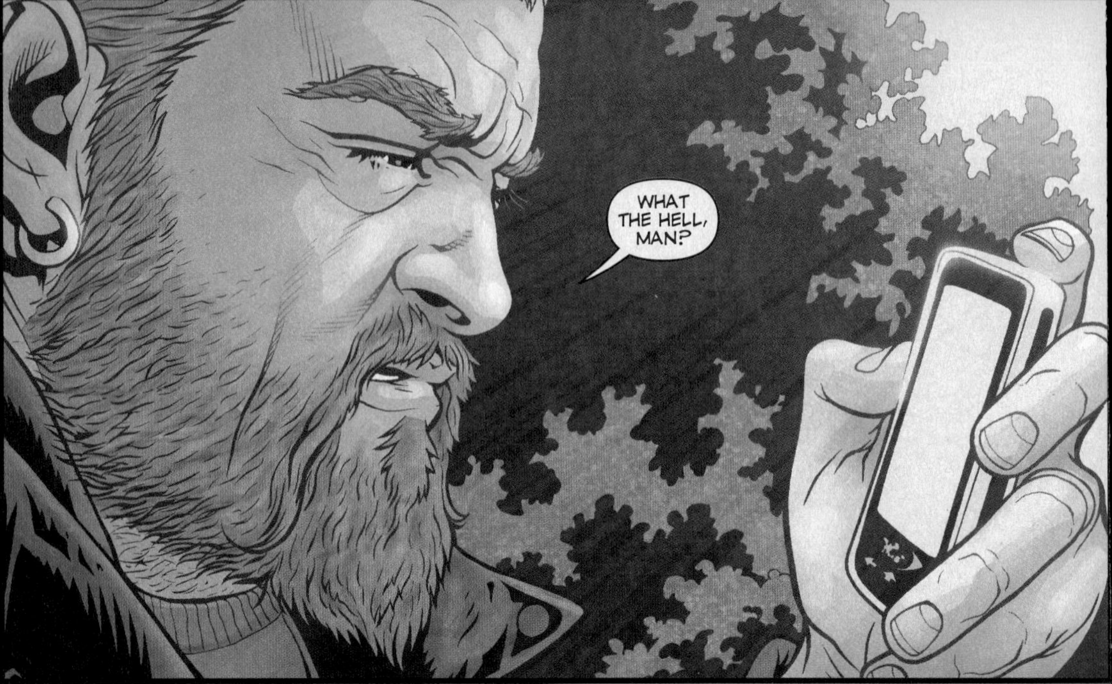
WHAT THE HELL, MAN?

WEDNESDAY, OCTOBER 6, 2004

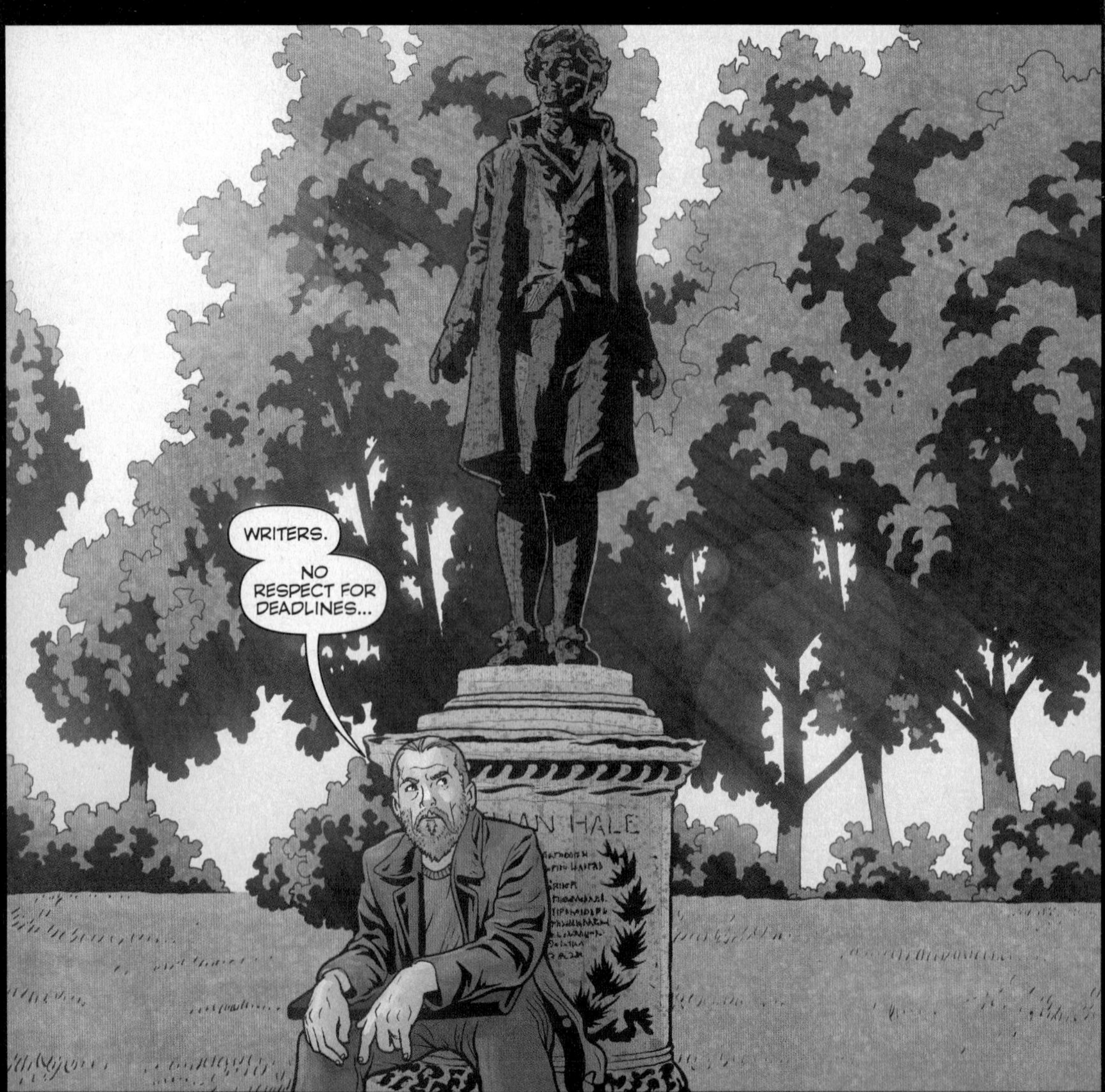
WRITERS.
NO RESPECT FOR DEADLINES...

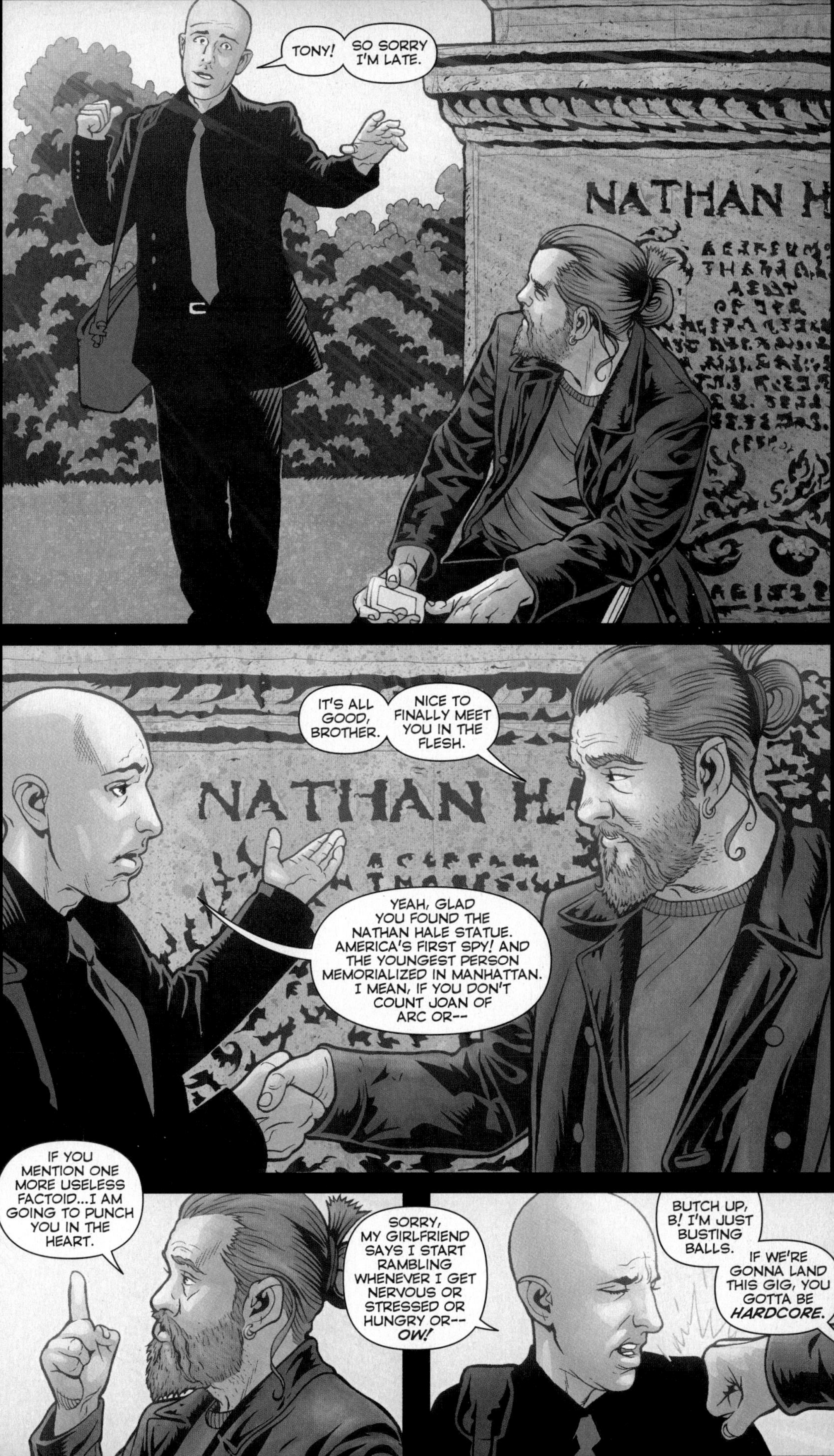
TONY!
SO SORRY I'M LATE.
NATHAN H
IT'S ALL GOOD, BROTHER.
NICE TO FINALLY MEET YOU IN THE FLESH.
NATHAN H
YEAH, GLAD YOU FOUND THE NATHAN HALE STATUE. AMERICA'S FIRST SPY! AND THE YOUNGEST PERSON MEMORIALIZED IN MANHATTAN. I MEAN, IF YOU DON'T COUNT JOAN OF ARC OR--
IF YOU MENTION ONE MORE USELESS FACTOID...I AM GOING TO PUNCH YOU IN THE HEART.
SORRY, MY GIRLFRIEND SAYS I START RAMBLING WHENEVER I GET NERVOUS OR STRESSED OR HUNGRY OR-- OW!
BUTCH UP, B! I'M JUST BUSTING BALLS.
IF WE'RE GONNA LAND THIS GIG, YOU GOTTA BE HARDCORE.

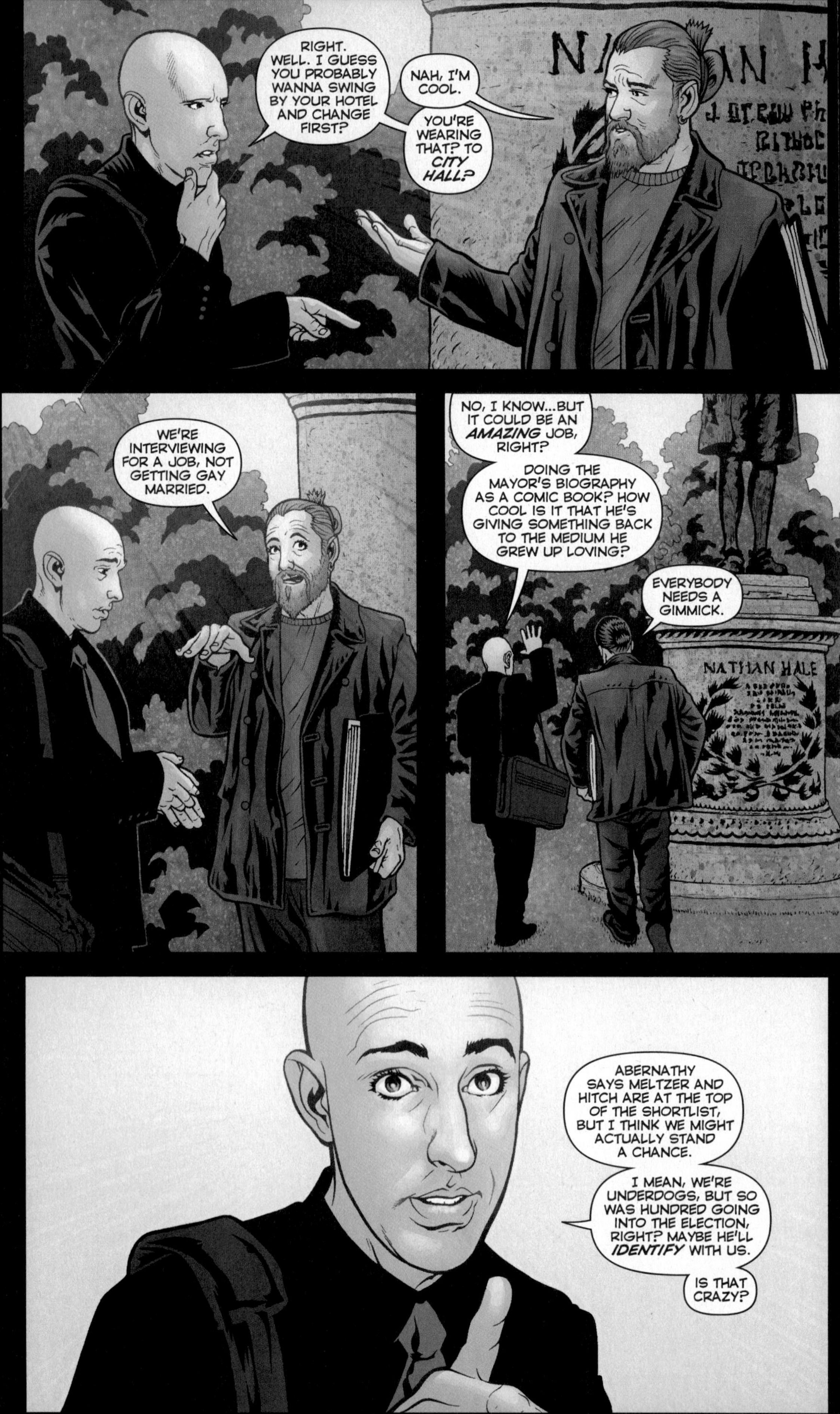
RIGHT. WELL. I GUESS YOU PROBABLY WANNA SWING BY YOUR HOTEL AND CHANGE FIRST?
NAH, I'M COOL.
YOU'RE WEARING THAT? TO CITY HALL?
WE'RE INTERVIEWING FOR A JOB, NOT GETTING GAY MARRIED.
NO, I KNOW...BUT IT COULD BE AN AMAZING JOB, RIGHT?
DOING THE MAYOR'S BIOGRAPHY AS A COMIC BOOK? HOW COOL IS IT THAT HE'S GIVING SOMETHING BACK TO THE MEDIUM HE GREW UP LOVING?
EVERYBODY NEEDS A GIMMICK.
NATHAN HALE
ABERNATHY SAYS MELTZER AND HITCH ARE AT THE TOP OF THE SHORTLIST, BUT I THINK WE MIGHT ACTUALLY STAND A CHANCE.
I MEAN, WE'RE UNDERDOGS, BUT SO WAS HUNDRED GOING INTO THE ELECTION, RIGHT? MAYBE HE'LL IDENTIFY WITH US.
IS THAT CRAZY?

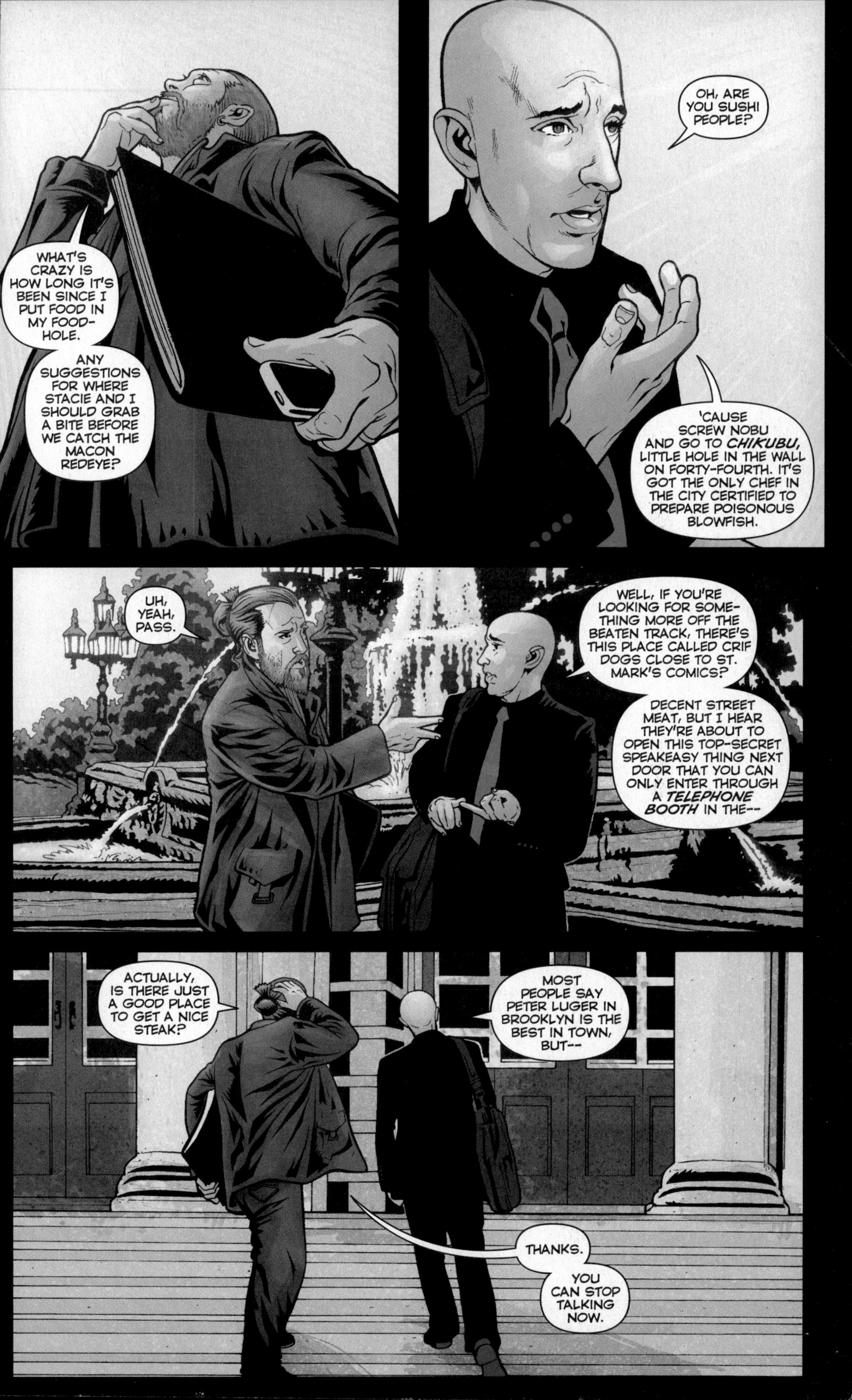
WHAT'S CRAZY IS HOW LONG IT'S BEEN SINCE I PUT FOOD IN MY FOOD-HOLE.
ANY SUGGESTIONS FOR WHERE STACIE AND I SHOULD GRAB A BITE BEFORE WE CATCH THE MACON REDEYE?
OH, ARE YOU SUSHI PEOPLE?
'CAUSE SCREW NOBU AND GO TO CHIKUBU, LITTLE HOLE IN THE WALL ON FORTY-FOURTH. IT'S GOT THE ONLY CHEF IN THE CITY CERTIFIED TO PREPARE POISONOUS BLOWFISH.
UH, YEAH, PASS.
WELL, IF YOU'RE LOOKING FOR SOMETHING MORE OFF THE BEATEN TRACK, THERE'S THIS PLACE CALLED CRIF DOGS CLOSE TO ST. MARK'S COMICS?
DECENT STREET MEAT, BUT I HEAR THEY'RE ABOUT TO OPEN THIS TOP-SECRET SPEAKEASY THING NEXT DOOR THAT YOU CAN ONLY ENTER THROUGH A TELEPHONE BOOTH IN THE--
ACTUALLY, IS THERE JUST A GOOD PLACE TO GET A NICE STEAK?
MOST PEOPLE SAY PETER LUGER IN BROOKLYN IS THE BEST IN TOWN, BUT--
THANKS.
YOU CAN STOP TALKING NOW.

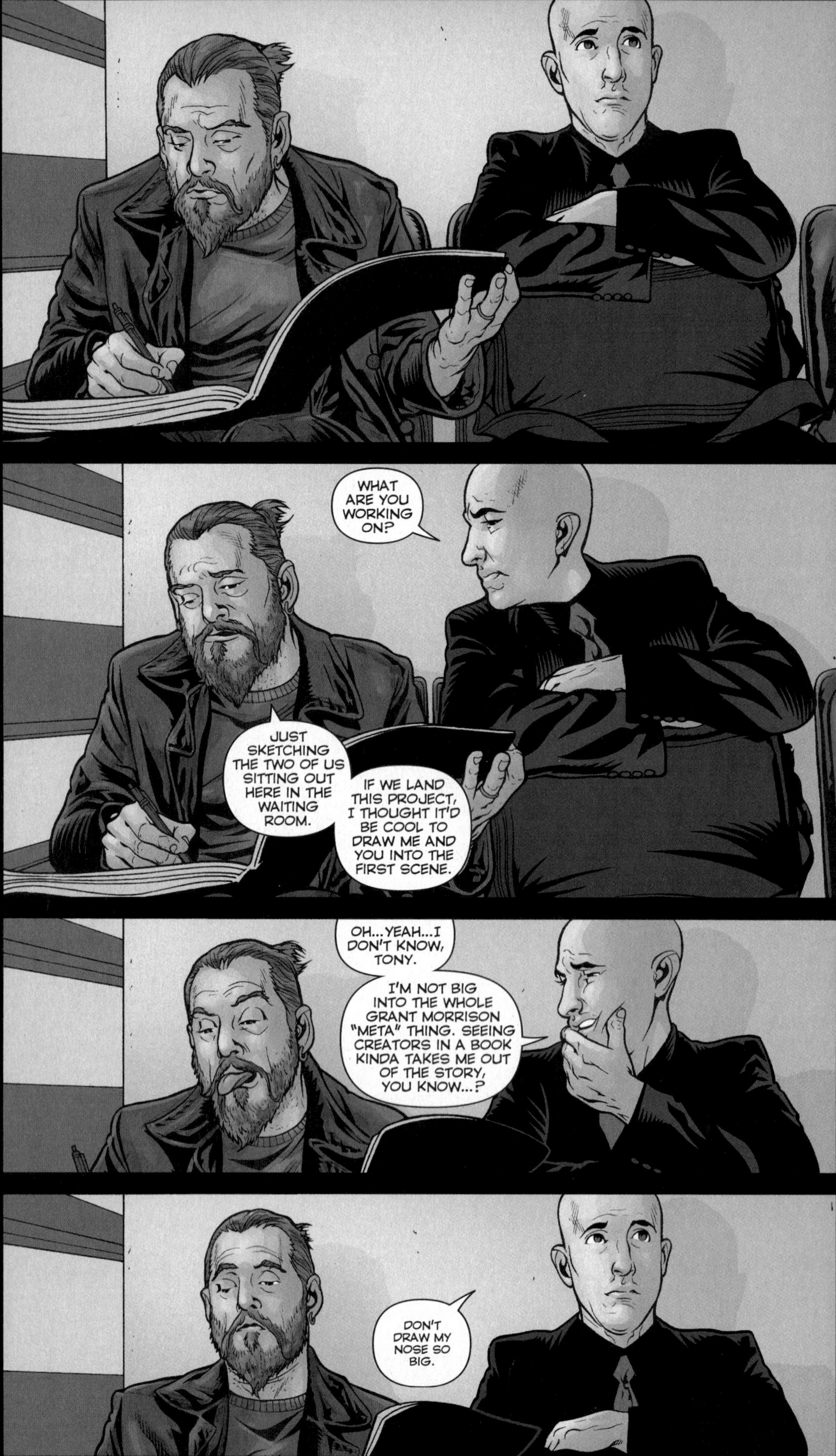
WHAT ARE YOU WORKING ON?
JUST SKETCHING THE TWO OF US SITTING OUT HERE IN THE WAITING ROOM.
IF WE LAND THIS PROJECT, I THOUGHT IT'D BE COOL TO DRAW ME AND YOU INTO THE FIRST SCENE.
OH...YEAH...I DON'T KNOW, TONY.
I'M NOT BIG INTO THE WHOLE GRANT MORRISON "META" THING. SEEING CREATORS IN A BOOK KINDA TAKES ME OUT OF THE STORY, YOU KNOW...?
DON'T DRAW MY NOSE SO BIG.

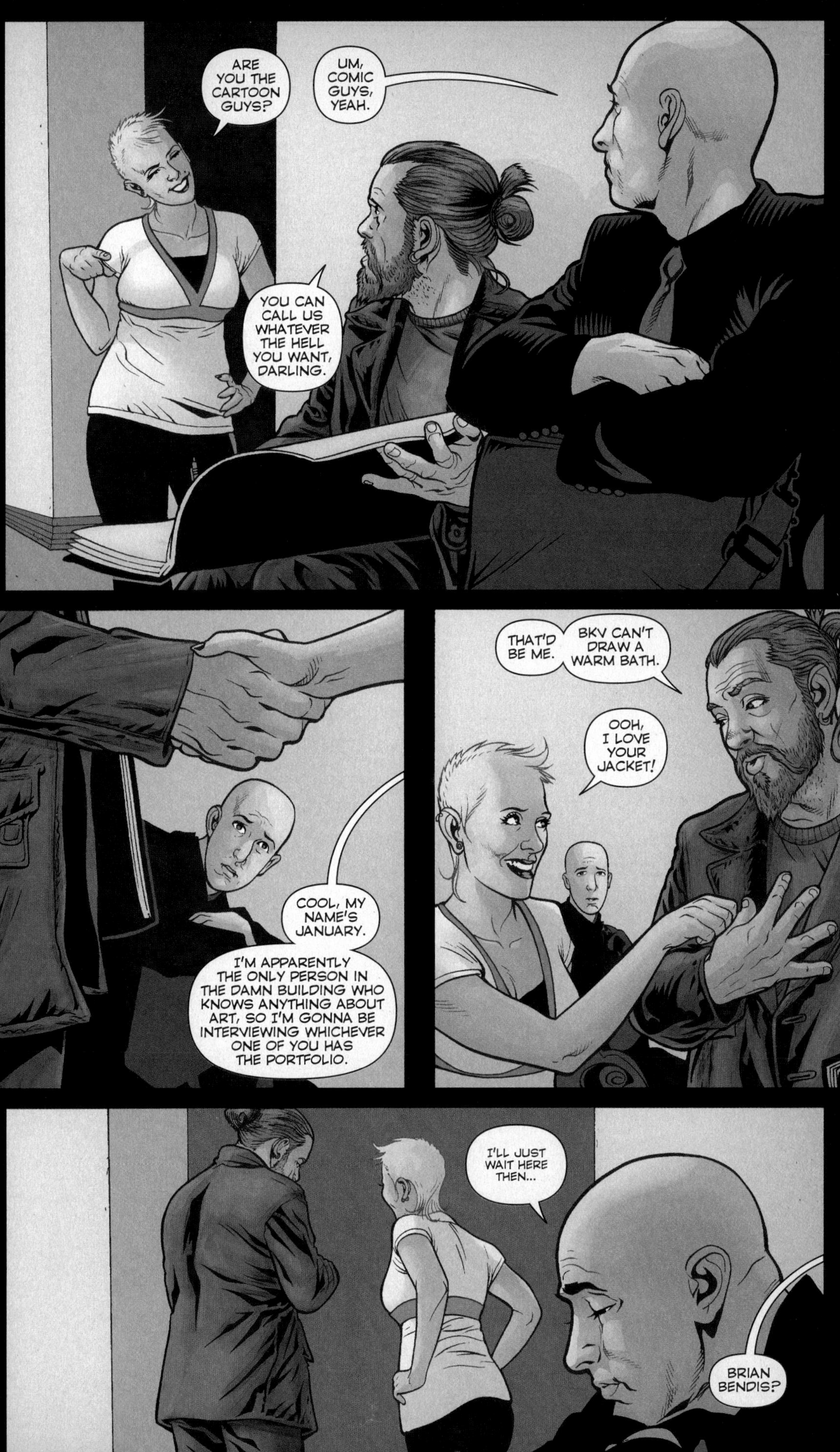

ARE YOU THE CARTOON GUYS?
UM, COMIC GUYS, YEAH.
YOU CAN CALL US WHATEVER THE HELL YOU WANT, DARLING.
COOL, MY NAME'S JANUARY.
I'M APPARENTLY THE ONLY PERSON IN THE DAMN BUILDING WHO KNOWS ANYTHING ABOUT ART, SO I'M GONNA BE INTERVIEWING WHICHEVER ONE OF YOU HAS THE PORTFOLIO.
THAT'D BE ME.
BKV CAN'T DRAW A WARM BATH.
OOH, I LOVE YOUR JACKET!
I'LL JUST WAIT HERE THEN...
BRIAN BENDIS?

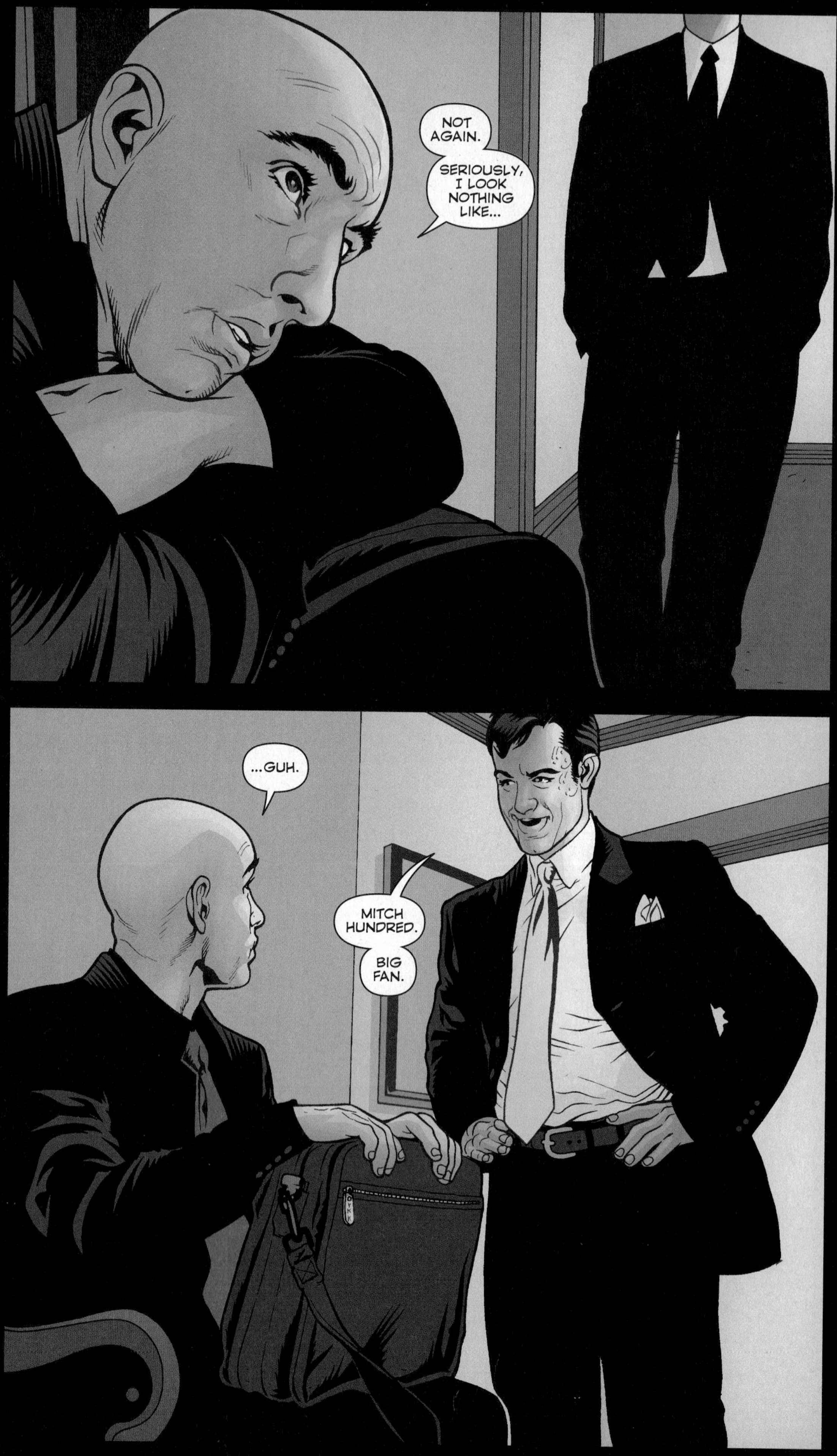
NOT AGAIN.
SERIOUSLY, I LOOK NOTHING LIKE...
...GUH.
MITCH HUNDRED.
BIG FAN.

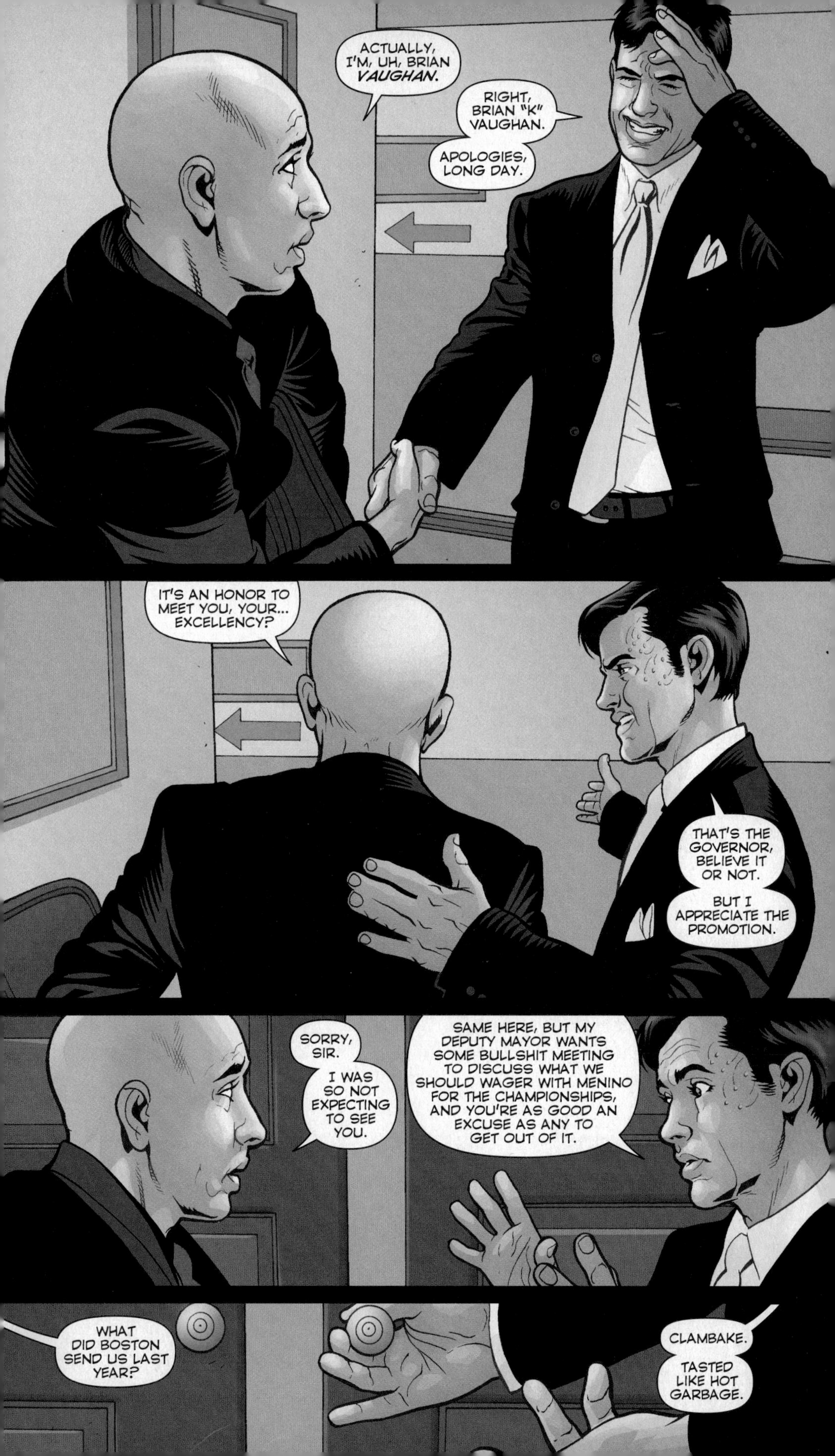
ACTUALLY, I'M, UH, BRIAN *VAUGHAN.*
RIGHT, BRIAN "K" VAUGHAN.
APOLOGIES, LONG DAY.
IT'S AN HONOR TO MEET YOU, YOUR... EXCELLENCY?
THAT'S THE GOVERNOR, BELIEVE IT OR NOT.
BUT I APPRECIATE THE PROMOTION.
SORRY, SIR.
I WAS SO NOT EXPECTING TO SEE YOU.
SAME HERE, BUT MY DEPUTY MAYOR WANTS SOME BULLSHIT MEETING TO DISCUSS WHAT WE SHOULD WAGER WITH MENINO FOR THE CHAMPIONSHIPS, AND YOU'RE AS GOOD AN EXCUSE AS ANY TO GET OUT OF IT.
WHAT DID BOSTON SEND US LAST YEAR?
CLAMBAKE.
TASTED LIKE HOT GARBAGE.

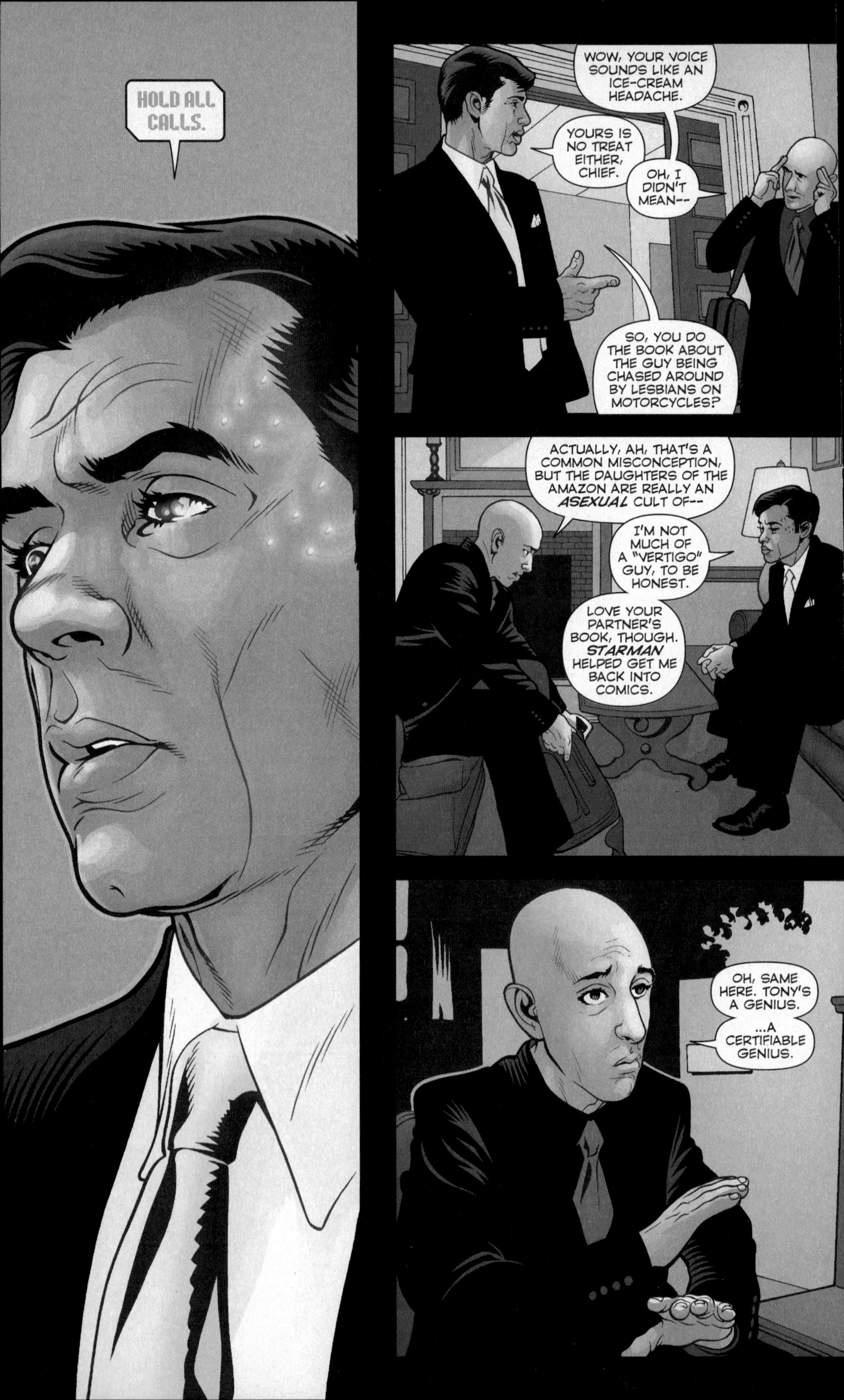
HOLD ALL CALLS.
WOW, YOUR VOICE SOUNDS LIKE AN ICE-CREAM HEADACHE.
YOURS IS NO TREAT EITHER, CHIEF.
OH, I DIDN'T MEAN--
SO, YOU DO THE BOOK ABOUT THE GUY BEING CHASED AROUND BY LESBIANS ON MOTORCYCLES?
ACTUALLY, AH, THAT'S A COMMON MISCONCEPTION, BUT THE DAUGHTERS OF THE AMAZON ARE REALLY AN ASEXUAL CULT OF--
I'M NOT MUCH OF A "VERTIGO" GUY, TO BE HONEST.
LOVE YOUR PARTNER'S BOOK, THOUGH. STARMAN HELPED GET ME BACK INTO COMICS.
OH, SAME HERE. TONY'S A GENIUS.
...A CERTIFIABLE GENIUS.

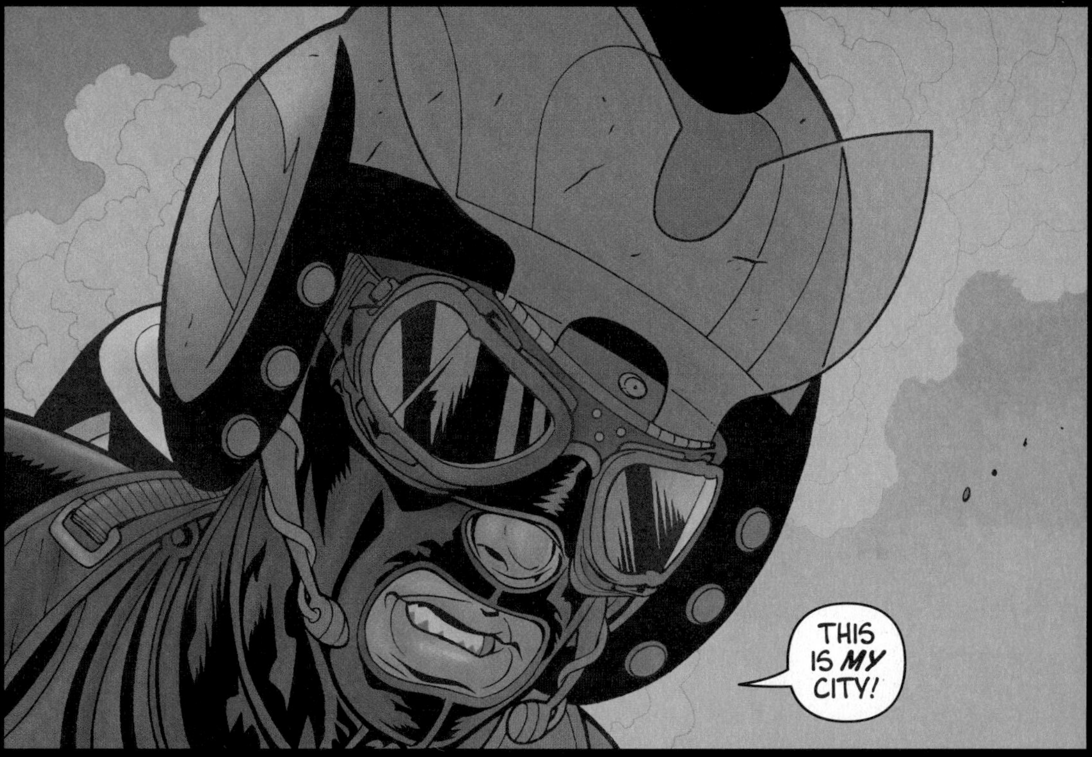
THIS IS MY CITY!

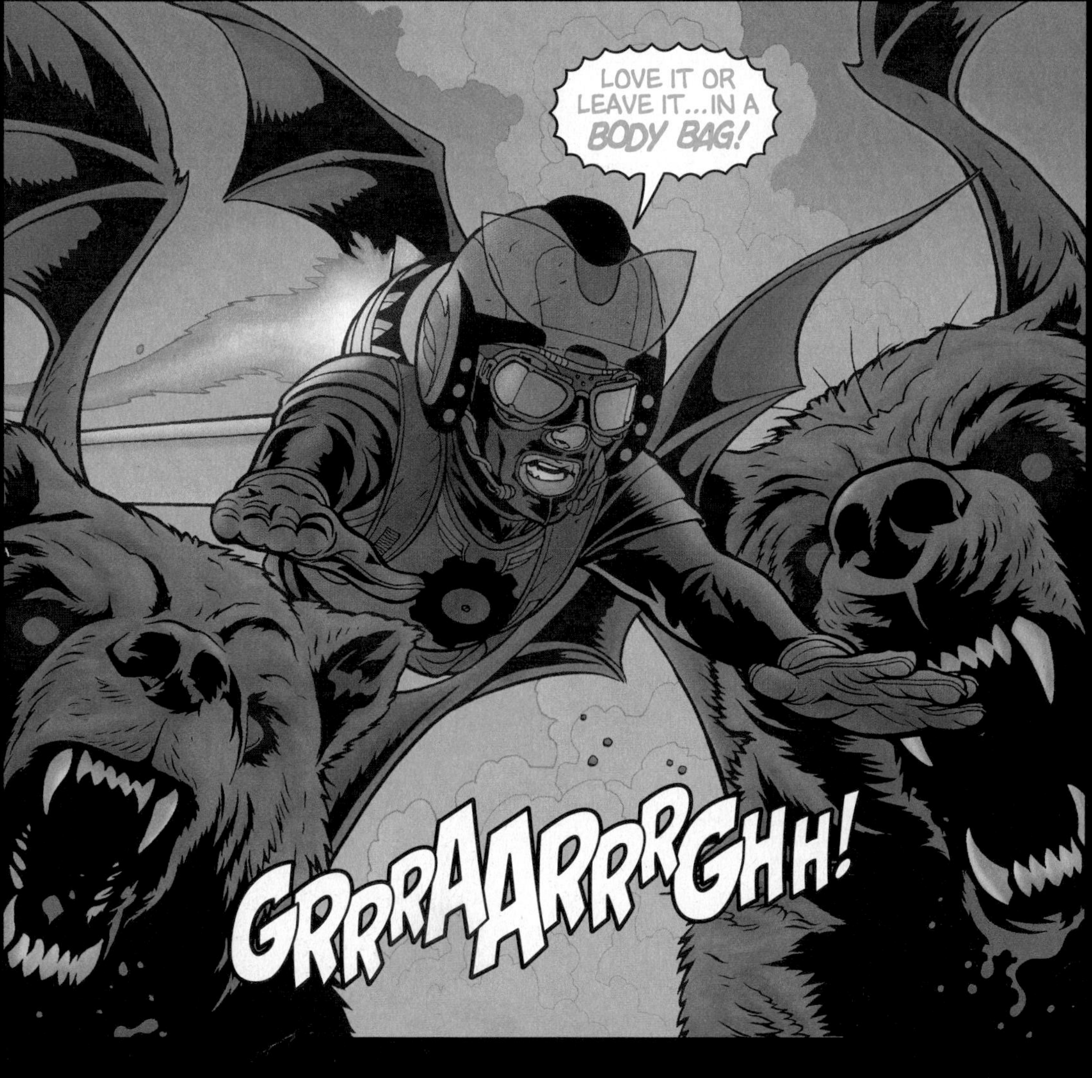
LOVE IT OR LEAVE IT...IN A BODY BAG!
GRRRAARRRGHH!

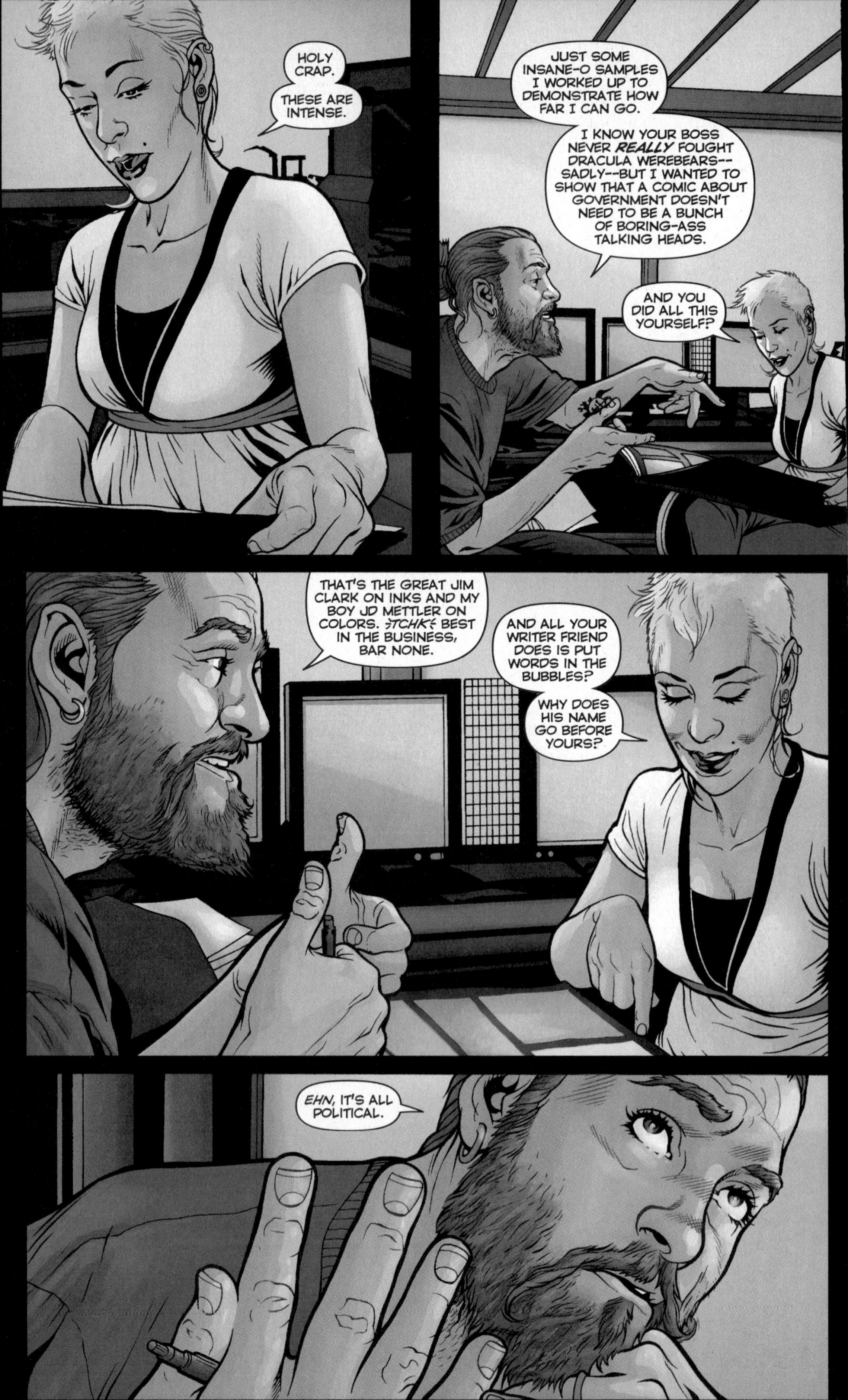
HOLY CRAP.
THESE ARE INTENSE.
JUST SOME INSANE-O SAMPLES I WORKED UP TO DEMONSTRATE HOW FAR I CAN GO.
I KNOW YOUR BOSS NEVER *REALLY* FOUGHT DRACULA WEREBEARS--SADLY--BUT I WANTED TO SHOW THAT A COMIC ABOUT GOVERNMENT DOESN'T NEED TO BE A BUNCH OF BORING-ASS TALKING HEADS.
AND YOU DID ALL THIS YOURSELF?
THAT'S THE GREAT JIM CLARK ON INKS AND MY BOY JD METTLER ON COLORS. *TCHK* BEST IN THE BUSINESS, BAR NONE.
AND ALL YOUR WRITER FRIEND DOES IS PUT WORDS IN THE BUBBLES?
WHY DOES HIS NAME GO BEFORE YOURS?
EHN, IT'S ALL POLITICAL.

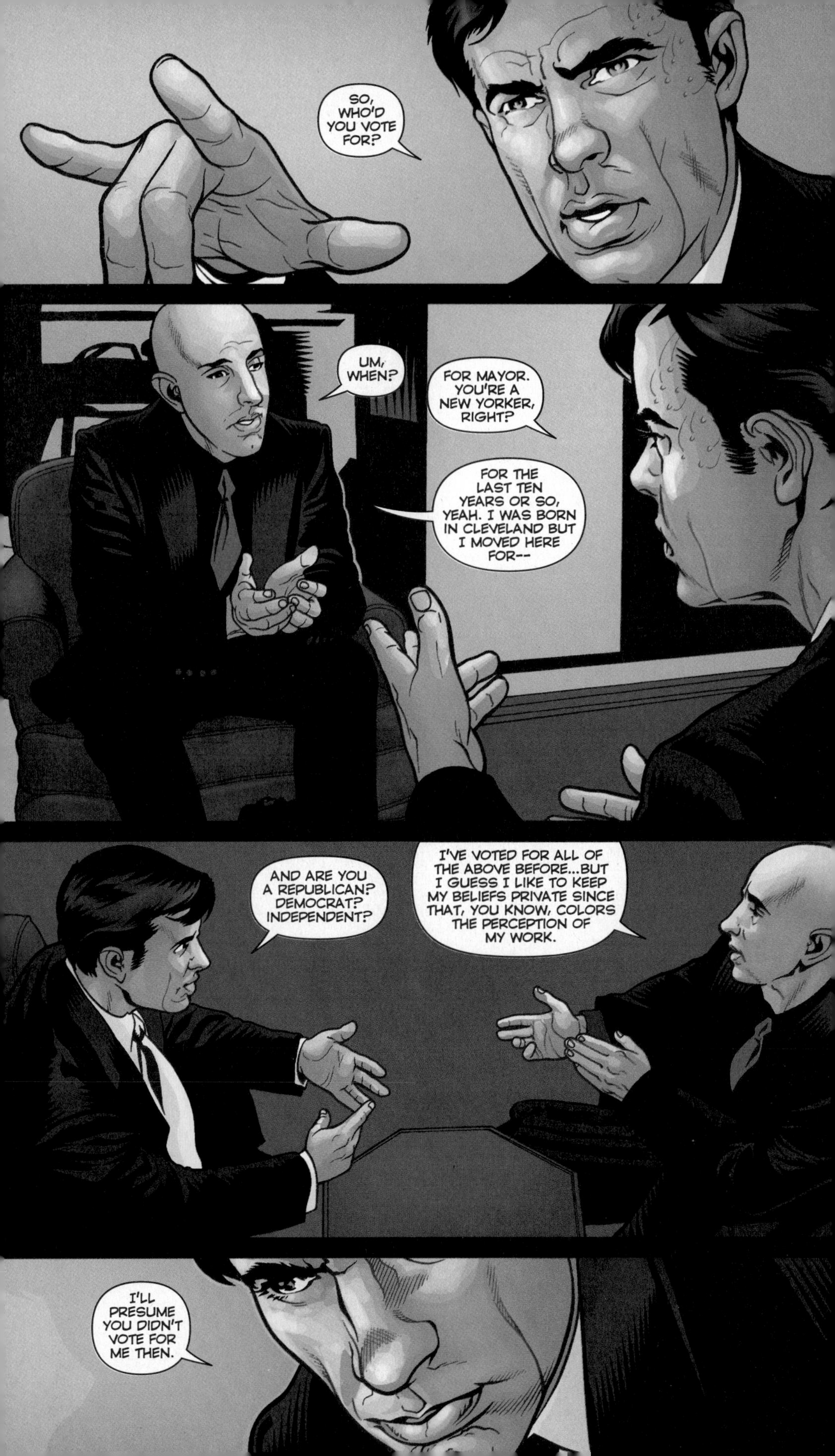
SO, WHO'D YOU VOTE FOR?
UM, WHEN?
FOR MAYOR. YOU'RE A NEW YORKER, RIGHT?
FOR THE LAST TEN YEARS OR SO, YEAH. I WAS BORN IN CLEVELAND BUT I MOVED HERE FOR--
AND ARE YOU A REPUBLICAN? DEMOCRAT? INDEPENDENT?
I'VE VOTED FOR ALL OF THE ABOVE BEFORE...BUT I GUESS I LIKE TO KEEP MY BELIEFS PRIVATE SINCE THAT, YOU KNOW, COLORS THE PERCEPTION OF MY WORK.
I'LL PRESUME YOU DIDN'T VOTE FOR ME THEN.

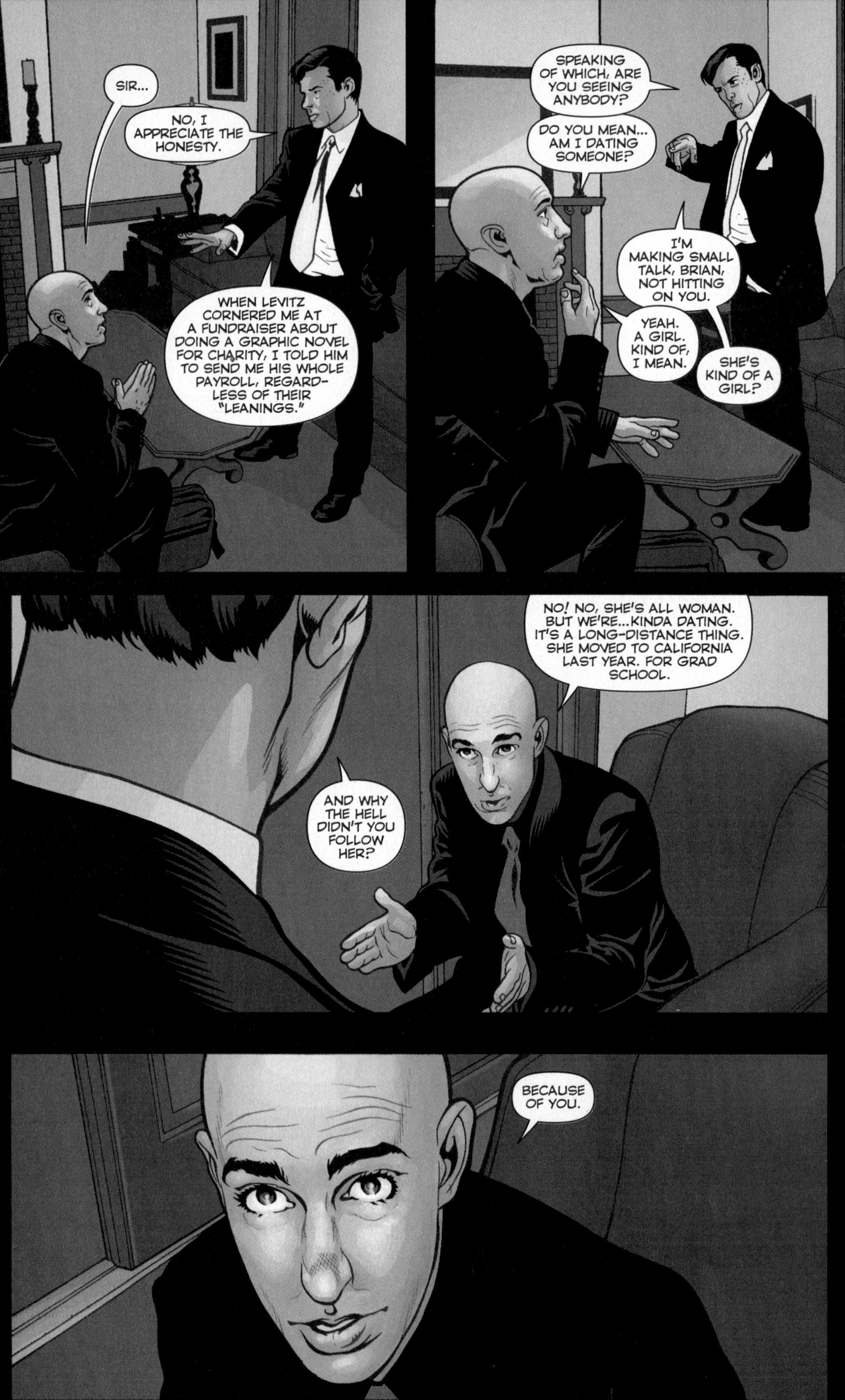
SIR...
NO, I APPRECIATE THE HONESTY.
WHEN LEVITZ CORNERED ME AT A FUNDRAISER ABOUT DOING A GRAPHIC NOVEL FOR CHARITY, I TOLD HIM TO SEND ME HIS WHOLE PAYROLL, REGARDLESS OF THEIR "LEANINGS."
SPEAKING OF WHICH, ARE YOU SEEING ANYBODY?
DO YOU MEAN... AM I DATING SOMEONE?
I'M MAKING SMALL TALK, BRIAN, NOT HITTING ON YOU.
YEAH. A GIRL. KIND OF, I MEAN.
SHE'S KIND OF A GIRL?
NO! NO, SHE'S ALL WOMAN. BUT WE'RE...KINDA DATING. IT'S A LONG-DISTANCE THING. SHE MOVED TO CALIFORNIA LAST YEAR. FOR GRAD SCHOOL.
AND WHY THE HELL DIDN'T YOU FOLLOW HER?
BECAUSE OF YOU.

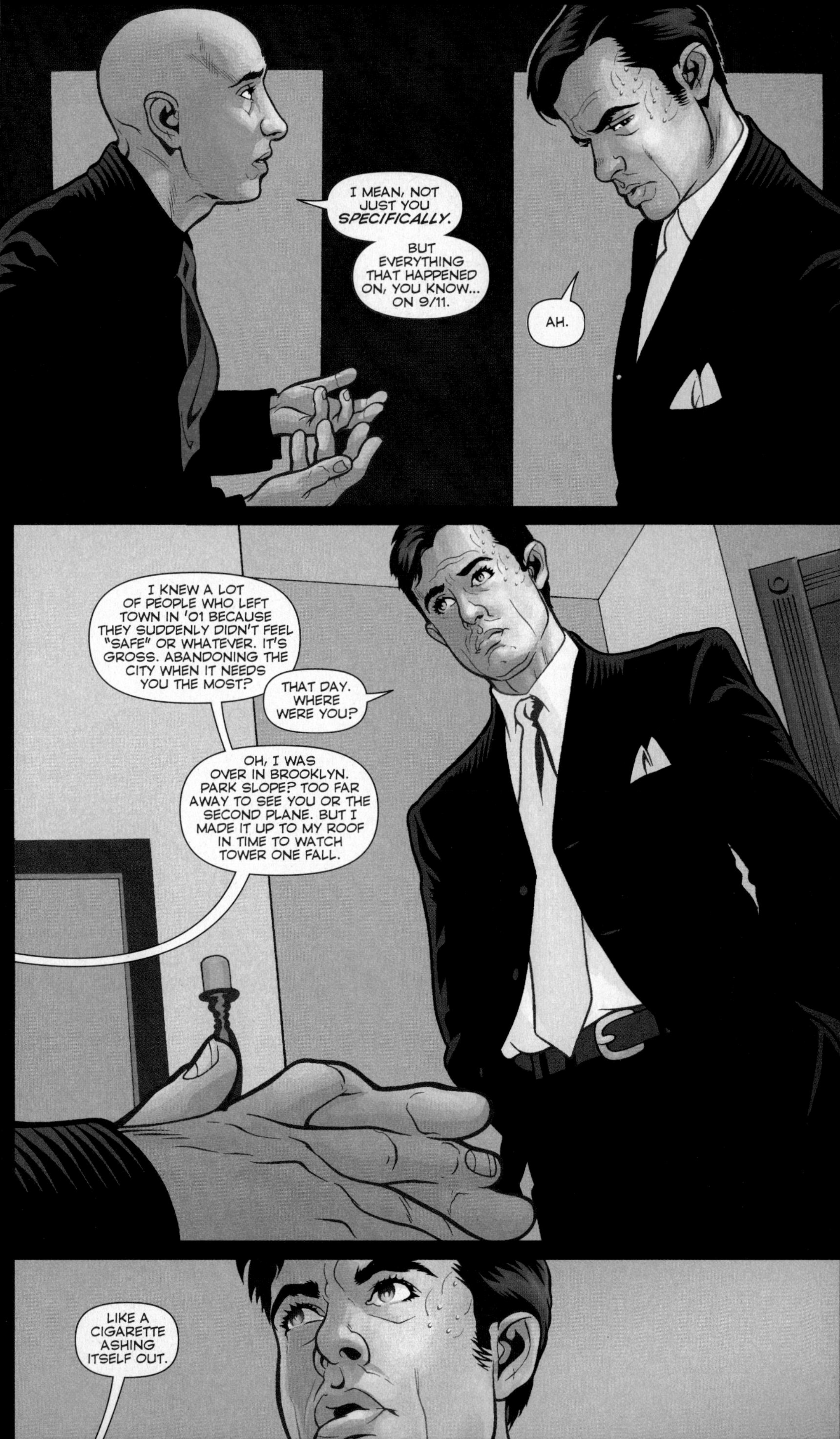
I MEAN, NOT JUST YOU *SPECIFICALLY*.
BUT EVERYTHING THAT HAPPENED ON, YOU KNOW... ON 9/11.
AH.
I KNEW A LOT OF PEOPLE WHO LEFT TOWN IN '01 BECAUSE THEY SUDDENLY DIDN'T FEEL "SAFE" OR WHATEVER. IT'S GROSS. ABANDONING THE CITY WHEN IT NEEDS YOU THE MOST?
THAT DAY. WHERE WERE YOU?
OH, I WAS OVER IN BROOKLYN. PARK SLOPE? TOO FAR AWAY TO SEE YOU OR THE SECOND PLANE. BUT I MADE IT UP TO MY ROOF IN TIME TO WATCH TOWER ONE FALL.
LIKE A CIGARETTE ASHING ITSELF OUT.

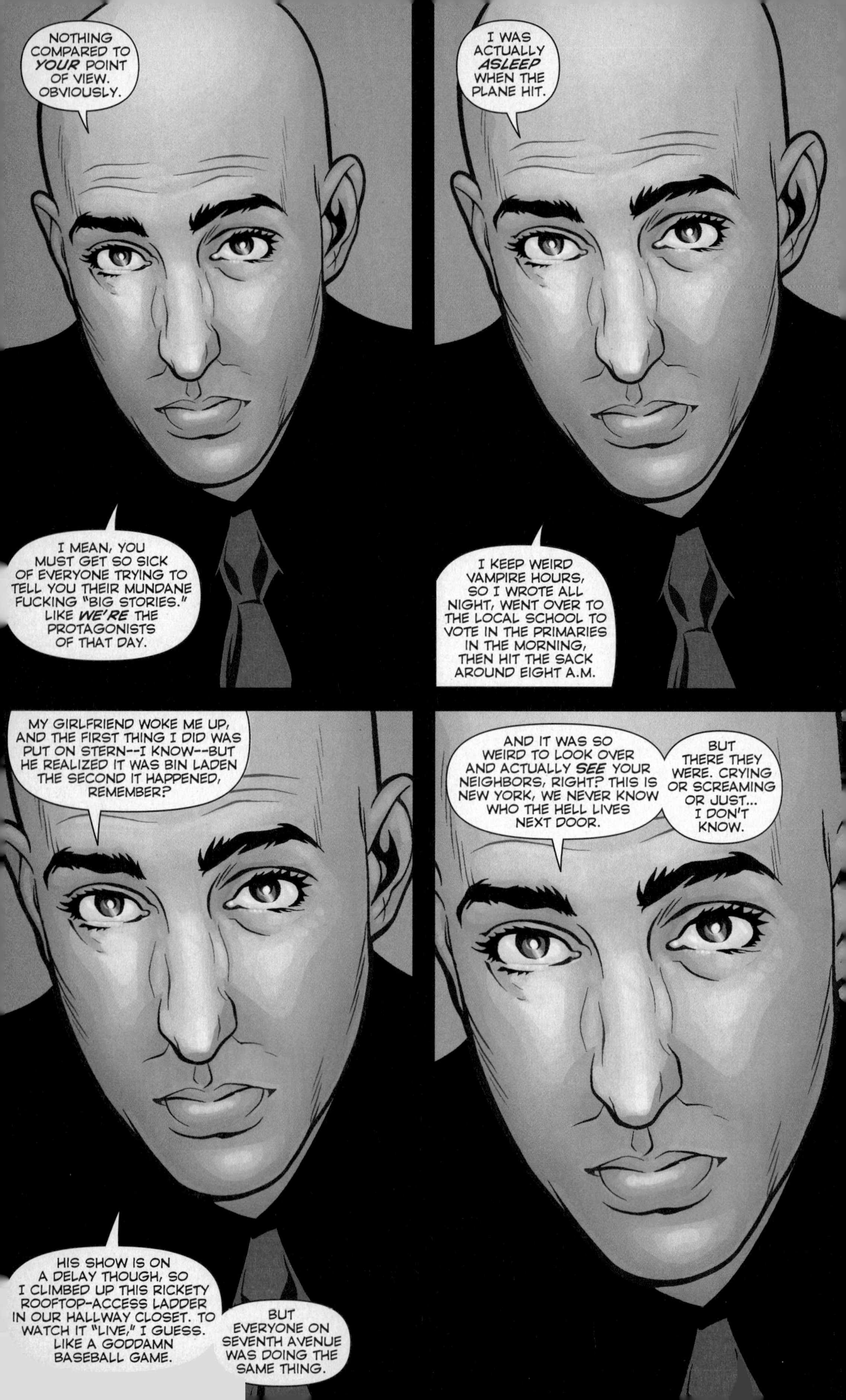
NOTHING COMPARED TO *YOUR* POINT OF VIEW. OBVIOUSLY.
I MEAN, YOU MUST GET SO SICK OF EVERYONE TRYING TO TELL YOU THEIR MUNDANE FUCKING "BIG STORIES." LIKE *WE'RE* THE PROTAGONISTS OF THAT DAY.
I WAS ACTUALLY *ASLEEP* WHEN THE PLANE HIT.
I KEEP WEIRD VAMPIRE HOURS, SO I WROTE ALL NIGHT, WENT OVER TO THE LOCAL SCHOOL TO VOTE IN THE PRIMARIES IN THE MORNING, THEN HIT THE SACK AROUND EIGHT A.M.
MY GIRLFRIEND WOKE ME UP, AND THE FIRST THING I DID WAS PUT ON STERN--I KNOW--BUT HE REALIZED IT WAS BIN LADEN THE SECOND IT HAPPENED, REMEMBER?
HIS SHOW IS ON A DELAY THOUGH, SO I CLIMBED UP THIS RICKETY ROOFTOP-ACCESS LADDER IN OUR HALLWAY CLOSET. TO WATCH IT "LIVE," I GUESS. LIKE A GODDAMN BASEBALL GAME.
BUT EVERYONE ON SEVENTH AVENUE WAS DOING THE SAME THING.
AND IT WAS SO WEIRD TO LOOK OVER AND ACTUALLY *SEE* YOUR NEIGHBORS, RIGHT? THIS IS NEW YORK, WE NEVER KNOW WHO THE HELL LIVES NEXT DOOR.
BUT THERE THEY WERE. CRYING OR SCREAMING OR JUST... I DON'T KNOW.

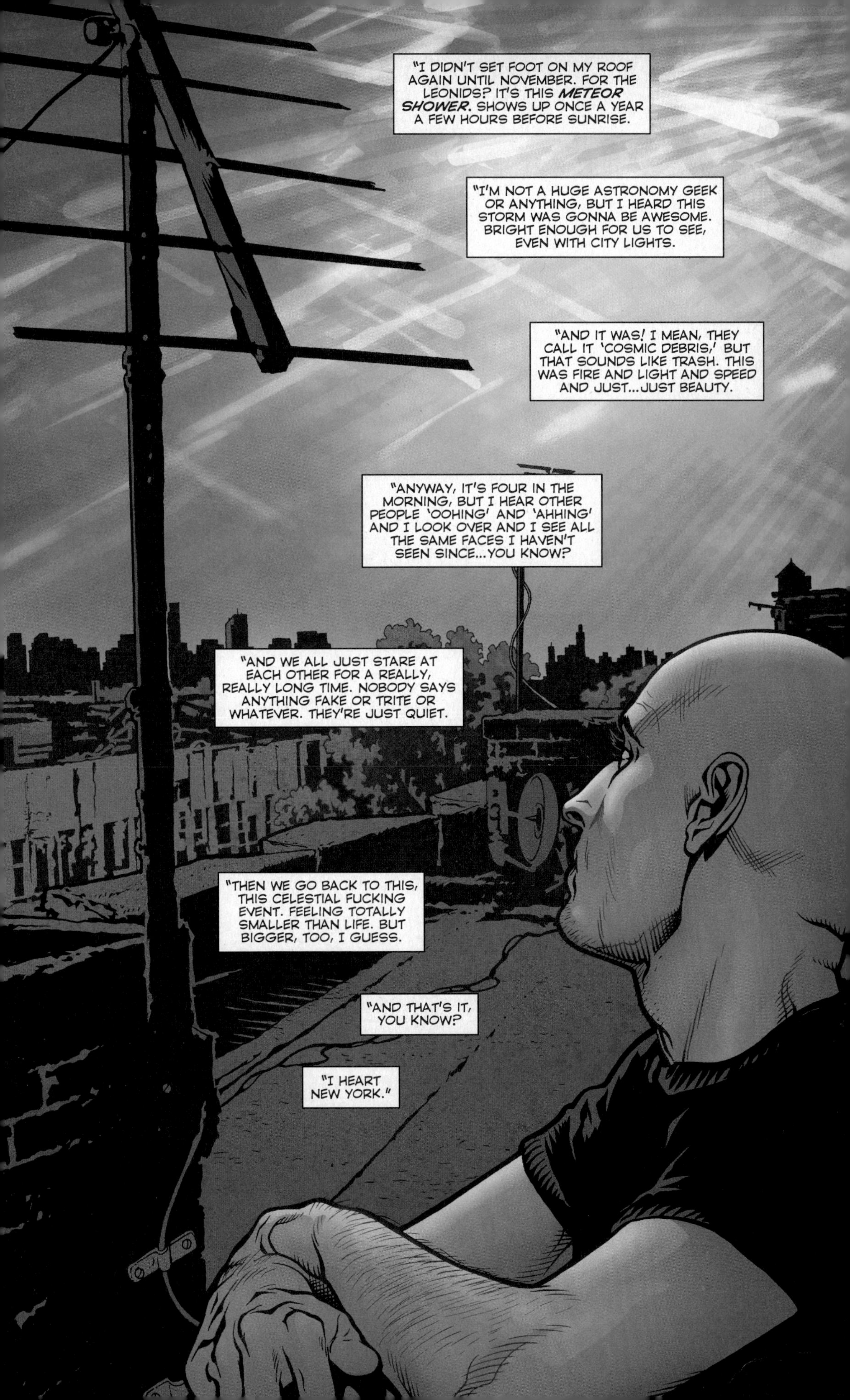
"I DIDN'T SET FOOT ON MY ROOF AGAIN UNTIL NOVEMBER. FOR THE LEONIDS? IT'S THIS *METEOR SHOWER.* SHOWS UP ONCE A YEAR A FEW HOURS BEFORE SUNRISE.
"I'M NOT A HUGE ASTRONOMY GEEK OR ANYTHING, BUT I HEARD THIS STORM WAS GONNA BE AWESOME. BRIGHT ENOUGH FOR US TO SEE, EVEN WITH CITY LIGHTS.
"AND IT WAS! I MEAN, THEY CALL IT 'COSMIC DEBRIS,' BUT THAT SOUNDS LIKE TRASH. THIS WAS FIRE AND LIGHT AND SPEED AND JUST...JUST BEAUTY.
"ANYWAY, IT'S FOUR IN THE MORNING, BUT I HEAR OTHER PEOPLE 'OOHING' AND 'AHHING' AND I LOOK OVER AND I SEE ALL THE SAME FACES I HAVEN'T SEEN SINCE...YOU KNOW?
"AND WE ALL JUST STARE AT EACH OTHER FOR A REALLY, REALLY LONG TIME. NOBODY SAYS ANYTHING FAKE OR TRITE OR WHATEVER. THEY'RE JUST QUIET.
"THEN WE GO BACK TO THIS, THIS CELESTIAL FUCKING EVENT. FEELING TOTALLY SMALLER THAN LIFE. BUT BIGGER, TOO, I GUESS.
"AND THAT'S IT, YOU KNOW?
"I HEART NEW YORK."

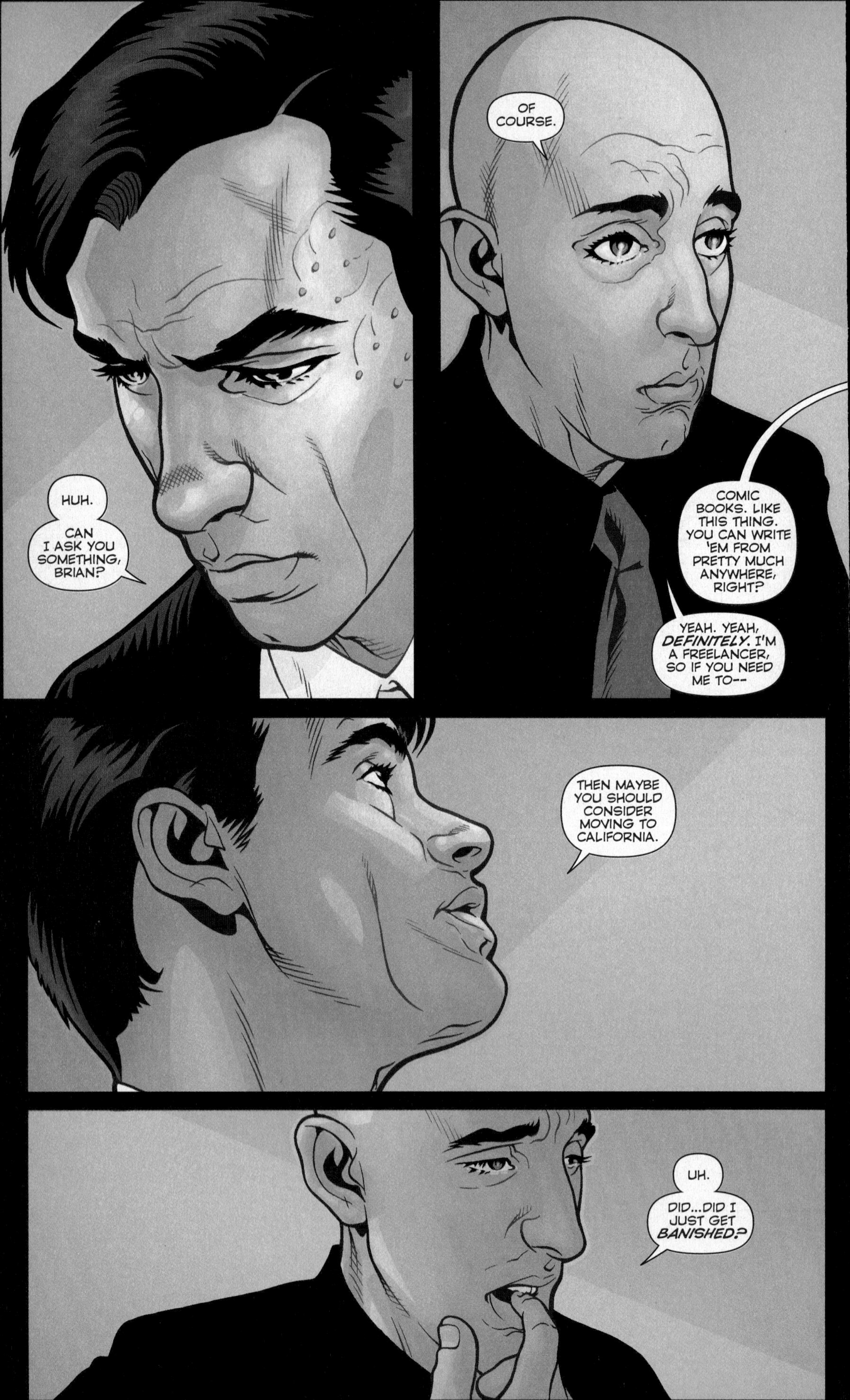
OF COURSE.
HUH.
CAN I ASK YOU SOMETHING, BRIAN?
COMIC BOOKS. LIKE THIS THING. YOU CAN WRITE 'EM FROM PRETTY MUCH ANYWHERE, RIGHT?
YEAH. YEAH, DEFINITELY. I'M A FREELANCER, SO IF YOU NEED ME TO--
THEN MAYBE YOU SHOULD CONSIDER MOVING TO CALIFORNIA.
UH.
DID...DID I JUST GET BANISHED?

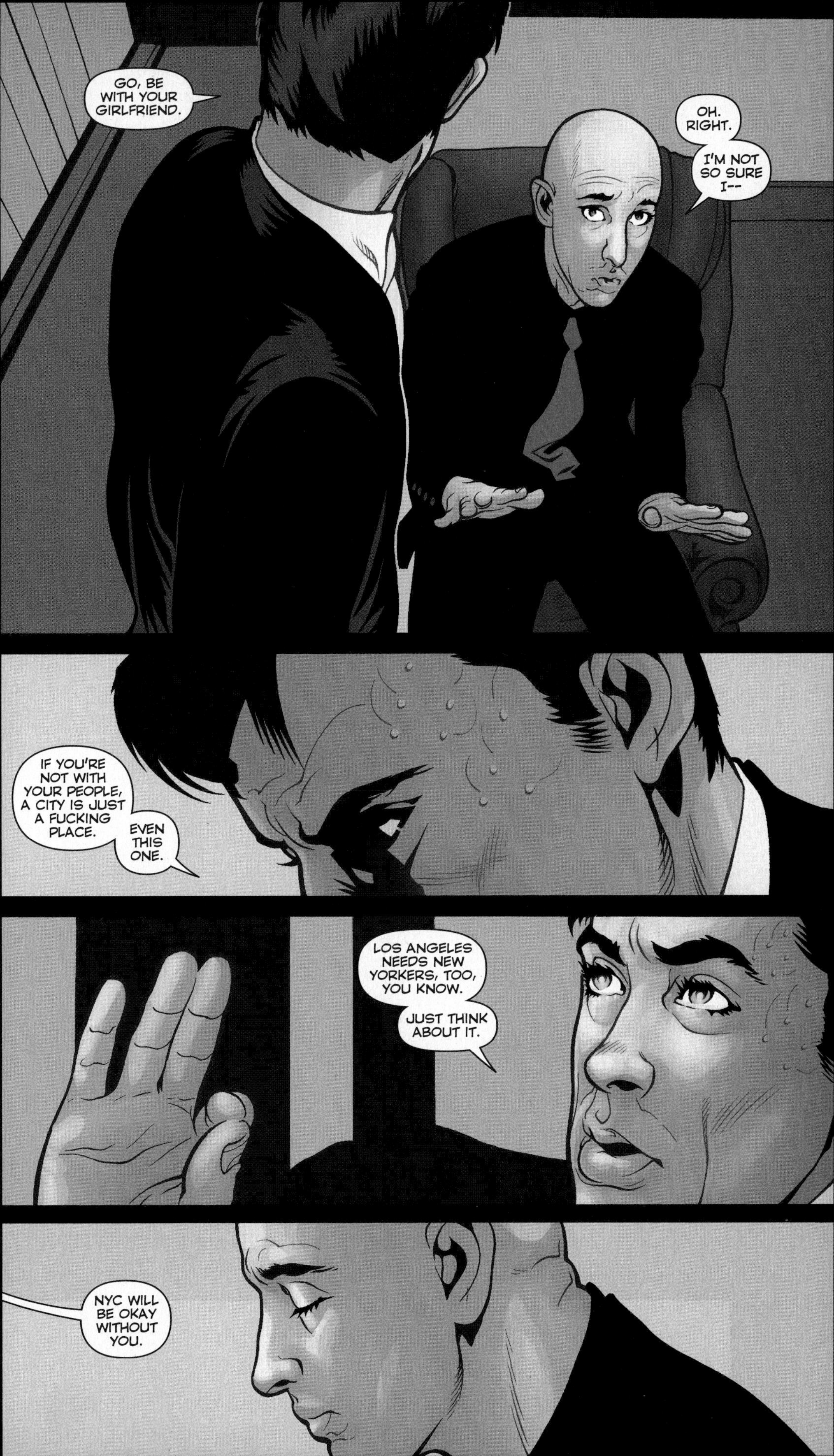
GO, BE WITH YOUR GIRLFRIEND.
OH. RIGHT.
I'M NOT SO SURE I--
IF YOU'RE NOT WITH YOUR PEOPLE, A CITY IS JUST A FUCKING PLACE.
EVEN THIS ONE.
LOS ANGELES NEEDS NEW YORKERS, TOO, YOU KNOW.
JUST THINK ABOUT IT.
NYC WILL BE OKAY WITHOUT YOU.

FREEZE, DICKBAG!

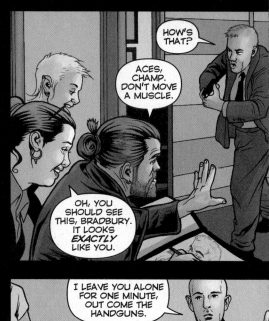

HOW'S THAT?

ACES, CHAMP. DON'T MOVE A MUSCLE.

OH, YOU SHOULD SEE THIS, BRADBURY. IT LOOKS *EXACTLY* LIKE YOU.

I LEAVE YOU ALONE FOR ONE MINUTE, OUT COME THE HANDGUNS.

HO, IT'S THE MAN OF THE HOUR! HOW'D IT GO, B?

ACTUALLY?

NOT BAD.

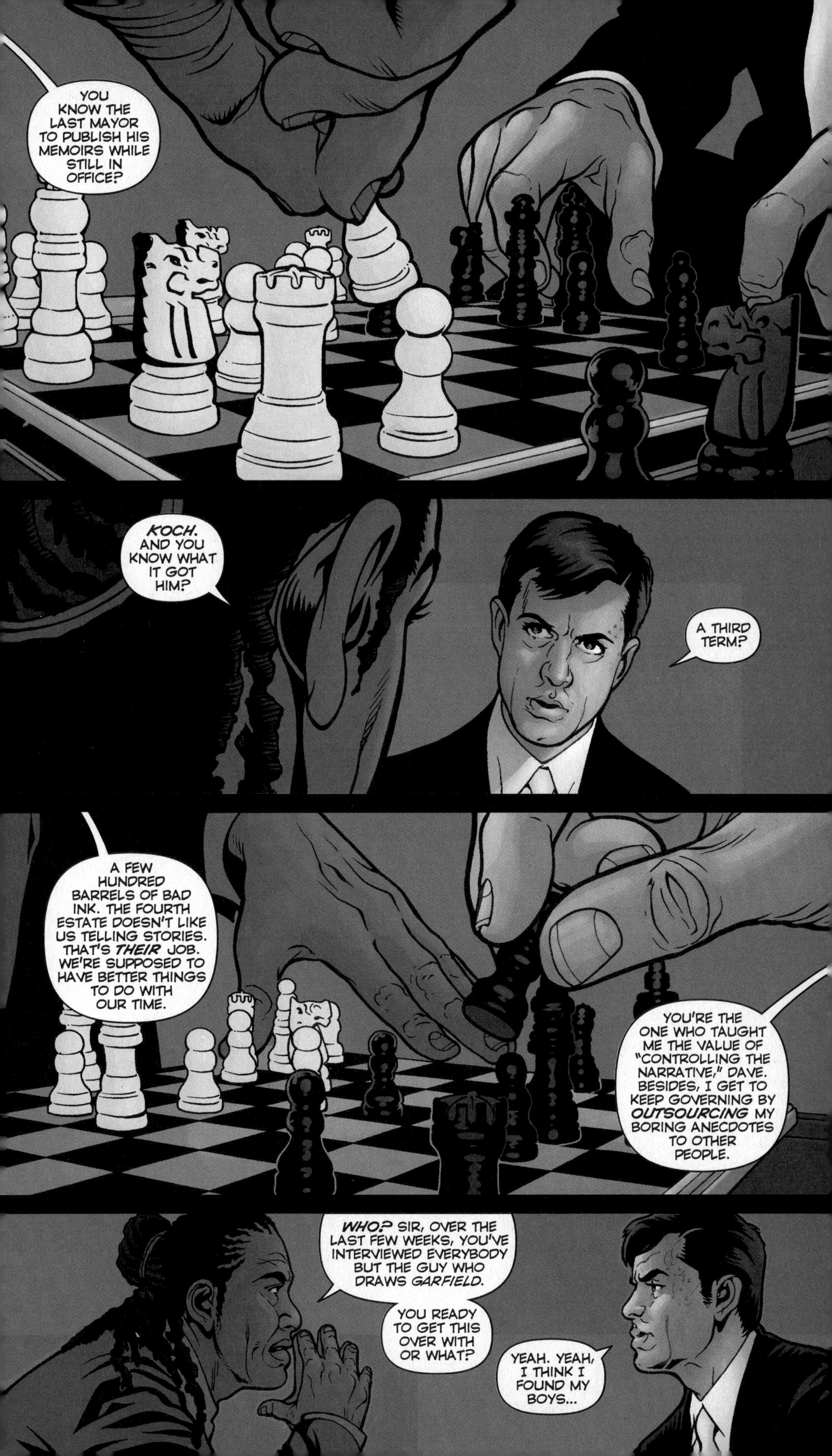

YOU KNOW THE LAST MAYOR TO PUBLISH HIS MEMOIRS WHILE STILL IN OFFICE?
KOCH. AND YOU KNOW WHAT IT GOT HIM?
A THIRD TERM?
A FEW HUNDRED BARRELS OF BAD INK. THE FOURTH ESTATE DOESN'T LIKE US TELLING STORIES. THAT'S *THEIR* JOB. WE'RE SUPPOSED TO HAVE BETTER THINGS TO DO WITH OUR TIME.
YOU'RE THE ONE WHO TAUGHT ME THE VALUE OF "CONTROLLING THE NARRATIVE," DAVE. BESIDES, I GET TO KEEP GOVERNING BY *OUTSOURCING* MY BORING ANECDOTES TO OTHER PEOPLE.
WHO? SIR, OVER THE LAST FEW WEEKS, YOU'VE INTERVIEWED EVERYBODY BUT THE GUY WHO DRAWS *GARFIELD*.
YOU READY TO GET THIS OVER WITH OR WHAT?
YEAH. YEAH, I THINK I FOUND MY BOYS...

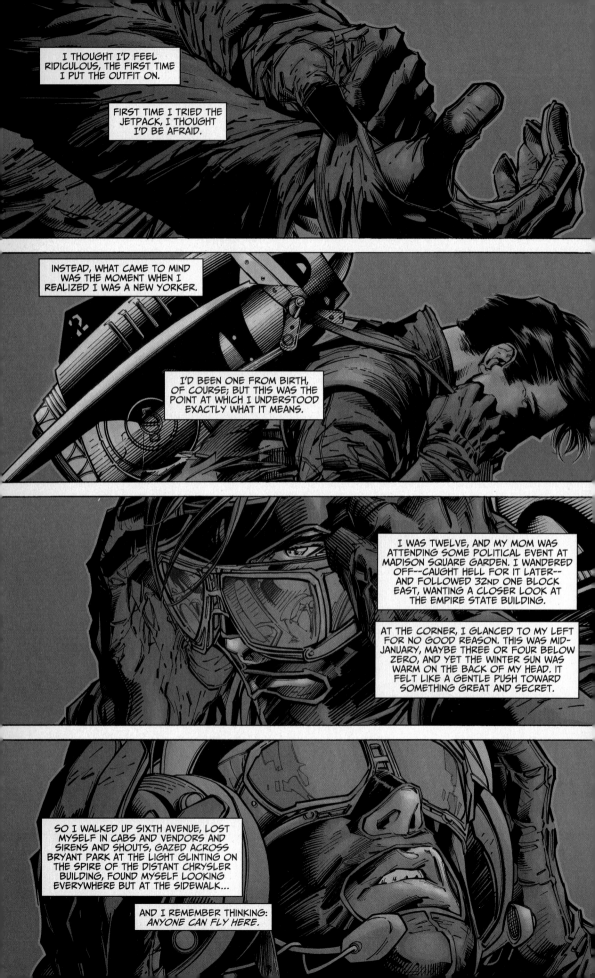

I THOUGHT I'D FEEL RIDICULOUS, THE FIRST TIME I PUT THE OUTFIT ON.

FIRST TIME I TRIED THE JETPACK, I THOUGHT I'D BE AFRAID.

INSTEAD, WHAT CAME TO MIND WAS THE MOMENT WHEN I REALIZED I WAS A NEW YORKER.

I'D BEEN ONE FROM BIRTH, OF COURSE; BUT THIS WAS THE POINT AT WHICH I UNDERSTOOD EXACTLY WHAT IT MEANS.

I WAS TWELVE, AND MY MOM WAS ATTENDING SOME POLITICAL EVENT AT MADISON SQUARE GARDEN. I WANDERED OFF--CAUGHT HELL FOR IT LATER-- AND FOLLOWED 32ND ONE BLOCK EAST, WANTING A CLOSER LOOK AT THE EMPIRE STATE BUILDING.

AT THE CORNER, I GLANCED TO MY LEFT FOR NO GOOD REASON. THIS WAS MID-JANUARY, MAYBE THREE OR FOUR BELOW ZERO, AND YET THE WINTER SUN WAS WARM ON THE BACK OF MY HEAD. IT FELT LIKE A GENTLE PUSH TOWARD SOMETHING GREAT AND SECRET.

SO I WALKED UP SIXTH AVENUE, LOST MYSELF IN CABS AND VENDORS AND SIRENS AND SHOUTS, GAZED ACROSS BRYANT PARK AT THE LIGHT GLINTING ON THE SPIRE OF THE DISTANT CHRYSLER BUILDING, FOUND MYSELF LOOKING EVERYWHERE BUT AT THE SIDEWALK...

AND I REMEMBER THINKING: *ANYONE CAN FLY HERE.*

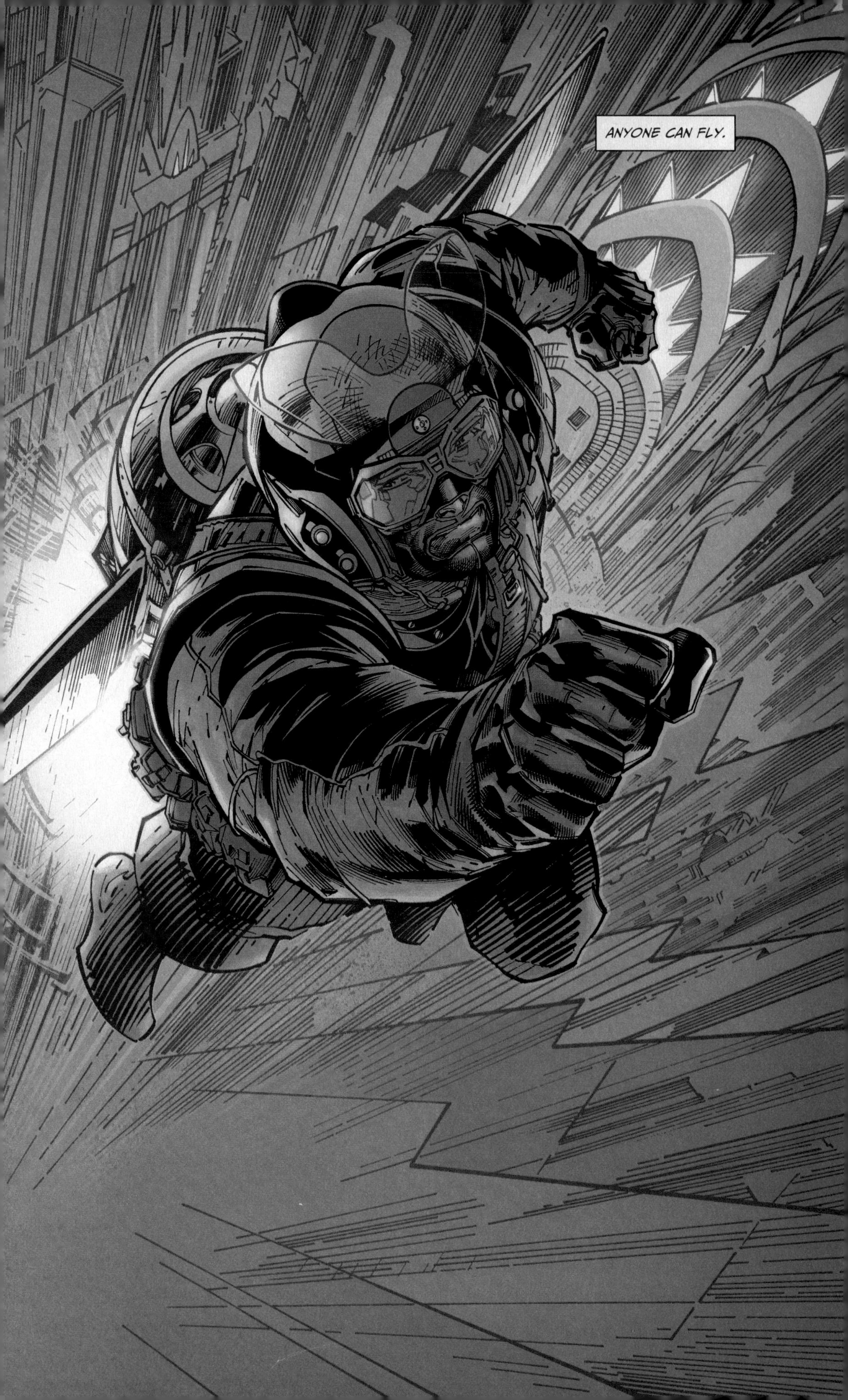
ANYONE CAN FLY.

Green

Chapter 2

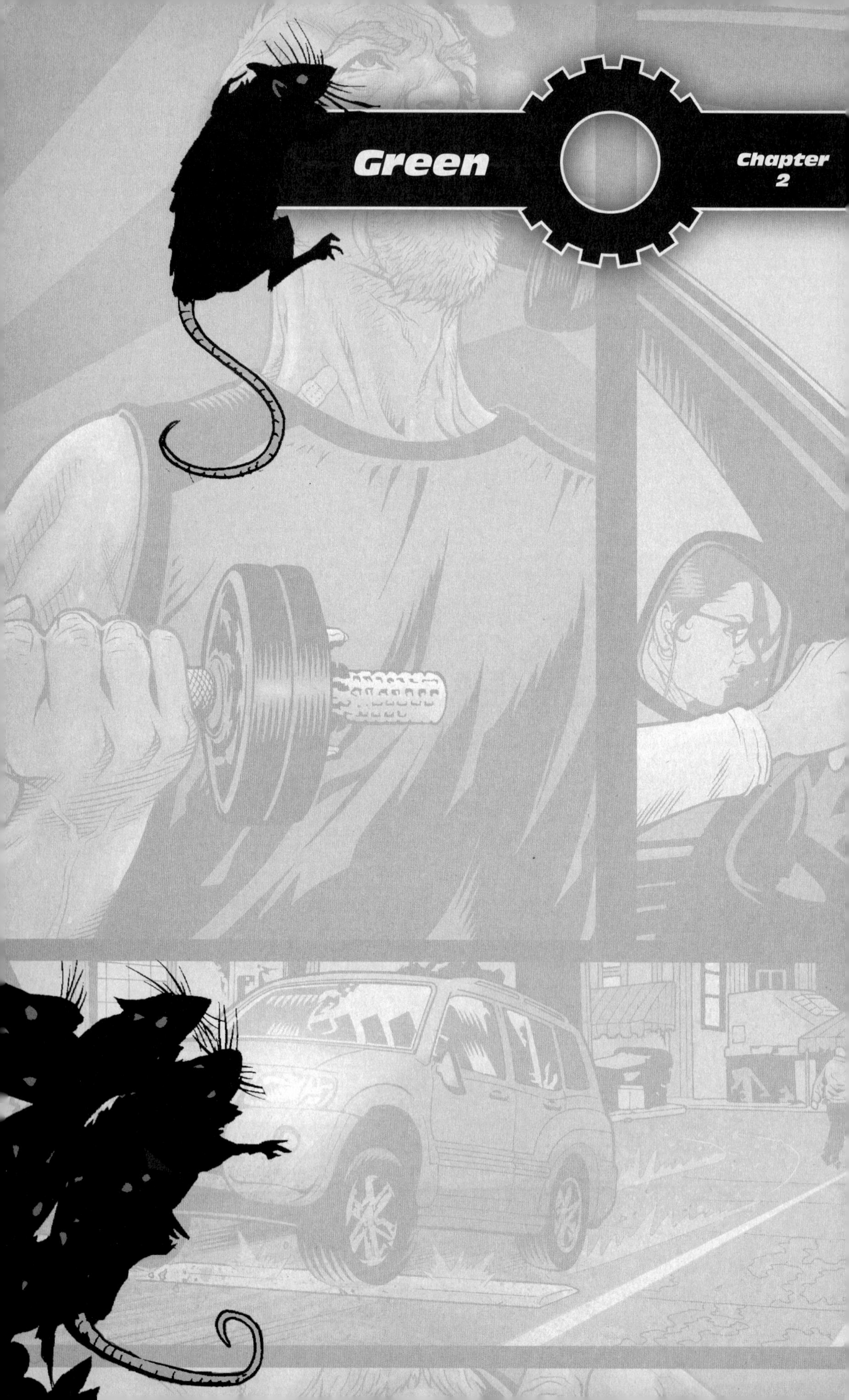

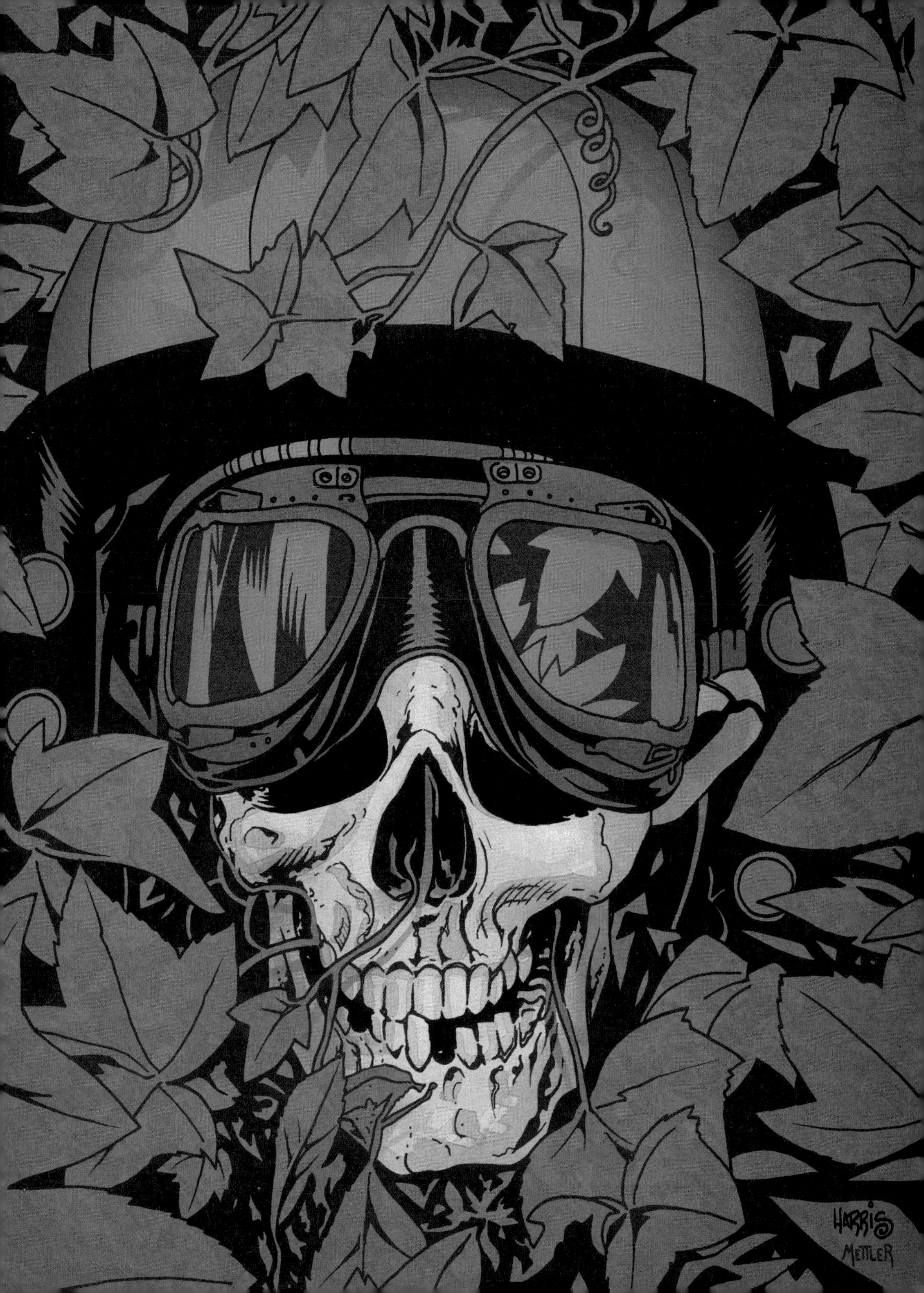
HARRIS
METTLER

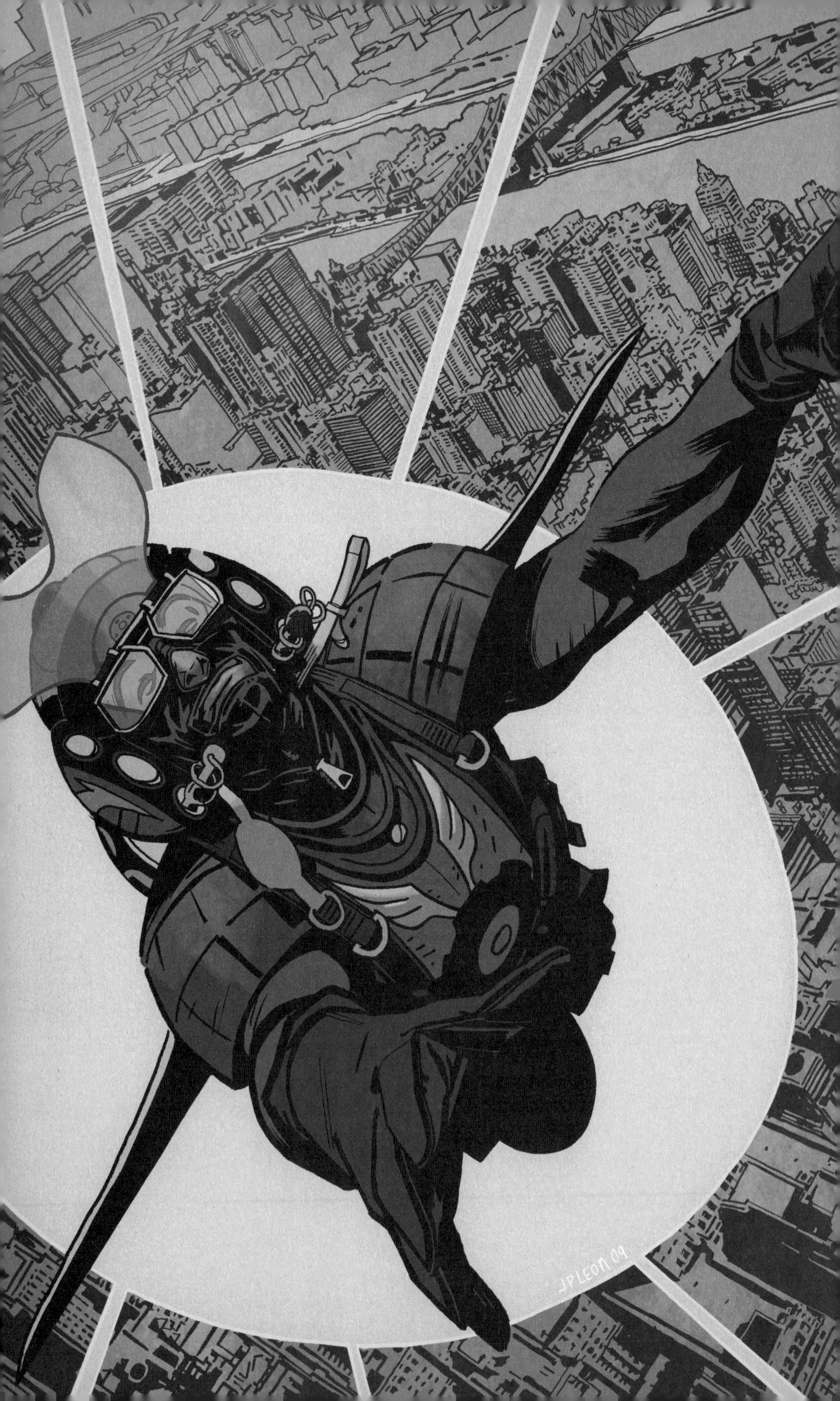
JPLEON 09

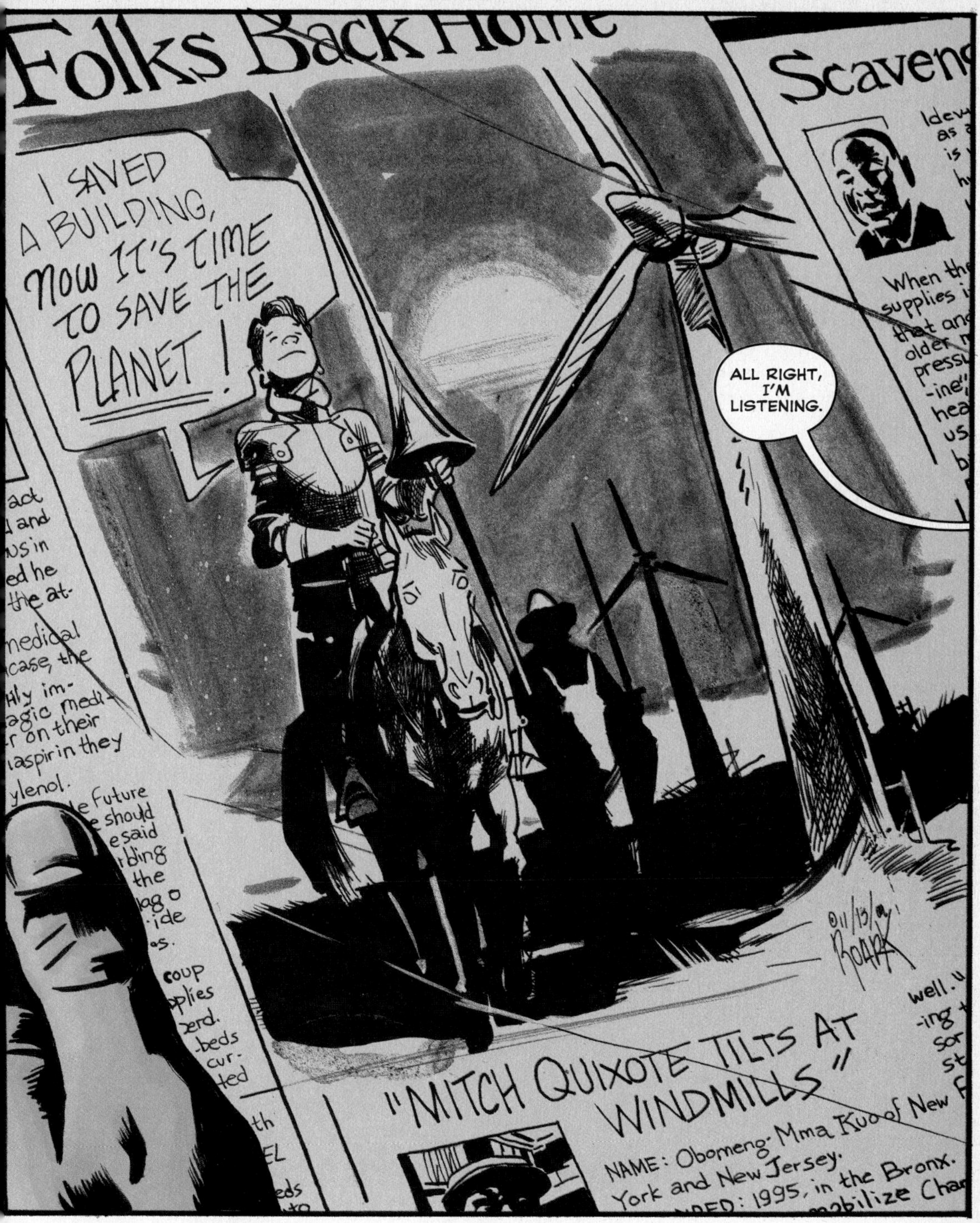
Folks Back Home
I SAVED A BUILDING, NOW IT'S TIME TO SAVE THE PLANET!
ALL RIGHT, I'M LISTENING.
"MITCH QUIXOTE TILTS AT WINDMILLS"
NAME: Obomeng-Mma Kuo of New York and New Jersey.

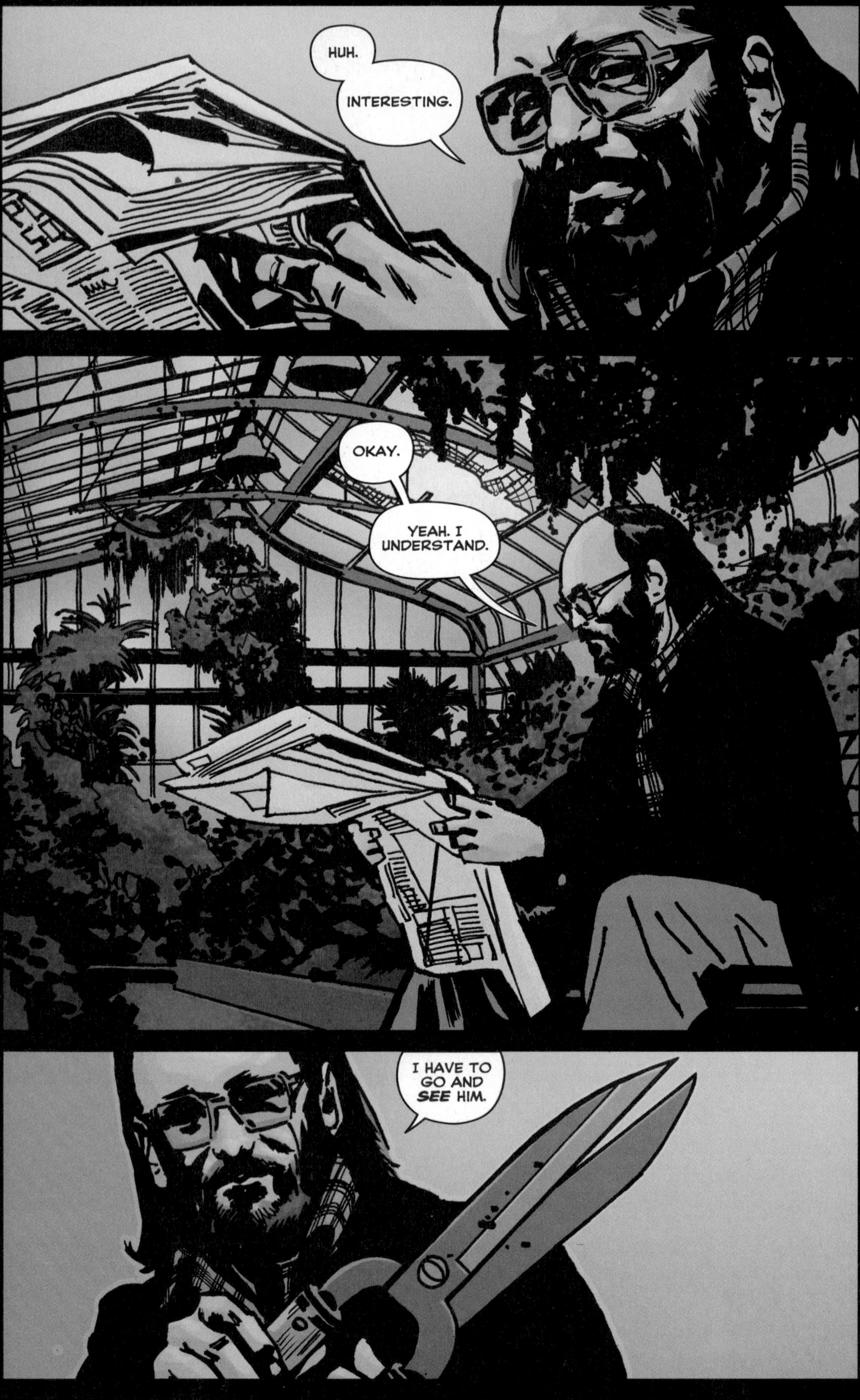
HUH.
INTERESTING.
OKAY.
YEAH. I UNDERSTAND.
I HAVE TO GO AND *SEE* HIM.

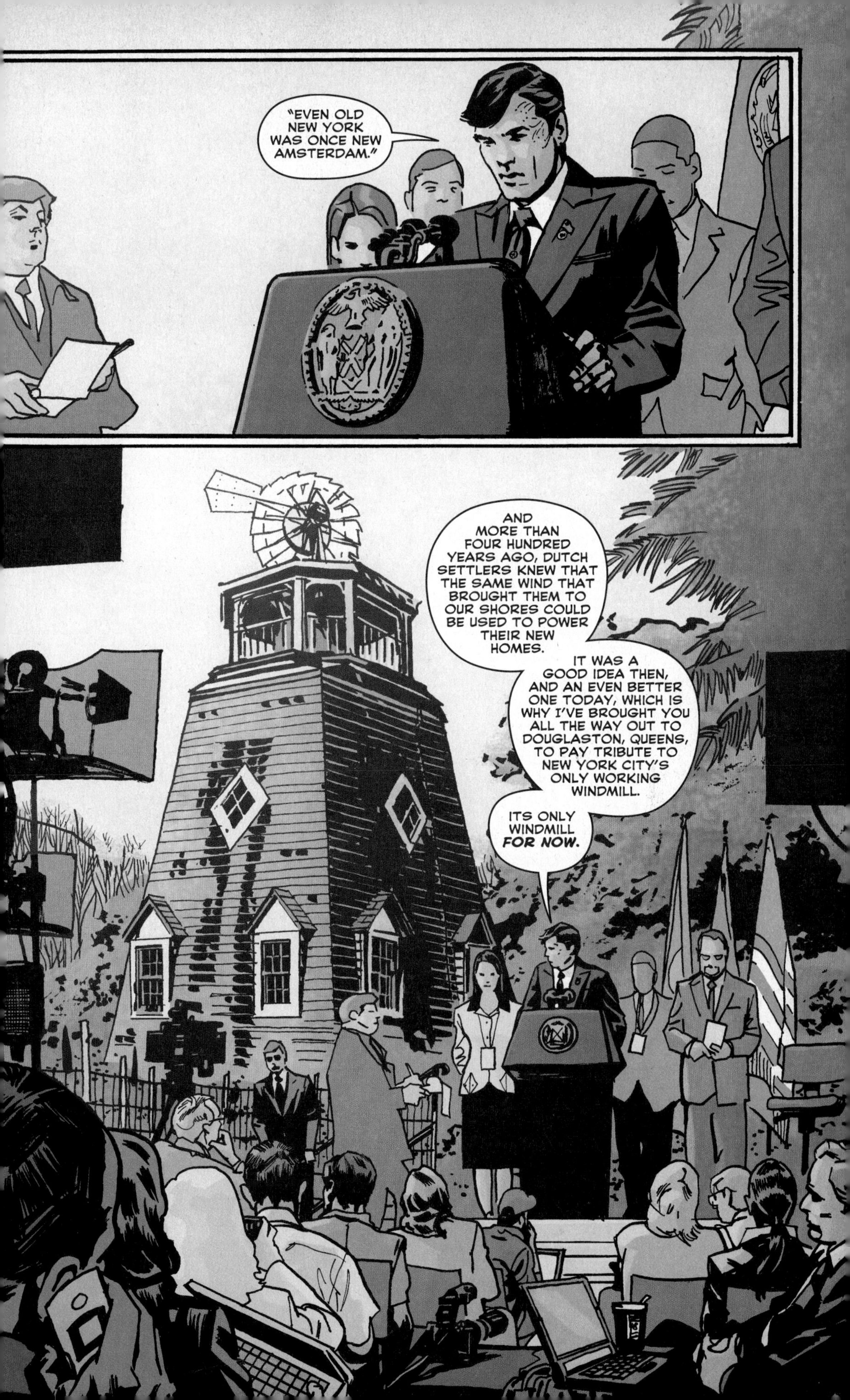
"EVEN OLD NEW YORK WAS ONCE NEW AMSTERDAM."
AND MORE THAN FOUR HUNDRED YEARS AGO, DUTCH SETTLERS KNEW THAT THE SAME WIND THAT BROUGHT THEM TO OUR SHORES COULD BE USED TO POWER THEIR NEW HOMES.
IT WAS A GOOD IDEA THEN, AND AN EVEN BETTER ONE TODAY, WHICH IS WHY I'VE BROUGHT YOU ALL THE WAY OUT TO DOUGLASTON, QUEENS, TO PAY TRIBUTE TO NEW YORK CITY'S ONLY WORKING WINDMILL.
ITS ONLY WINDMILL *FOR NOW.*

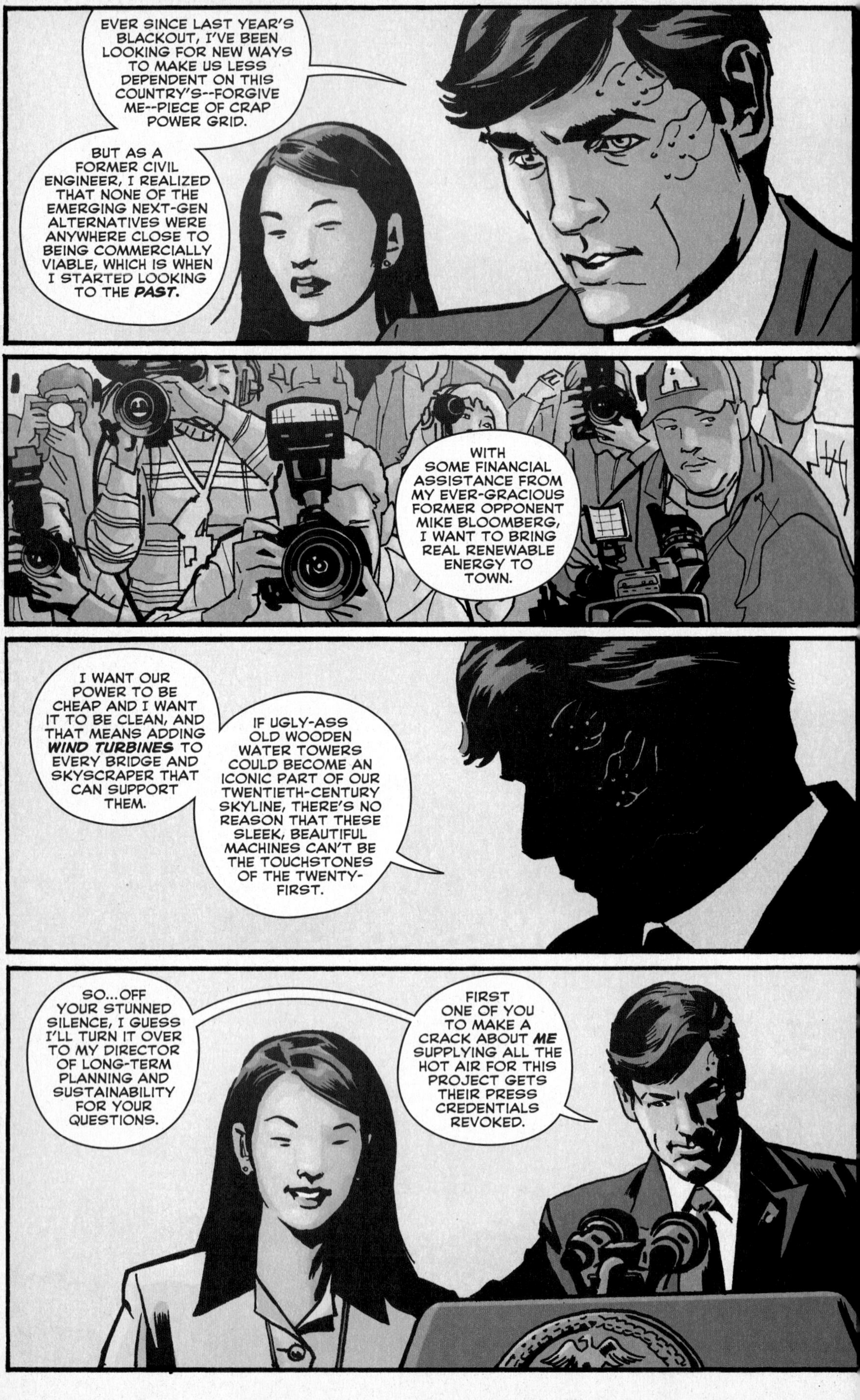
EVER SINCE LAST YEAR'S BLACKOUT, I'VE BEEN LOOKING FOR NEW WAYS TO MAKE US LESS DEPENDENT ON THIS COUNTRY'S--FORGIVE ME--PIECE OF CRAP POWER GRID.
BUT AS A FORMER CIVIL ENGINEER, I REALIZED THAT NONE OF THE EMERGING NEXT-GEN ALTERNATIVES WERE ANYWHERE CLOSE TO BEING COMMERCIALLY VIABLE, WHICH IS WHEN I STARTED LOOKING TO THE *PAST.*
WITH SOME FINANCIAL ASSISTANCE FROM MY EVER-GRACIOUS FORMER OPPONENT MIKE BLOOMBERG, I WANT TO BRING REAL RENEWABLE ENERGY TO TOWN.
I WANT OUR POWER TO BE CHEAP AND I WANT IT TO BE CLEAN, AND THAT MEANS ADDING ***WIND TURBINES*** TO EVERY BRIDGE AND SKYSCRAPER THAT CAN SUPPORT THEM.
IF UGLY-ASS OLD WOODEN WATER TOWERS COULD BECOME AN ICONIC PART OF OUR TWENTIETH-CENTURY SKYLINE, THERE'S NO REASON THAT THESE SLEEK, BEAUTIFUL MACHINES CAN'T BE THE TOUCHSTONES OF THE TWENTY-FIRST.
SO...OFF YOUR STUNNED SILENCE, I GUESS I'LL TURN IT OVER TO MY DIRECTOR OF LONG-TERM PLANNING AND SUSTAINABILITY FOR YOUR QUESTIONS.
FIRST ONE OF YOU TO MAKE A CRACK ABOUT ***ME*** SUPPLYING ALL THE HOT AIR FOR THIS PROJECT GETS THEIR PRESS CREDENTIALS REVOKED.

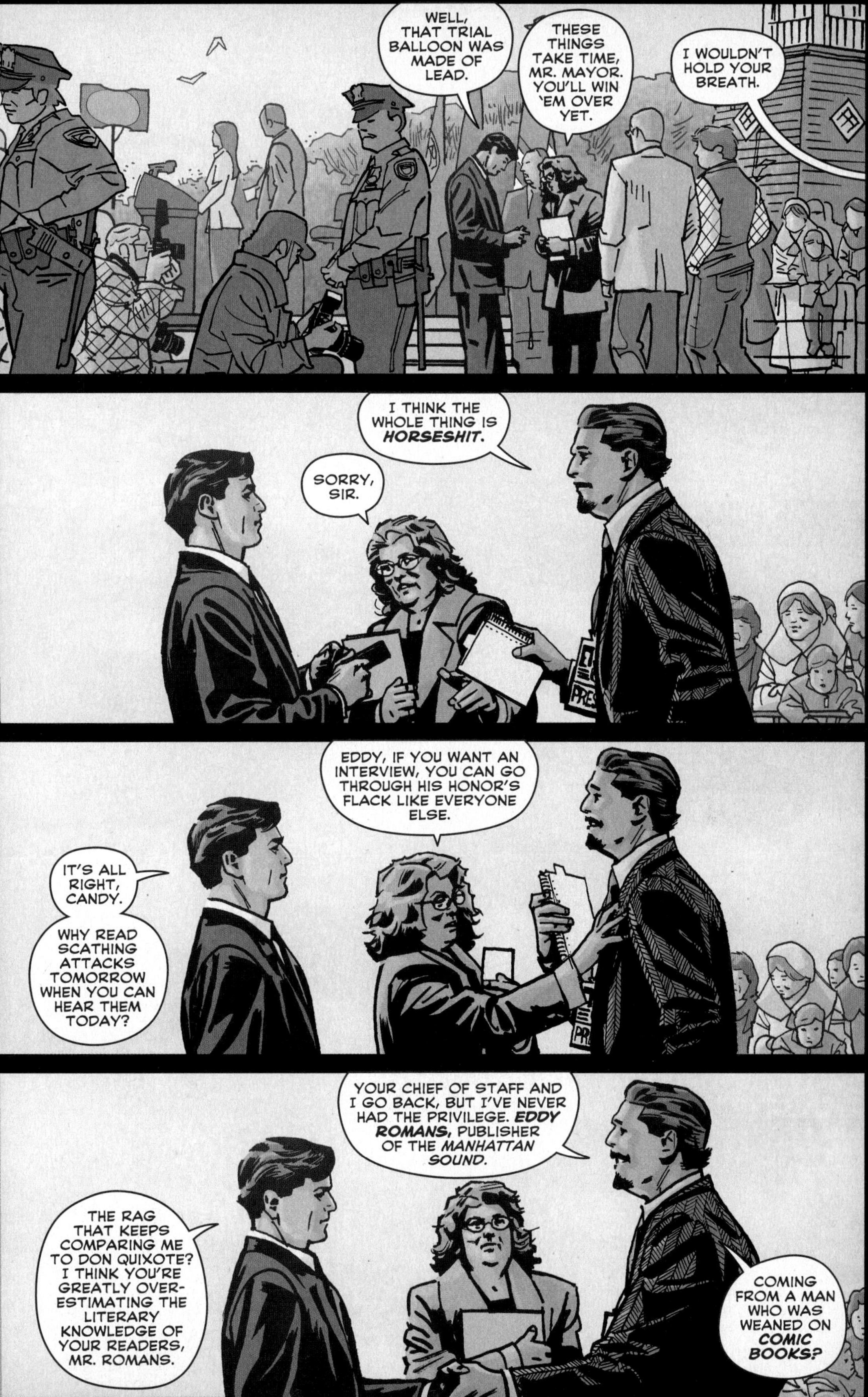
WELL, THAT TRIAL BALLOON WAS MADE OF LEAD.
THESE THINGS TAKE TIME, MR. MAYOR. YOU'LL WIN 'EM OVER YET.
I WOULDN'T HOLD YOUR BREATH.
I THINK THE WHOLE THING IS *HORSESHIT*.
SORRY, SIR.
EDDY, IF YOU WANT AN INTERVIEW, YOU CAN GO THROUGH HIS HONOR'S FLACK LIKE EVERYONE ELSE.
IT'S ALL RIGHT, CANDY.
WHY READ SCATHING ATTACKS TOMORROW WHEN YOU CAN HEAR THEM TODAY?
YOUR CHIEF OF STAFF AND I GO BACK, BUT I'VE NEVER HAD THE PRIVILEGE. *EDDY ROMANS,* PUBLISHER OF THE *MANHATTAN SOUND.*
THE RAG THAT KEEPS COMPARING ME TO DON QUIXOTE? I THINK YOU'RE GREATLY OVER-ESTIMATING THE LITERARY KNOWLEDGE OF YOUR READERS, MR. ROMANS.
COMING FROM A MAN WHO WAS WEANED ON *COMIC BOOKS?*

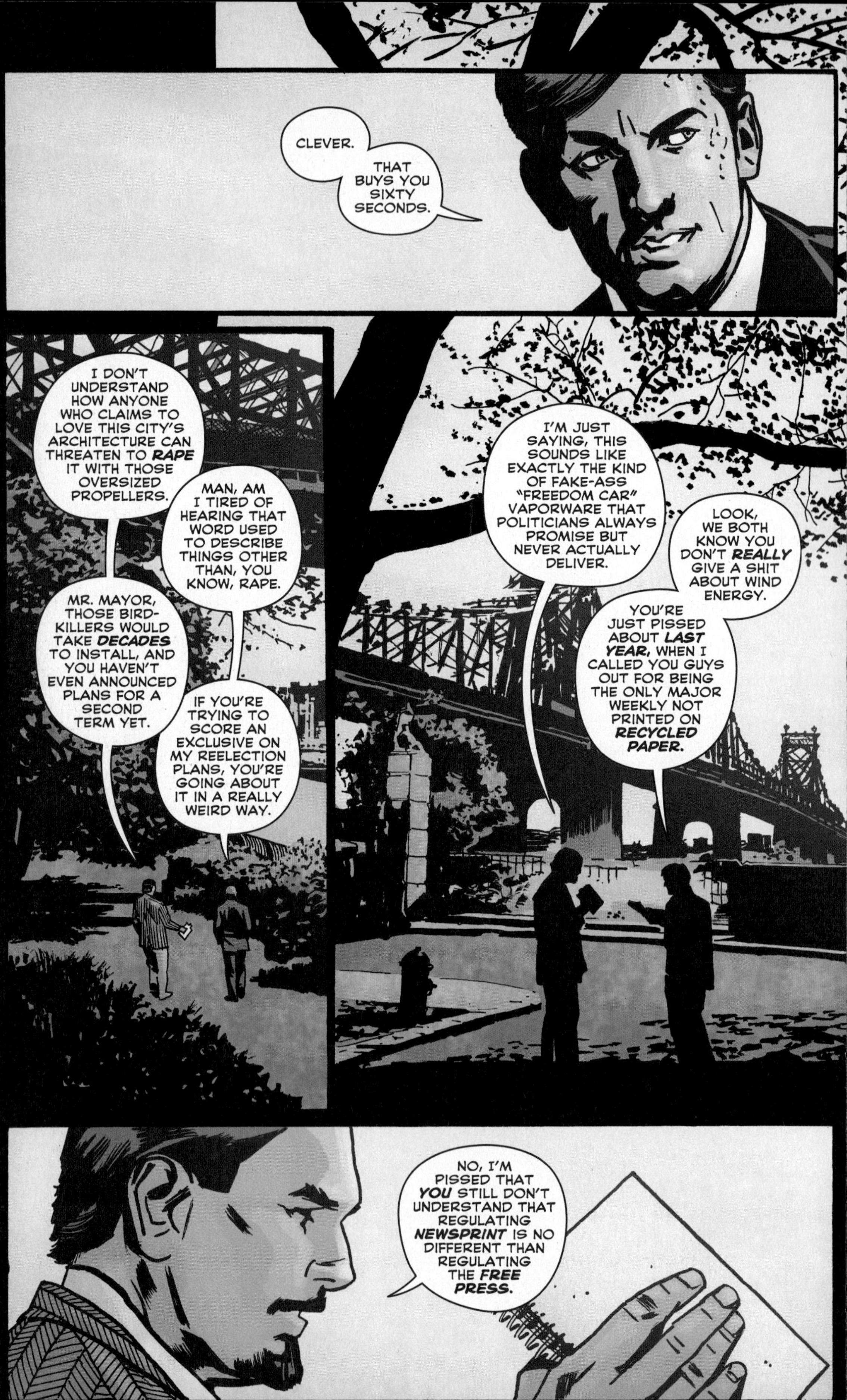
CLEVER.
THAT BUYS YOU SIXTY SECONDS.
I DON'T UNDERSTAND HOW ANYONE WHO CLAIMS TO LOVE THIS CITY'S ARCHITECTURE CAN THREATEN TO ***RAPE*** IT WITH THOSE OVERSIZED PROPELLERS.
MAN, AM I TIRED OF HEARING THAT WORD USED TO DESCRIBE THINGS OTHER THAN, YOU KNOW, RAPE.
MR. MAYOR, THOSE BIRD-KILLERS WOULD TAKE ***DECADES*** TO INSTALL, AND YOU HAVEN'T EVEN ANNOUNCED PLANS FOR A SECOND TERM YET.
IF YOU'RE TRYING TO SCORE AN EXCLUSIVE ON MY REELECTION PLANS, YOU'RE GOING ABOUT IT IN A REALLY WEIRD WAY.
I'M JUST SAYING, THIS SOUNDS LIKE EXACTLY THE KIND OF FAKE-ASS "FREEDOM CAR" VAPORWARE THAT POLITICIANS ALWAYS PROMISE BUT NEVER ACTUALLY DELIVER.
LOOK, WE BOTH KNOW YOU DON'T ***REALLY*** GIVE A SHIT ABOUT WIND ENERGY.
YOU'RE JUST PISSED ABOUT ***LAST YEAR,*** WHEN I CALLED YOU GUYS OUT FOR BEING THE ONLY MAJOR WEEKLY NOT PRINTED ON ***RECYCLED PAPER.***
NO, I'M PISSED THAT ***YOU*** STILL DON'T UNDERSTAND THAT REGULATING ***NEWSPRINT*** IS NO DIFFERENT THAN REGULATING THE ***FREE PRESS.***

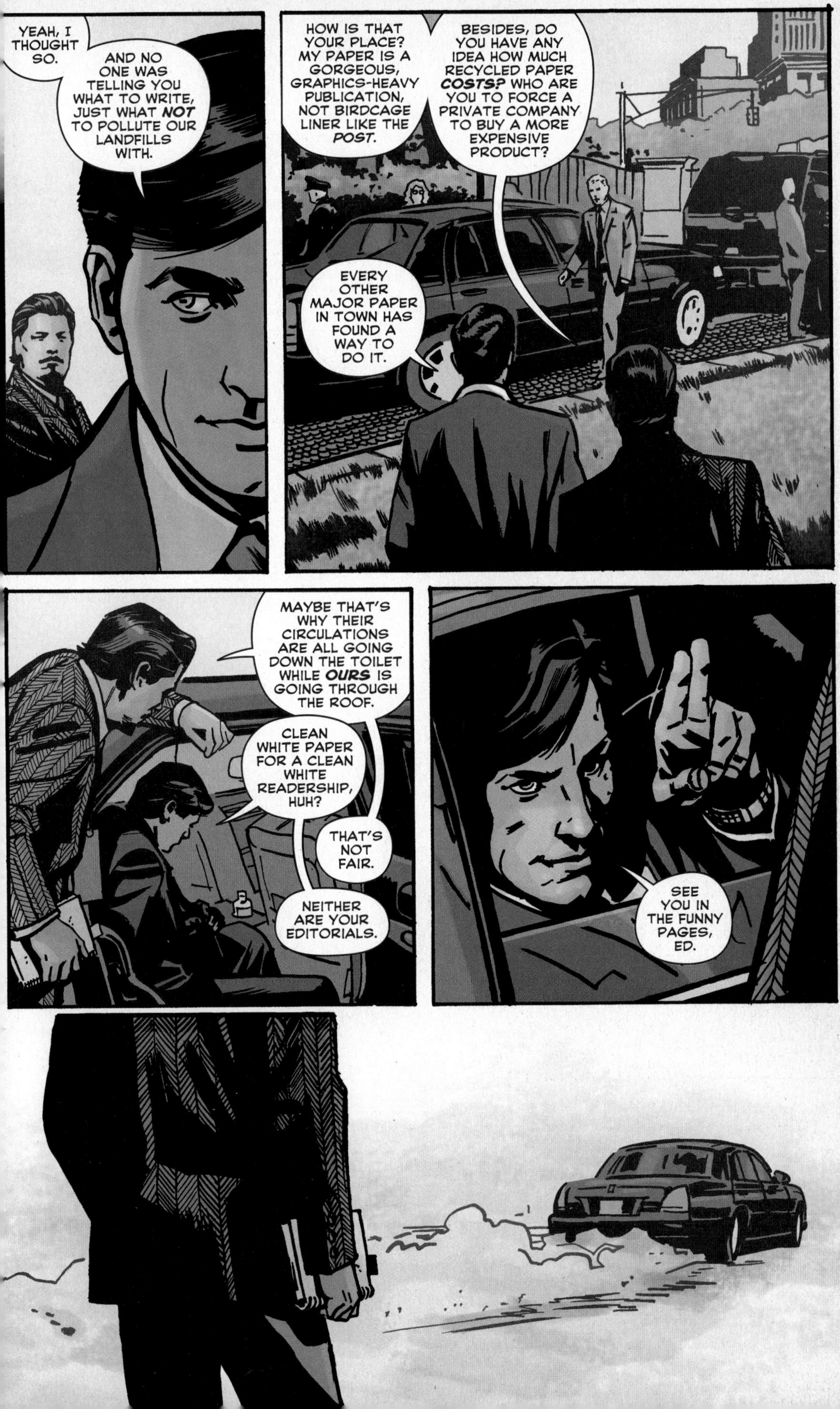
YEAH, I THOUGHT SO.
AND NO ONE WAS TELLING YOU WHAT TO WRITE, JUST WHAT NOT TO POLLUTE OUR LANDFILLS WITH.
HOW IS THAT YOUR PLACE? MY PAPER IS A GORGEOUS, GRAPHICS-HEAVY PUBLICATION, NOT BIRDCAGE LINER LIKE THE POST.
BESIDES, DO YOU HAVE ANY IDEA HOW MUCH RECYCLED PAPER COSTS? WHO ARE YOU TO FORCE A PRIVATE COMPANY TO BUY A MORE EXPENSIVE PRODUCT?
EVERY OTHER MAJOR PAPER IN TOWN HAS FOUND A WAY TO DO IT.
MAYBE THAT'S WHY THEIR CIRCULATIONS ARE ALL GOING DOWN THE TOILET WHILE OURS IS GOING THROUGH THE ROOF.
CLEAN WHITE PAPER FOR A CLEAN WHITE READERSHIP, HUH?
THAT'S NOT FAIR.
NEITHER ARE YOUR EDITORIALS.
SEE YOU IN THE FUNNY PAGES, ED.

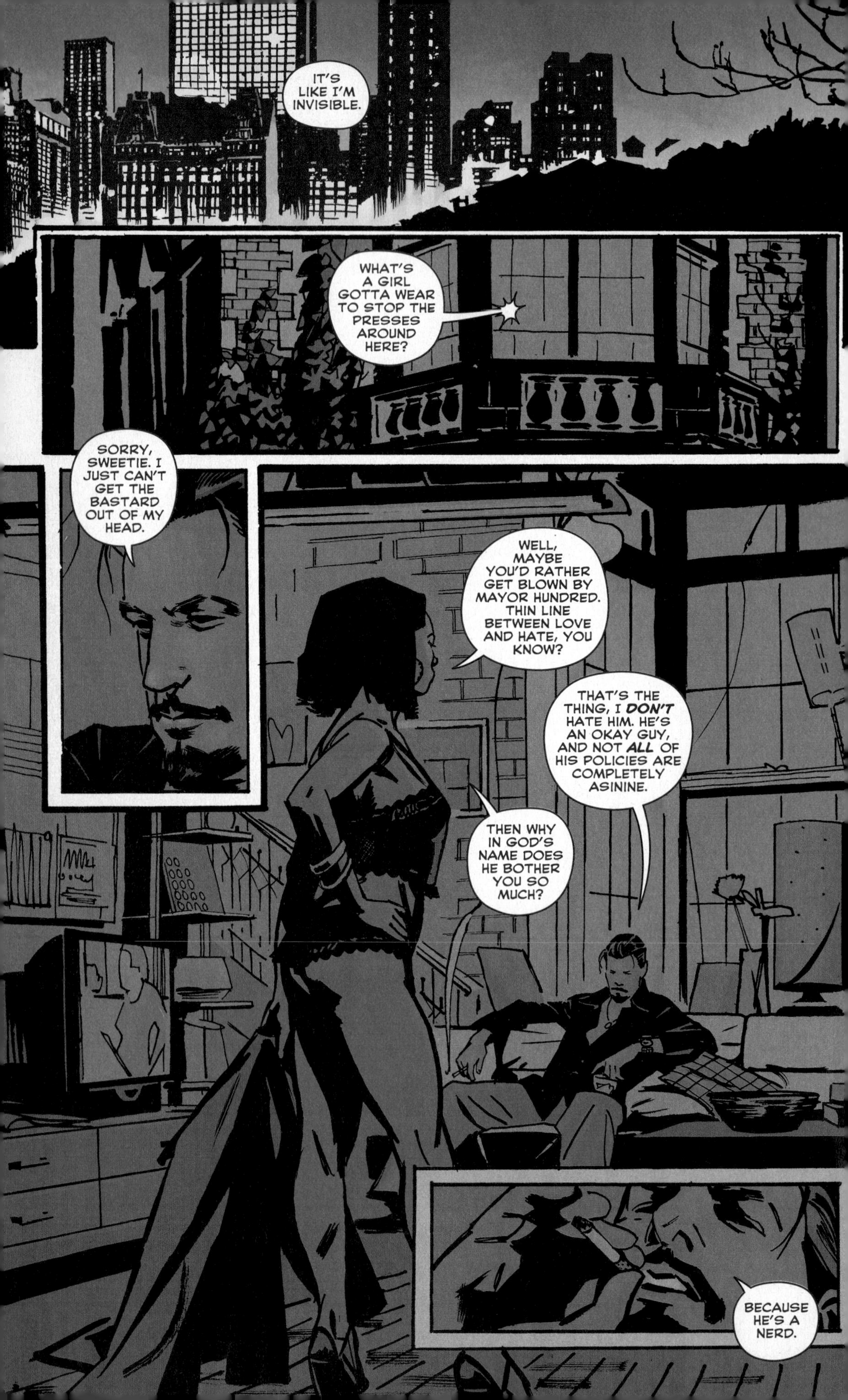
IT'S LIKE I'M INVISIBLE.
WHAT'S A GIRL GOTTA WEAR TO STOP THE PRESSES AROUND HERE?
SORRY, SWEETIE. I JUST CAN'T GET THE BASTARD OUT OF MY HEAD.
WELL, MAYBE YOU'D RATHER GET BLOWN BY MAYOR HUNDRED. THIN LINE BETWEEN LOVE AND HATE, YOU KNOW?
THAT'S THE THING, I DON'T HATE HIM. HE'S AN OKAY GUY, AND NOT ALL OF HIS POLICIES ARE COMPLETELY ASININE.
THEN WHY IN GOD'S NAME DOES HE BOTHER YOU SO MUCH?
BECAUSE HE'S A NERD.

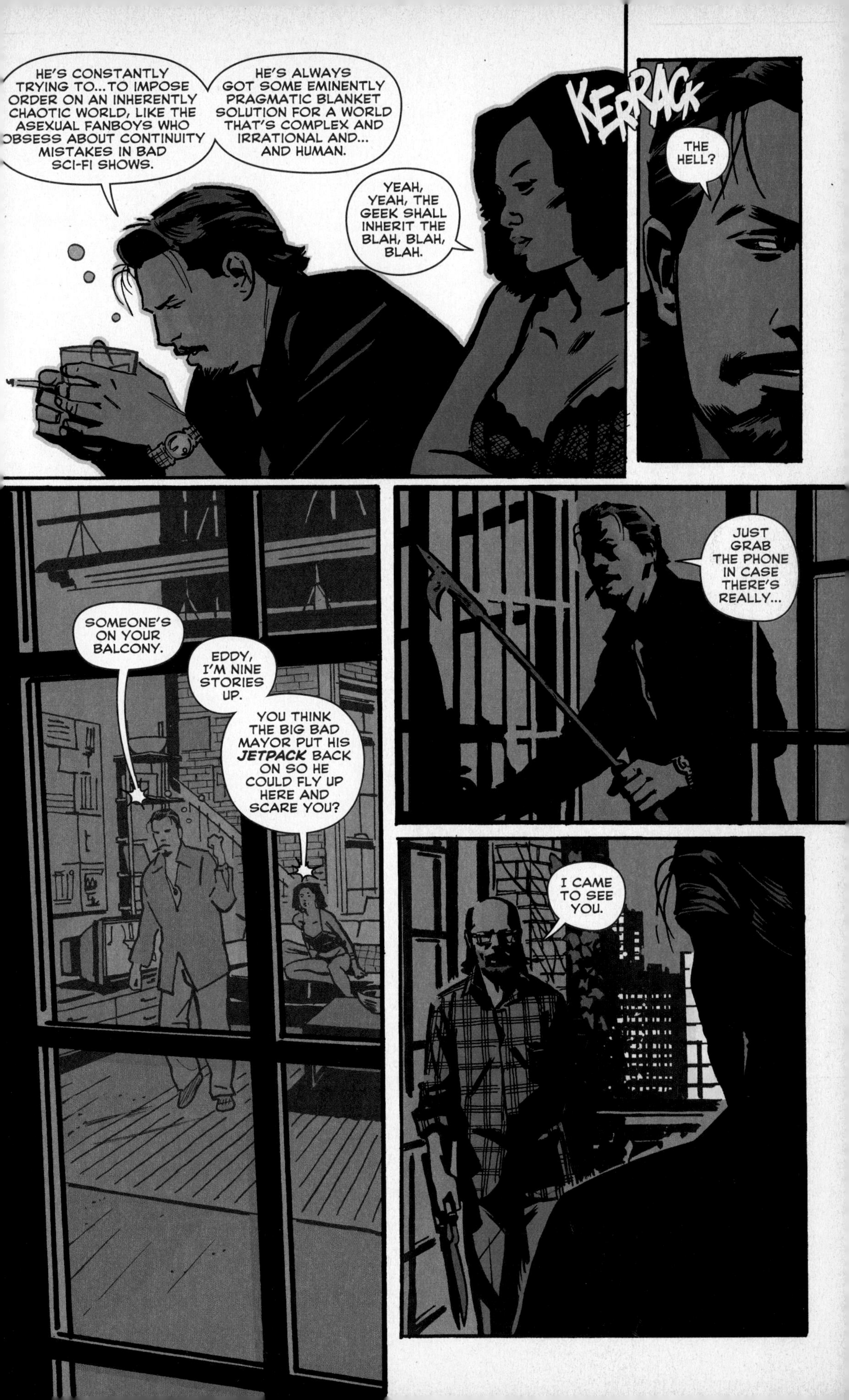
HE'S CONSTANTLY TRYING TO...TO IMPOSE ORDER ON AN INHERENTLY CHAOTIC WORLD, LIKE THE ASEXUAL FANBOYS WHO OBSESS ABOUT CONTINUITY MISTAKES IN BAD SCI-FI SHOWS.
HE'S ALWAYS GOT SOME EMINENTLY PRAGMATIC BLANKET SOLUTION FOR A WORLD THAT'S COMPLEX AND IRRATIONAL AND... AND HUMAN.
YEAH, YEAH, THE GEEK SHALL INHERIT THE BLAH, BLAH, BLAH.
KERRACK
THE HELL?
SOMEONE'S ON YOUR BALCONY.
EDDY, I'M NINE STORIES UP.
YOU THINK THE BIG BAD MAYOR PUT HIS *JETPACK* BACK ON SO HE COULD FLY UP HERE AND SCARE YOU?
JUST GRAB THE PHONE IN CASE THERE'S REALLY...
I CAME TO SEE YOU.

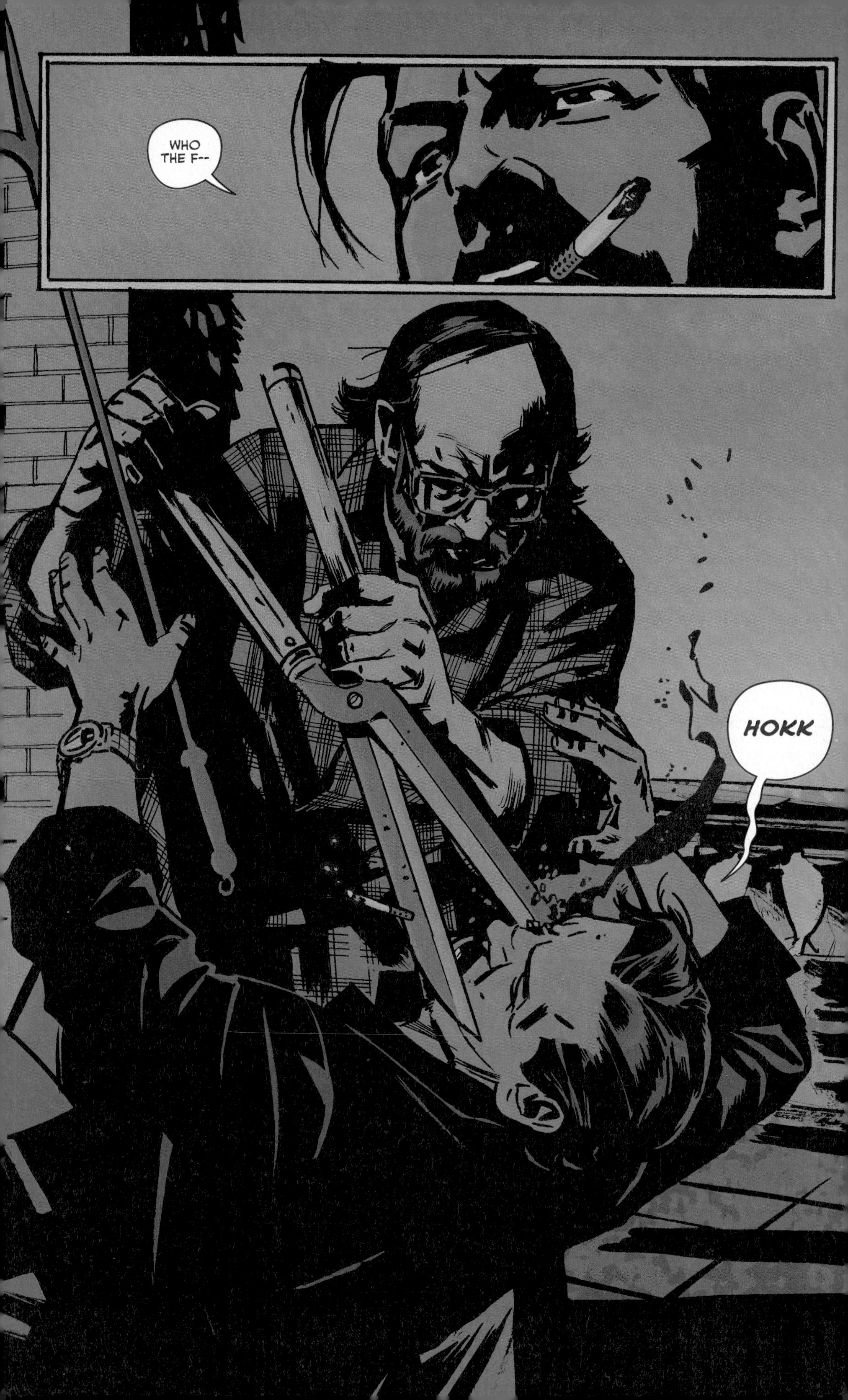
WHO THE F--
HOKK

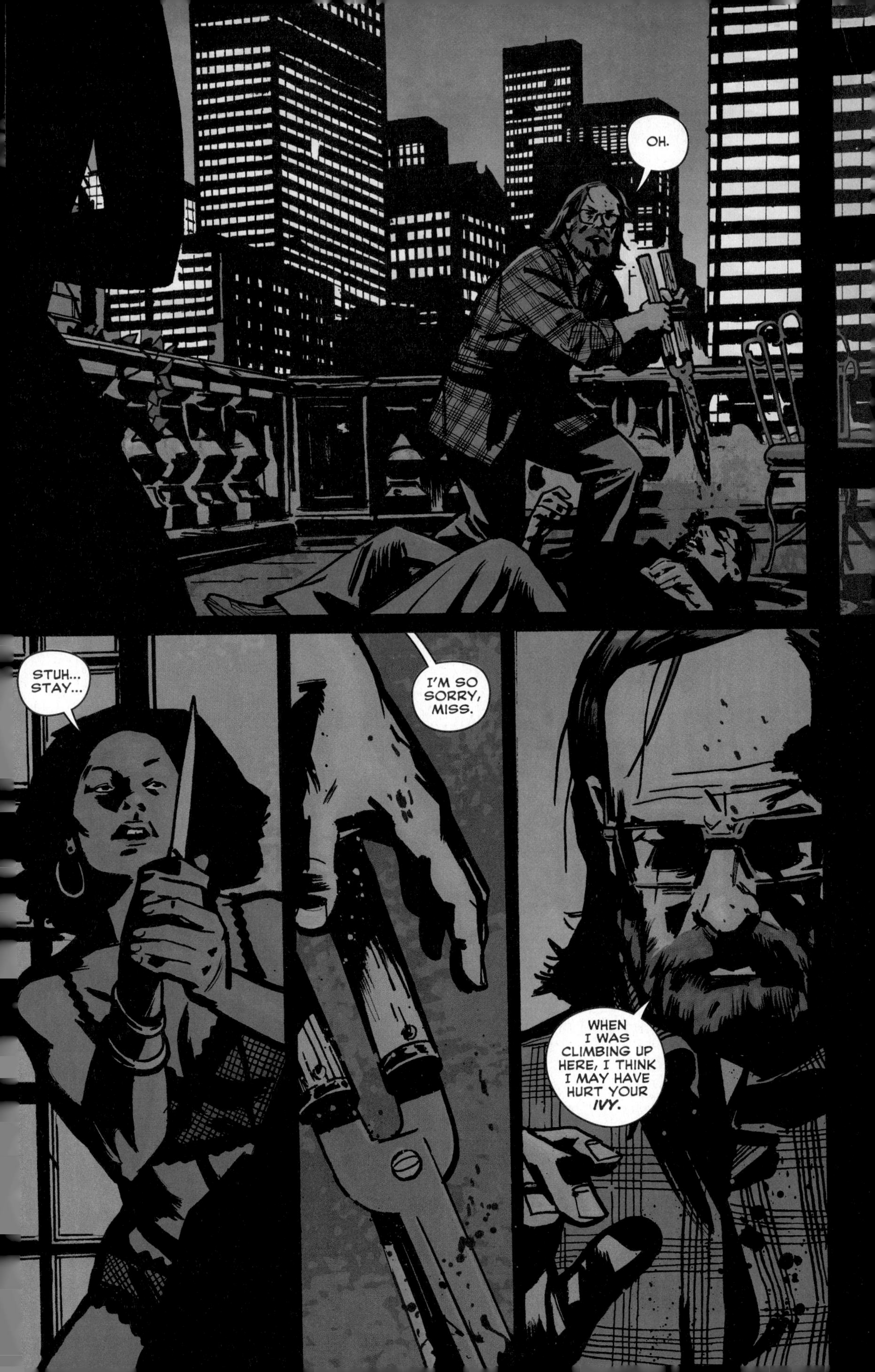
OH.
STUH... STAY...
I'M SO SORRY, MISS.
WHEN I WAS CLIMBING UP HERE, I THINK I MAY HAVE HURT YOUR *IVY*.

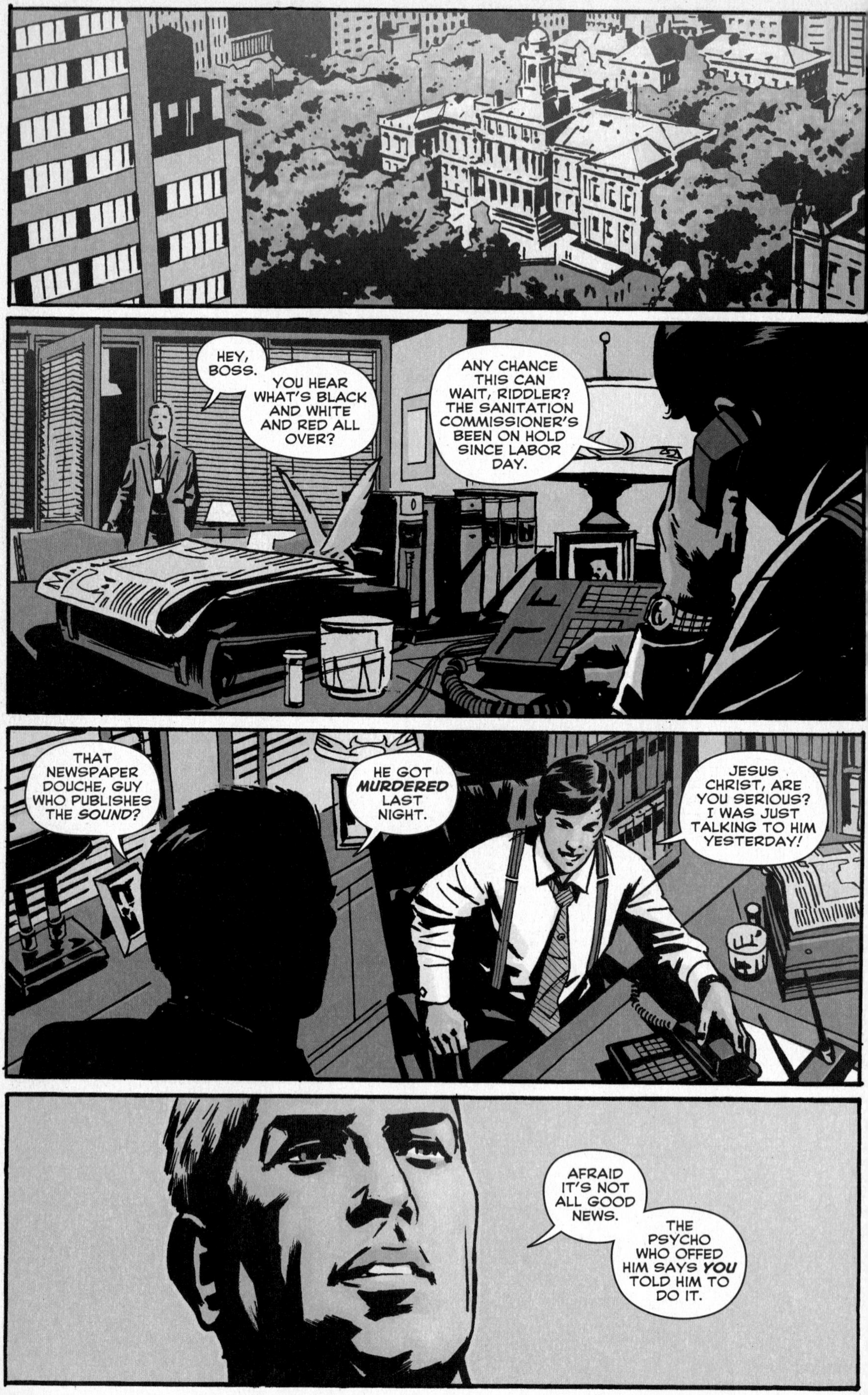
HEY, BOSS.
YOU HEAR WHAT'S BLACK AND WHITE AND RED ALL OVER?
ANY CHANCE THIS CAN WAIT, RIDDLER? THE SANITATION COMMISSIONER'S BEEN ON HOLD SINCE LABOR DAY.
THAT NEWSPAPER DOUCHE, GUY WHO PUBLISHES THE *SOUND*?
HE GOT ***MURDERED*** LAST NIGHT.
JESUS CHRIST, ARE YOU SERIOUS? I WAS JUST TALKING TO HIM YESTERDAY!
AFRAID IT'S NOT ALL GOOD NEWS.
THE PSYCHO WHO OFFED HIM SAYS ***YOU*** TOLD HIM TO DO IT.

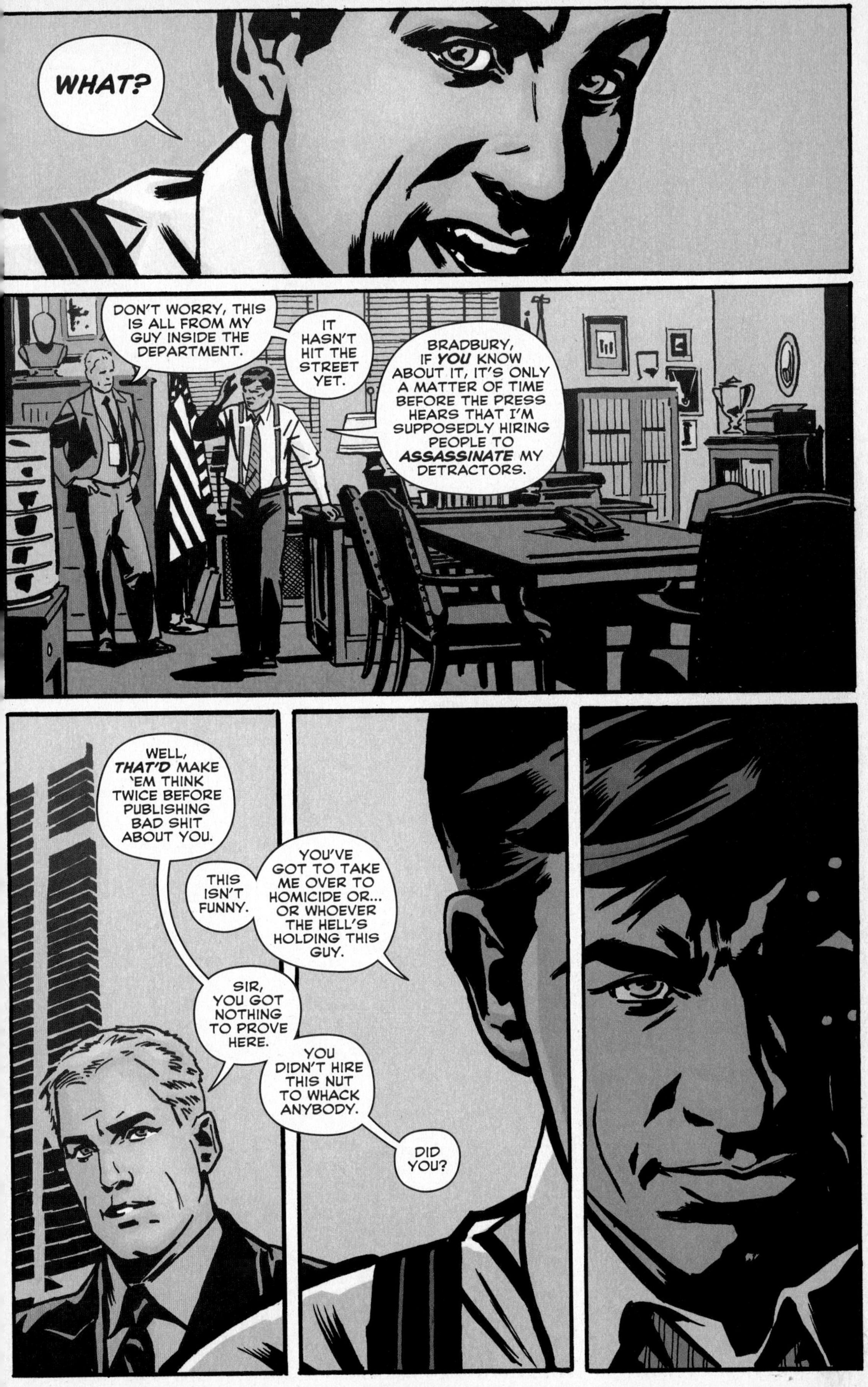
WHAT?
DON'T WORRY, THIS IS ALL FROM MY GUY INSIDE THE DEPARTMENT.
IT HASN'T HIT THE STREET YET.
BRADBURY, IF YOU KNOW ABOUT IT, IT'S ONLY A MATTER OF TIME BEFORE THE PRESS HEARS THAT I'M SUPPOSEDLY HIRING PEOPLE TO ASSASSINATE MY DETRACTORS.
WELL, THAT'D MAKE 'EM THINK TWICE BEFORE PUBLISHING BAD SHIT ABOUT YOU.
THIS ISN'T FUNNY.
YOU'VE GOT TO TAKE ME OVER TO HOMICIDE OR... OR WHOEVER THE HELL'S HOLDING THIS GUY.
SIR, YOU GOT NOTHING TO PROVE HERE.
YOU DIDN'T HIRE THIS NUT TO WHACK ANYBODY.
DID YOU?

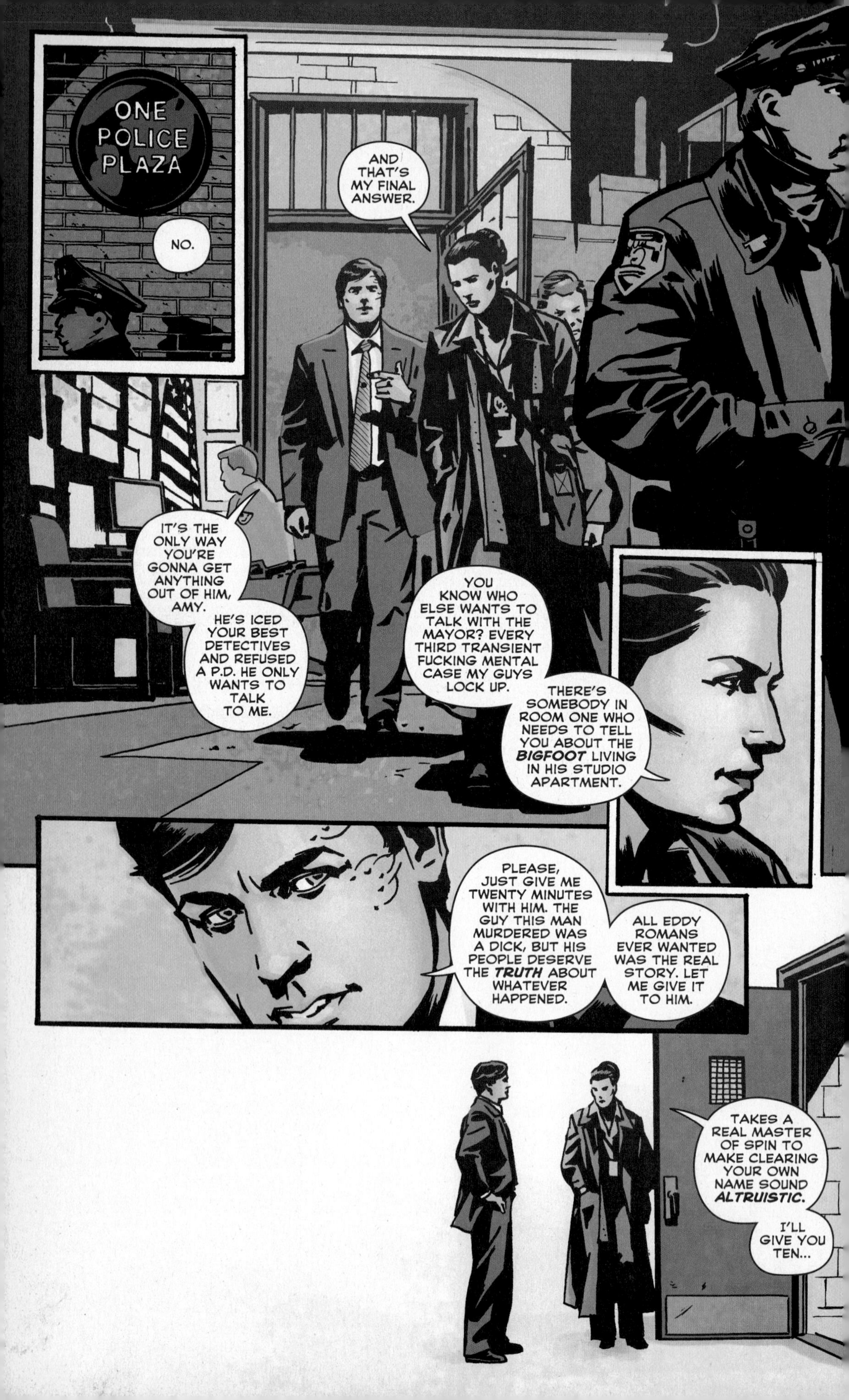
ONE POLICE PLAZA
NO.
AND THAT'S MY FINAL ANSWER.
IT'S THE ONLY WAY YOU'RE GONNA GET ANYTHING OUT OF HIM, AMY.
HE'S ICED YOUR BEST DETECTIVES AND REFUSED A P.D. HE ONLY WANTS TO TALK TO ME.
YOU KNOW WHO ELSE WANTS TO TALK WITH THE MAYOR? EVERY THIRD TRANSIENT FUCKING MENTAL CASE MY GUYS LOCK UP.
THERE'S SOMEBODY IN ROOM ONE WHO NEEDS TO TELL YOU ABOUT THE *BIGFOOT* LIVING IN HIS STUDIO APARTMENT.
PLEASE, JUST GIVE ME TWENTY MINUTES WITH HIM. THE GUY THIS MAN MURDERED WAS A DICK, BUT HIS PEOPLE DESERVE THE *TRUTH* ABOUT WHATEVER HAPPENED.
ALL EDDY ROMANS EVER WANTED WAS THE REAL STORY. LET ME GIVE IT TO HIM.
TAKES A REAL MASTER OF SPIN TO MAKE CLEARING YOUR OWN NAME SOUND *ALTRUISTIC.*
I'LL GIVE YOU TEN...

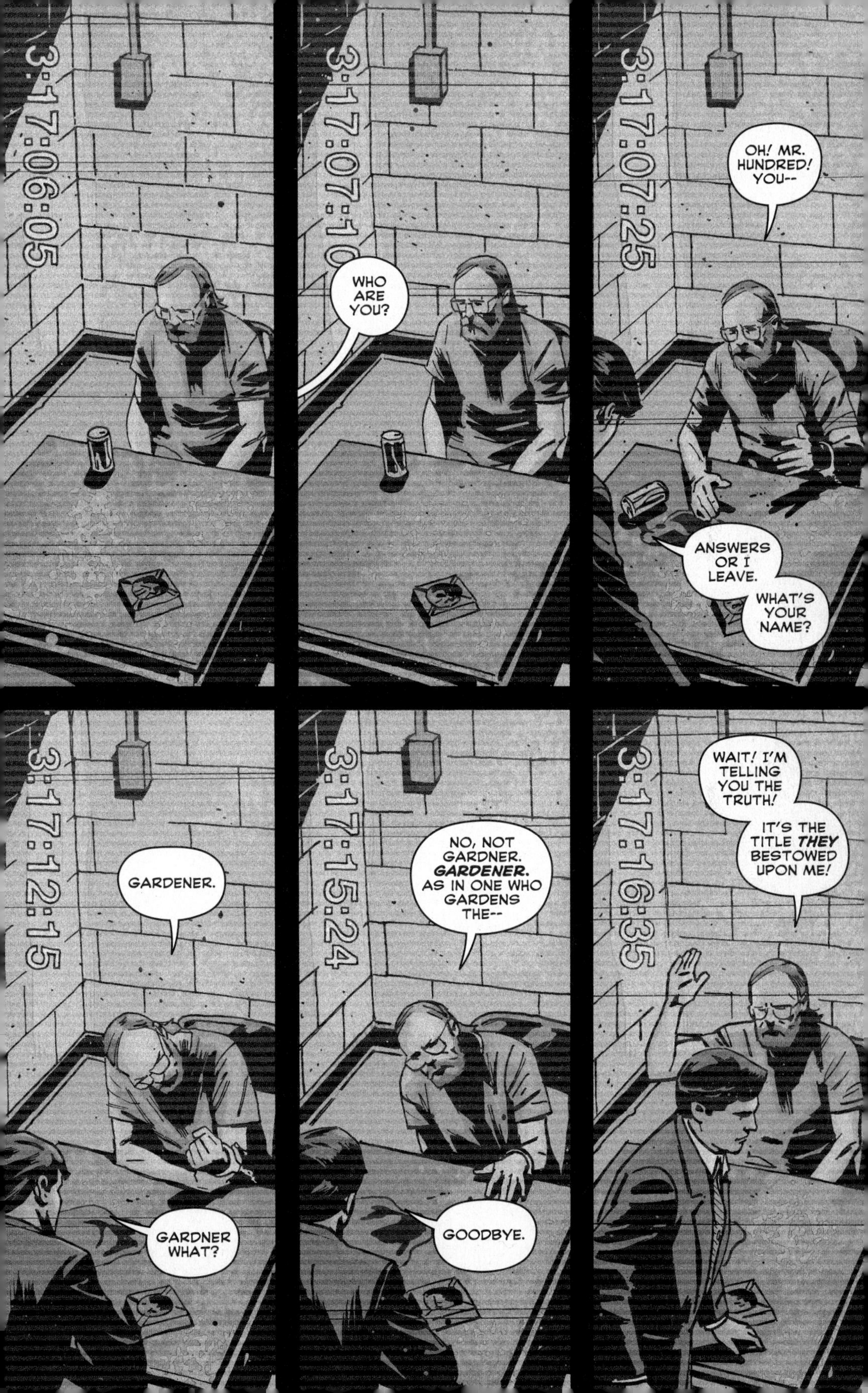
3:17:06:05
3:17:07:10
WHO ARE YOU?
3:17:07:25
OH! MR. HUNDRED! YOU--
ANSWERS OR I LEAVE.
WHAT'S YOUR NAME?
3:17:12:15
GARDENER.
GARDNER WHAT?
3:17:15:24
NO, NOT GARDNER. ***GARDENER.*** AS IN ONE WHO GARDENS THE--
GOODBYE.
3:17:16:35
WAIT! I'M TELLING YOU THE TRUTH!
IT'S THE TITLE ***THEY*** BESTOWED UPON ME!

3:17:19:42
THEY WHO?
3:17:21:15
THE PLANTS. I...I CAN COMMUNICATE WITH THEM.
JUST LIKE YOU CAN COMMUNICATE WITH MACHINES.
3:17:24:26
IS THAT RIGHT, SWAMP THING?
TELL ME, WHERE DID YOU GET YOUR AWESOMELY UNORIGINAL POWERS?
3:17:25:38
YOU GAVE THEM TO ME.
3:17:30:15
CAMERA. GIVE US A MOMENT. WOULD YOU?

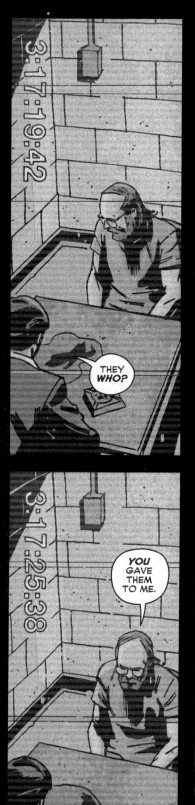

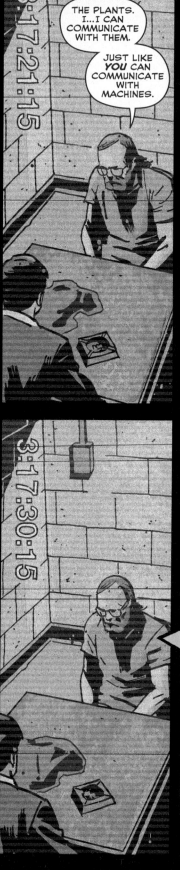

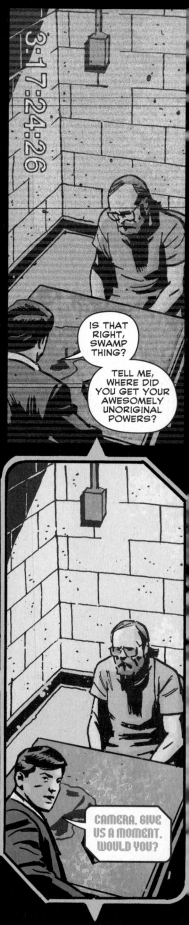

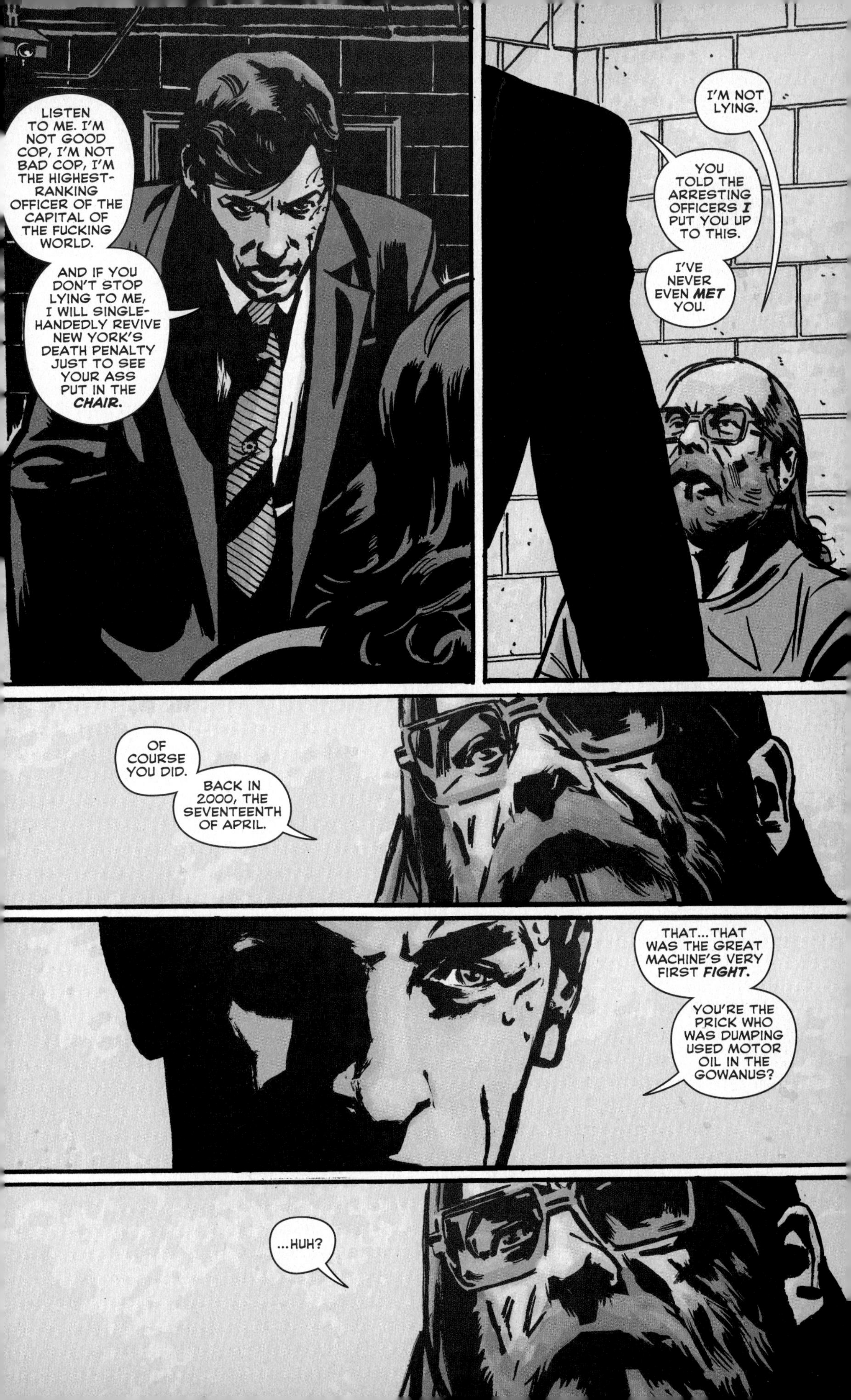
LISTEN TO ME. I'M NOT GOOD COP, I'M NOT BAD COP, I'M THE HIGHEST-RANKING OFFICER OF THE CAPITAL OF THE FUCKING WORLD.
AND IF YOU DON'T STOP LYING TO ME, I WILL SINGLE-HANDEDLY REVIVE NEW YORK'S DEATH PENALTY JUST TO SEE YOUR ASS PUT IN THE ***CHAIR.***
I'M NOT LYING.
YOU TOLD THE ARRESTING OFFICERS ***I*** PUT YOU UP TO THIS.
I'VE NEVER EVEN ***MET*** YOU.
OF COURSE YOU DID.
BACK IN 2000, THE SEVENTEENTH OF APRIL.
THAT...THAT WAS THE GREAT MACHINE'S VERY FIRST ***FIGHT.***
YOU'RE THE PRICK WHO WAS DUMPING USED MOTOR OIL IN THE GOWANUS?
...HUH?

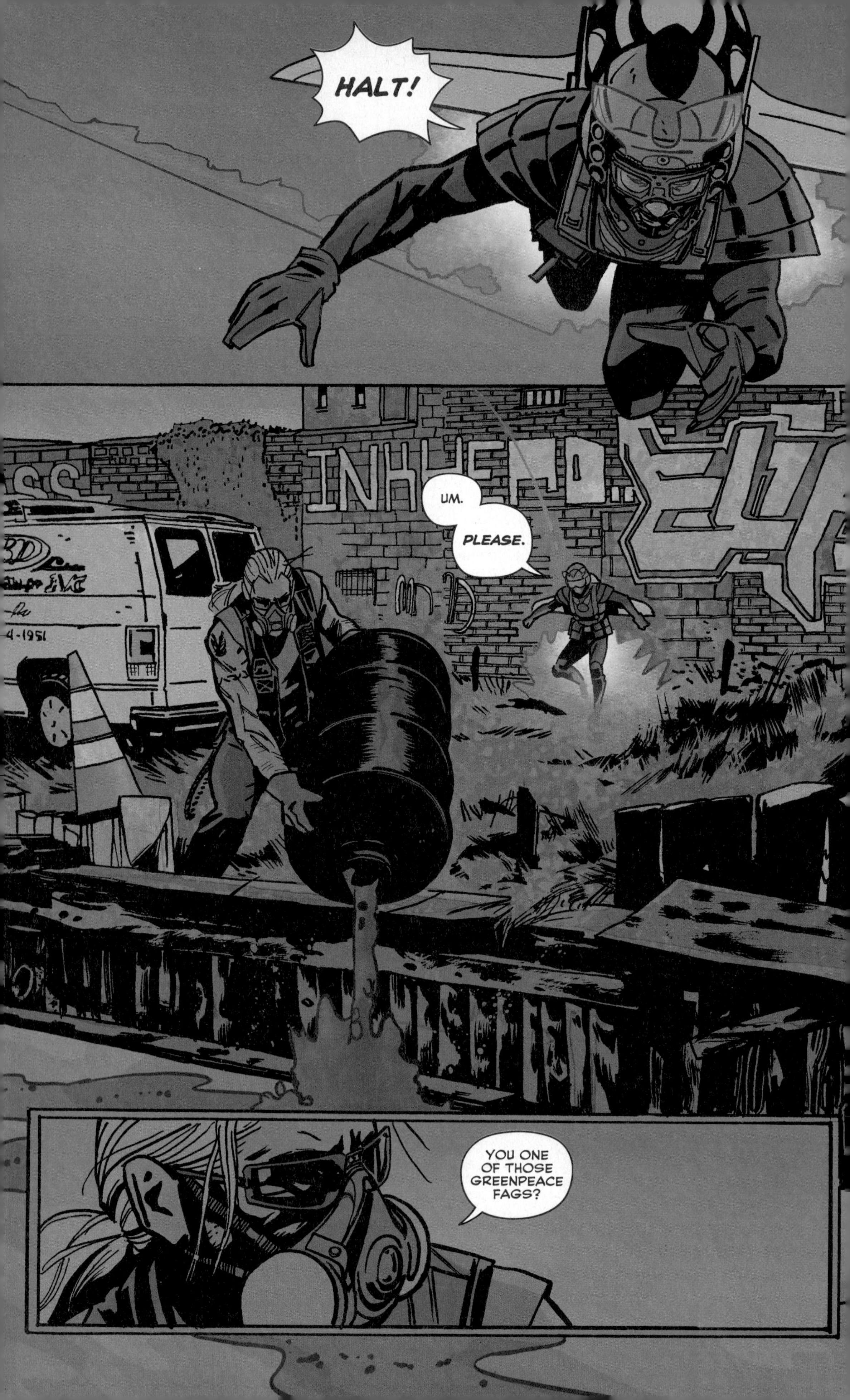
HALT!
UM.
PLEASE.
YOU ONE OF THOSE GREENPEACE FAGS?

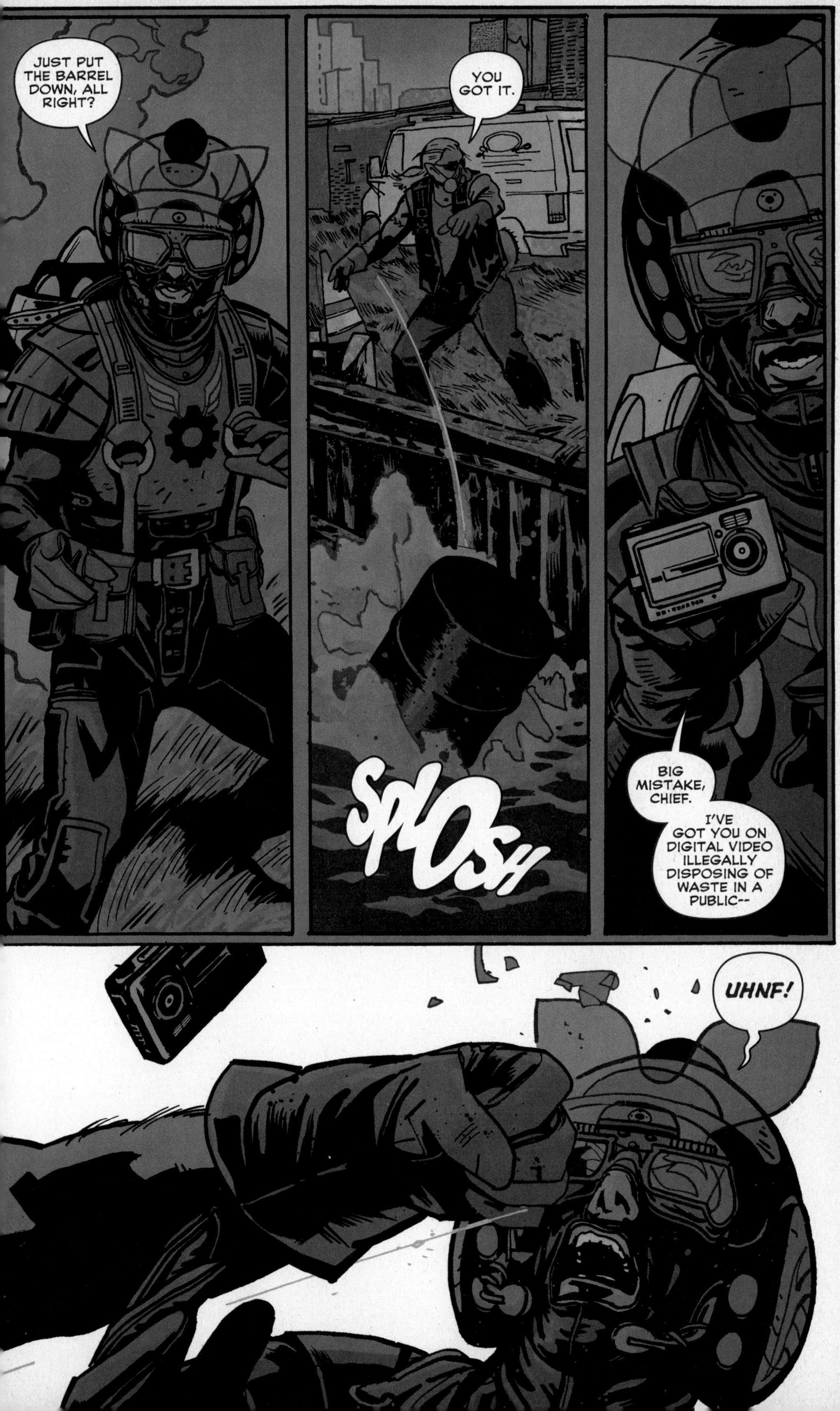
JUST PUT THE BARREL DOWN, ALL RIGHT?
YOU GOT IT.
SPLOSH
BIG MISTAKE, CHIEF.
I'VE GOT YOU ON DIGITAL VIDEO ILLEGALLY DISPOSING OF WASTE IN A PUBLIC--
UHNF!

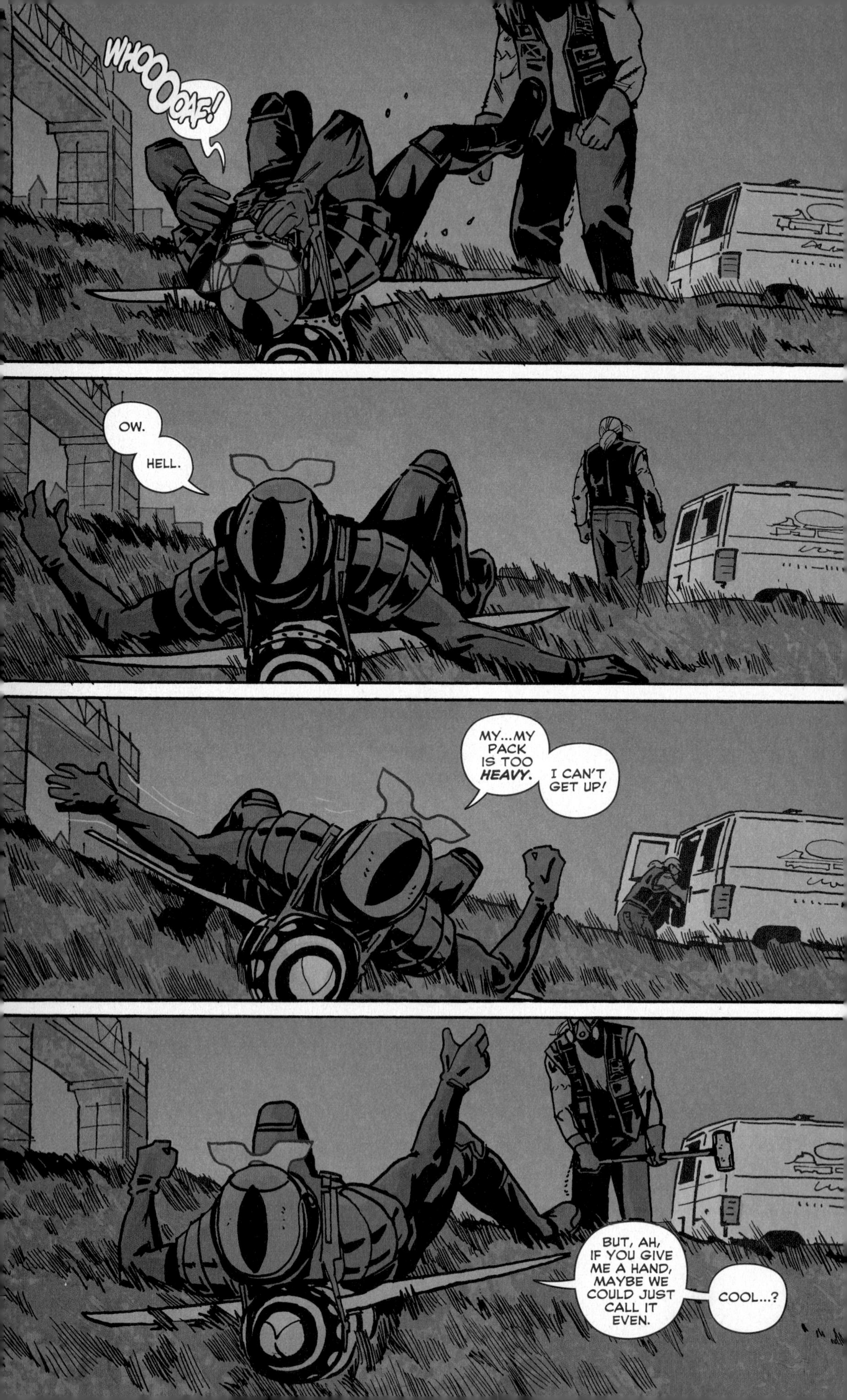
WHOOOOAF!
OW.
HELL.
MY...MY PACK IS TOO HEAVY.
I CAN'T GET UP!
BUT, AH, IF YOU GIVE ME A HAND, MAYBE WE COULD JUST CALL IT EVEN.
COOL...?

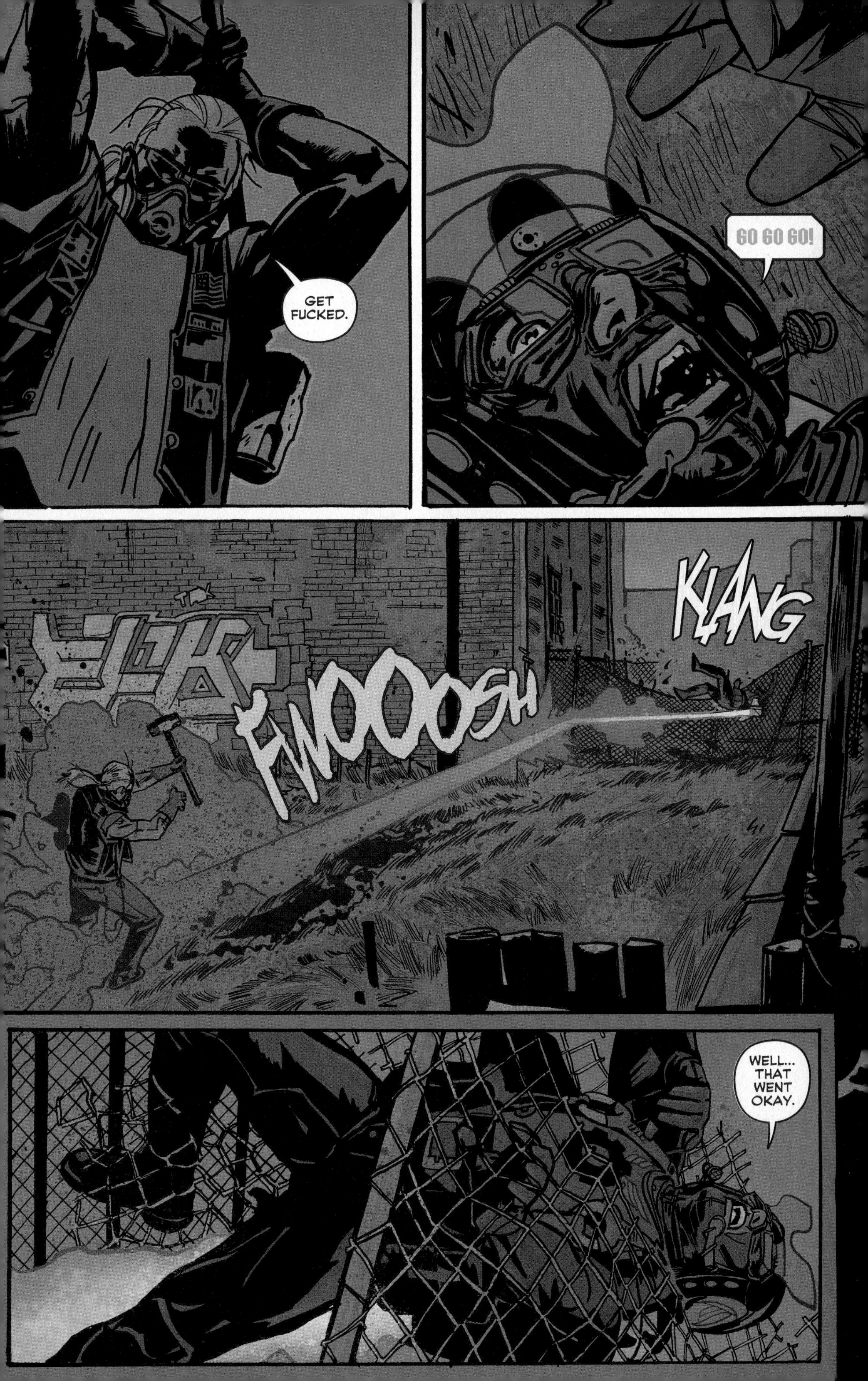
GET FUCKED.
GO GO GO!
KLANG
FWOOOSH
WELL... THAT WENT OKAY.

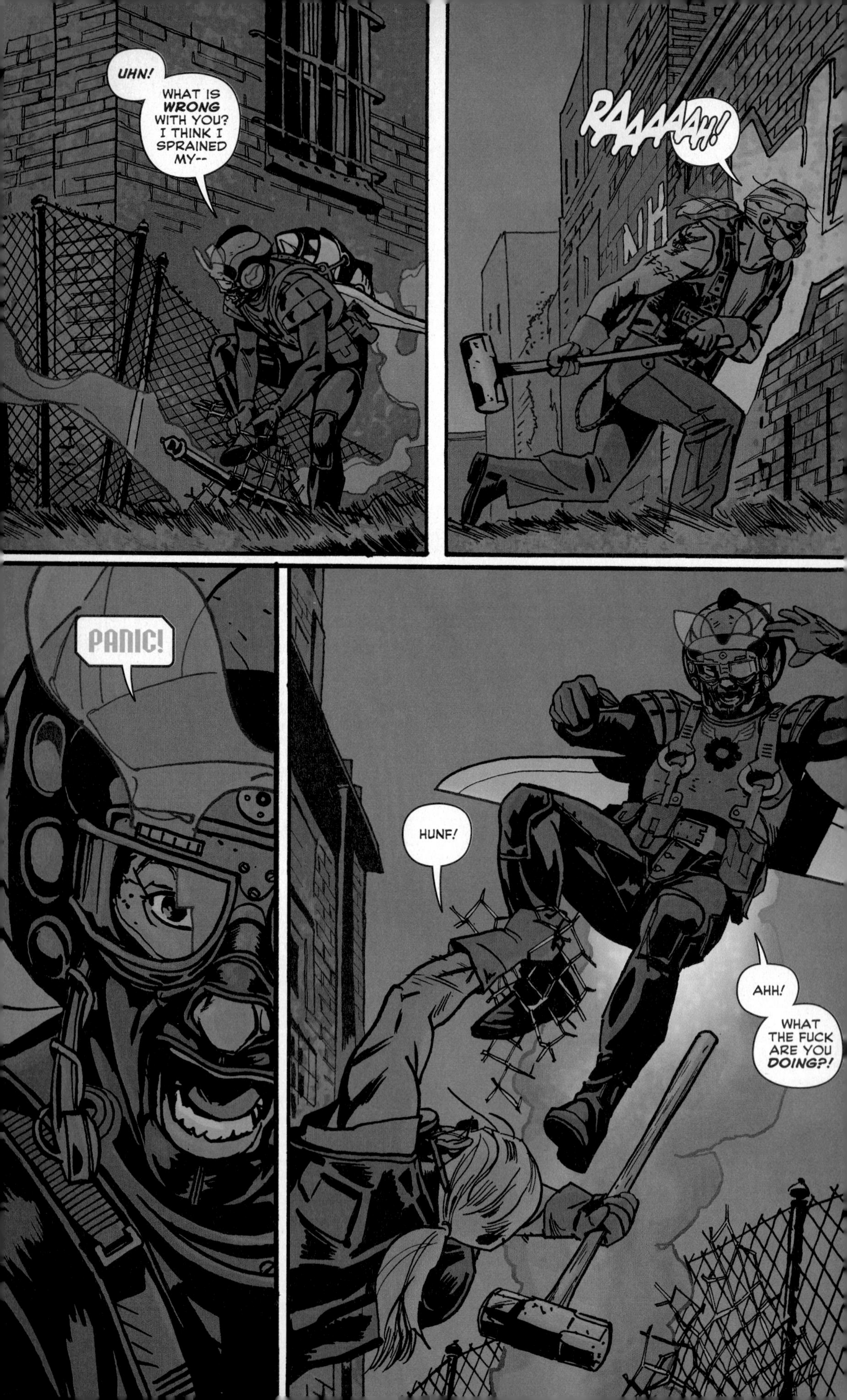
UHN!
WHAT IS WRONG WITH YOU? I THINK I SPRAINED MY--
RAAAAAH!
PANIC!
HUNF!
AHH!
WHAT THE FUCK ARE YOU DOING?!

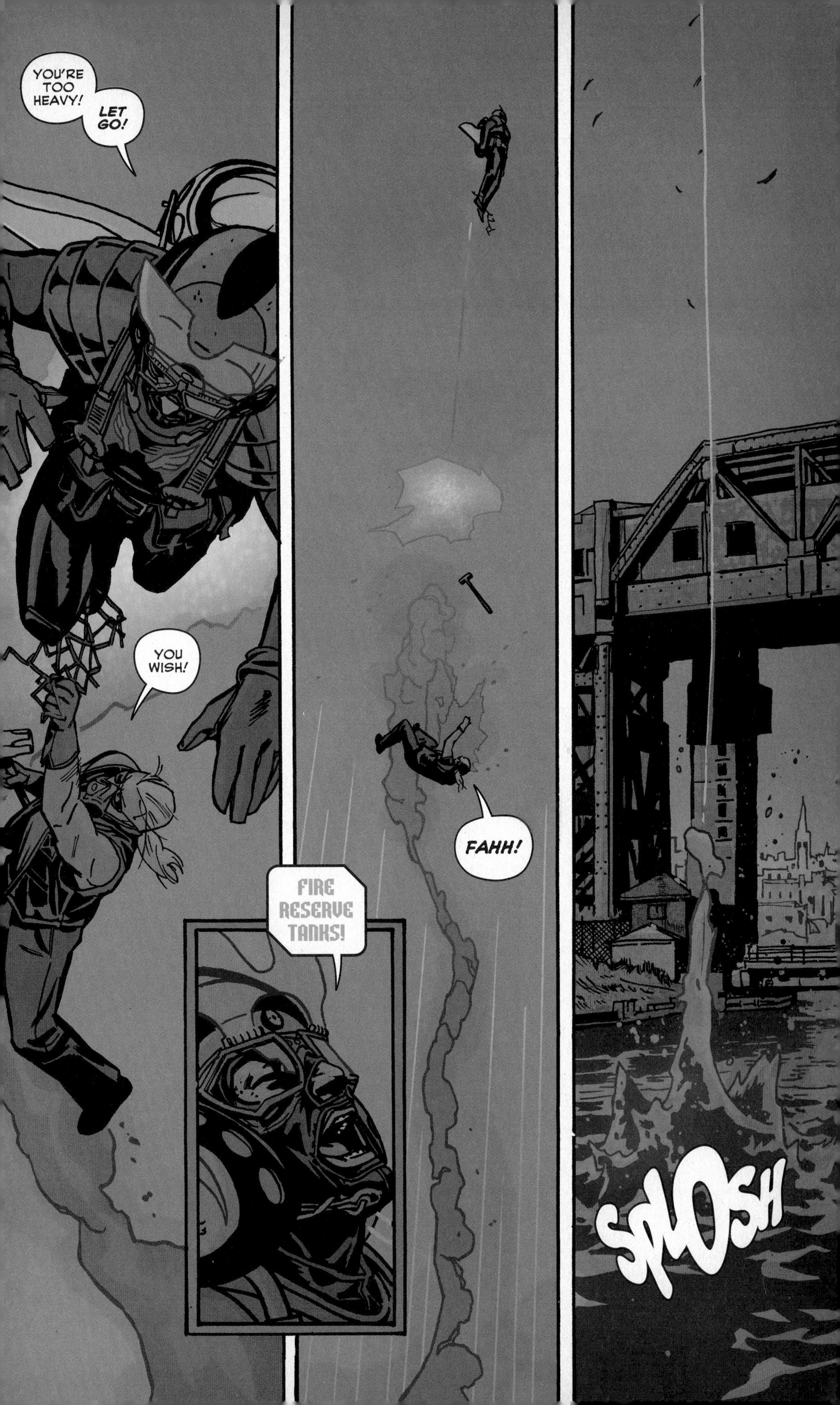

YOU'RE TOO HEAVY!
LET GO!
YOU WISH!
FIRE RESERVE TANKS!
FAHH!
SPLOSH

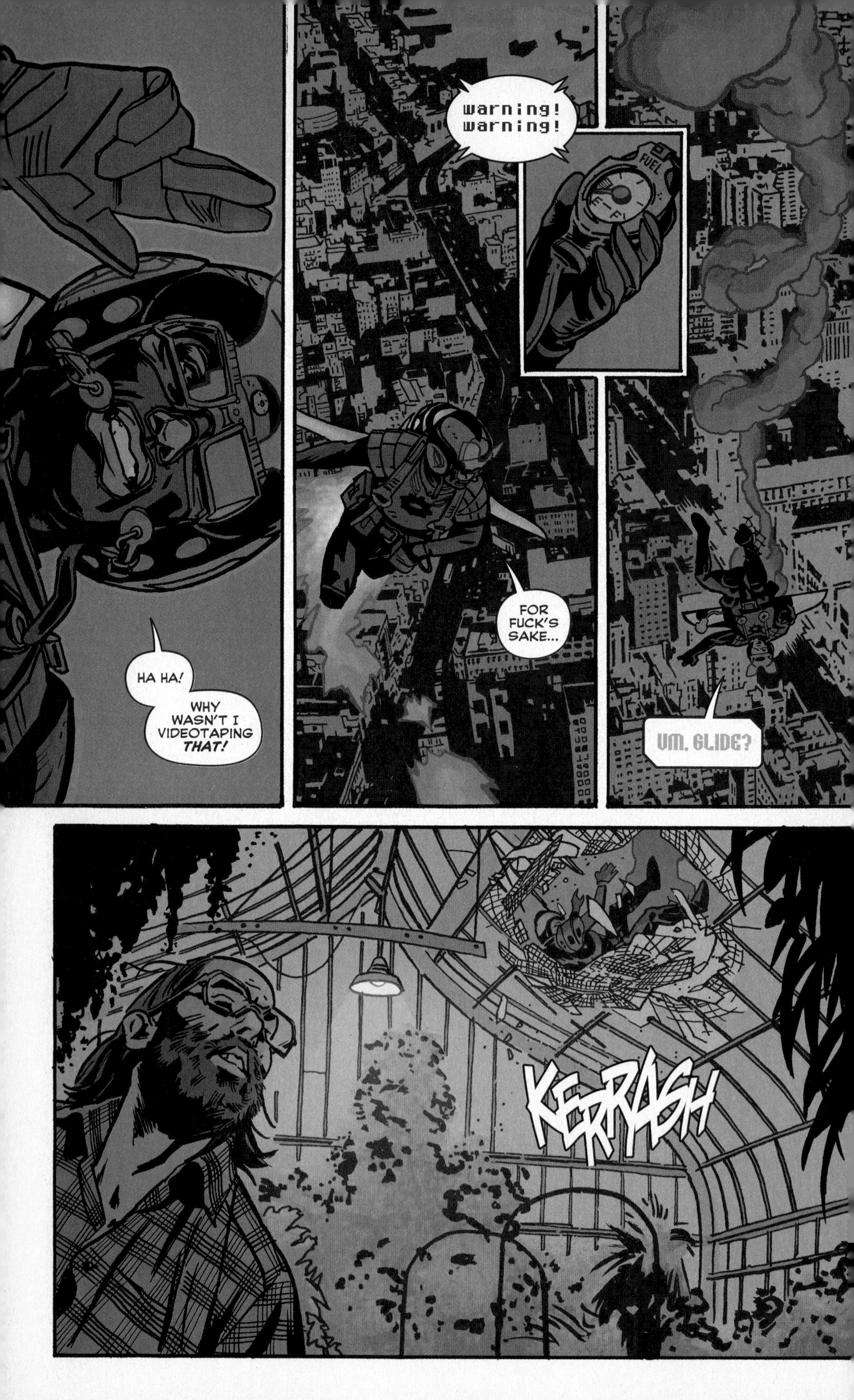
HA HA!
WHY WASN'T I VIDEOTAPING THAT!
warning! warning!
FUEL
FOR FUCK'S SAKE...
UM, GLIDE?
KERRASH

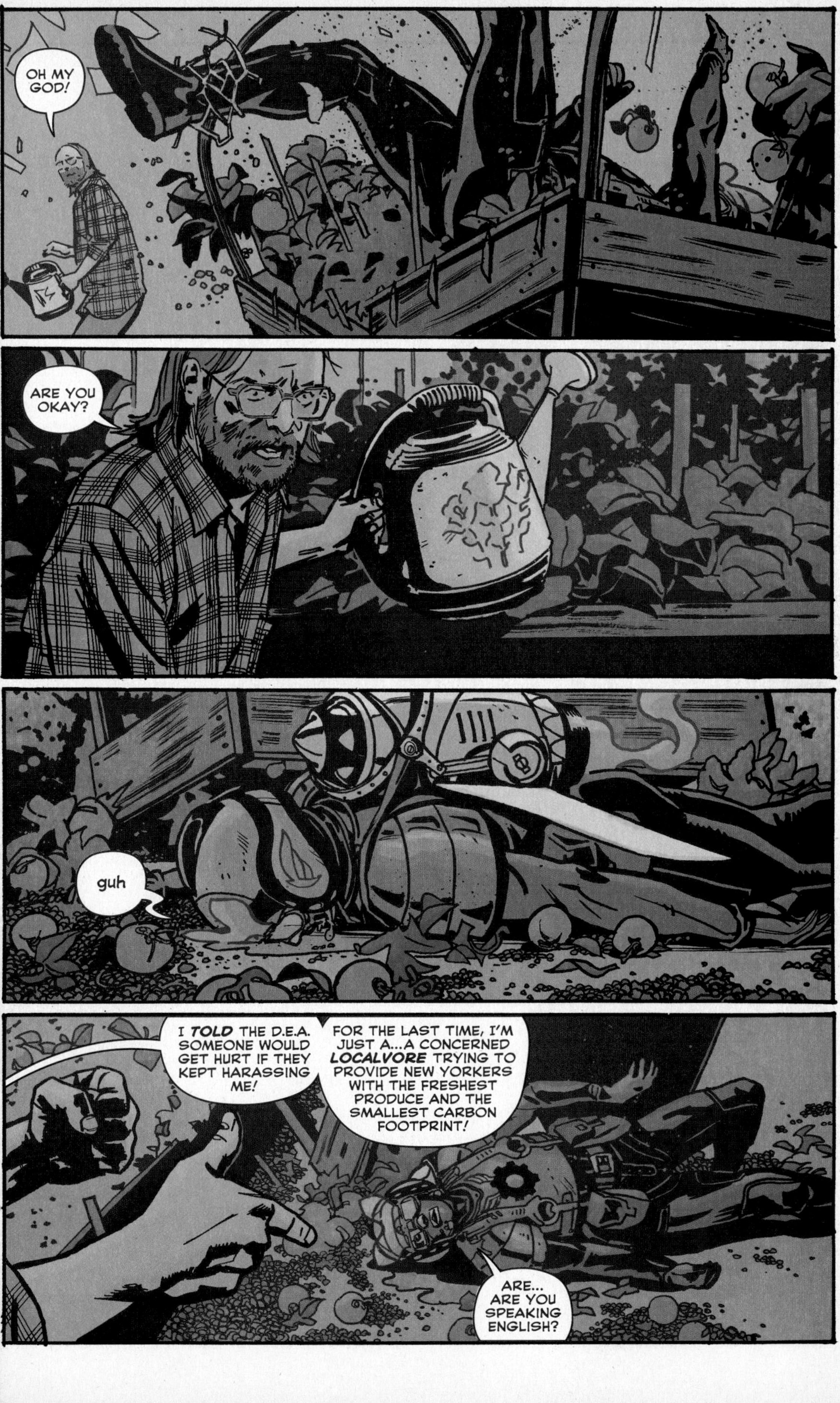
OH MY GOD!
ARE YOU OKAY?
guh
I TOLD THE D.E.A. SOMEONE WOULD GET HURT IF THEY KEPT HARASSING ME!
FOR THE LAST TIME, I'M JUST A...A CONCERNED LOCALVORE TRYING TO PROVIDE NEW YORKERS WITH THE FRESHEST PRODUCE AND THE SMALLEST CARBON FOOTPRINT!
ARE... ARE YOU SPEAKING ENGLISH?

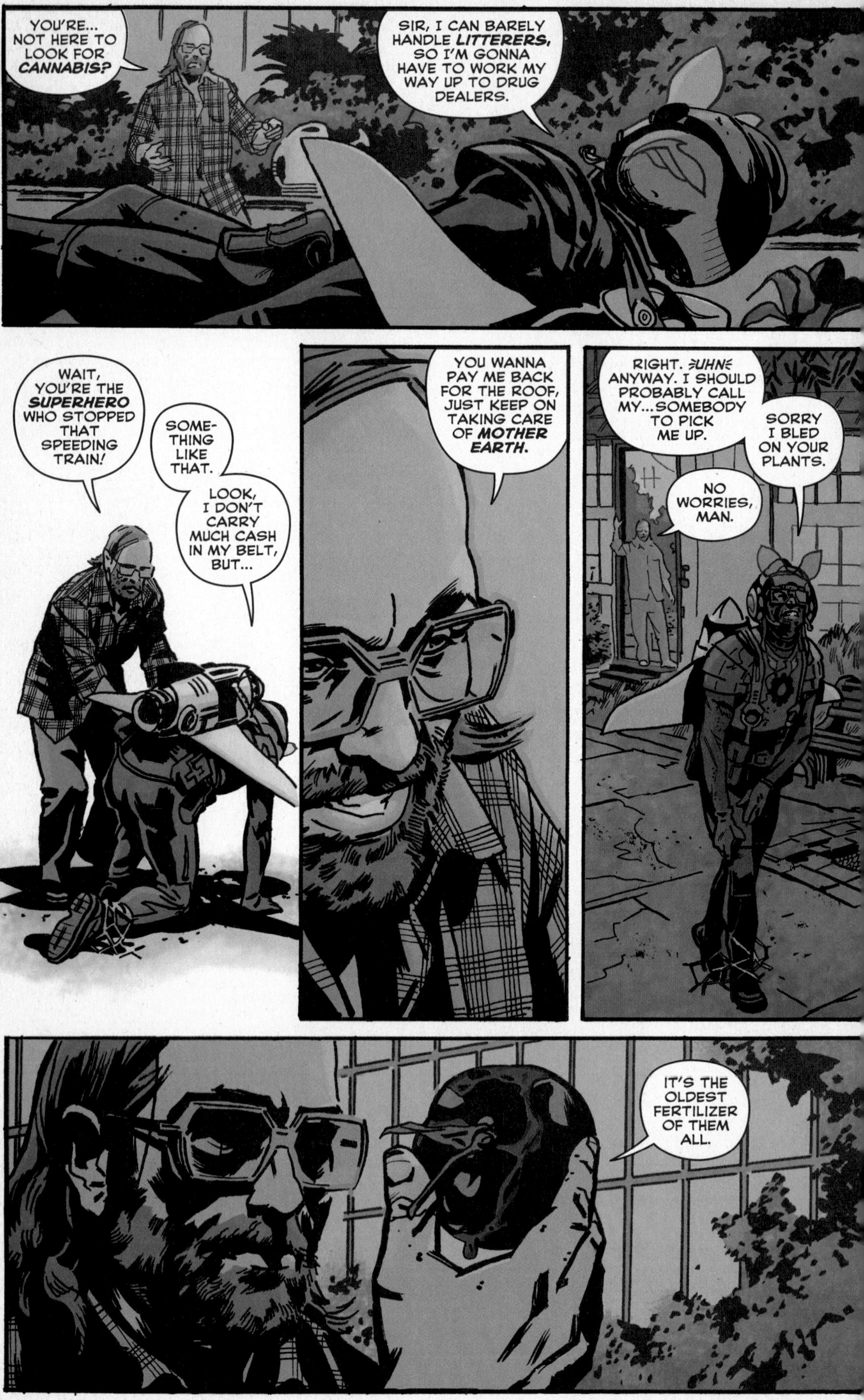
YOU'RE... NOT HERE TO LOOK FOR CANNABIS?
SIR, I CAN BARELY HANDLE LITTERERS, SO I'M GONNA HAVE TO WORK MY WAY UP TO DRUG DEALERS.
WAIT, YOU'RE THE SUPERHERO WHO STOPPED THAT SPEEDING TRAIN!
SOME-THING LIKE THAT.
LOOK, I DON'T CARRY MUCH CASH IN MY BELT, BUT...
YOU WANNA PAY ME BACK FOR THE ROOF, JUST KEEP ON TAKING CARE OF MOTHER EARTH.
RIGHT. UHN ANYWAY. I SHOULD PROBABLY CALL MY...SOMEBODY TO PICK ME UP.
SORRY I BLED ON YOUR PLANTS.
NO WORRIES, MAN.
IT'S THE OLDEST FERTILIZER OF THEM ALL.

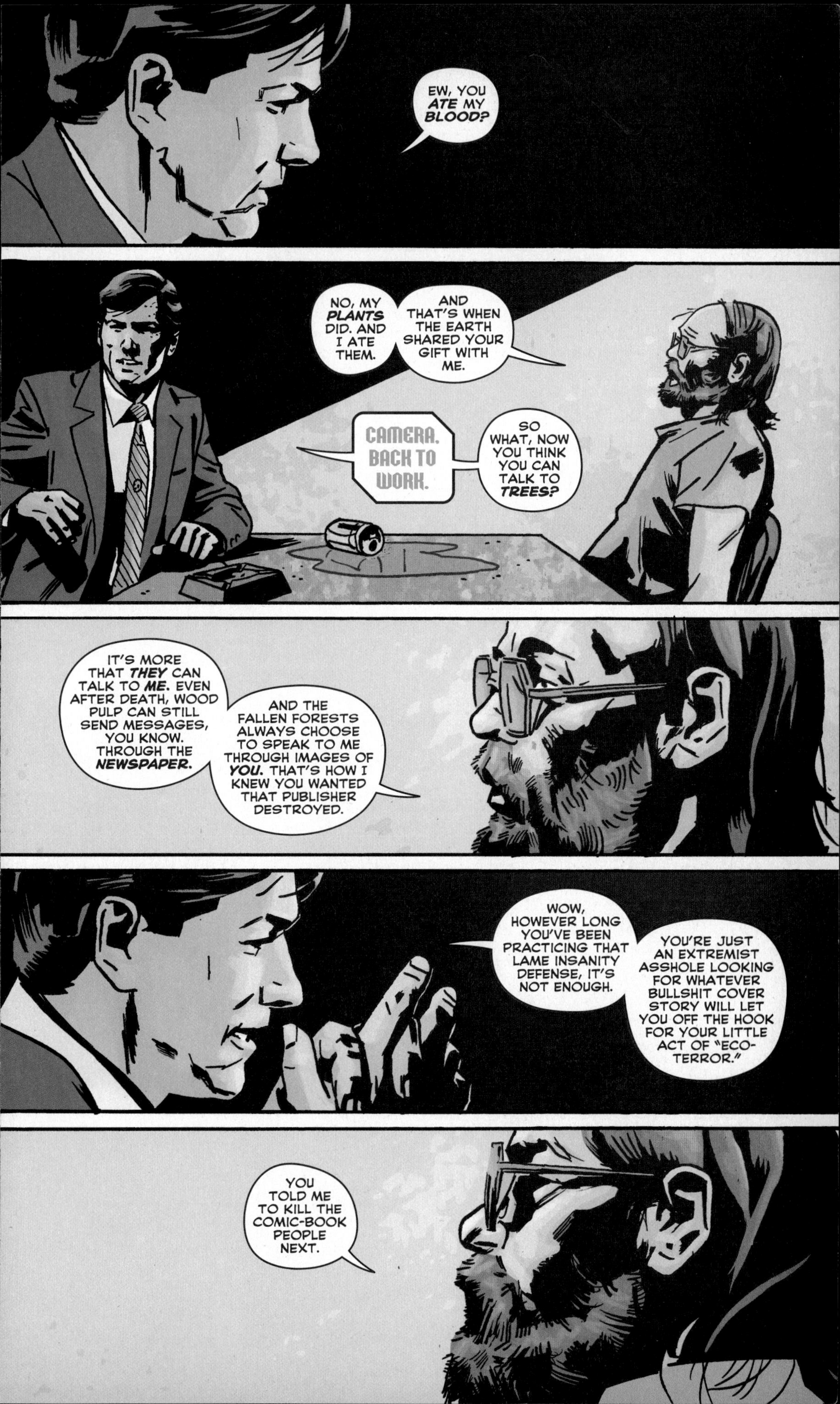

EW, YOU ATE MY BLOOD?
NO, MY PLANTS DID. AND I ATE THEM.
AND THAT'S WHEN THE EARTH SHARED YOUR GIFT WITH ME.
SO WHAT, NOW YOU THINK YOU CAN TALK TO TREES?
CAMERA. BACK TO WORK.
IT'S MORE THAT THEY CAN TALK TO ME. EVEN AFTER DEATH, WOOD PULP CAN STILL SEND MESSAGES, YOU KNOW. THROUGH THE NEWSPAPER.
AND THE FALLEN FORESTS ALWAYS CHOOSE TO SPEAK TO ME THROUGH IMAGES OF YOU. THAT'S HOW I KNEW YOU WANTED THAT PUBLISHER DESTROYED.
WOW, HOWEVER LONG YOU'VE BEEN PRACTICING THAT LAME INSANITY DEFENSE, IT'S NOT ENOUGH.
YOU'RE JUST AN EXTREMIST ASSHOLE LOOKING FOR WHATEVER BULLSHIT COVER STORY WILL LET YOU OFF THE HOOK FOR YOUR LITTLE ACT OF "ECO-TERROR."
YOU TOLD ME TO KILL THE COMIC-BOOK PEOPLE NEXT.

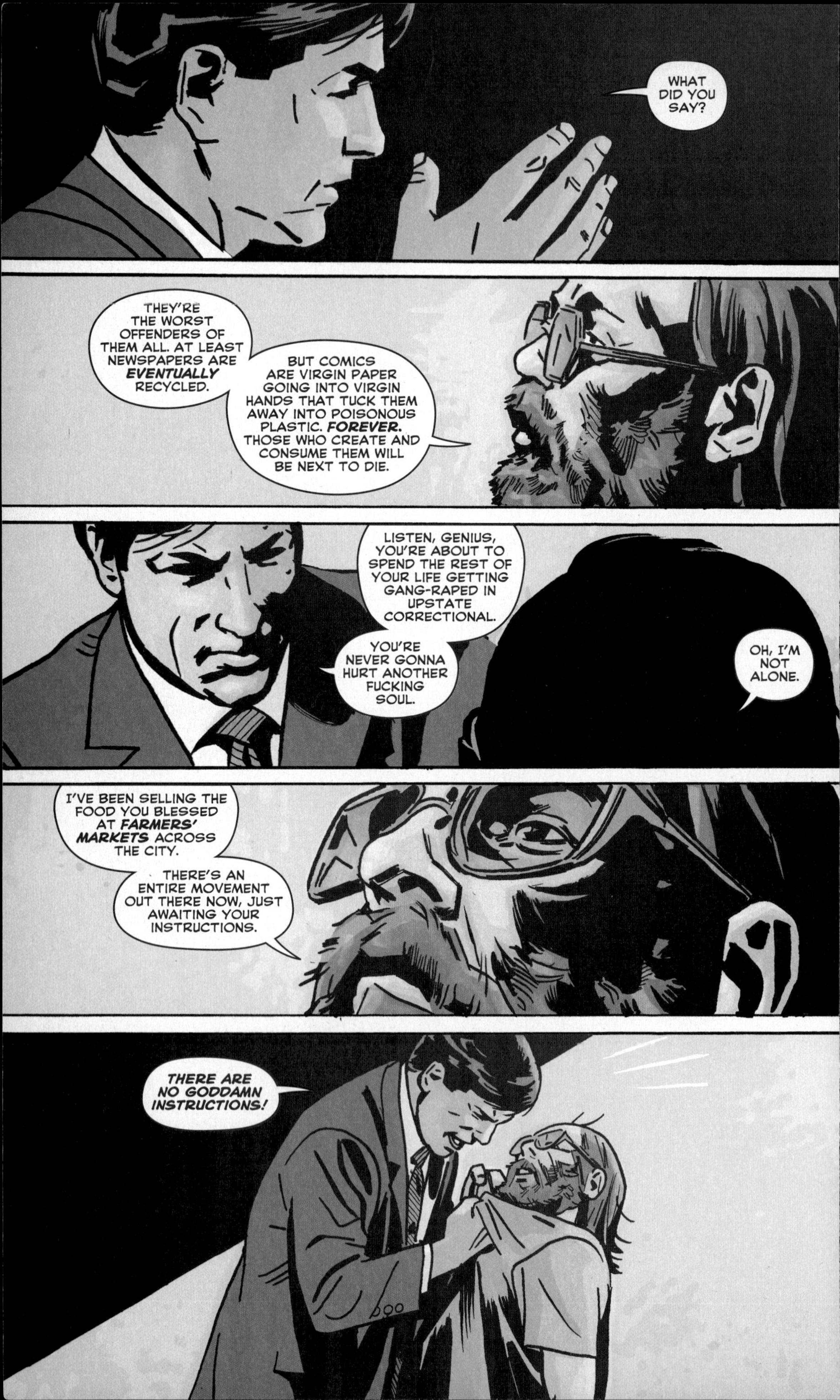
WHAT DID YOU SAY?
THEY'RE THE WORST OFFENDERS OF THEM ALL. AT LEAST NEWSPAPERS ARE *EVENTUALLY* RECYCLED.
BUT COMICS ARE VIRGIN PAPER GOING INTO VIRGIN HANDS THAT TUCK THEM AWAY INTO POISONOUS PLASTIC. *FOREVER.* THOSE WHO CREATE AND CONSUME THEM WILL BE NEXT TO DIE.
LISTEN, GENIUS, YOU'RE ABOUT TO SPEND THE REST OF YOUR LIFE GETTING GANG-RAPED IN UPSTATE CORRECTIONAL.
YOU'RE NEVER GONNA HURT ANOTHER FUCKING SOUL.
OH, I'M NOT ALONE.
I'VE BEEN SELLING THE FOOD YOU BLESSED AT *FARMERS' MARKETS* ACROSS THE CITY.
THERE'S AN ENTIRE MOVEMENT OUT THERE NOW, JUST AWAITING YOUR INSTRUCTIONS.
THERE ARE NO GODDAMN INSTRUCTIONS!

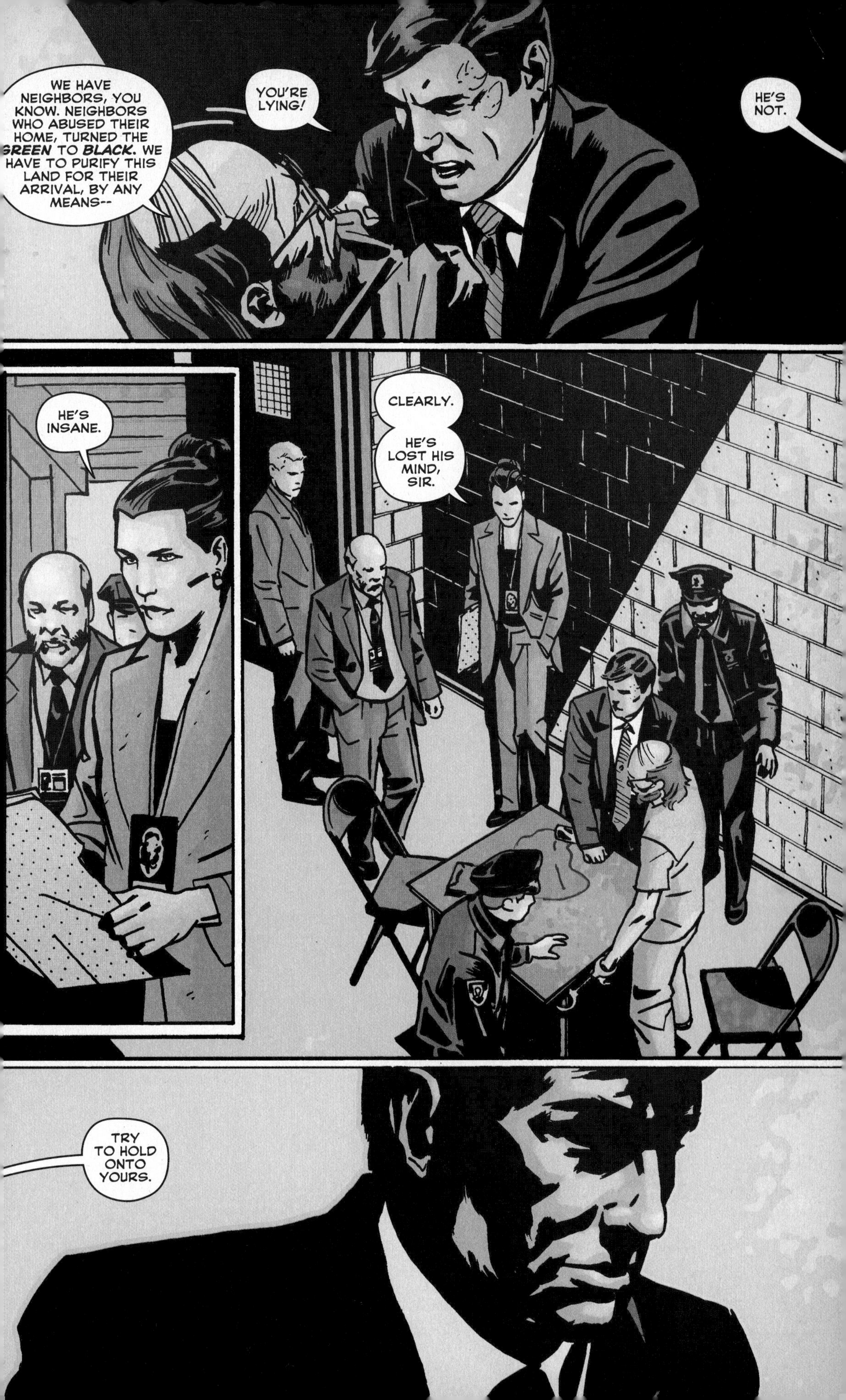
WE HAVE NEIGHBORS, YOU KNOW. NEIGHBORS WHO ABUSED THEIR HOME, TURNED THE **GREEN** TO **BLACK.** WE HAVE TO PURIFY THIS LAND FOR THEIR ARRIVAL, BY ANY MEANS--
YOU'RE LYING!
HE'S NOT.
HE'S INSANE.
CLEARLY.
HE'S LOST HIS MIND, SIR.
TRY TO HOLD ONTO YOURS.

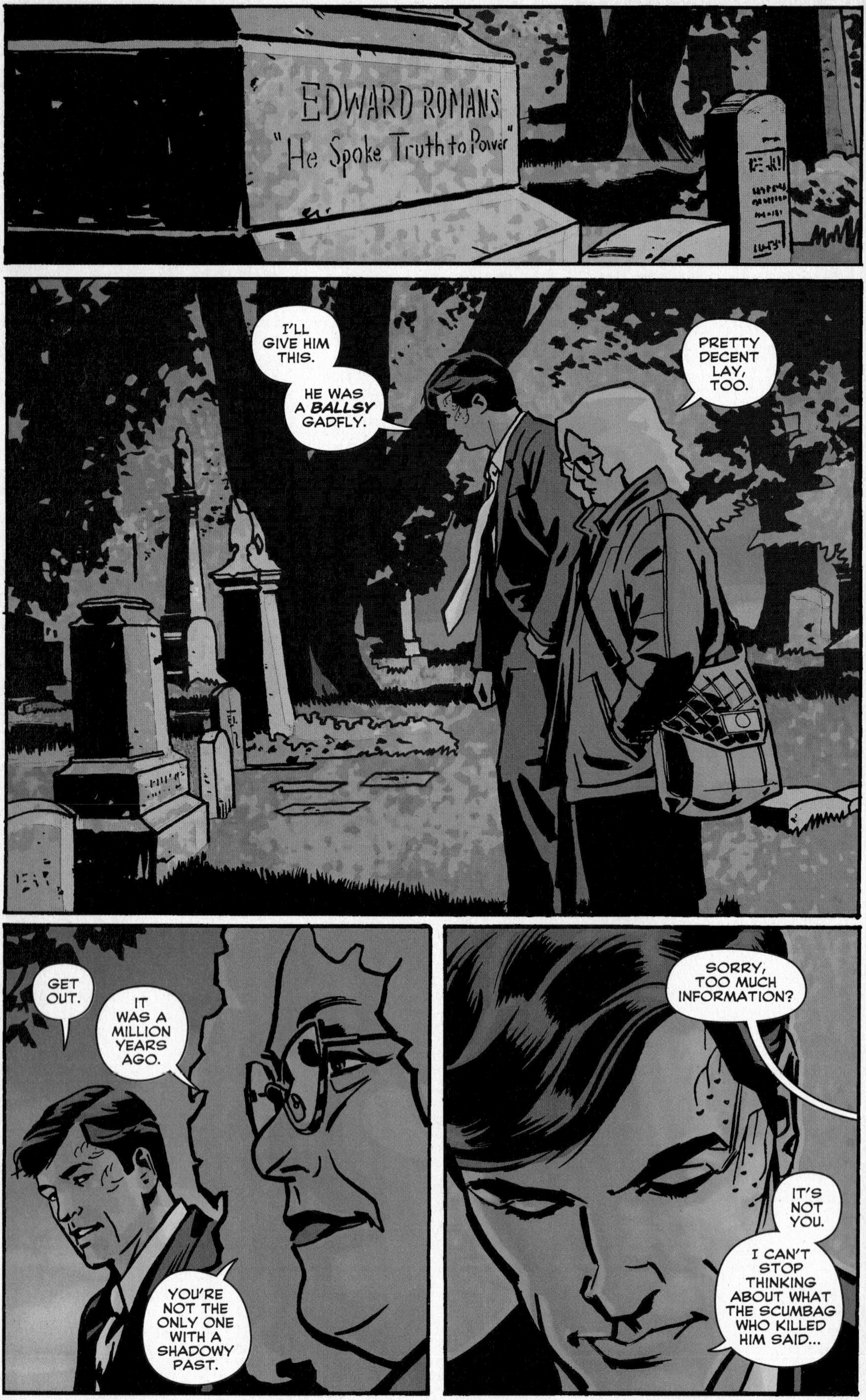
EDWARD ROMANS
"He Spoke Truth to Power"
I'LL GIVE HIM THIS.
HE WAS A ***BALLSY*** GADFLY.
PRETTY DECENT LAY, TOO.
GET OUT.
IT WAS A MILLION YEARS AGO.
YOU'RE NOT THE ONLY ONE WITH A SHADOWY PAST.
SORRY, TOO MUCH INFORMATION?
IT'S NOT YOU.
I CAN'T STOP THINKING ABOUT WHAT THE SCUMBAG WHO KILLED HIM SAID...

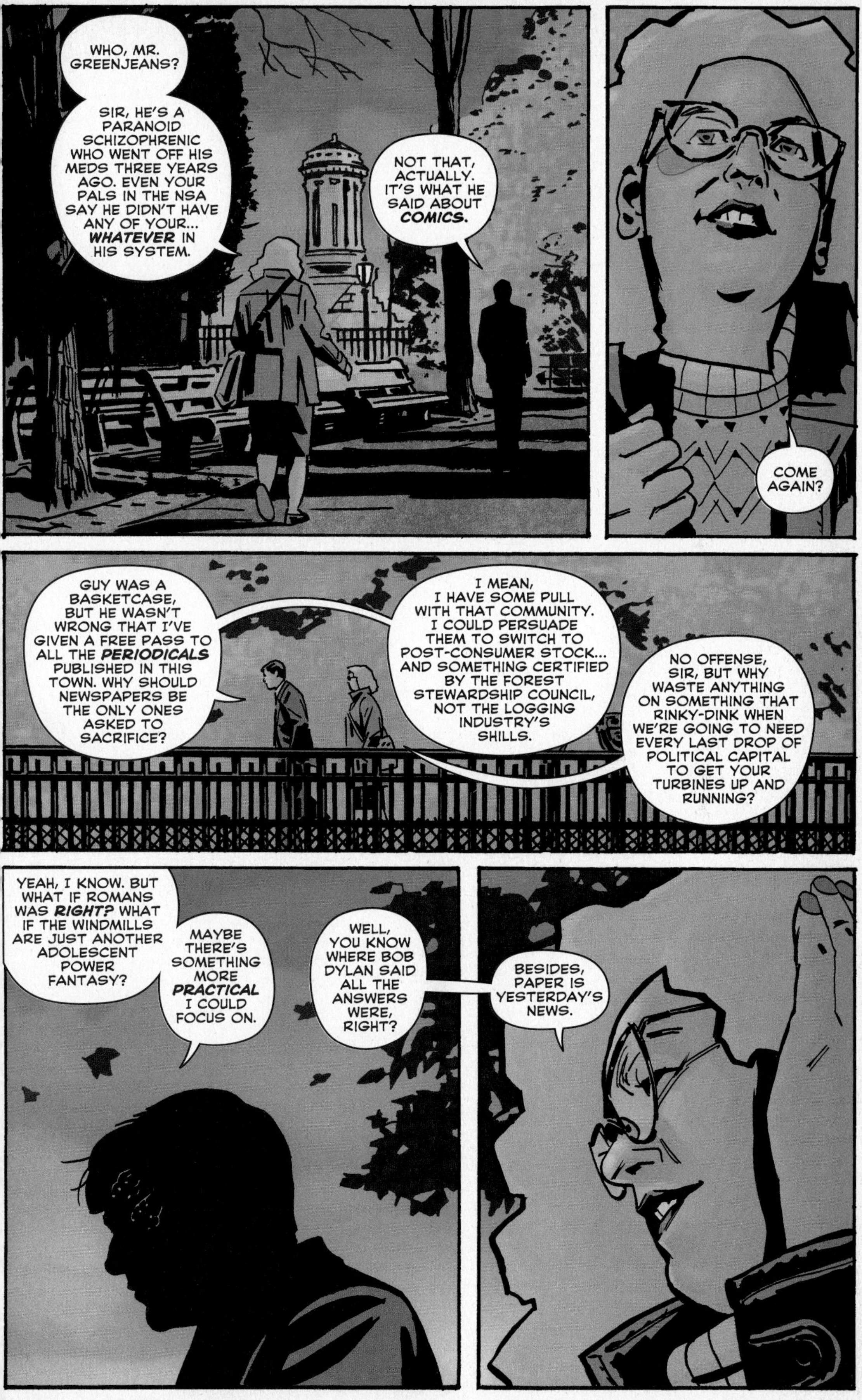
WHO, MR. GREENJEANS?
SIR, HE'S A PARANOID SCHIZOPHRENIC WHO WENT OFF HIS MEDS THREE YEARS AGO. EVEN YOUR PALS IN THE NSA SAY HE DIDN'T HAVE ANY OF YOUR... ***WHATEVER*** IN HIS SYSTEM.
NOT THAT, ACTUALLY. IT'S WHAT HE SAID ABOUT ***COMICS.***
COME AGAIN?
GUY WAS A BASKETCASE, BUT HE WASN'T WRONG THAT I'VE GIVEN A FREE PASS TO ALL THE ***PERIODICALS*** PUBLISHED IN THIS TOWN. WHY SHOULD NEWSPAPERS BE THE ONLY ONES ASKED TO SACRIFICE?
I MEAN, I HAVE SOME PULL WITH THAT COMMUNITY. I COULD PERSUADE THEM TO SWITCH TO POST-CONSUMER STOCK... AND SOMETHING CERTIFIED BY THE FOREST STEWARDSHIP COUNCIL, NOT THE LOGGING INDUSTRY'S SHILLS.
NO OFFENSE, SIR, BUT WHY WASTE ANYTHING ON SOMETHING THAT RINKY-DINK WHEN WE'RE GOING TO NEED EVERY LAST DROP OF POLITICAL CAPITAL TO GET YOUR TURBINES UP AND RUNNING?
YEAH, I KNOW. BUT WHAT IF ROMANS WAS ***RIGHT?*** WHAT IF THE WINDMILLS ARE JUST ANOTHER ADOLESCENT POWER FANTASY?
MAYBE THERE'S SOMETHING MORE ***PRACTICAL*** I COULD FOCUS ON.
WELL, YOU KNOW WHERE BOB DYLAN SAID ALL THE ANSWERS WERE, RIGHT?
BESIDES, PAPER IS YESTERDAY'S NEWS.

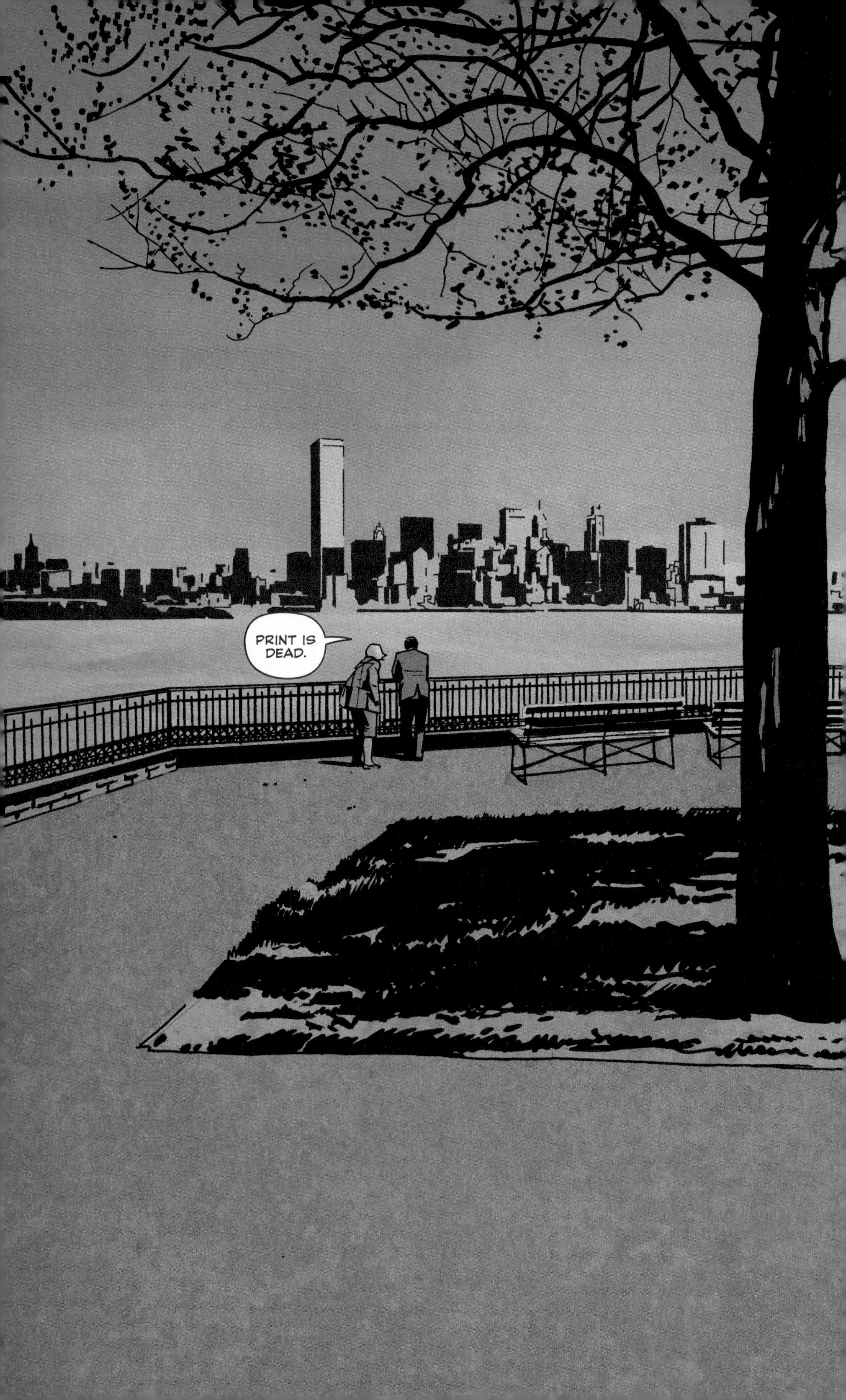
PRINT IS DEAD.

Ring Out the Old
part 1

Chapter 3

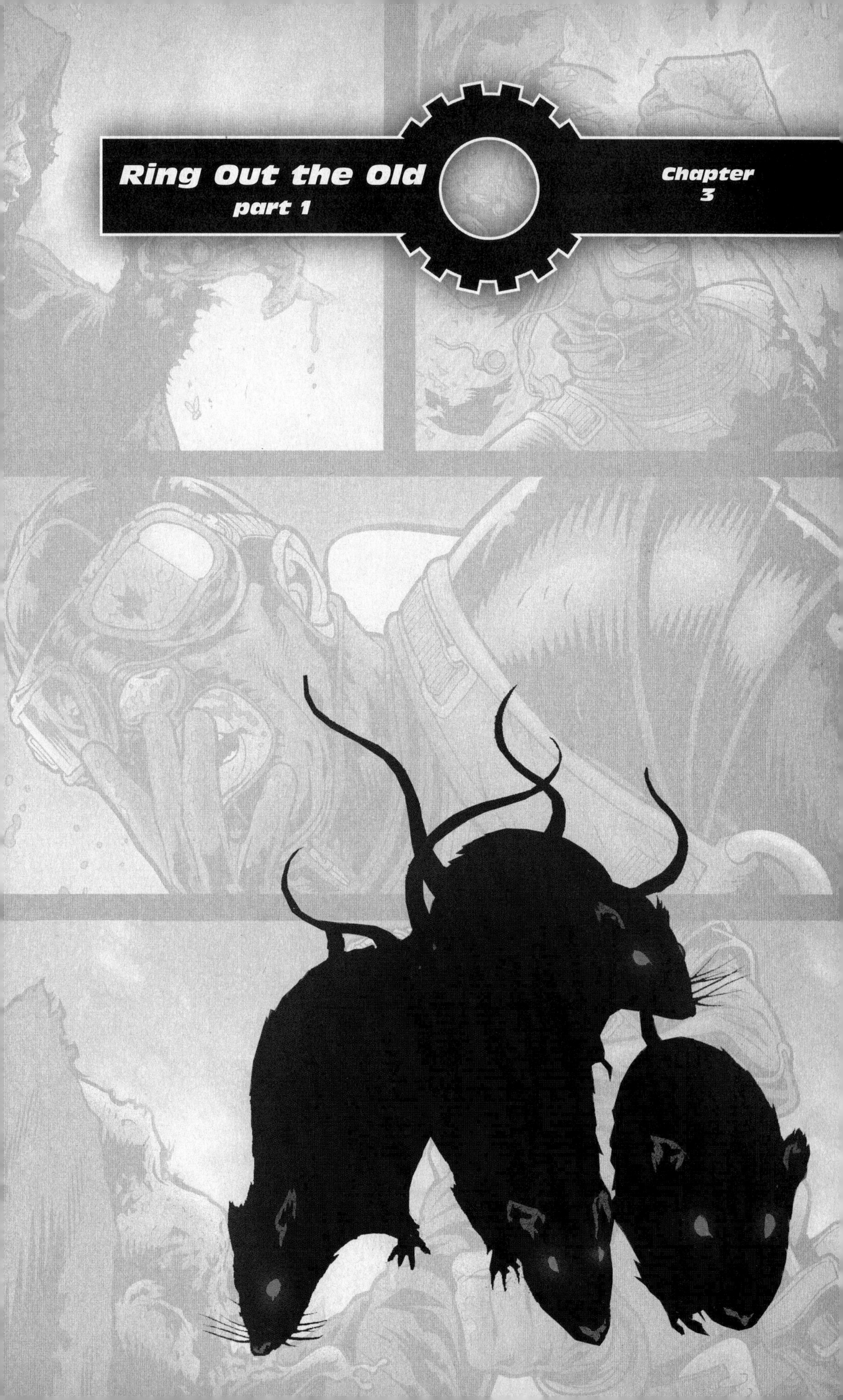

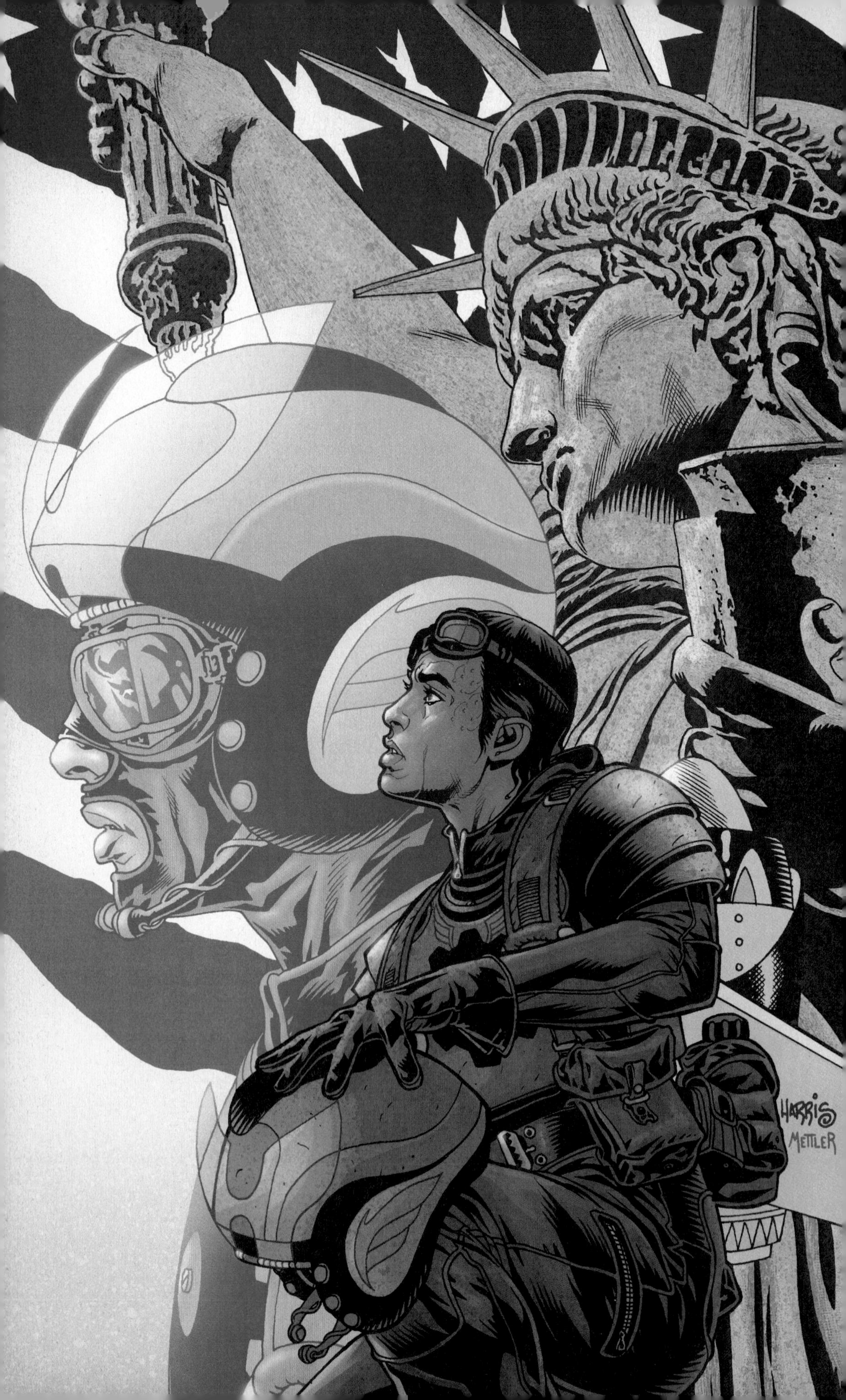
HARRIS
METTLER

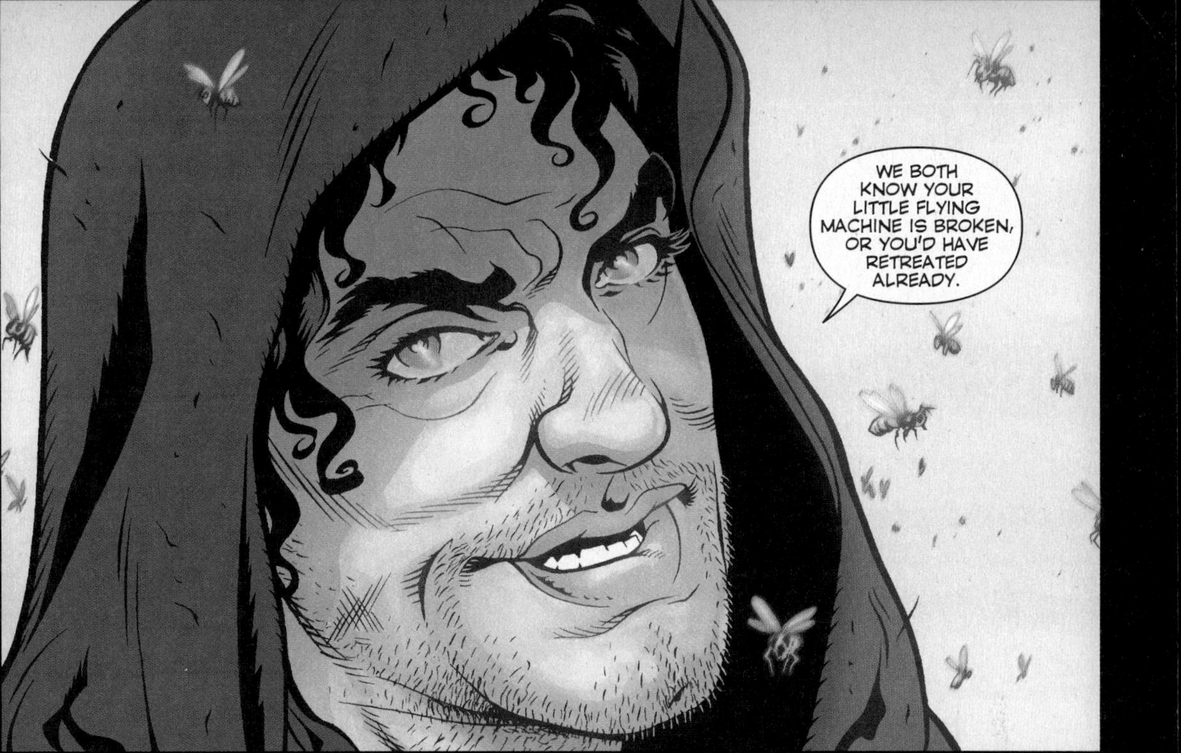
WE BOTH KNOW YOUR LITTLE FLYING MACHINE IS BROKEN, OR YOU'D HAVE RETREATED ALREADY.

TUESDAY, MARCH 27, 2001

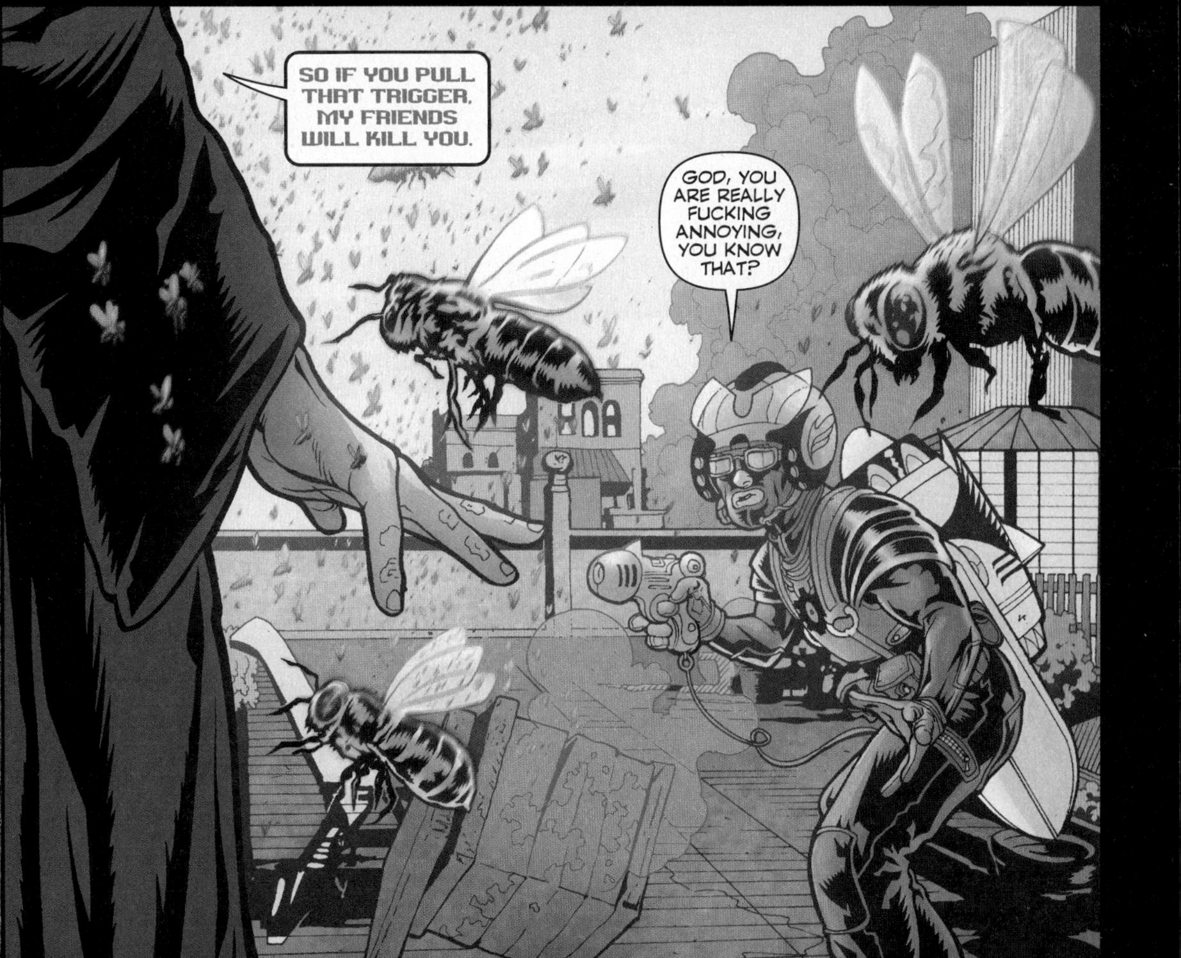
SO IF YOU PULL THAT TRIGGER, MY FRIENDS WILL KILL YOU.
GOD, YOU ARE REALLY FUCKING ANNOYING, YOU KNOW THAT?

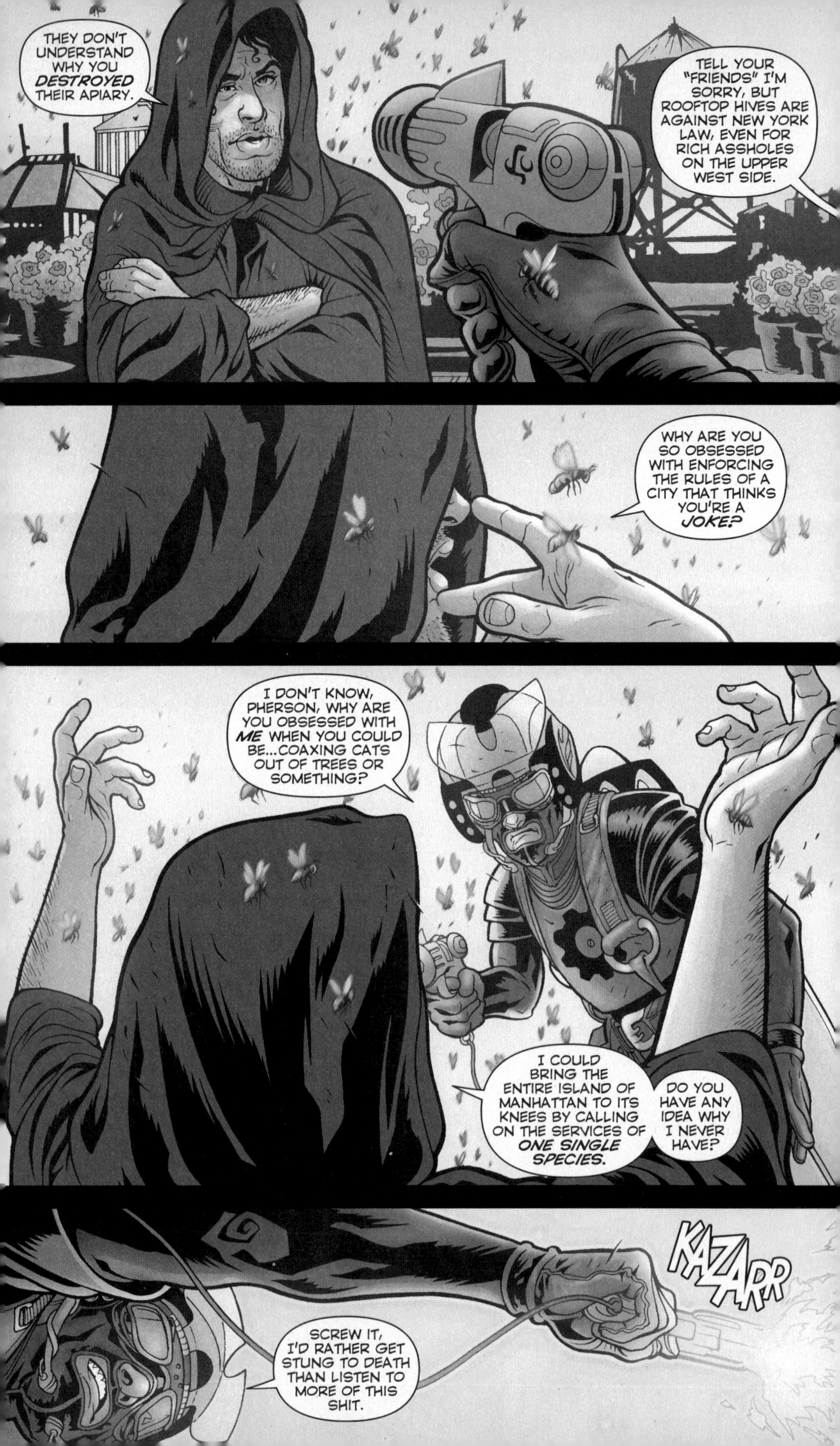
THEY DON'T UNDERSTAND WHY YOU DESTROYED THEIR APIARY.
TELL YOUR "FRIENDS" I'M SORRY, BUT ROOFTOP HIVES ARE AGAINST NEW YORK LAW, EVEN FOR RICH ASSHOLES ON THE UPPER WEST SIDE.
WHY ARE YOU SO OBSESSED WITH ENFORCING THE RULES OF A CITY THAT THINKS YOU'RE A JOKE?
I DON'T KNOW, PHERSON, WHY ARE YOU OBSESSED WITH ME WHEN YOU COULD BE...COAXING CATS OUT OF TREES OR SOMETHING?
I COULD BRING THE ENTIRE ISLAND OF MANHATTAN TO ITS KNEES BY CALLING ON THE SERVICES OF ONE SINGLE SPECIES.
DO YOU HAVE ANY IDEA WHY I NEVER HAVE?
KAZARR
SCREW IT, I'D RATHER GET STUNG TO DEATH THAN LISTEN TO MORE OF THIS SHIT.

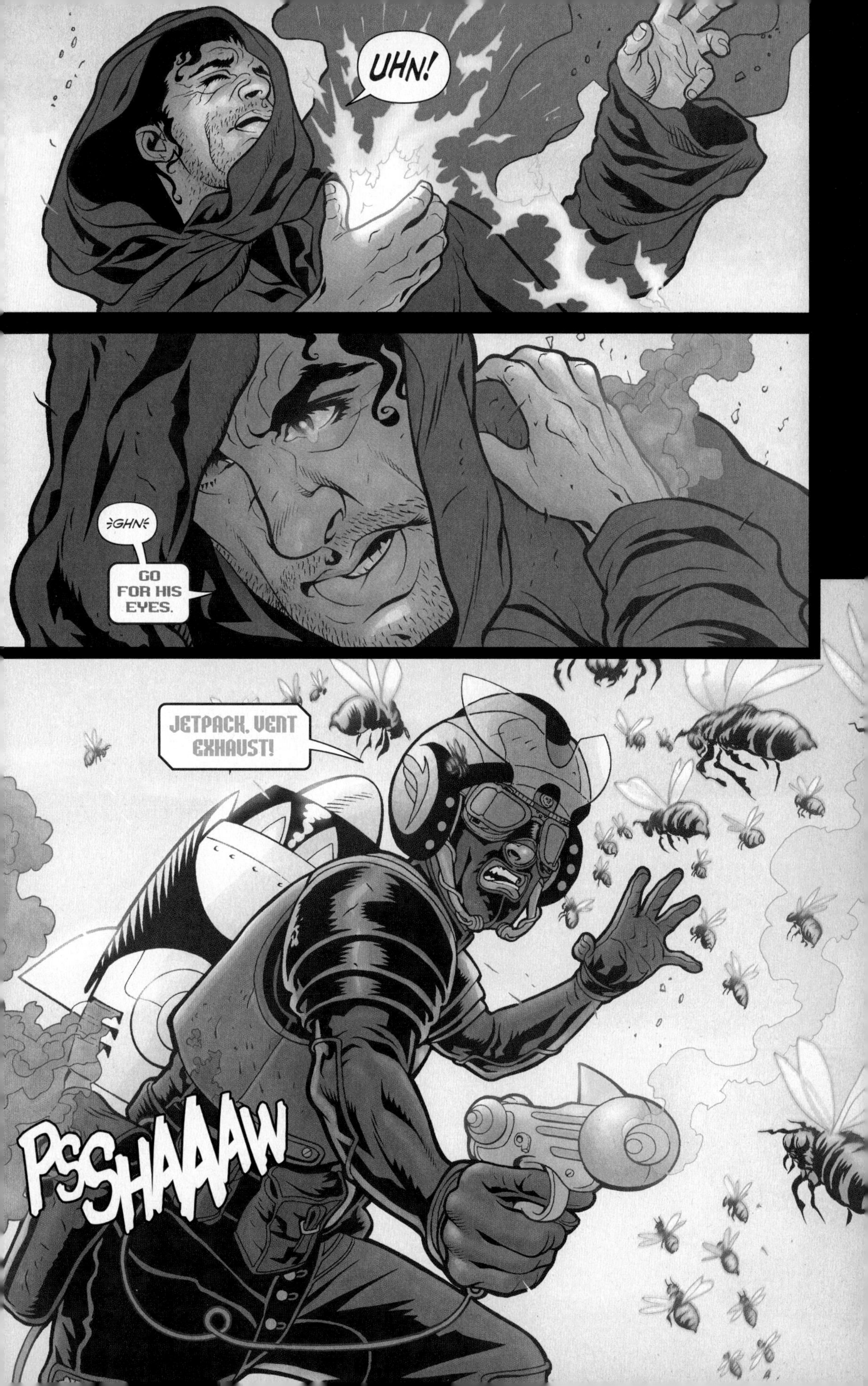
UHN!
GHN
GO FOR HIS EYES.
JETPACK, VENT EXHAUST!
PSSHAAAAW

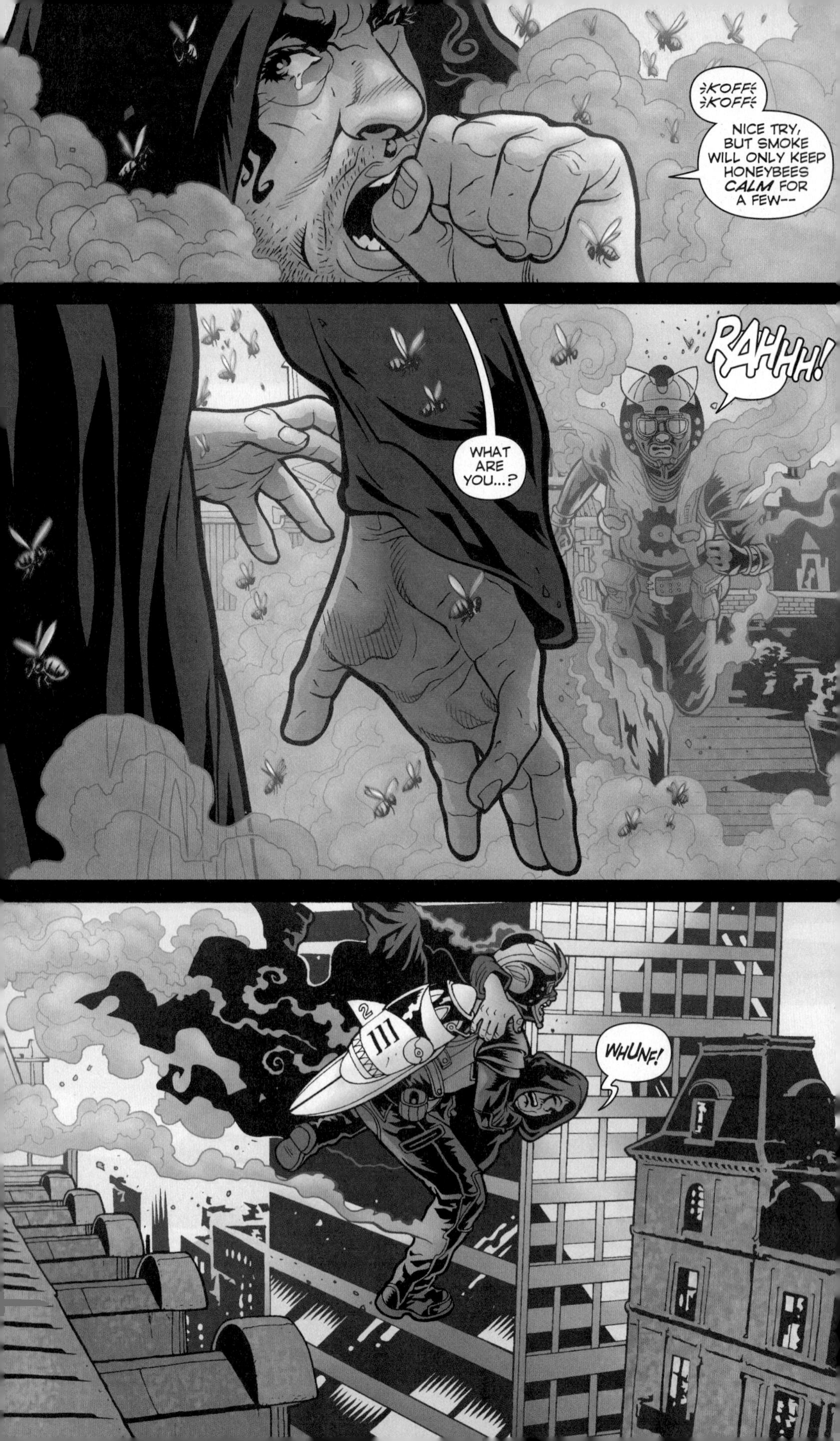

KOFF KOFF
NICE TRY, BUT SMOKE WILL ONLY KEEP HONEYBEES CALM FOR A FEW--
RAHHH!
WHAT ARE YOU...?
WHUNF!

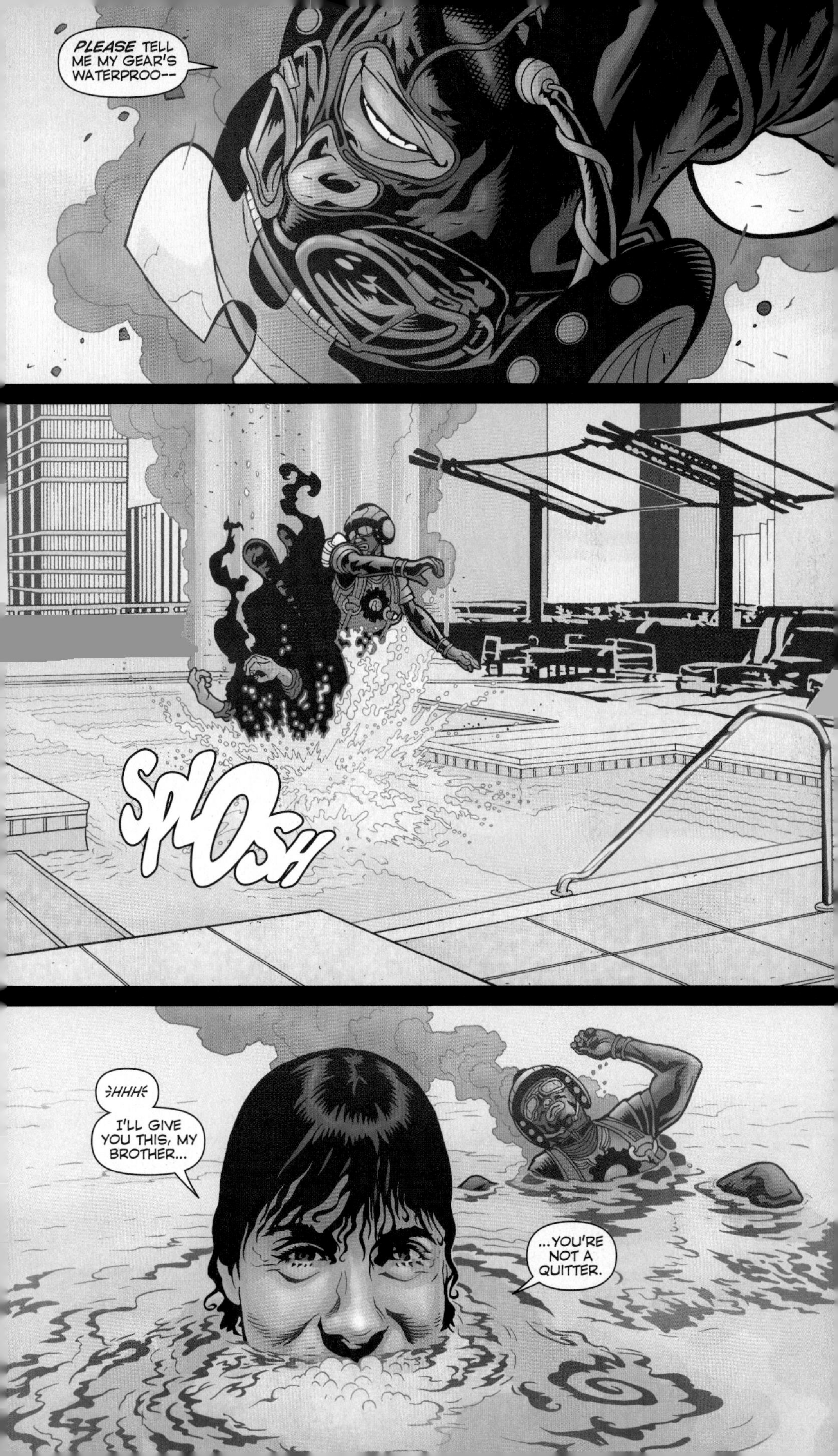
PLEASE TELL ME MY GEAR'S WATERPROO--
SPLOSH
HHH
I'LL GIVE YOU THIS, MY BROTHER...
...YOU'RE NOT A QUITTER.

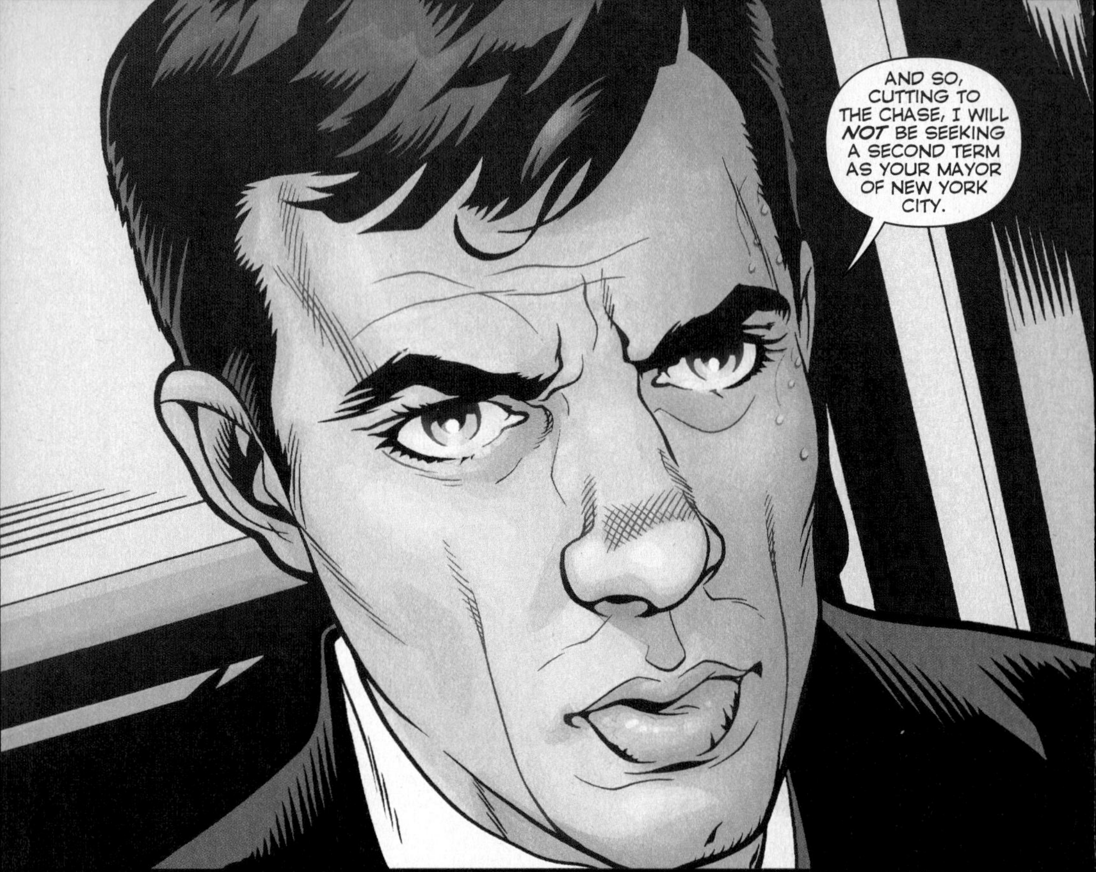
AND SO, CUTTING TO THE CHASE, I WILL NOT BE SEEKING A SECOND TERM AS YOUR MAYOR OF NEW YORK CITY.

WEDNESDAY, DECEMBER 29, 2004

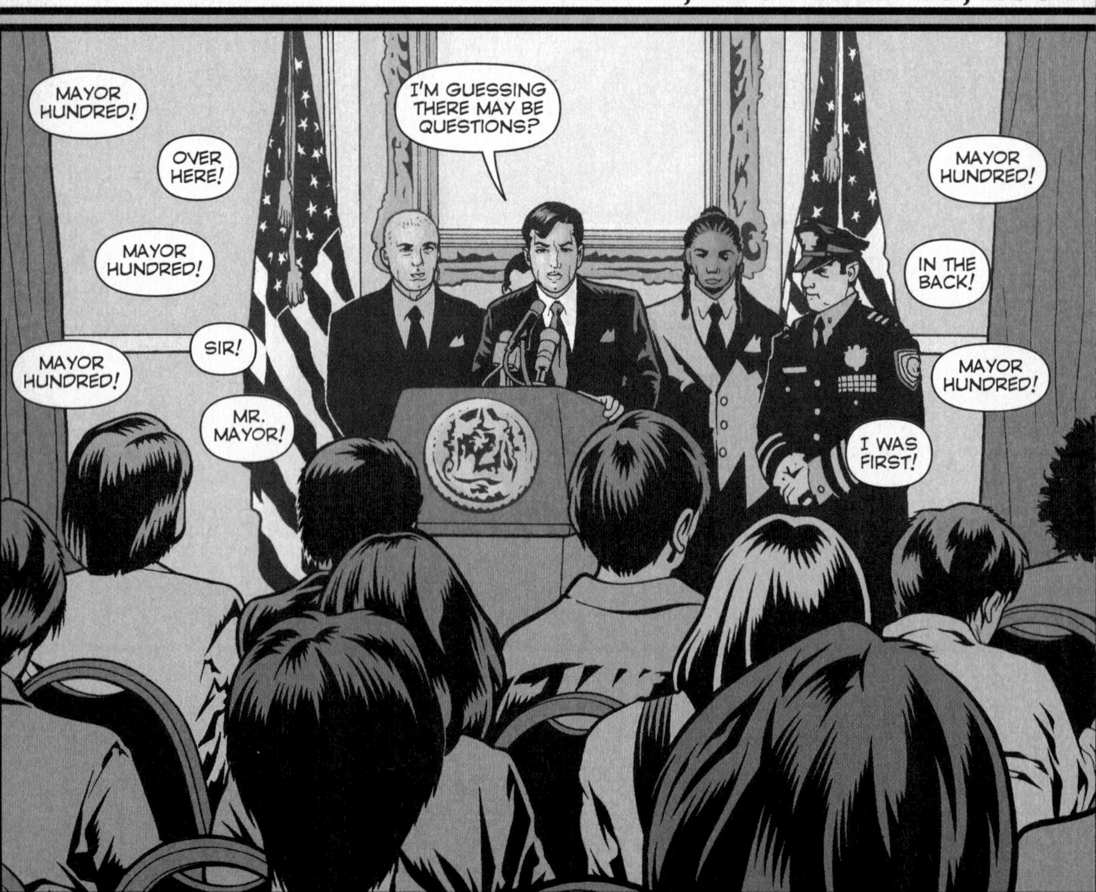
I'M GUESSING THERE MAY BE QUESTIONS?
MAYOR HUNDRED!
OVER HERE!
MAYOR HUNDRED!
SIR!
MAYOR HUNDRED!
MR. MAYOR!
MAYOR HUNDRED!
IN THE BACK!
MAYOR HUNDRED!
I WAS FIRST!

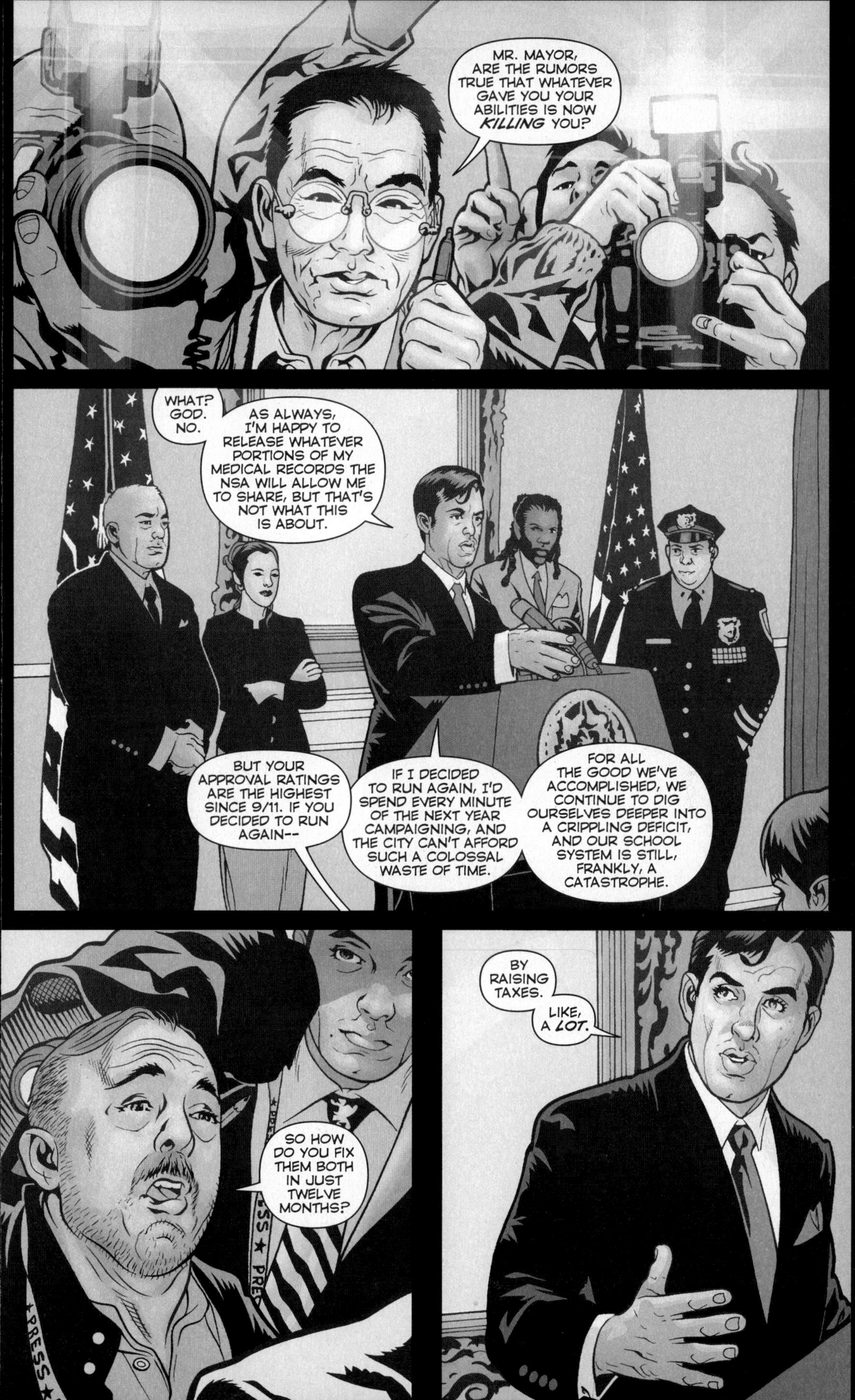

MR. MAYOR, ARE THE RUMORS TRUE THAT WHATEVER GAVE YOU YOUR ABILITIES IS NOW *KILLING* YOU?
WHAT? GOD. NO.
AS ALWAYS, I'M HAPPY TO RELEASE WHATEVER PORTIONS OF MY MEDICAL RECORDS THE NSA WILL ALLOW ME TO SHARE, BUT THAT'S NOT WHAT THIS IS ABOUT.
BUT YOUR APPROVAL RATINGS ARE THE HIGHEST SINCE 9/11. IF YOU DECIDED TO RUN AGAIN--
IF I DECIDED TO RUN AGAIN, I'D SPEND EVERY MINUTE OF THE NEXT YEAR CAMPAIGNING, AND THE CITY CAN'T AFFORD SUCH A COLOSSAL WASTE OF TIME.
FOR ALL THE GOOD WE'VE ACCOMPLISHED, WE CONTINUE TO DIG OURSELVES DEEPER INTO A CRIPPLING DEFICIT, AND OUR SCHOOL SYSTEM IS STILL, FRANKLY, A CATASTROPHE.
SO HOW DO YOU FIX THEM BOTH IN JUST TWELVE MONTHS?
BY RAISING TAXES.
LIKE, A *LOT*.

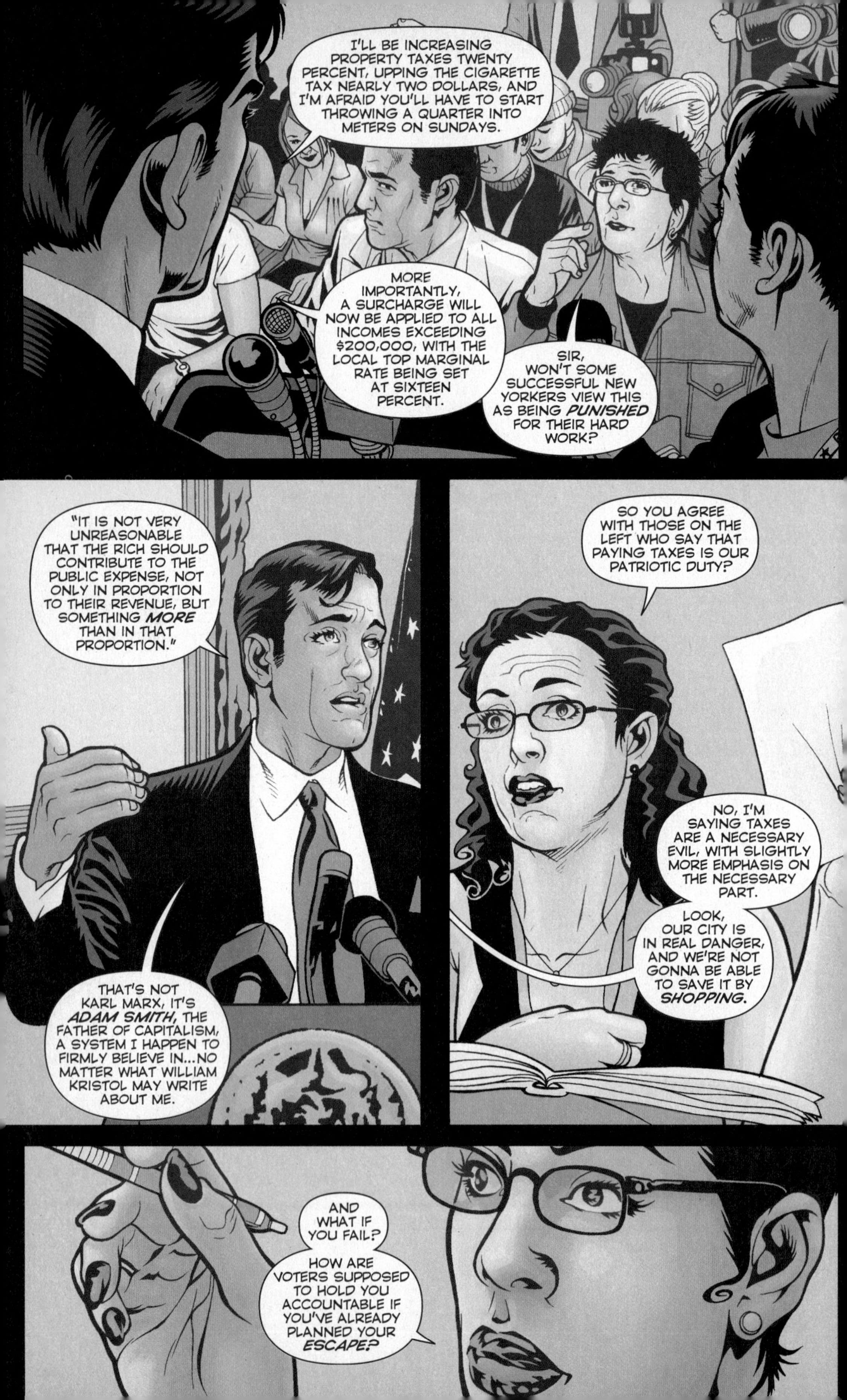
I'LL BE INCREASING PROPERTY TAXES TWENTY PERCENT, UPPING THE CIGARETTE TAX NEARLY TWO DOLLARS, AND I'M AFRAID YOU'LL HAVE TO START THROWING A QUARTER INTO METERS ON SUNDAYS.
MORE IMPORTANTLY, A SURCHARGE WILL NOW BE APPLIED TO ALL INCOMES EXCEEDING $200,000, WITH THE LOCAL TOP MARGINAL RATE BEING SET AT SIXTEEN PERCENT.
SIR, WON'T SOME SUCCESSFUL NEW YORKERS VIEW THIS AS BEING *PUNISHED* FOR THEIR HARD WORK?
"IT IS NOT VERY UNREASONABLE THAT THE RICH SHOULD CONTRIBUTE TO THE PUBLIC EXPENSE, NOT ONLY IN PROPORTION TO THEIR REVENUE, BUT SOMETHING *MORE* THAN IN THAT PROPORTION."
THAT'S NOT KARL MARX, IT'S *ADAM SMITH*, THE FATHER OF CAPITALISM, A SYSTEM I HAPPEN TO FIRMLY BELIEVE IN...NO MATTER WHAT WILLIAM KRISTOL MAY WRITE ABOUT ME.
SO YOU AGREE WITH THOSE ON THE LEFT WHO SAY THAT PAYING TAXES IS OUR PATRIOTIC DUTY?
NO, I'M SAYING TAXES ARE A NECESSARY EVIL, WITH SLIGHTLY MORE EMPHASIS ON THE NECESSARY PART.
LOOK, OUR CITY IS IN REAL DANGER, AND WE'RE NOT GONNA BE ABLE TO SAVE IT BY *SHOPPING*.
AND WHAT IF YOU FAIL?
HOW ARE VOTERS SUPPOSED TO HOLD YOU ACCOUNTABLE IF YOU'VE ALREADY PLANNED YOUR *ESCAPE?*

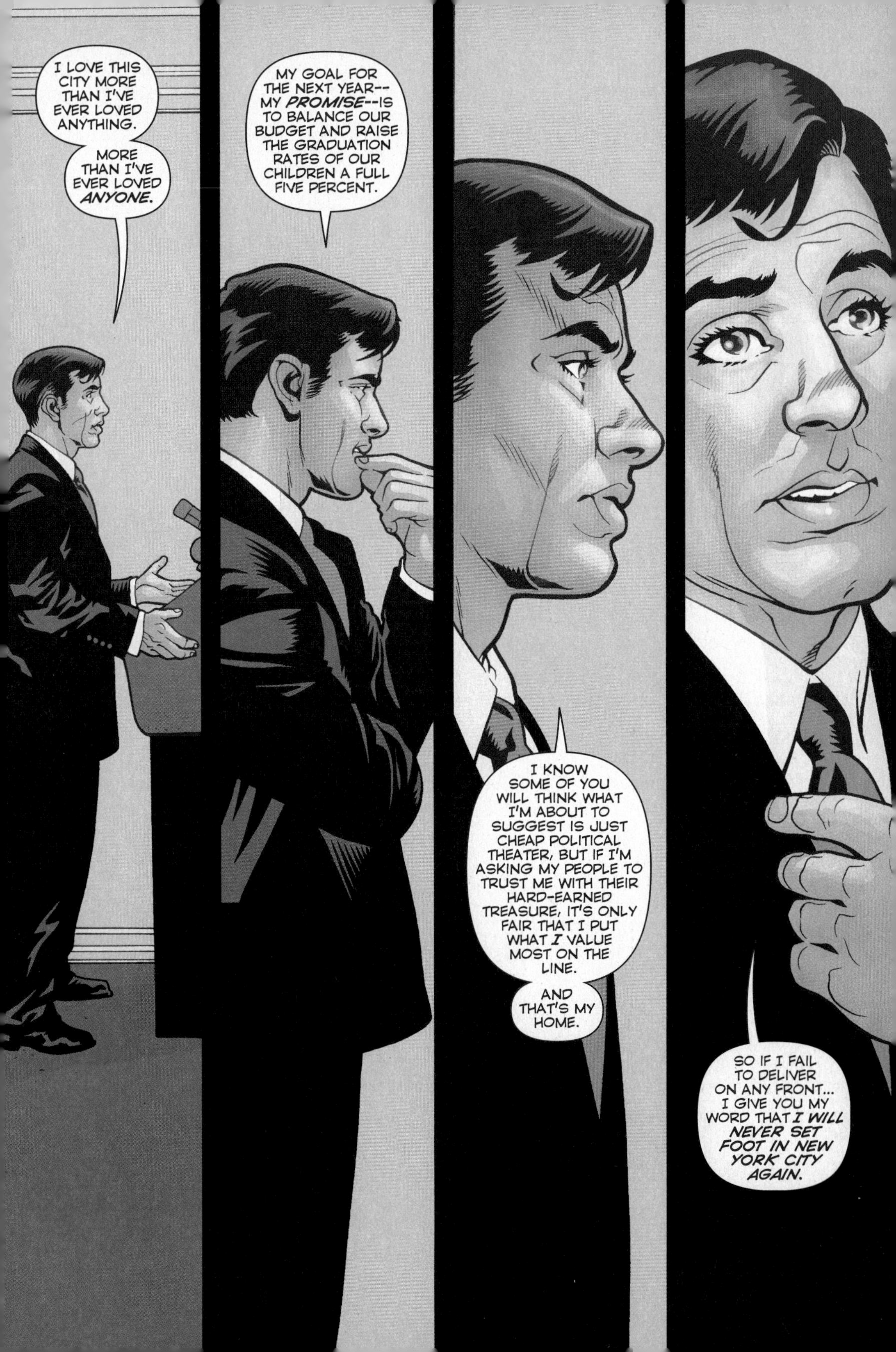
I LOVE THIS CITY MORE THAN I'VE EVER LOVED ANYTHING.
MORE THAN I'VE EVER LOVED *ANYONE*.
MY GOAL FOR THE NEXT YEAR-- MY *PROMISE*--IS TO BALANCE OUR BUDGET AND RAISE THE GRADUATION RATES OF OUR CHILDREN A FULL FIVE PERCENT.
I KNOW SOME OF YOU WILL THINK WHAT I'M ABOUT TO SUGGEST IS JUST CHEAP POLITICAL THEATER, BUT IF I'M ASKING MY PEOPLE TO TRUST ME WITH THEIR HARD-EARNED TREASURE, IT'S ONLY FAIR THAT I PUT WHAT *I* VALUE MOST ON THE LINE.
AND THAT'S MY HOME.
SO IF I FAIL TO DELIVER ON ANY FRONT... I GIVE YOU MY WORD THAT *I WILL NEVER SET FOOT IN NEW YORK CITY AGAIN.*

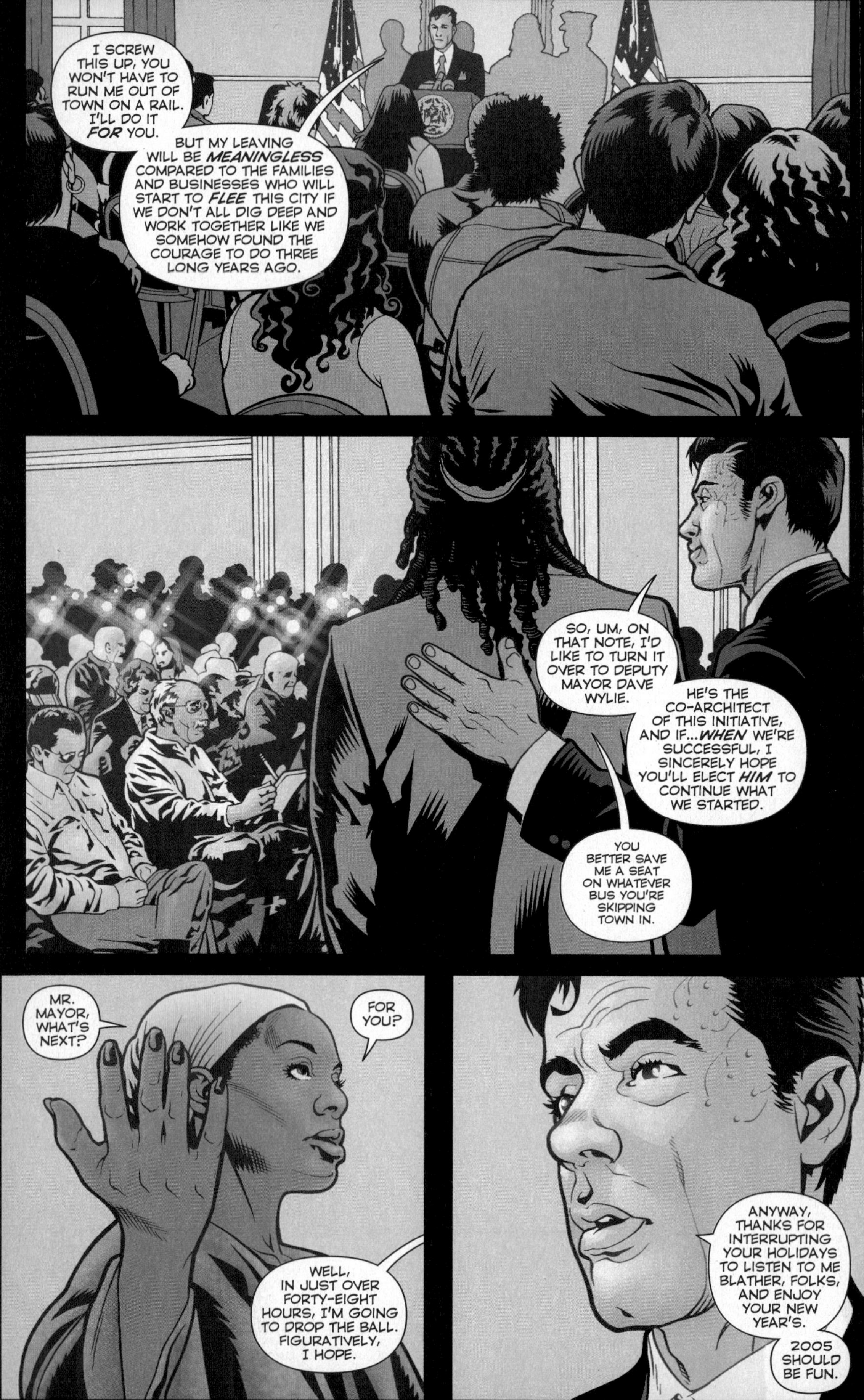

I SCREW THIS UP, YOU WON'T HAVE TO RUN ME OUT OF TOWN ON A RAIL. I'LL DO IT *FOR* YOU.
BUT MY LEAVING WILL BE *MEANINGLESS* COMPARED TO THE FAMILIES AND BUSINESSES WHO WILL START TO *FLEE* THIS CITY IF WE DON'T ALL DIG DEEP AND WORK TOGETHER LIKE WE SOMEHOW FOUND THE COURAGE TO DO THREE LONG YEARS AGO.
SO, UM, ON THAT NOTE, I'D LIKE TO TURN IT OVER TO DEPUTY MAYOR DAVE WYLIE.
HE'S THE CO-ARCHITECT OF THIS INITIATIVE, AND IF...*WHEN* WE'RE SUCCESSFUL, I SINCERELY HOPE YOU'LL ELECT *HIM* TO CONTINUE WHAT WE STARTED.
YOU BETTER SAVE ME A SEAT ON WHATEVER BUS YOU'RE SKIPPING TOWN IN.
MR. MAYOR, WHAT'S NEXT?
FOR YOU?
WELL, IN JUST OVER FORTY-EIGHT HOURS, I'M GOING TO DROP THE BALL. FIGURATIVELY, I HOPE.
ANYWAY, THANKS FOR INTERRUPTING YOUR HOLIDAYS TO LISTEN TO ME BLATHER, FOLKS, AND ENJOY YOUR NEW YEAR'S.
2005 SHOULD BE FUN.

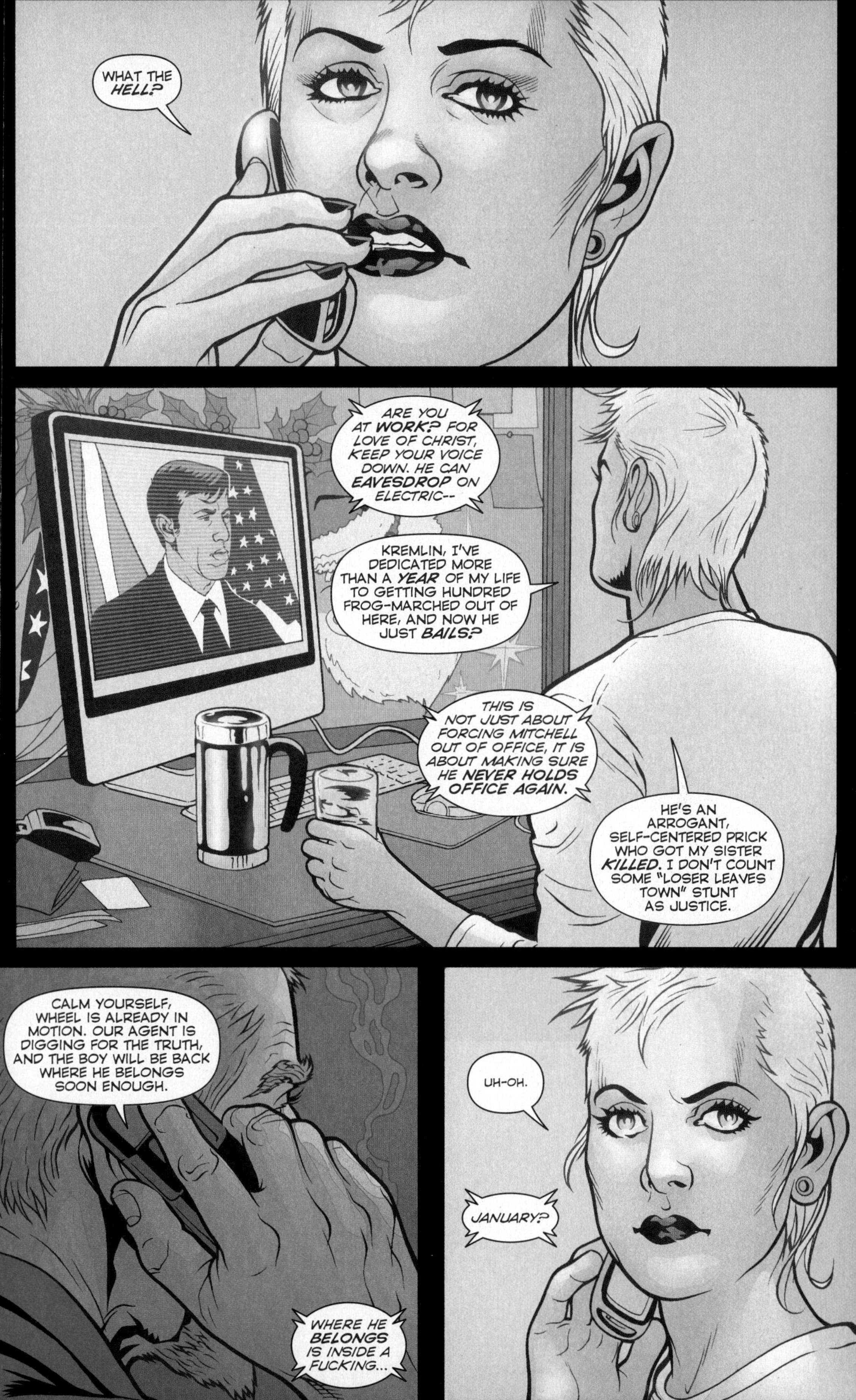
WHAT THE HELL?
ARE YOU AT WORK? FOR LOVE OF CHRIST, KEEP YOUR VOICE DOWN. HE CAN EAVESDROP ON ELECTRIC--
KREMLIN, I'VE DEDICATED MORE THAN A YEAR OF MY LIFE TO GETTING HUNDRED FROG-MARCHED OUT OF HERE, AND NOW HE JUST BAILS?
THIS IS NOT JUST ABOUT FORCING MITCHELL OUT OF OFFICE, IT IS ABOUT MAKING SURE HE NEVER HOLDS OFFICE AGAIN.
HE'S AN ARROGANT, SELF-CENTERED PRICK WHO GOT MY SISTER KILLED. I DON'T COUNT SOME "LOSER LEAVES TOWN" STUNT AS JUSTICE.
CALM YOURSELF, WHEEL IS ALREADY IN MOTION. OUR AGENT IS DIGGING FOR THE TRUTH, AND THE BOY WILL BE BACK WHERE HE BELONGS SOON ENOUGH.
WHERE HE BELONGS IS INSIDE A FUCKING...
UH-OH.
JANUARY?

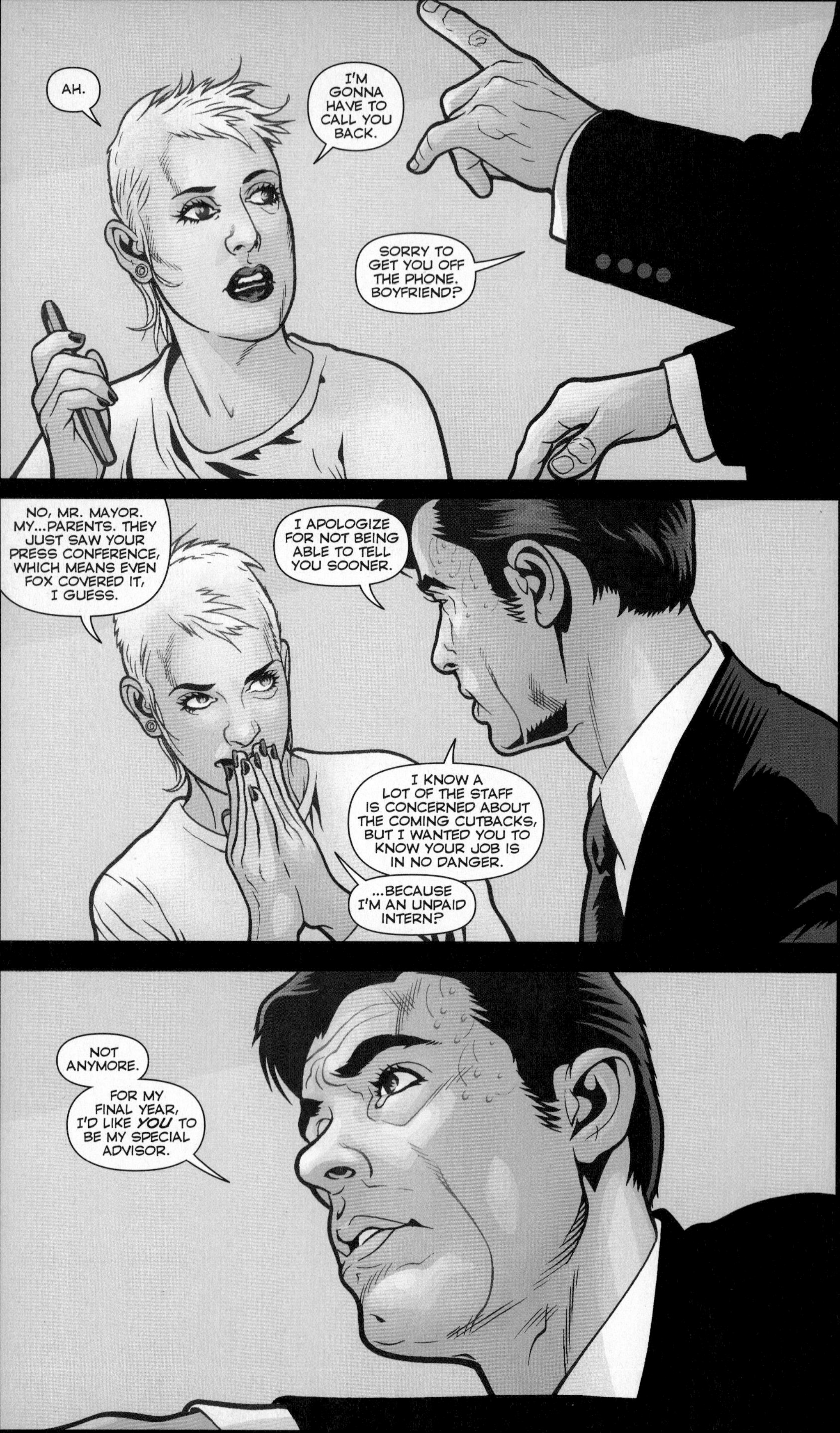
AH.
I'M GONNA HAVE TO CALL YOU BACK.
SORRY TO GET YOU OFF THE PHONE. BOYFRIEND?
NO, MR. MAYOR. MY...PARENTS. THEY JUST SAW YOUR PRESS CONFERENCE, WHICH MEANS EVEN FOX COVERED IT, I GUESS.
I APOLOGIZE FOR NOT BEING ABLE TO TELL YOU SOONER.
I KNOW A LOT OF THE STAFF IS CONCERNED ABOUT THE COMING CUTBACKS, BUT I WANTED YOU TO KNOW YOUR JOB IS IN NO DANGER.
...BECAUSE I'M AN UNPAID INTERN?
NOT ANYMORE.
FOR MY FINAL YEAR, I'D LIKE *YOU* TO BE MY SPECIAL ADVISOR.

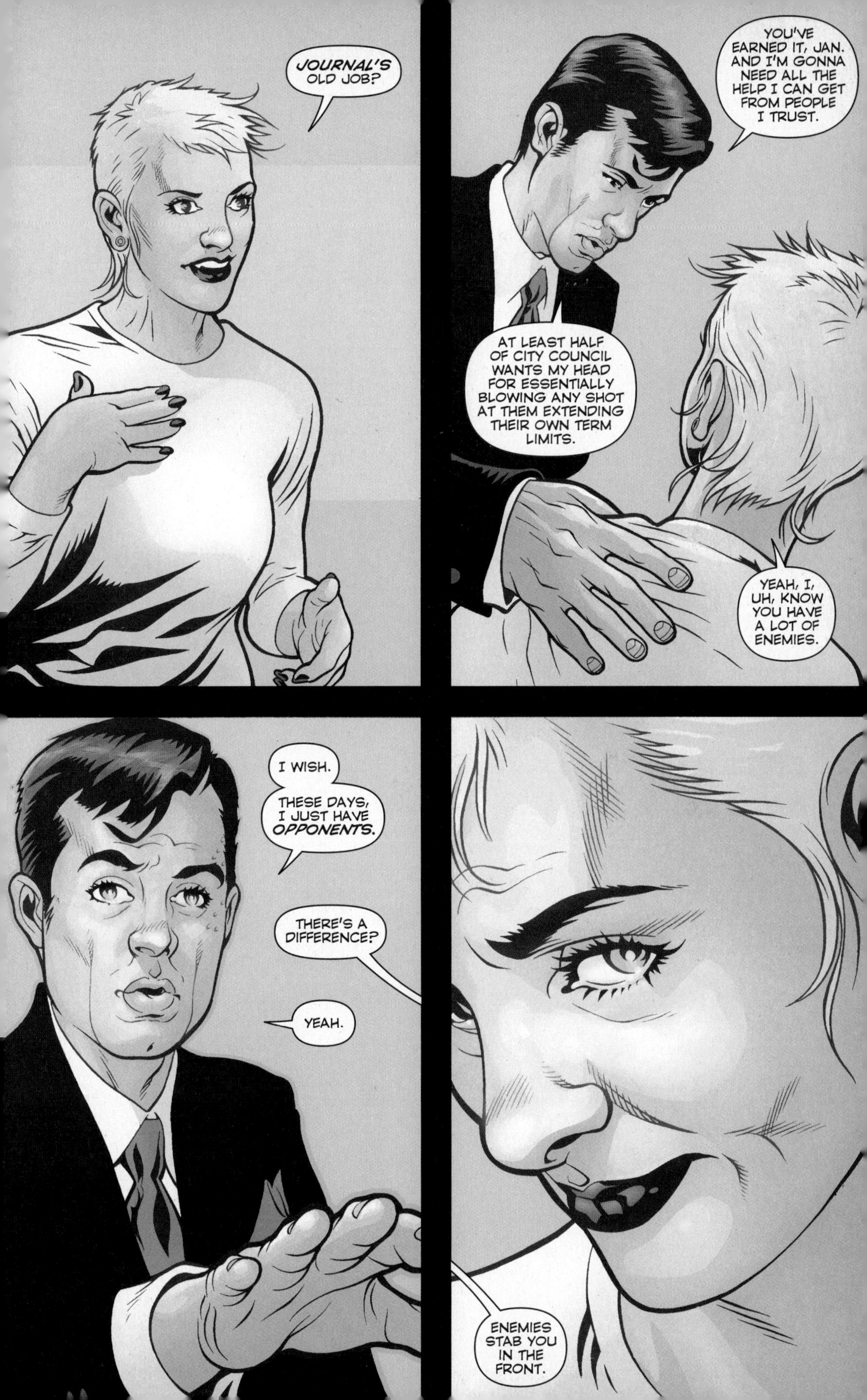
JOURNAL'S OLD JOB?
YOU'VE EARNED IT, JAN. AND I'M GONNA NEED ALL THE HELP I CAN GET FROM PEOPLE I TRUST.
AT LEAST HALF OF CITY COUNCIL WANTS MY HEAD FOR ESSENTIALLY BLOWING ANY SHOT AT THEM EXTENDING THEIR OWN TERM LIMITS.
YEAH, I, UH, KNOW YOU HAVE A LOT OF ENEMIES.
I WISH.
THESE DAYS, I JUST HAVE OPPONENTS.
THERE'S A DIFFERENCE?
YEAH.
ENEMIES STAB YOU IN THE FRONT.

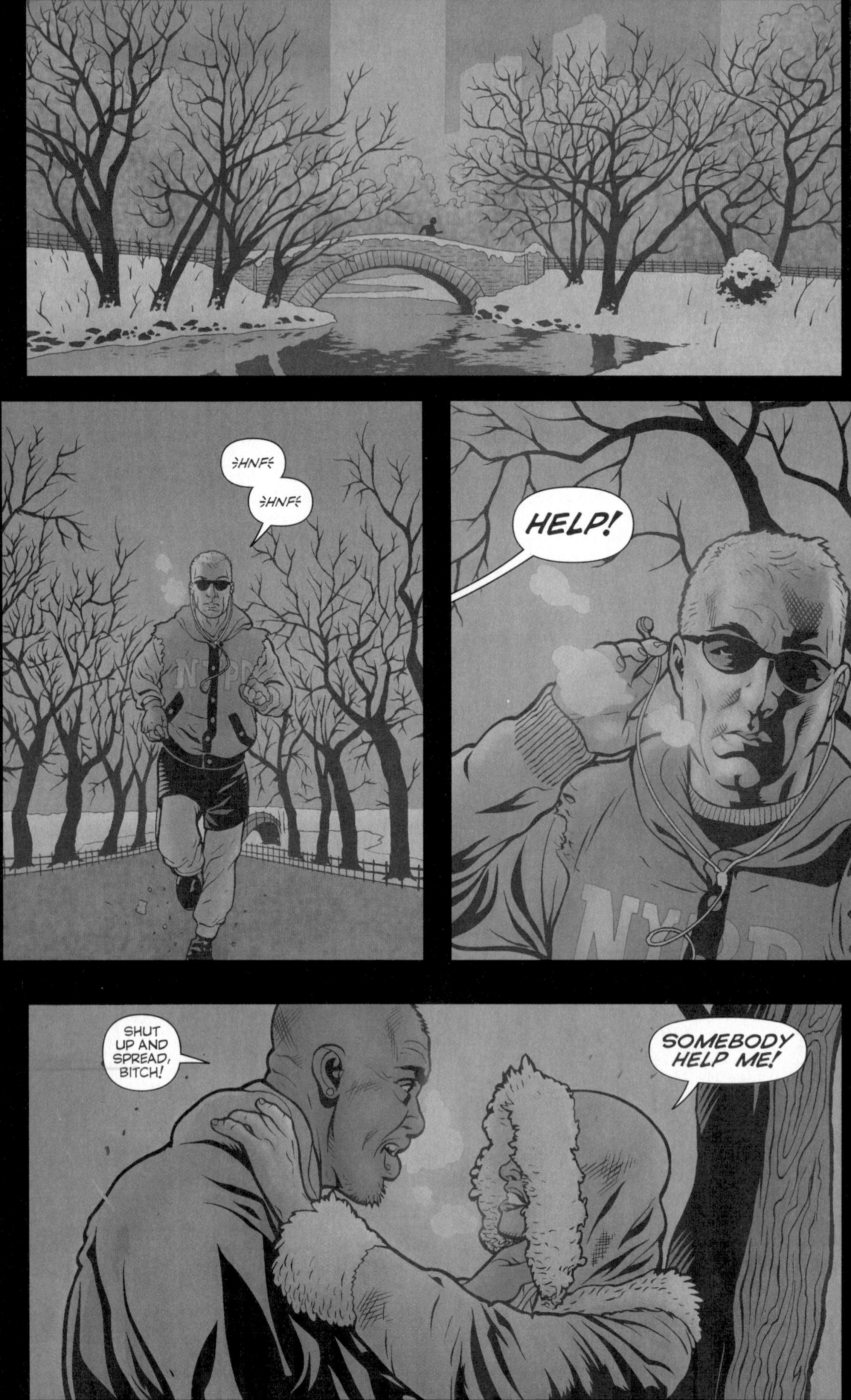
HNF
HNF
HELP!
SHUT UP AND SPREAD, BITCH!
SOMEBODY HELP ME!

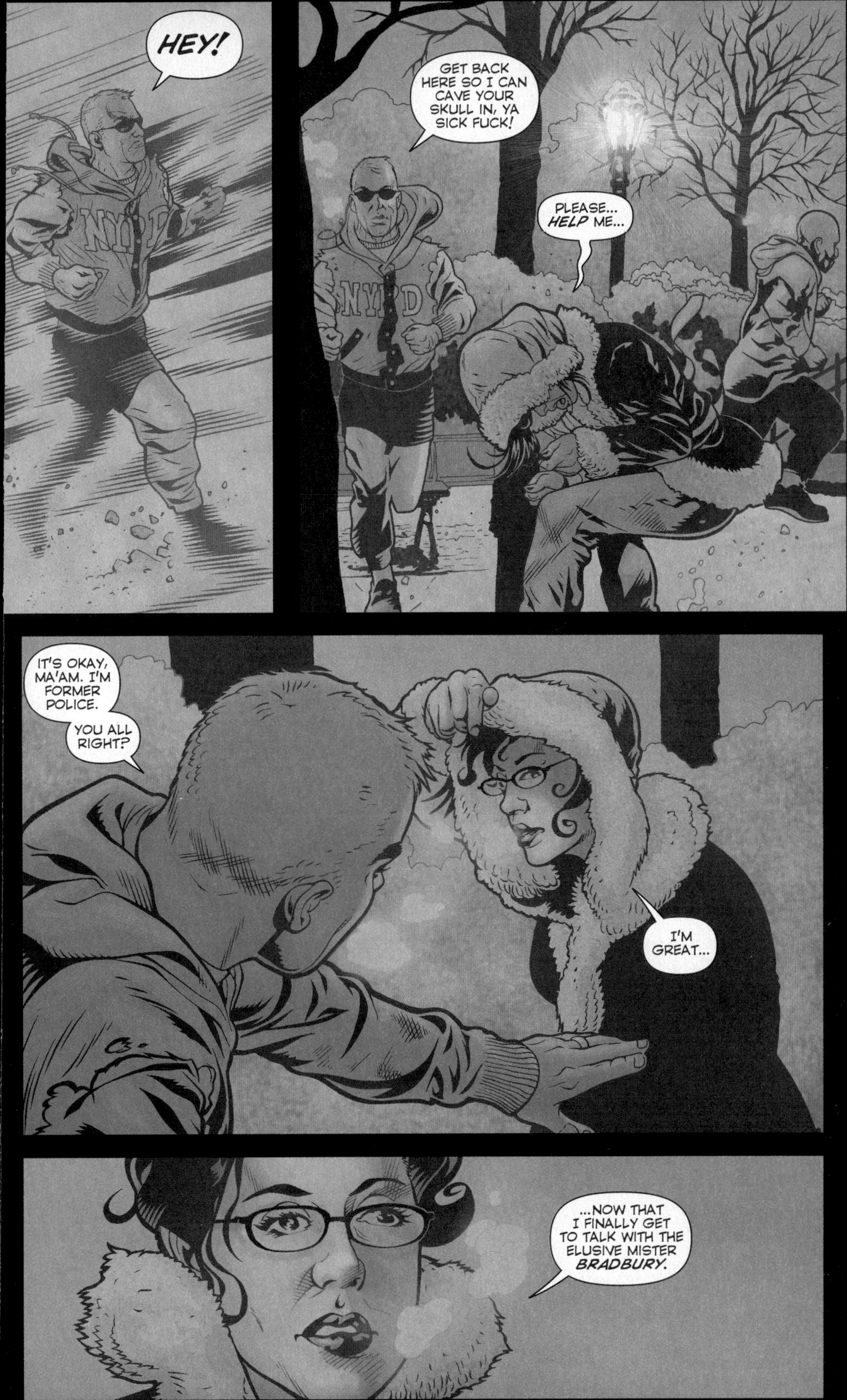
HEY!
GET BACK HERE SO I CAN CAVE YOUR SKULL IN, YA SICK FUCK!
PLEASE... HELP ME...
IT'S OKAY, MA'AM. I'M FORMER POLICE.
YOU ALL RIGHT?
I'M GREAT...
...NOW THAT I FINALLY GET TO TALK WITH THE ELUSIVE MISTER BRADBURY.

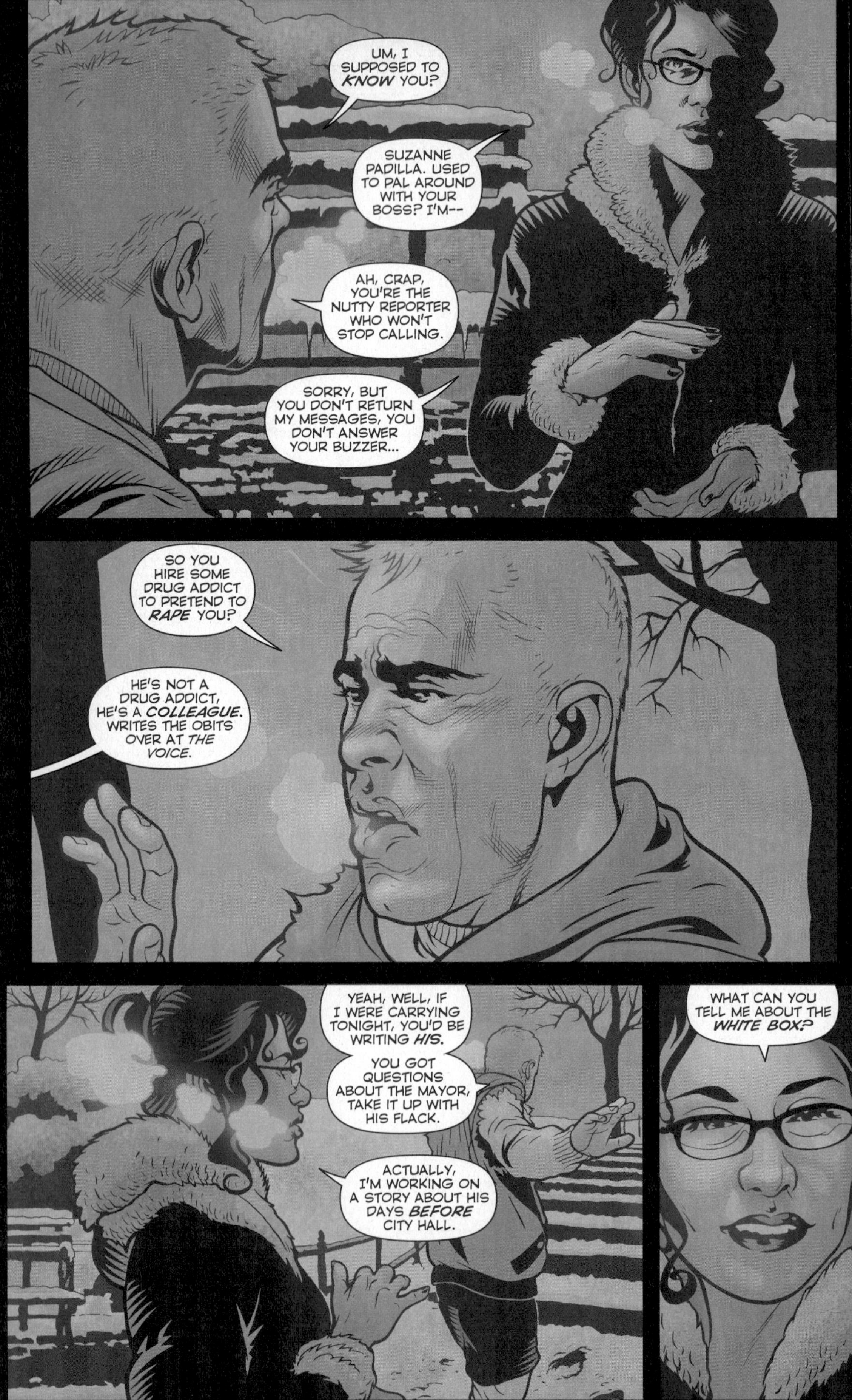
UM, I SUPPOSED TO KNOW YOU?
SUZANNE PADILLA. USED TO PAL AROUND WITH YOUR BOSS? I'M--
AH, CRAP, YOU'RE THE NUTTY REPORTER WHO WON'T STOP CALLING.
SORRY, BUT YOU DON'T RETURN MY MESSAGES, YOU DON'T ANSWER YOUR BUZZER...
SO YOU HIRE SOME DRUG ADDICT TO PRETEND TO RAPE YOU?
HE'S NOT A DRUG ADDICT, HE'S A COLLEAGUE. WRITES THE OBITS OVER AT THE VOICE.
YEAH, WELL, IF I WERE CARRYING TONIGHT, YOU'D BE WRITING HIS.
YOU GOT QUESTIONS ABOUT THE MAYOR, TAKE IT UP WITH HIS FLACK.
ACTUALLY, I'M WORKING ON A STORY ABOUT HIS DAYS BEFORE CITY HALL.
WHAT CAN YOU TELL ME ABOUT THE WHITE BOX?

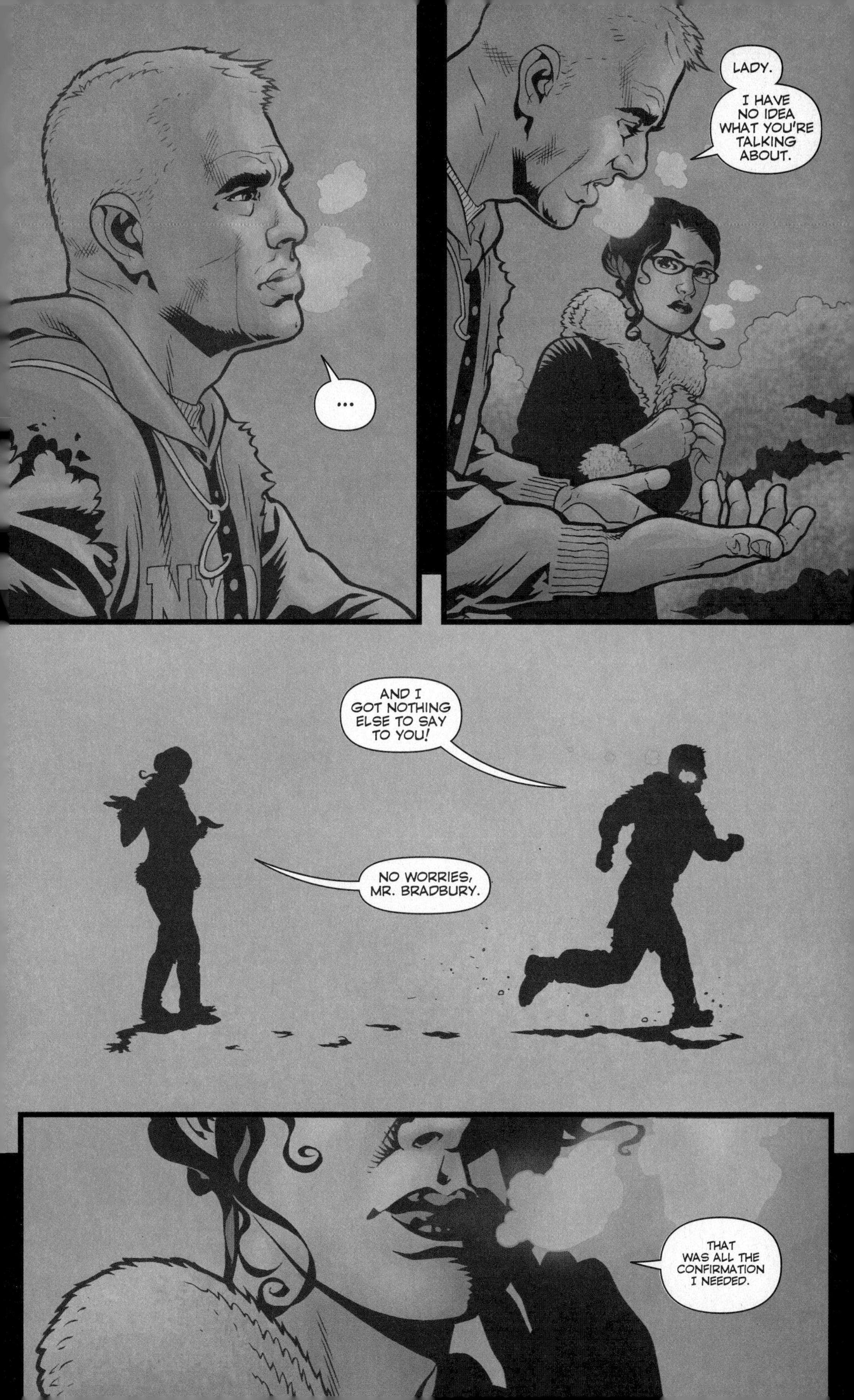
...
LADY.
I HAVE NO IDEA WHAT YOU'RE TALKING ABOUT.
AND I GOT NOTHING ELSE TO SAY TO YOU!
NO WORRIES, MR. BRADBURY.
THAT WAS ALL THE CONFIRMATION I NEEDED.

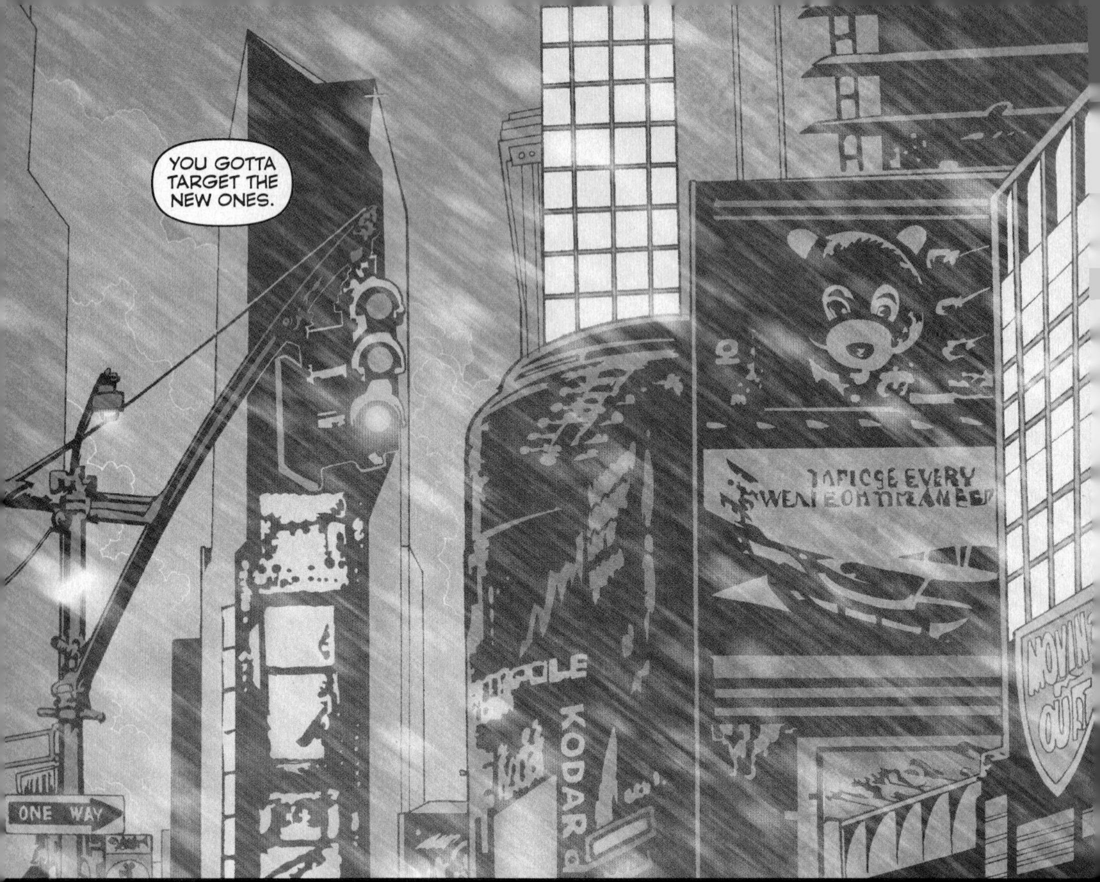
YOU GOTTA TARGET THE NEW ONES.
ONE WAY
KODAR

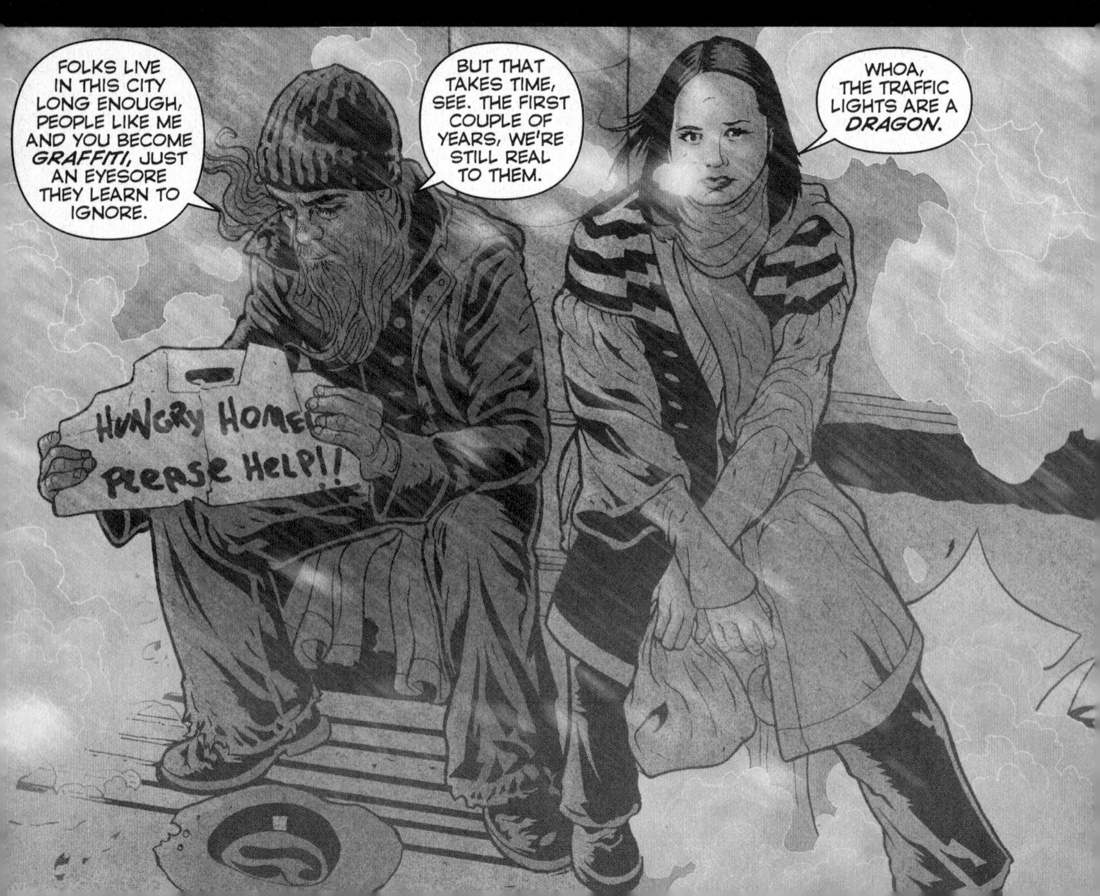
FOLKS LIVE IN THIS CITY LONG ENOUGH, PEOPLE LIKE ME AND YOU BECOME *GRAFFITI*, JUST AN EYESORE THEY LEARN TO IGNORE.
BUT THAT TAKES TIME, SEE. THE FIRST COUPLE OF YEARS, WE'RE STILL REAL TO THEM.
WHOA, THE TRAFFIC LIGHTS ARE A *DRAGON*.
HUNGRY HOME
PLEASE HELP!

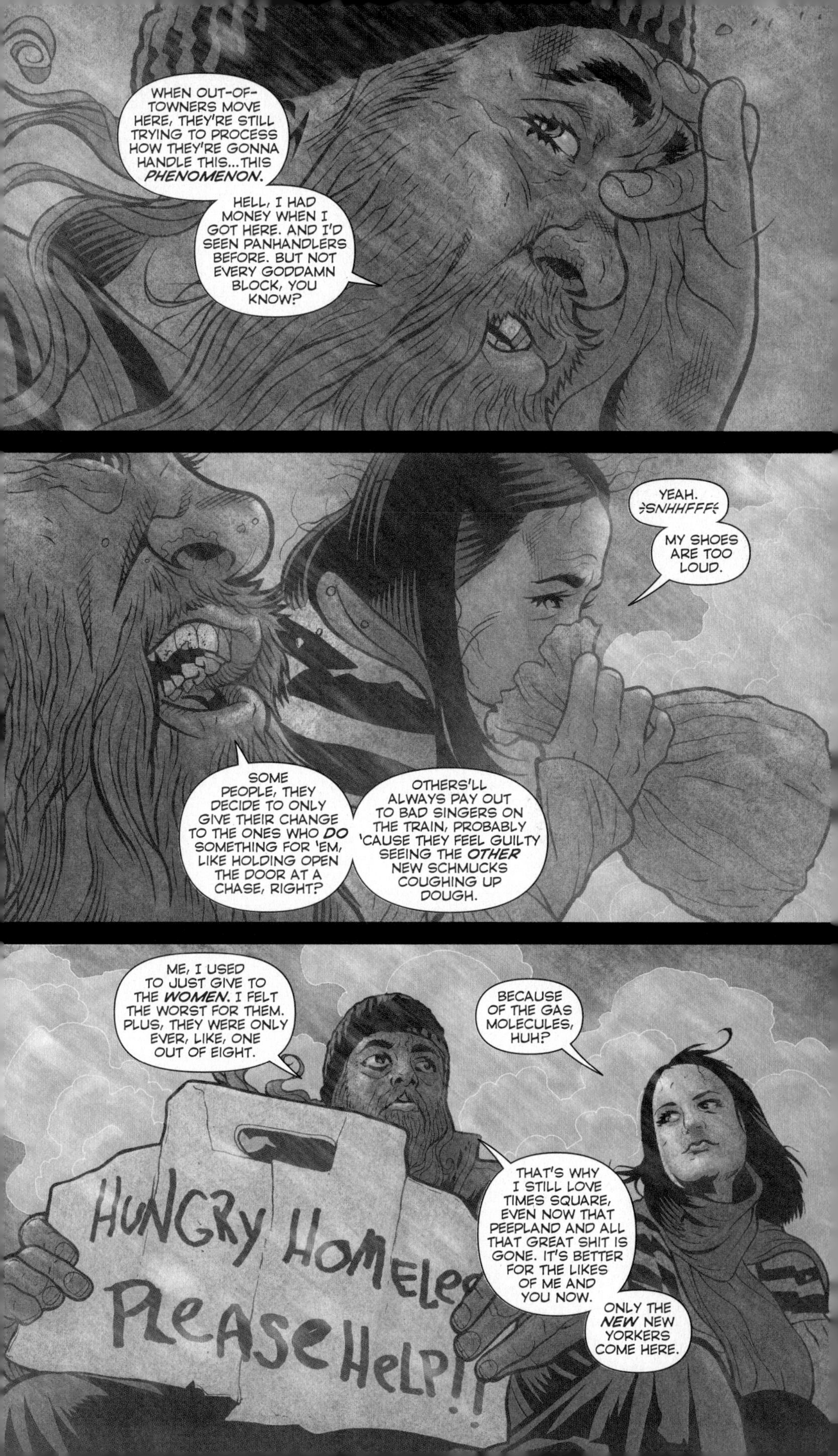
WHEN OUT-OF-TOWNERS MOVE HERE, THEY'RE STILL TRYING TO PROCESS HOW THEY'RE GONNA HANDLE THIS...THIS *PHENOMENON.*
HELL, I HAD MONEY WHEN I GOT HERE. AND I'D SEEN PANHANDLERS BEFORE. BUT NOT EVERY GODDAMN BLOCK, YOU KNOW?
YEAH. *SNHHFFF*
MY SHOES ARE TOO LOUD.
SOME PEOPLE, THEY DECIDE TO ONLY GIVE THEIR CHANGE TO THE ONES WHO *DO* SOMETHING FOR 'EM, LIKE HOLDING OPEN THE DOOR AT A CHASE, RIGHT?
OTHERS'LL ALWAYS PAY OUT TO BAD SINGERS ON THE TRAIN, PROBABLY 'CAUSE THEY FEEL GUILTY SEEING THE *OTHER* NEW SCHMUCKS COUGHING UP DOUGH.
ME, I USED TO JUST GIVE TO THE *WOMEN.* I FELT THE WORST FOR THEM. PLUS, THEY WERE ONLY EVER, LIKE, ONE OUT OF EIGHT.
BECAUSE OF THE GAS MOLECULES, HUH?
HUNGRY HOMELES
PLEASE HELP!!
THAT'S WHY I STILL LOVE TIMES SQUARE, EVEN NOW THAT PEEPLAND AND ALL THAT GREAT SHIT IS GONE. IT'S BETTER FOR THE LIKES OF ME AND YOU NOW.
ONLY THE *NEW* NEW YORKERS COME HERE.

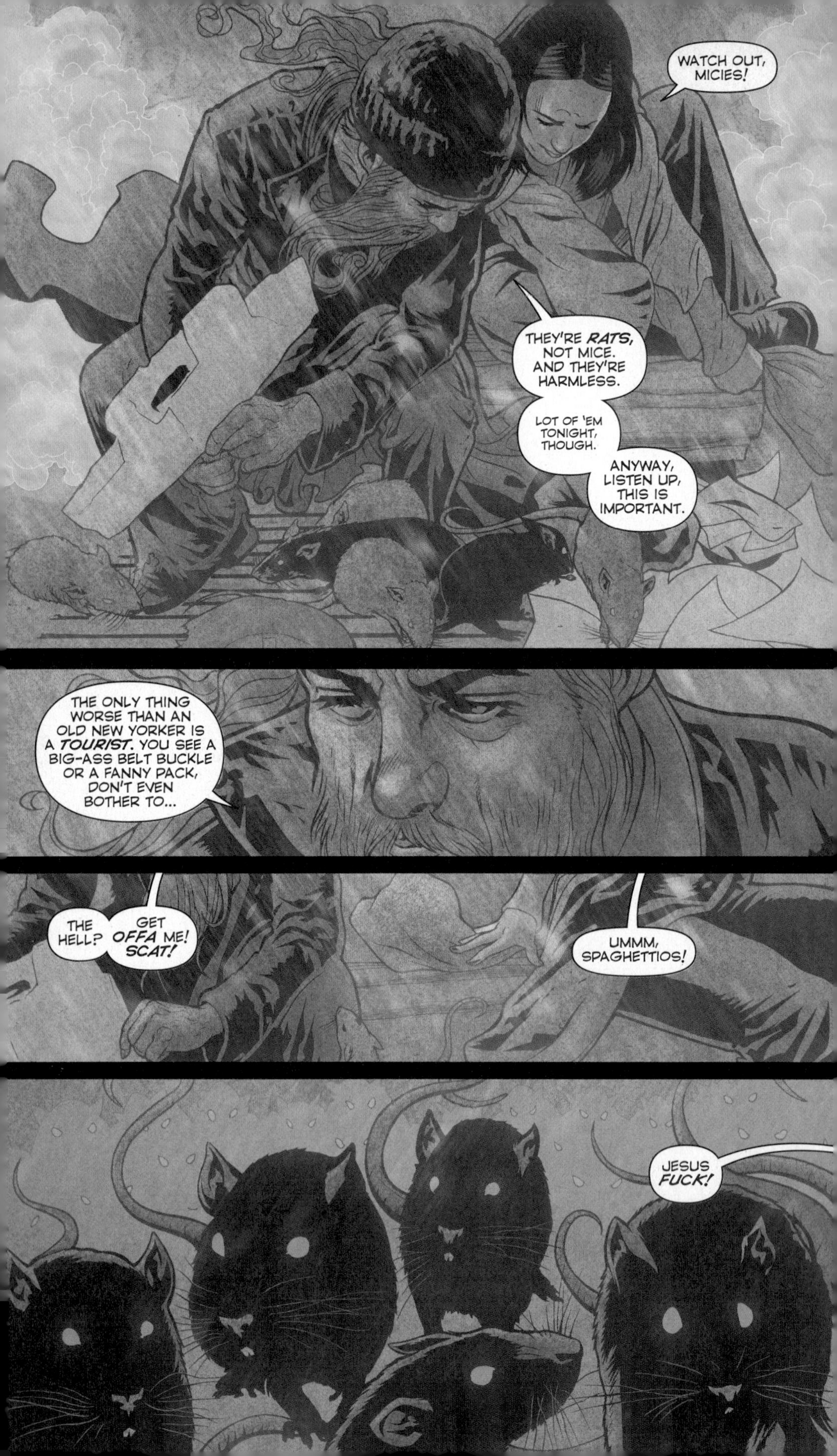
WATCH OUT, MICIES!
THEY'RE RATS, NOT MICE. AND THEY'RE HARMLESS.
LOT OF 'EM TONIGHT, THOUGH.
ANYWAY, LISTEN UP, THIS IS IMPORTANT.
THE ONLY THING WORSE THAN AN OLD NEW YORKER IS A TOURIST. YOU SEE A BIG-ASS BELT BUCKLE OR A FANNY PACK, DON'T EVEN BOTHER TO...
THE HELL?
GET OFFA ME! SCAT!
UMMM, SPAGHETTIOS!
JESUS FUCK!

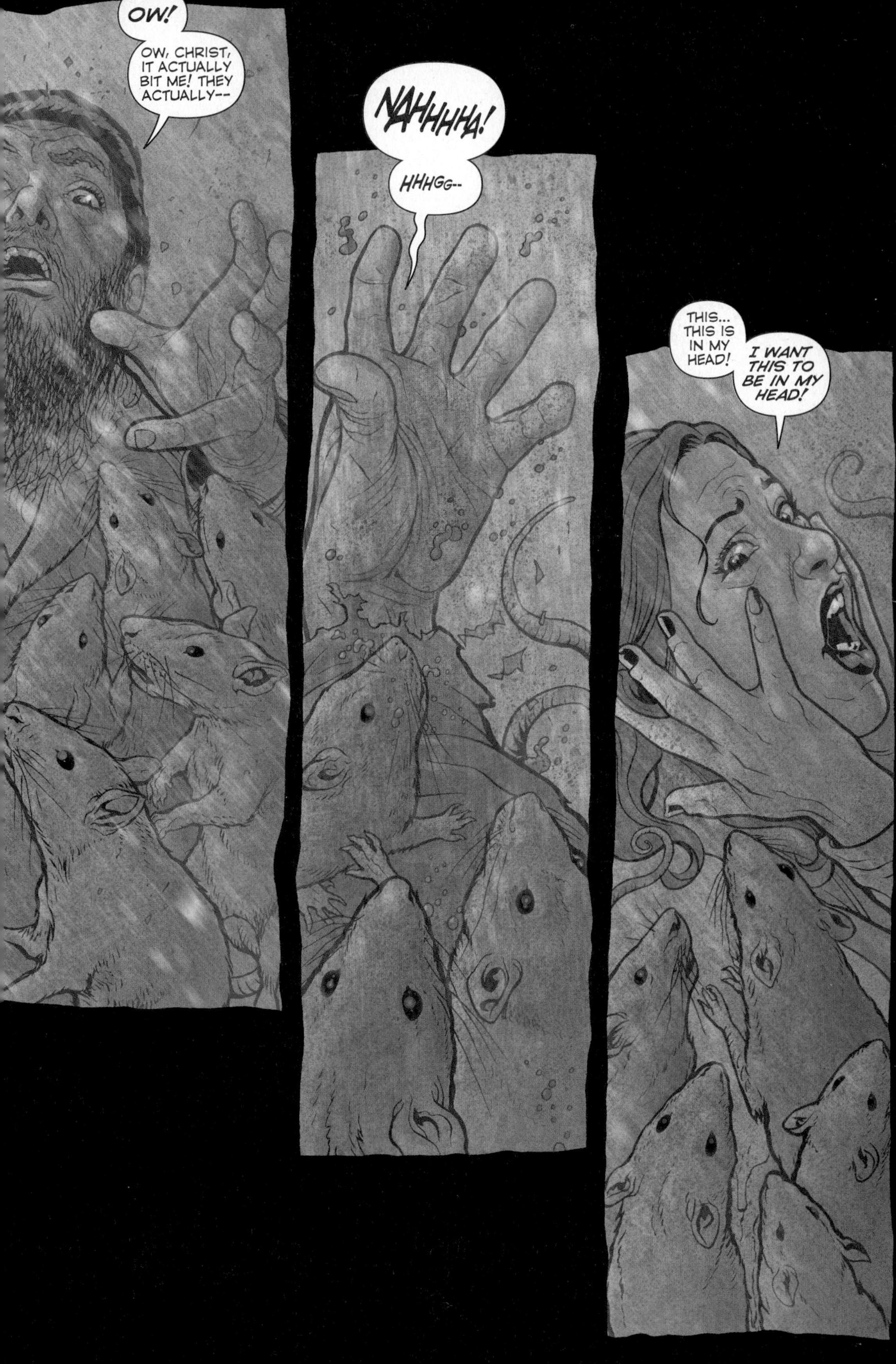
OW!
OW, CHRIST, IT ACTUALLY BIT ME! THEY ACTUALLY--
NAHHHHA!
HHHGG--
THIS... THIS IS IN MY HEAD!
I WANT THIS TO BE IN MY HEAD!

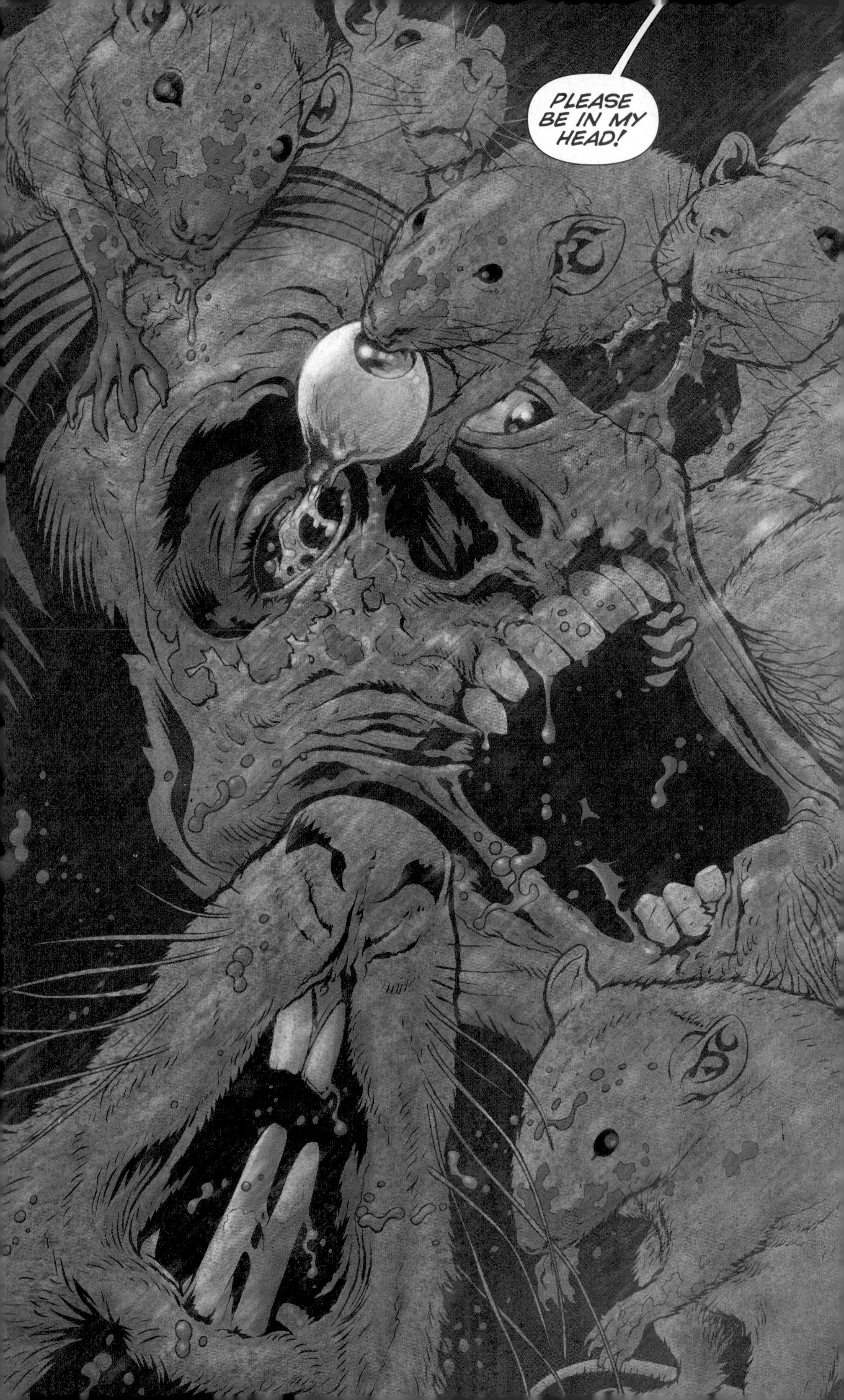
PLEASE BE IN MY HEAD!

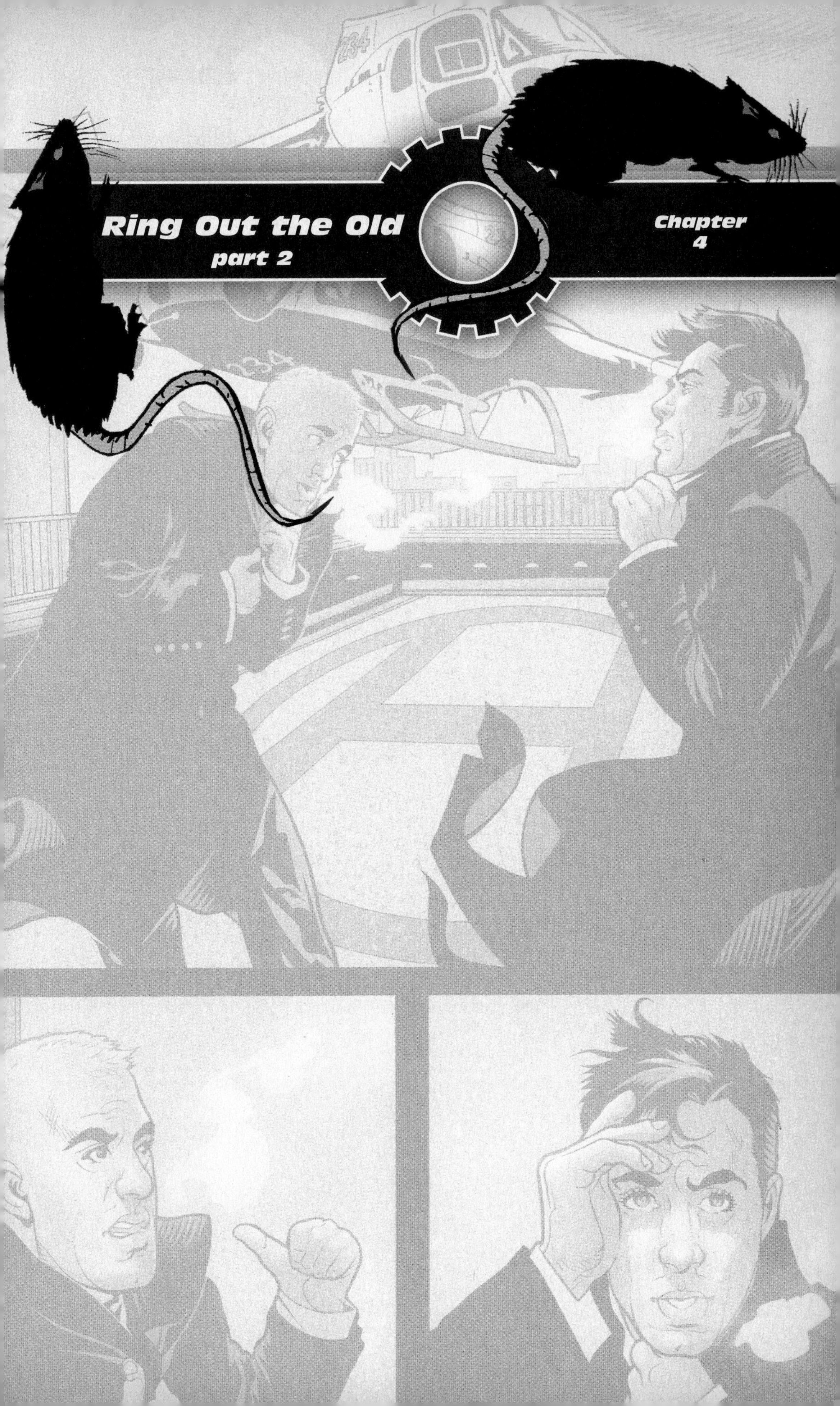
Ring Out the Old
part 2
Chapter
4

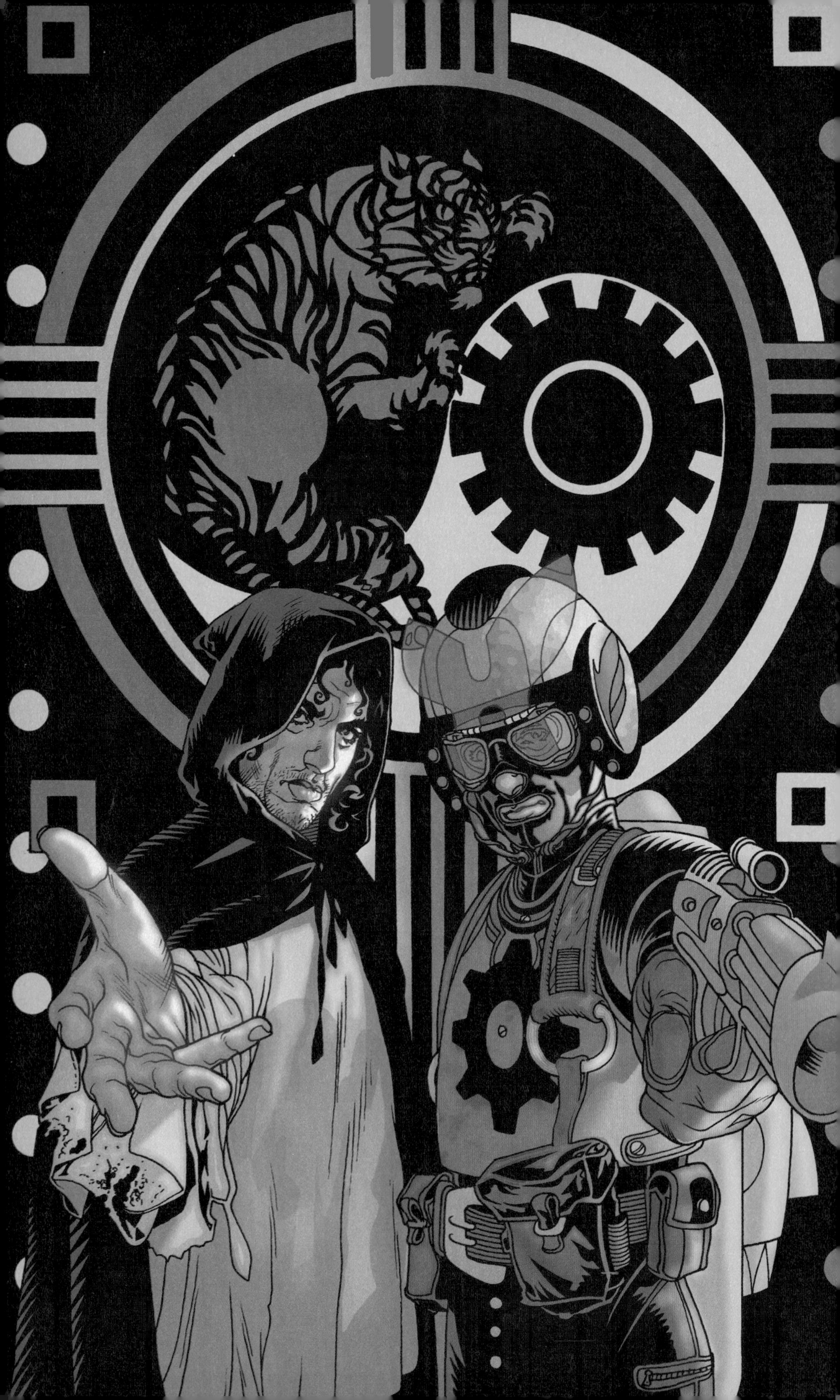

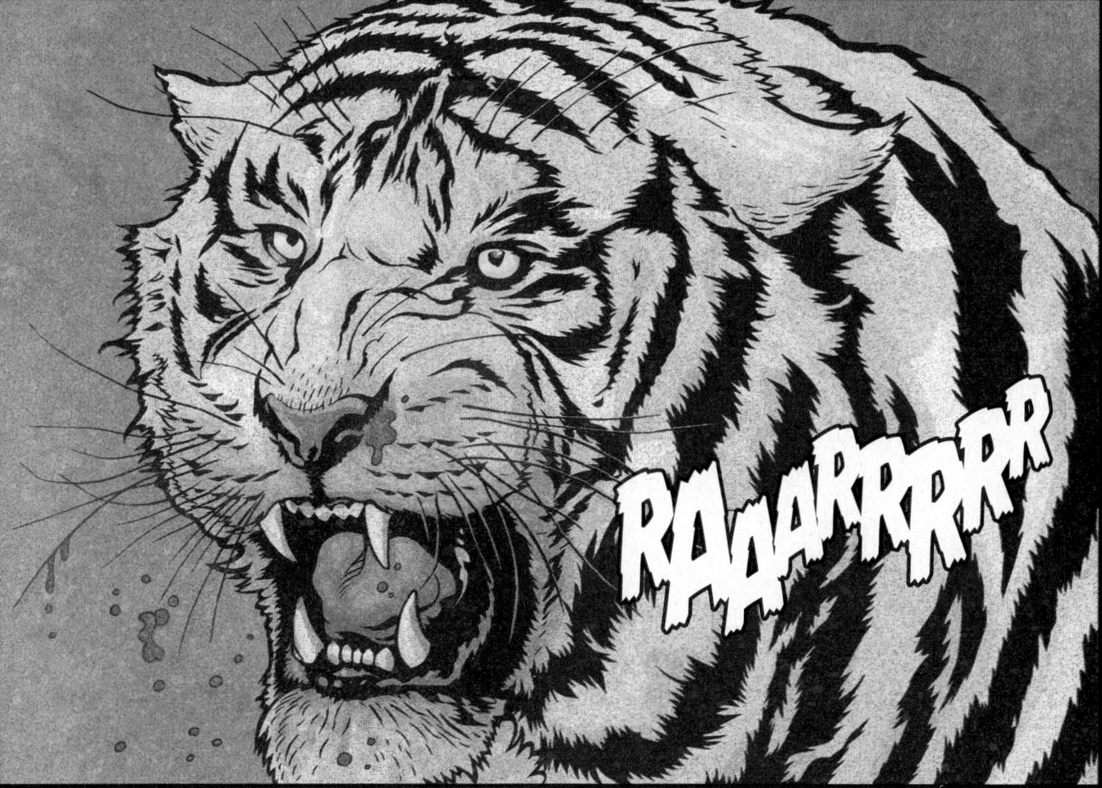
RAAARRRRRR

FRIDAY, MARCH 29, 2001

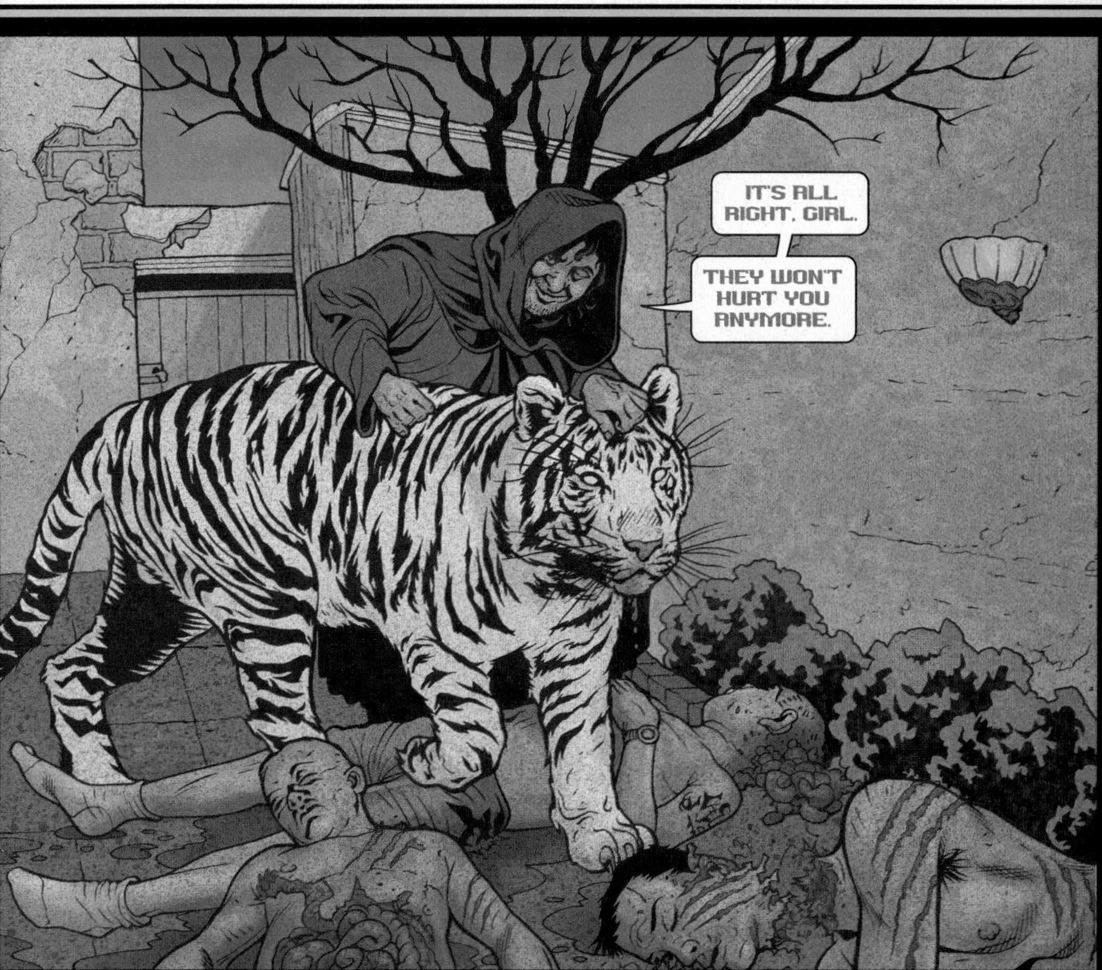
IT'S ALL RIGHT, GIRL.
THEY WON'T HURT YOU ANYMORE.

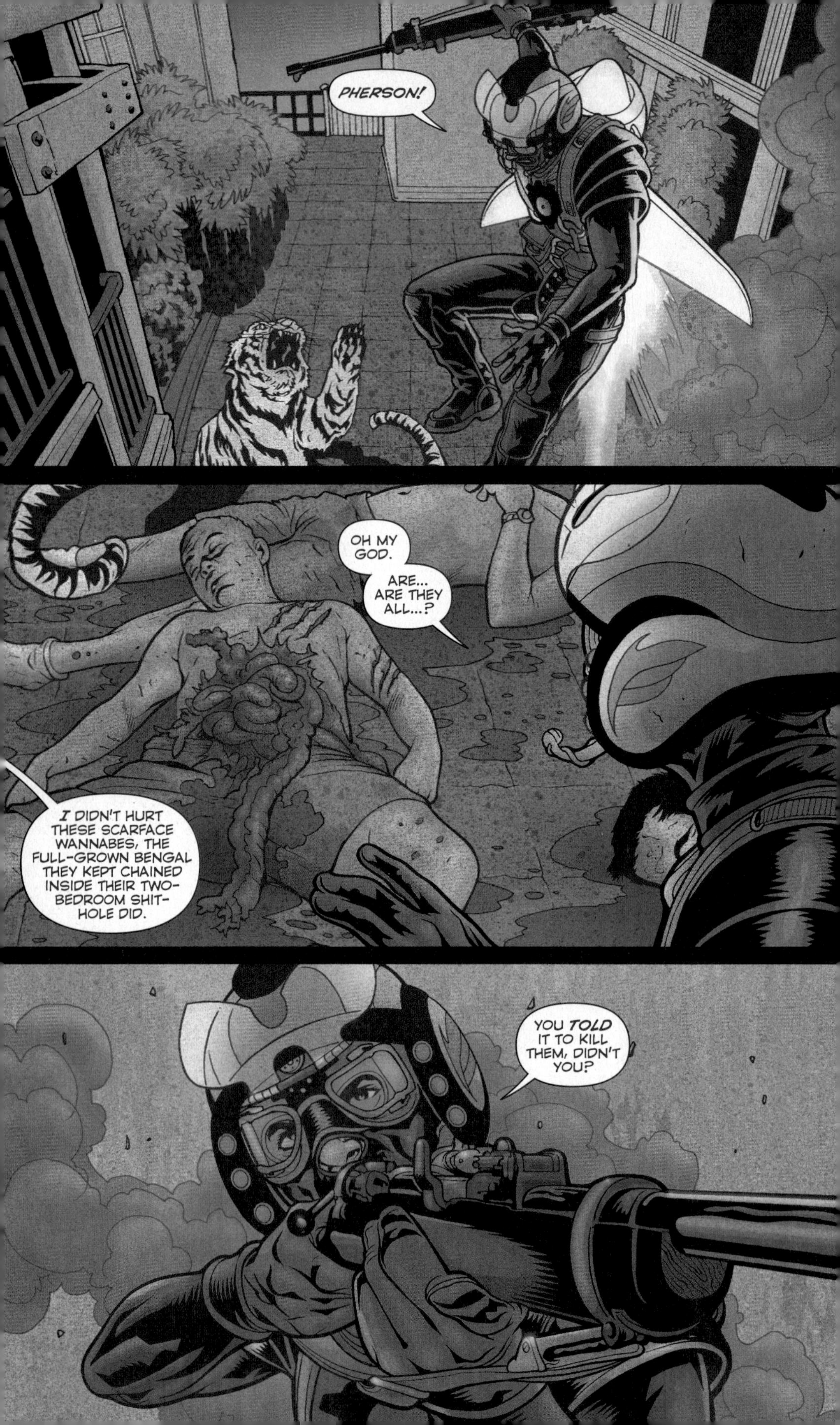
PHERSON!
OH MY GOD.
ARE... ARE THEY ALL...?
I DIDN'T HURT THESE SCARFACE WANNABES, THE FULL-GROWN BENGAL THEY KEPT CHAINED INSIDE THEIR TWO-BEDROOM SHIT-HOLE DID.
YOU TOLD IT TO KILL THEM, DIDN'T YOU?

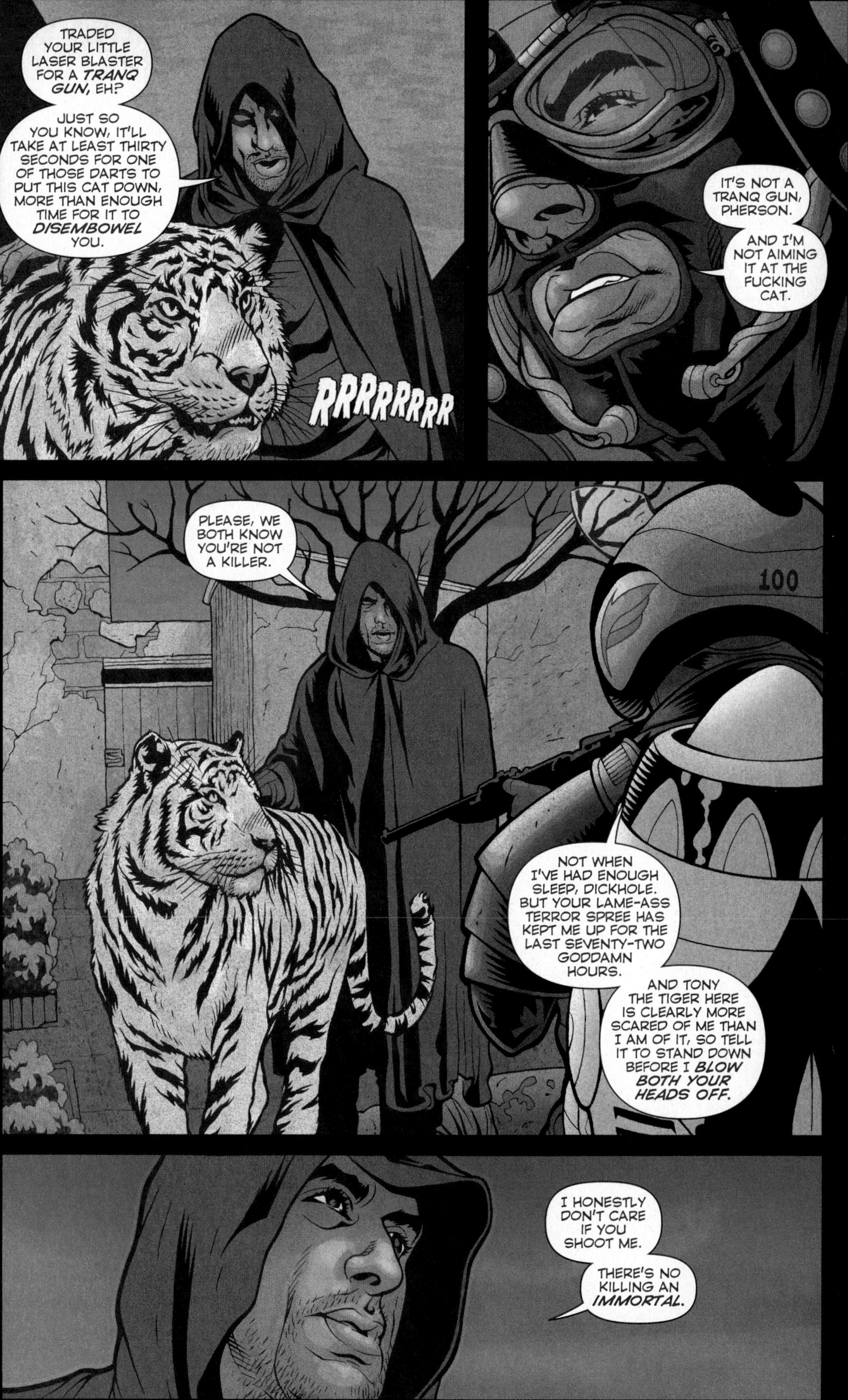
TRADED YOUR LITTLE LASER BLASTER FOR A *TRANQ GUN*, EH?
JUST SO YOU KNOW, IT'LL TAKE AT LEAST THIRTY SECONDS FOR ONE OF THOSE DARTS TO PUT THIS CAT DOWN, MORE THAN ENOUGH TIME FOR IT TO ***DISEMBOWEL*** YOU.
RRRRRRRR
IT'S NOT A TRANQ GUN, PHERSON.
AND I'M NOT AIMING IT AT THE FUCKING CAT.
PLEASE, WE BOTH KNOW YOU'RE NOT A KILLER.
100
NOT WHEN I'VE HAD ENOUGH SLEEP, DICKHOLE. BUT YOUR LAME-ASS TERROR SPREE HAS KEPT ME UP FOR THE LAST SEVENTY-TWO GODDAMN HOURS.
AND TONY THE TIGER HERE IS CLEARLY MORE SCARED OF ME THAN I AM OF IT, SO TELL IT TO STAND DOWN BEFORE I ***BLOW BOTH YOUR HEADS OFF***.
I HONESTLY DON'T CARE IF YOU SHOOT ME.
THERE'S NO KILLING AN *IMMORTAL*.

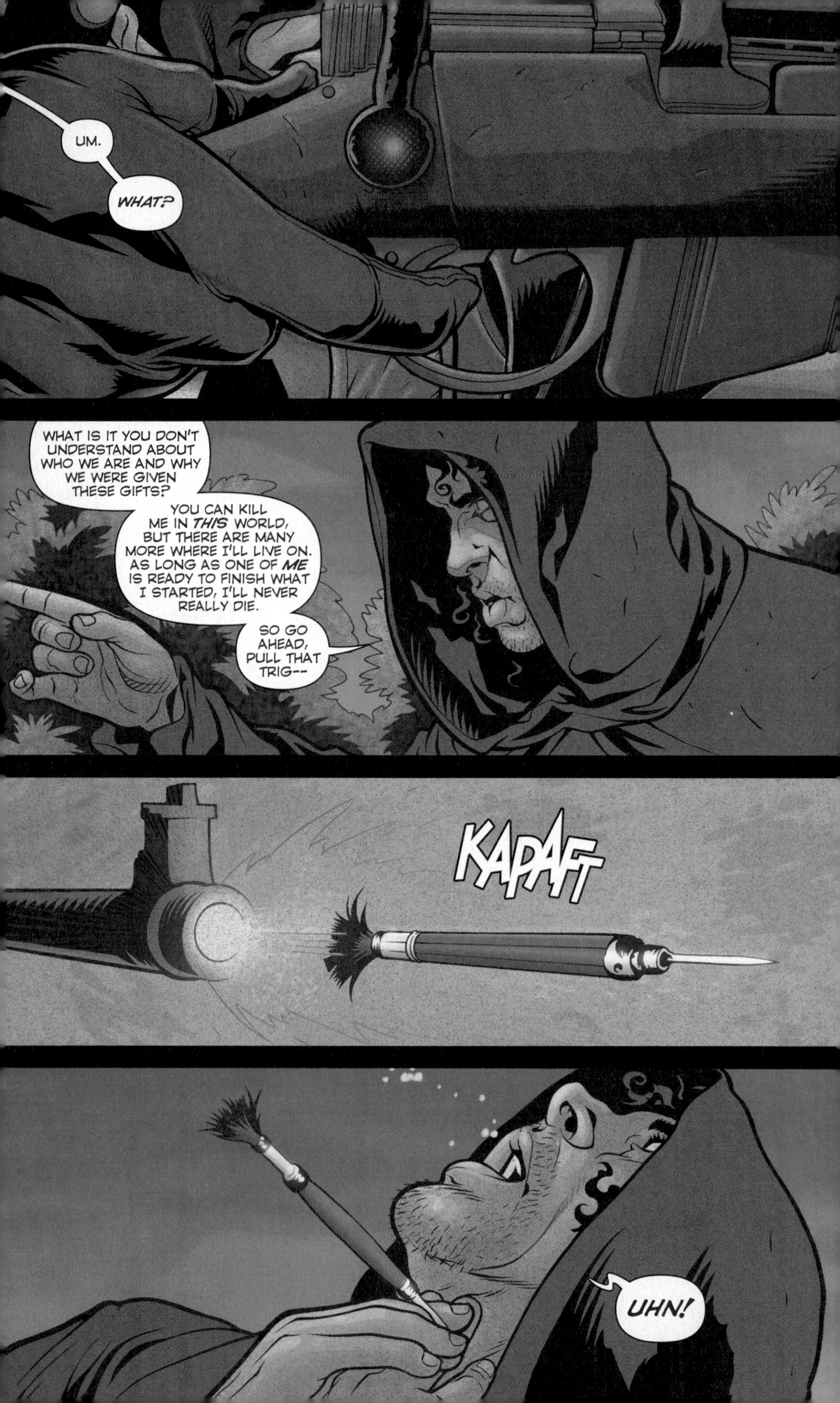

UM.
WHAT?
WHAT IS IT YOU DON'T UNDERSTAND ABOUT WHO WE ARE AND WHY WE WERE GIVEN THESE GIFTS?
YOU CAN KILL ME IN THIS WORLD, BUT THERE ARE MANY MORE WHERE I'LL LIVE ON. AS LONG AS ONE OF ME IS READY TO FINISH WHAT I STARTED, I'LL NEVER REALLY DIE.
SO GO AHEAD, PULL THAT TRIG--
KAPAFT
UHN!

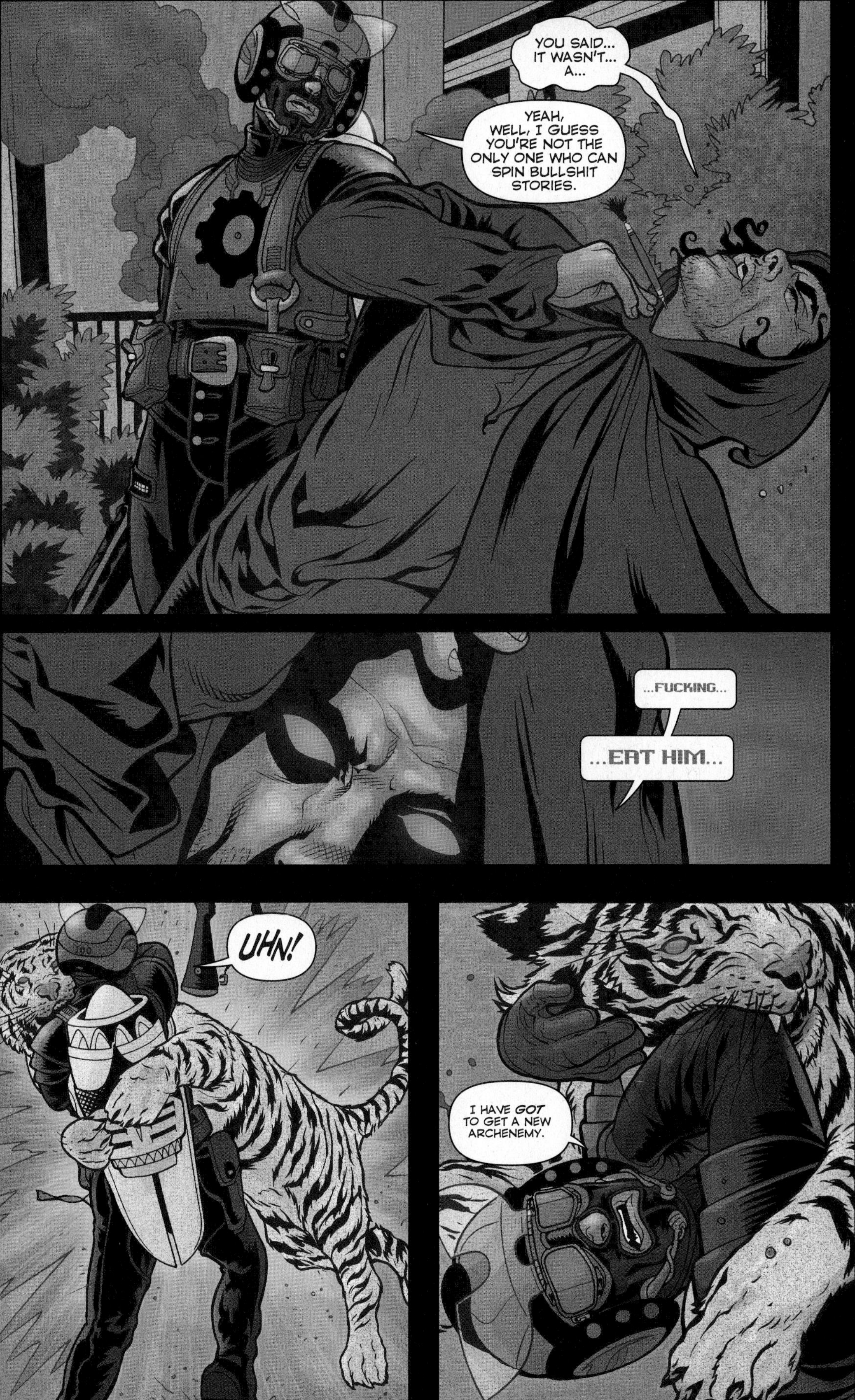
YOU SAID... IT WASN'T... A...
YEAH, WELL, I GUESS YOU'RE NOT THE ONLY ONE WHO CAN SPIN BULLSHIT STORIES.
...FUCKING...
...EAT HIM...
UHN!
I HAVE GOT TO GET A NEW ARCHENEMY.

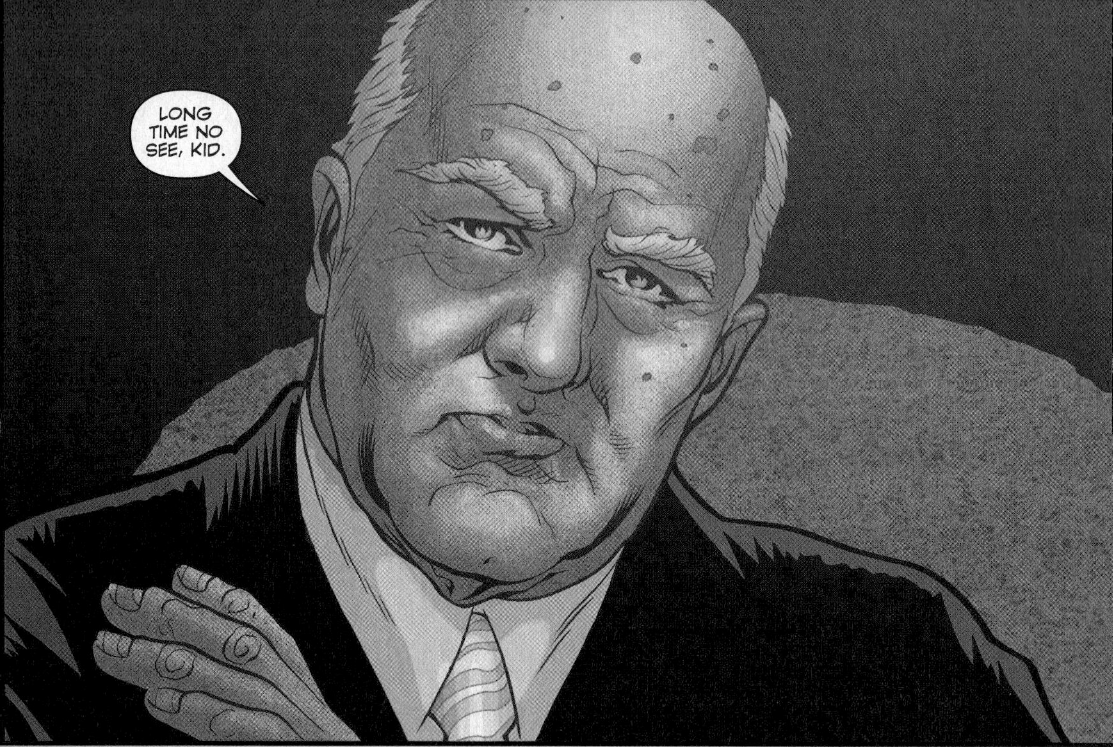
LONG TIME NO SEE, KID.

THURSDAY, DECEMBER 30, 2004

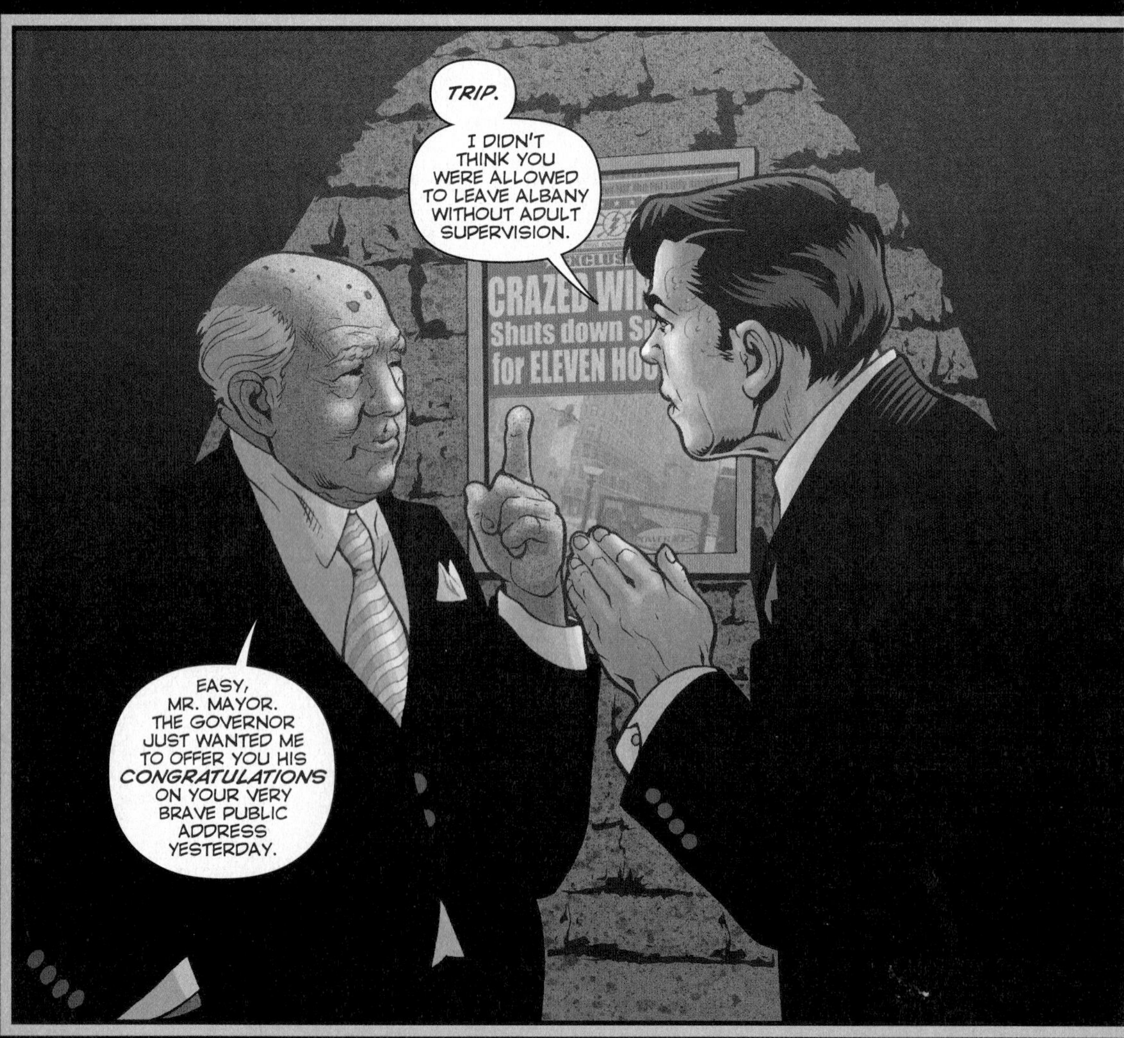
TRIP.
I DIDN'T THINK YOU WERE ALLOWED TO LEAVE ALBANY WITHOUT ADULT SUPERVISION.
EASY, MR. MAYOR. THE GOVERNOR JUST WANTED ME TO OFFER YOU HIS *CONGRATULATIONS* ON YOUR VERY BRAVE PUBLIC ADDRESS YESTERDAY.

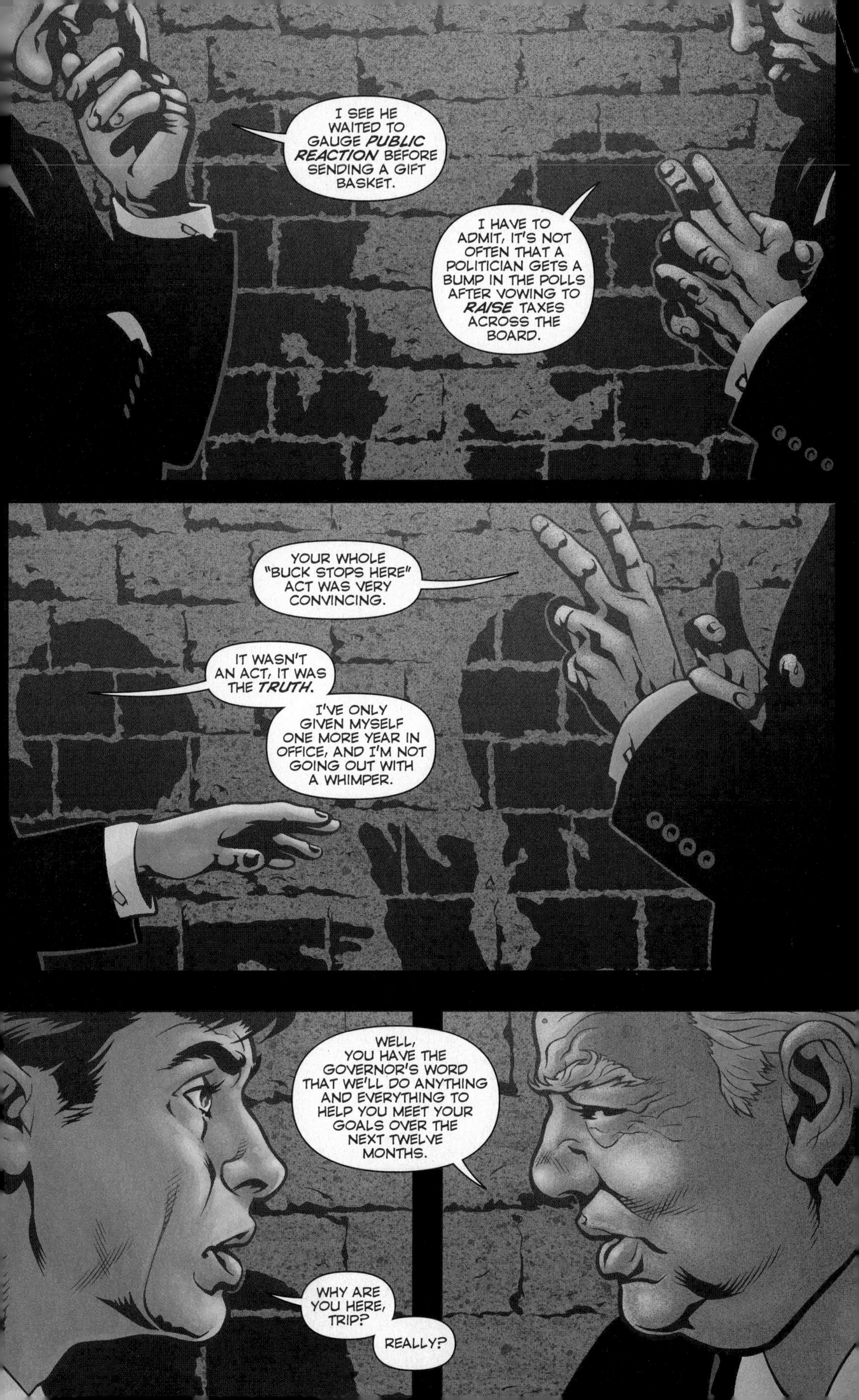
I SEE HE WAITED TO GAUGE PUBLIC REACTION BEFORE SENDING A GIFT BASKET.
I HAVE TO ADMIT, IT'S NOT OFTEN THAT A POLITICIAN GETS A BUMP IN THE POLLS AFTER VOWING TO RAISE TAXES ACROSS THE BOARD.
YOUR WHOLE "BUCK STOPS HERE" ACT WAS VERY CONVINCING.
IT WASN'T AN ACT, IT WAS THE TRUTH.
I'VE ONLY GIVEN MYSELF ONE MORE YEAR IN OFFICE, AND I'M NOT GOING OUT WITH A WHIMPER.
WELL, YOU HAVE THE GOVERNOR'S WORD THAT WE'LL DO ANYTHING AND EVERYTHING TO HELP YOU MEET YOUR GOALS OVER THE NEXT TWELVE MONTHS.
WHY ARE YOU HERE, TRIP?
REALLY?

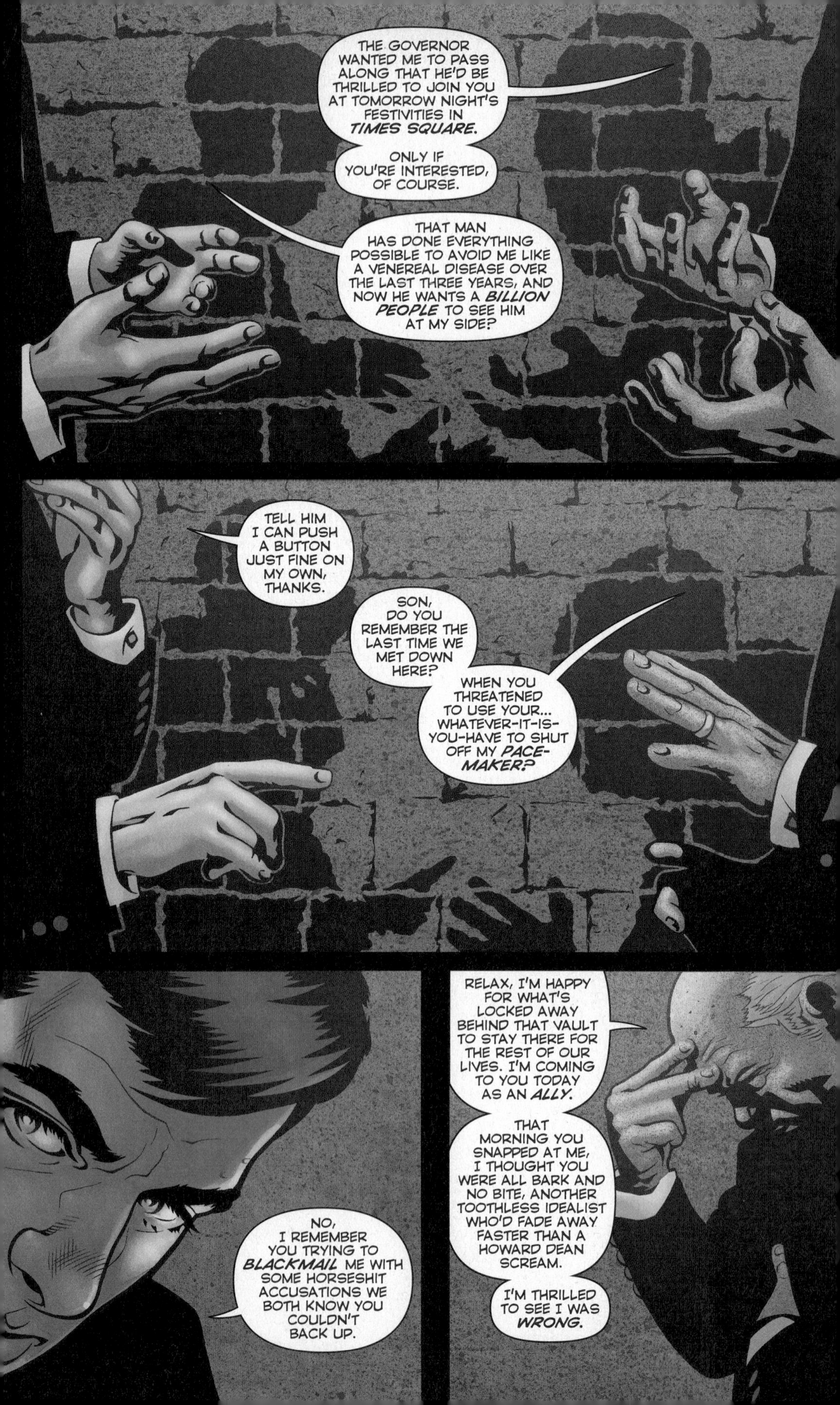
THE GOVERNOR WANTED ME TO PASS ALONG THAT HE'D BE THRILLED TO JOIN YOU AT TOMORROW NIGHT'S FESTIVITIES IN *TIMES SQUARE*.
ONLY IF YOU'RE INTERESTED, OF COURSE.
THAT MAN HAS DONE EVERYTHING POSSIBLE TO AVOID ME LIKE A VENEREAL DISEASE OVER THE LAST THREE YEARS, AND NOW HE WANTS A *BILLION PEOPLE* TO SEE HIM AT MY SIDE?
TELL HIM I CAN PUSH A BUTTON JUST FINE ON MY OWN, THANKS.
SON, DO YOU REMEMBER THE LAST TIME WE MET DOWN HERE?
WHEN YOU THREATENED TO USE YOUR... WHATEVER-IT-IS-YOU-HAVE TO SHUT OFF MY *PACE-MAKER?*
NO, I REMEMBER YOU TRYING TO *BLACKMAIL* ME WITH SOME HORSESHIT ACCUSATIONS WE BOTH KNOW YOU COULDN'T BACK UP.
RELAX, I'M HAPPY FOR WHAT'S LOCKED AWAY BEHIND THAT VAULT TO STAY THERE FOR THE REST OF OUR LIVES. I'M COMING TO YOU TODAY AS AN *ALLY*.
THAT MORNING YOU SNAPPED AT ME, I THOUGHT YOU WERE ALL BARK AND NO BITE, ANOTHER TOOTHLESS IDEALIST WHO'D FADE AWAY FASTER THAN A HOWARD DEAN SCREAM.
I'M THRILLED TO SEE I WAS *WRONG*.

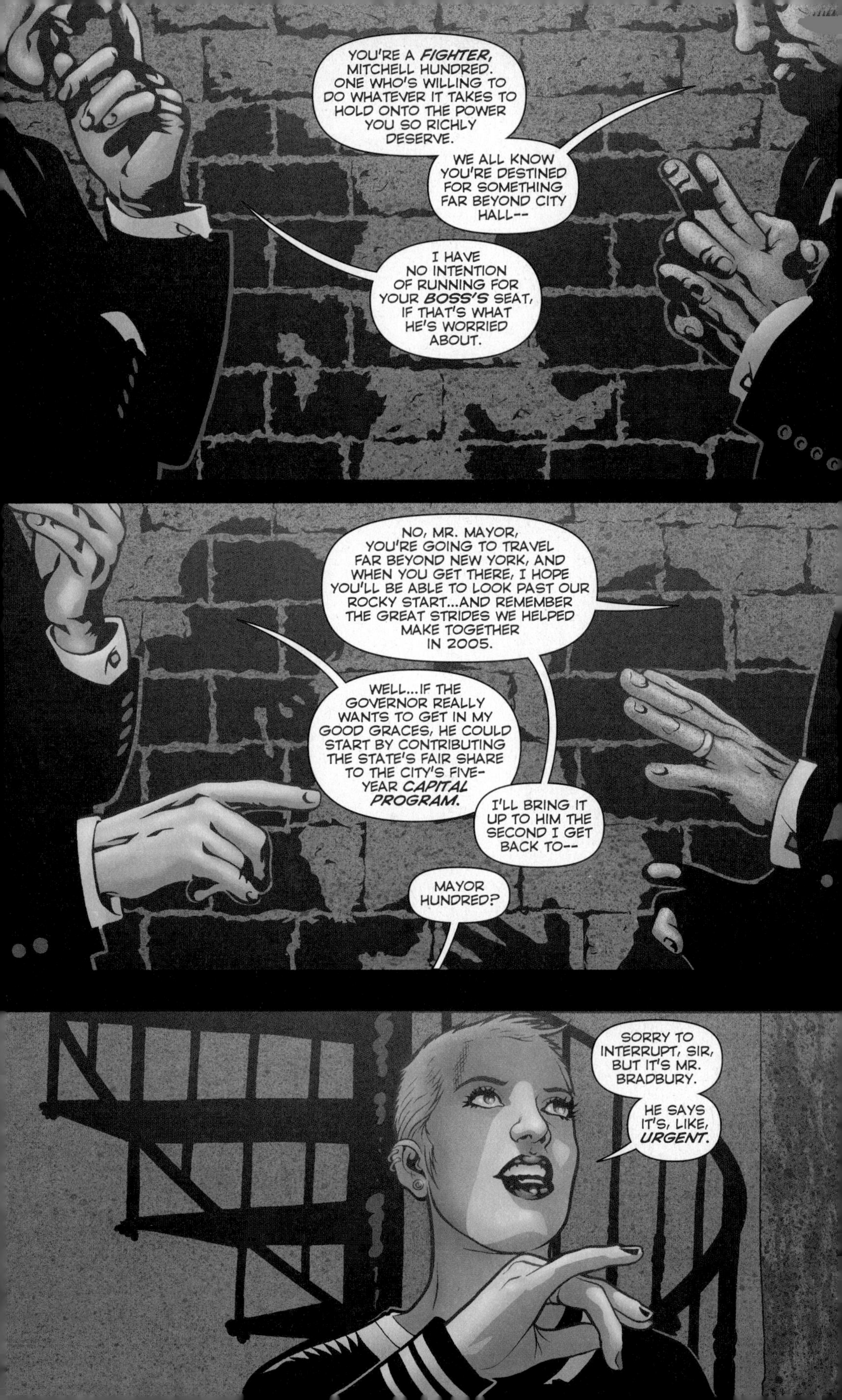
YOU'RE A *FIGHTER*, MITCHELL HUNDRED. ONE WHO'S WILLING TO DO WHATEVER IT TAKES TO HOLD ONTO THE POWER YOU SO RICHLY DESERVE.
WE ALL KNOW YOU'RE DESTINED FOR SOMETHING FAR BEYOND CITY HALL--
I HAVE NO INTENTION OF RUNNING FOR YOUR *BOSS'S* SEAT, IF THAT'S WHAT HE'S WORRIED ABOUT.
NO, MR. MAYOR, YOU'RE GOING TO TRAVEL FAR BEYOND NEW YORK, AND WHEN YOU GET THERE, I HOPE YOU'LL BE ABLE TO LOOK PAST OUR ROCKY START...AND REMEMBER THE GREAT STRIDES WE HELPED MAKE TOGETHER IN 2005.
WELL...IF THE GOVERNOR REALLY WANTS TO GET IN MY GOOD GRACES, HE COULD START BY CONTRIBUTING THE STATE'S FAIR SHARE TO THE CITY'S FIVE-YEAR *CAPITAL PROGRAM*.
I'LL BRING IT UP TO HIM THE SECOND I GET BACK TO--
MAYOR HUNDRED?
SORRY TO INTERRUPT, SIR, BUT IT'S MR. BRADBURY.
HE SAYS IT'S, LIKE, *URGENT*.

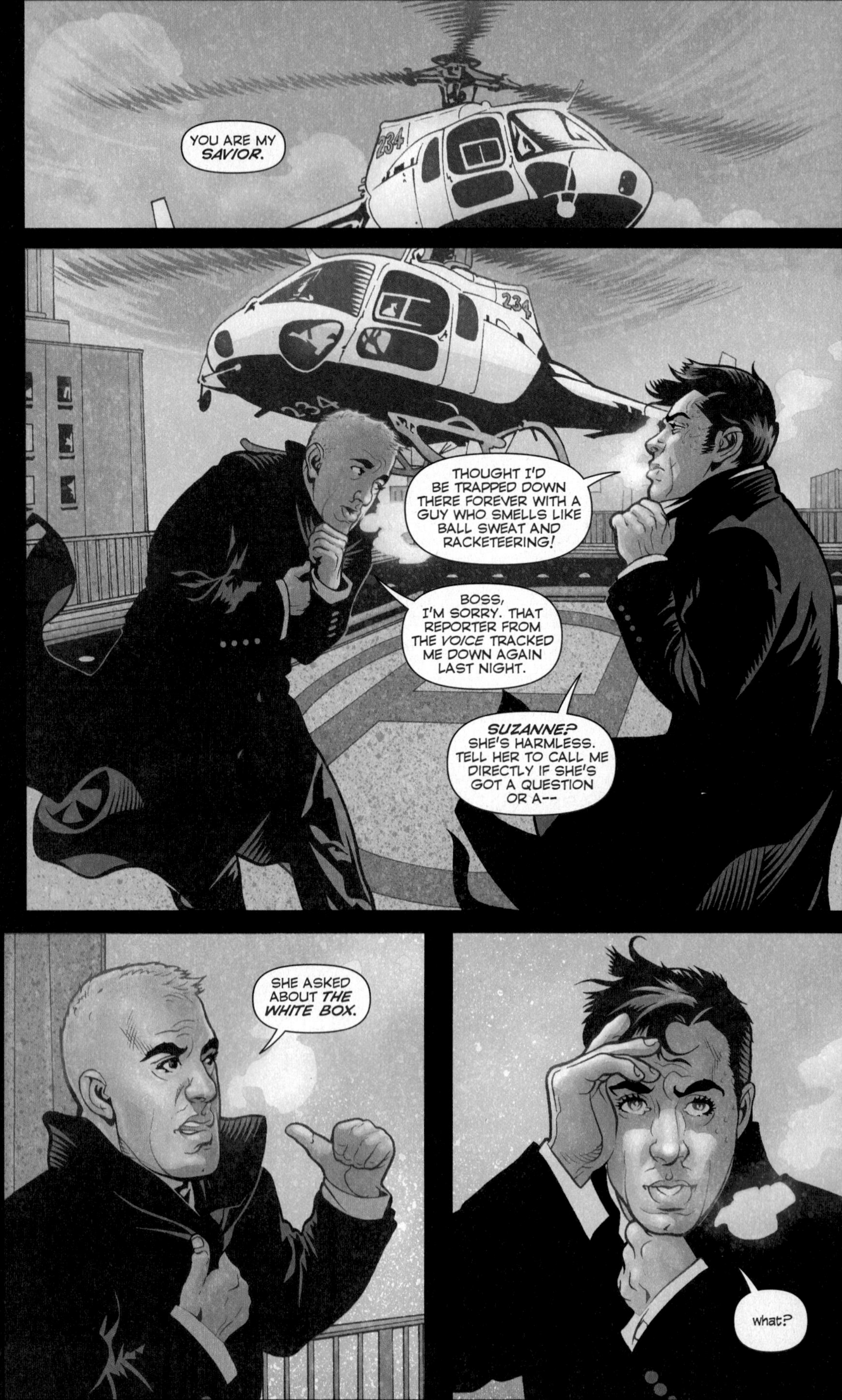
YOU ARE MY *SAVIOR*.
THOUGHT I'D BE TRAPPED DOWN THERE FOREVER WITH A GUY WHO SMELLS LIKE BALL SWEAT AND RACKETEERING!
BOSS, I'M SORRY. THAT REPORTER FROM THE *VOICE* TRACKED ME DOWN AGAIN LAST NIGHT.
SUZANNE? SHE'S HARMLESS. TELL HER TO CALL ME DIRECTLY IF SHE'S GOT A QUESTION OR A--
SHE ASKED ABOUT *THE WHITE BOX*.
what?

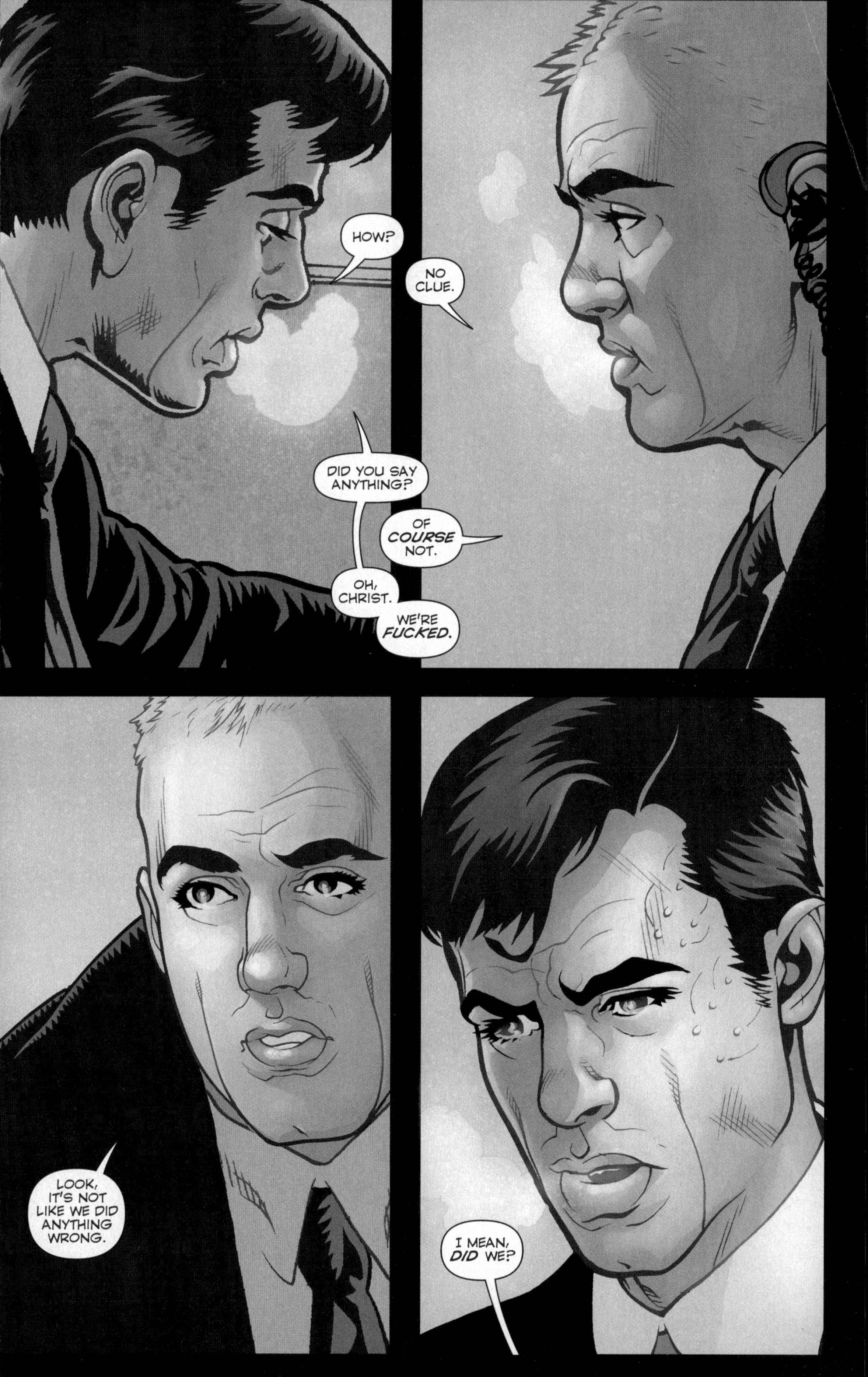

HOW?
NO CLUE.
DID YOU SAY ANYTHING?
OF *COURSE* NOT.
OH, CHRIST.
WE'RE *FUCKED*.
LOOK, IT'S NOT LIKE WE DID ANYTHING WRONG.
I MEAN, *DID* WE?

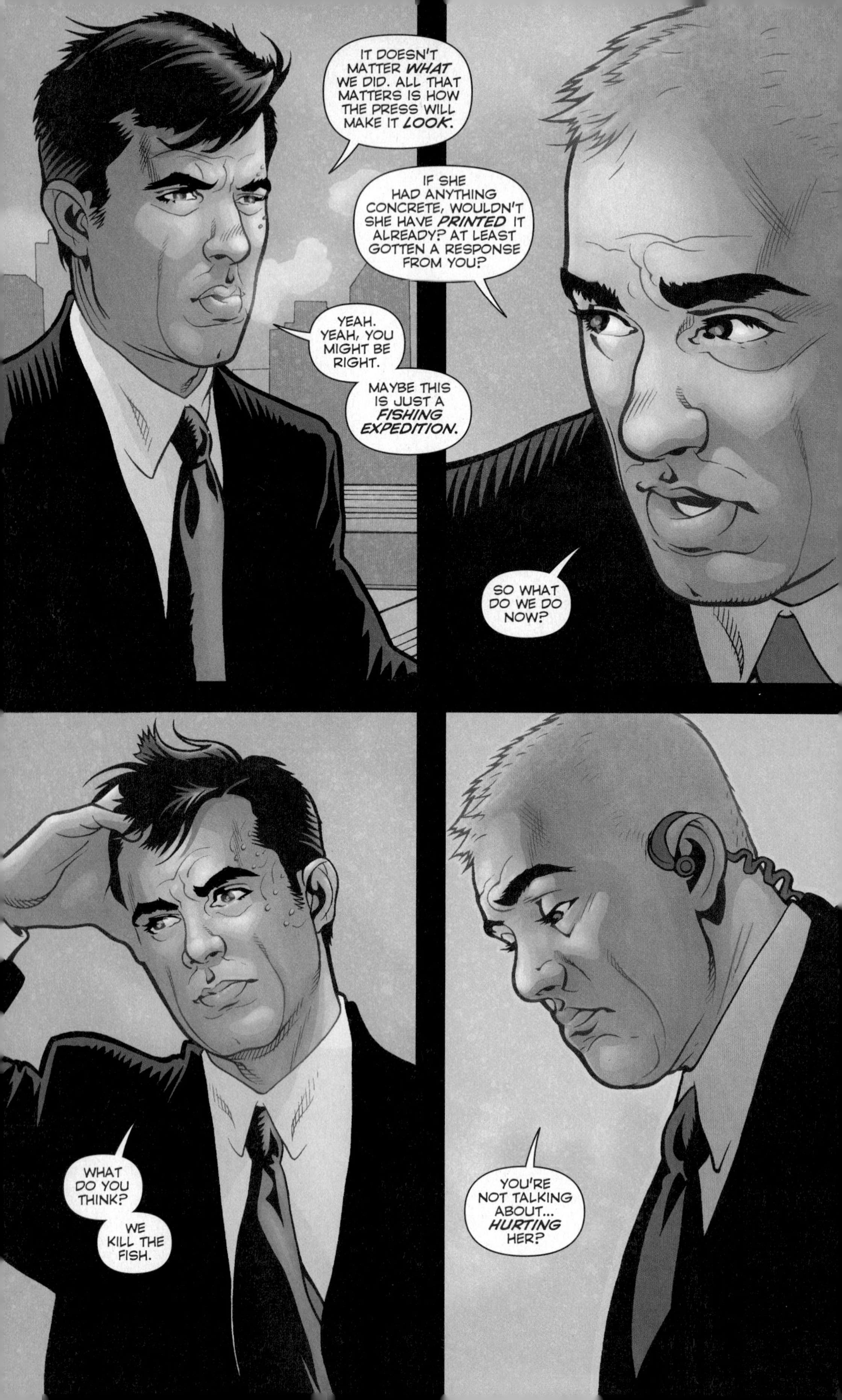
IT DOESN'T MATTER WHAT WE DID. ALL THAT MATTERS IS HOW THE PRESS WILL MAKE IT LOOK.
IF SHE HAD ANYTHING CONCRETE, WOULDN'T SHE HAVE PRINTED IT ALREADY? AT LEAST GOTTEN A RESPONSE FROM YOU?
YEAH. YEAH, YOU MIGHT BE RIGHT.
MAYBE THIS IS JUST A FISHING EXPEDITION.
SO WHAT DO WE DO NOW?
WHAT DO YOU THINK?
WE KILL THE FISH.
YOU'RE NOT TALKING ABOUT... HURTING HER?

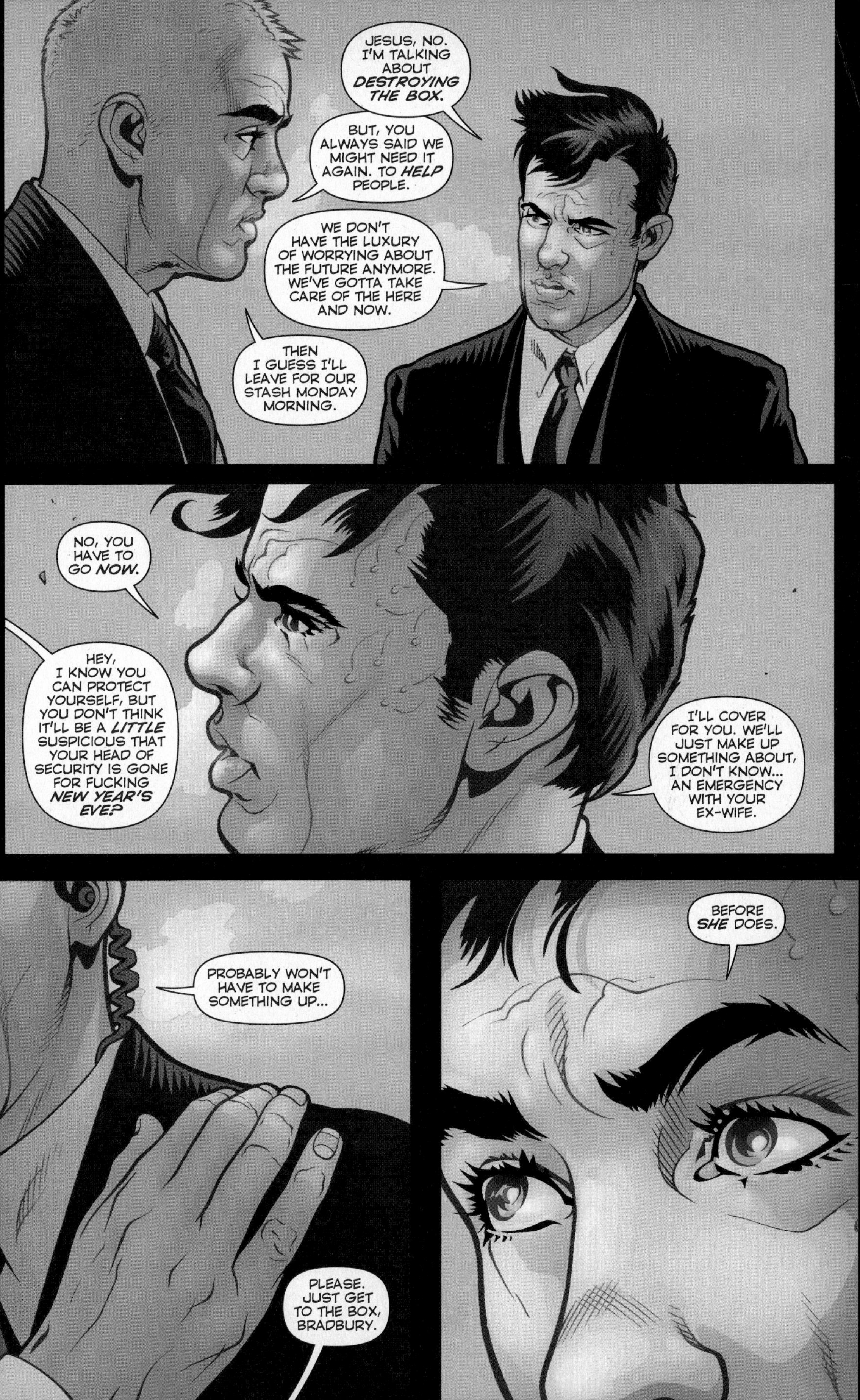
JESUS, NO. I'M TALKING ABOUT DESTROYING THE BOX.
BUT, YOU ALWAYS SAID WE MIGHT NEED IT AGAIN. TO HELP PEOPLE.
WE DON'T HAVE THE LUXURY OF WORRYING ABOUT THE FUTURE ANYMORE. WE'VE GOTTA TAKE CARE OF THE HERE AND NOW.
THEN I GUESS I'LL LEAVE FOR OUR STASH MONDAY MORNING.
NO, YOU HAVE TO GO NOW.
HEY, I KNOW YOU CAN PROTECT YOURSELF, BUT YOU DON'T THINK IT'LL BE A LITTLE SUSPICIOUS THAT YOUR HEAD OF SECURITY IS GONE FOR FUCKING NEW YEAR'S EVE?
I'LL COVER FOR YOU. WE'LL JUST MAKE UP SOMETHING ABOUT, I DON'T KNOW... AN EMERGENCY WITH YOUR EX-WIFE.
PROBABLY WON'T HAVE TO MAKE SOMETHING UP...
BEFORE SHE DOES.
PLEASE. JUST GET TO THE BOX, BRADBURY.

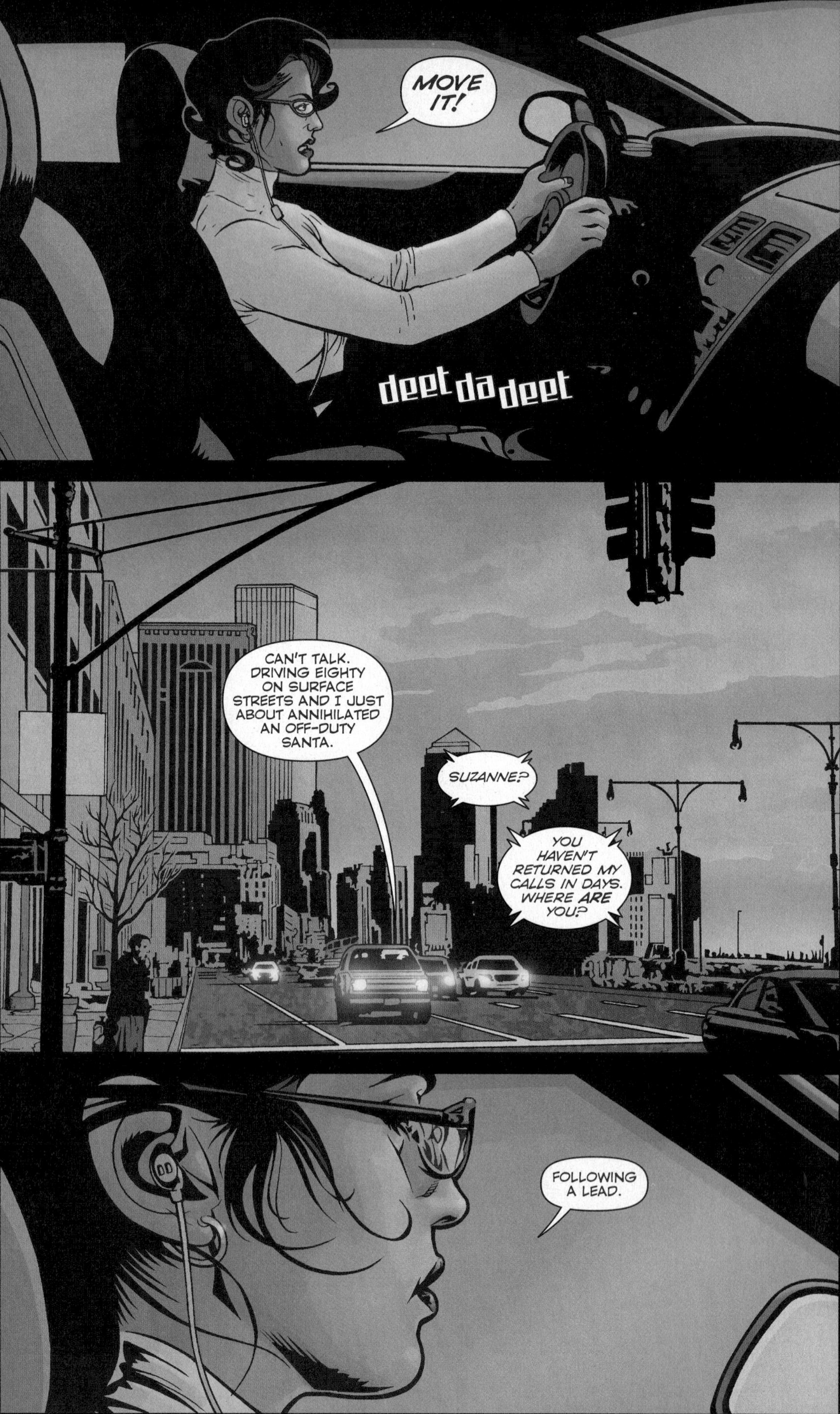
MOVE IT!
deet da deet
CAN'T TALK. DRIVING EIGHTY ON SURFACE STREETS AND I JUST ABOUT ANNIHILATED AN OFF-DUTY SANTA.
SUZANNE?
YOU HAVEN'T RETURNED MY CALLS IN DAYS. WHERE ARE YOU?
FOLLOWING A LEAD.

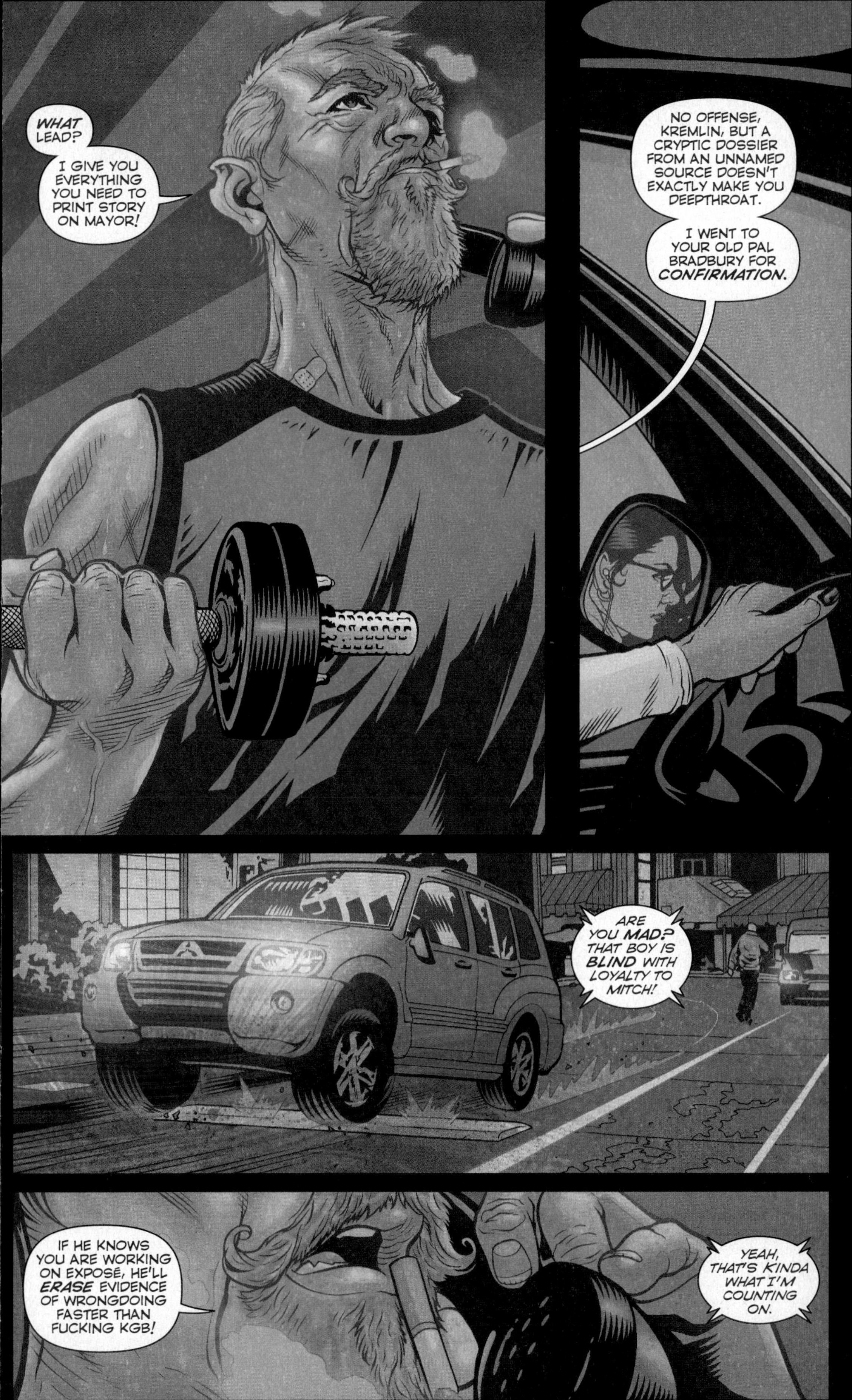
WHAT LEAD?
I GIVE YOU EVERYTHING YOU NEED TO PRINT STORY ON MAYOR!
NO OFFENSE, KREMLIN, BUT A CRYPTIC DOSSIER FROM AN UNNAMED SOURCE DOESN'T EXACTLY MAKE YOU DEEPTHROAT.
I WENT TO YOUR OLD PAL BRADBURY FOR CONFIRMATION.
ARE YOU MAD? THAT BOY IS BLIND WITH LOYALTY TO MITCH!
IF HE KNOWS YOU ARE WORKING ON EXPOSÉ, HE'LL ERASE EVIDENCE OF WRONGDOING FASTER THAN FUCKING KGB!
YEAH, THAT'S KINDA WHAT I'M COUNTING ON.

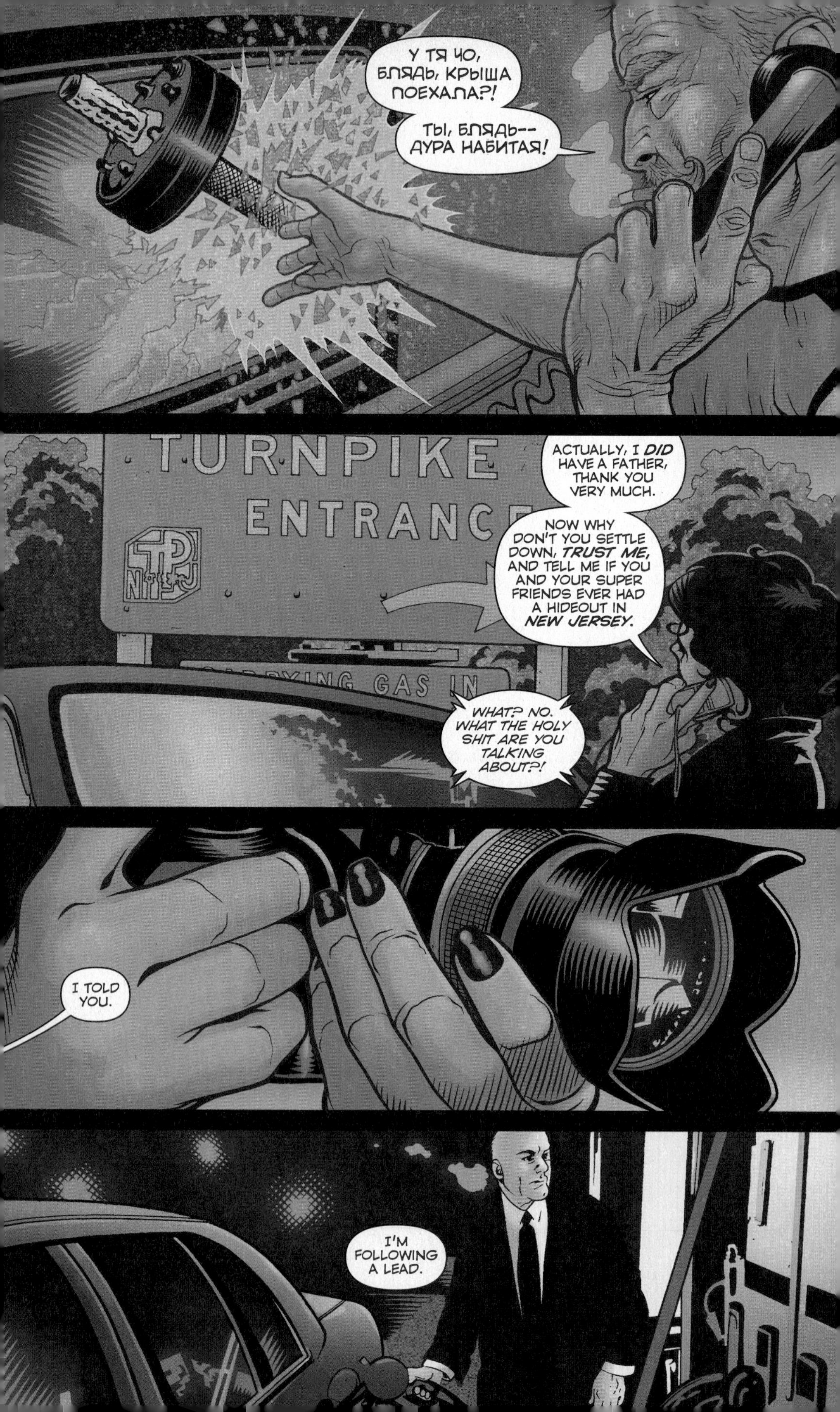
У ТЯ ЧО, БЛЯДЬ, КРЫША ПОЕХАЛА?!
ТЫ, БЛЯДЬ-- ДУРА НАБИТАЯ!
TURNPIKE ENTRANCE
ACTUALLY, I *DID* HAVE A FATHER, THANK YOU VERY MUCH.
NOW WHY DON'T YOU SETTLE DOWN, ***TRUST ME,*** AND TELL ME IF YOU AND YOUR SUPER FRIENDS EVER HAD A HIDEOUT IN ***NEW JERSEY.***
WHAT? NO. WHAT THE HOLY SHIT ARE YOU TALKING ABOUT?!
I TOLD YOU.
I'M FOLLOWING A LEAD.

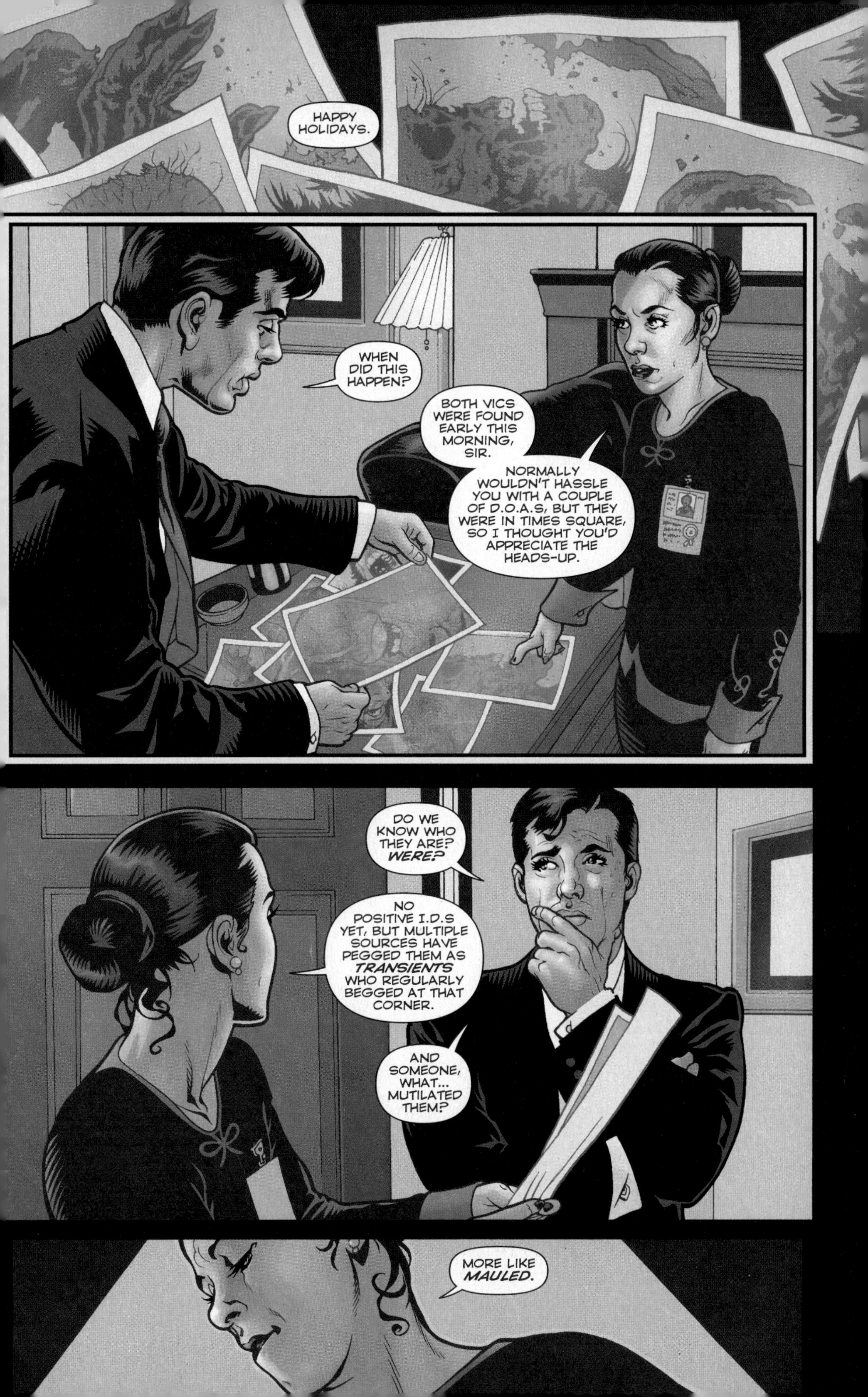
HAPPY HOLIDAYS.
WHEN DID THIS HAPPEN?
BOTH VICS WERE FOUND EARLY THIS MORNING, SIR.
NORMALLY WOULDN'T HASSLE YOU WITH A COUPLE OF D.O.A.S, BUT THEY WERE IN TIMES SQUARE, SO I THOUGHT YOU'D APPRECIATE THE HEADS-UP.
DO WE KNOW WHO THEY ARE? *WERE?*
NO POSITIVE I.D.S YET, BUT MULTIPLE SOURCES HAVE PEGGED THEM AS *TRANSIENTS* WHO REGULARLY BEGGED AT THAT CORNER.
AND SOMEONE, WHAT... MUTILATED THEM?
MORE LIKE *MAULED.*

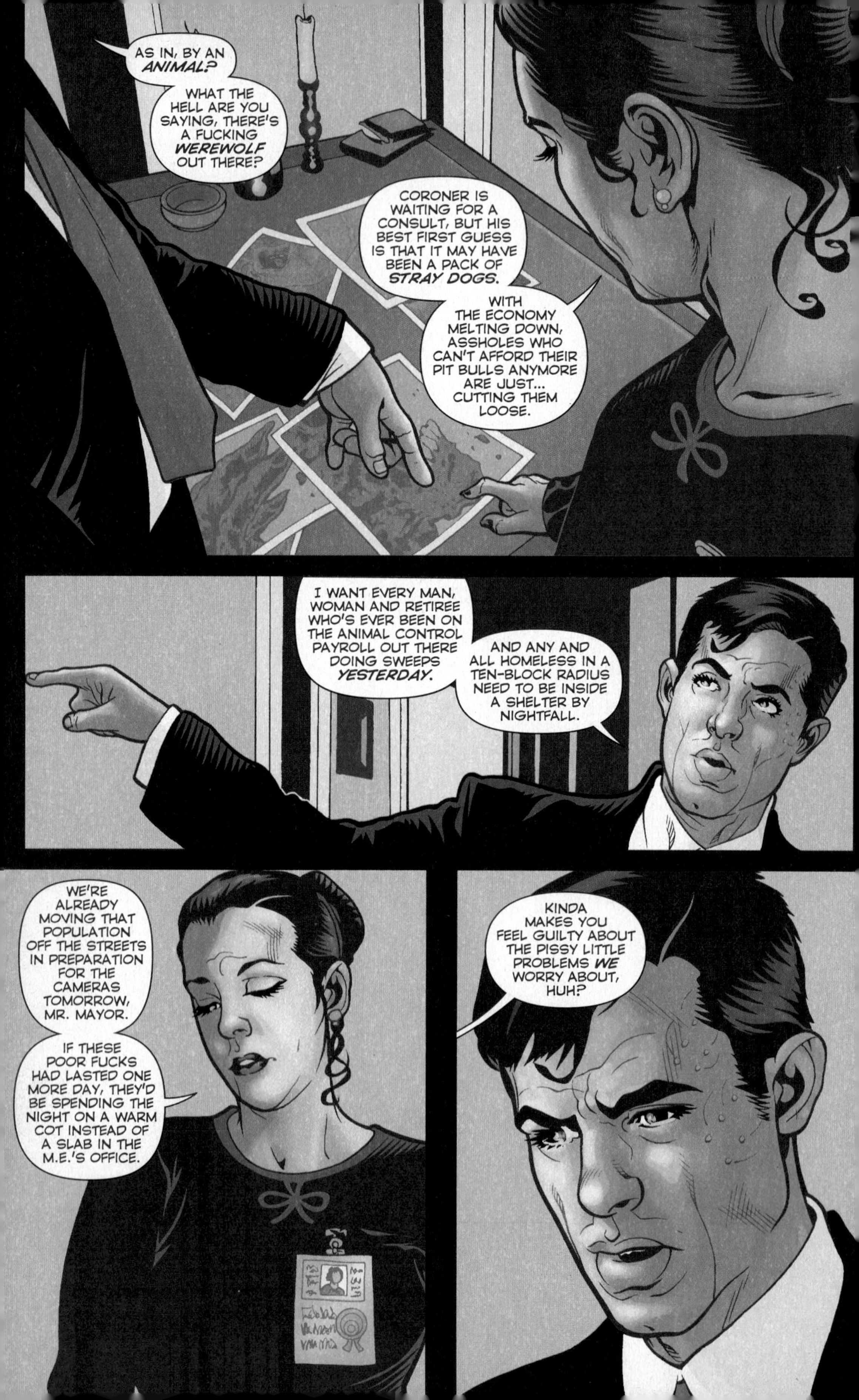
AS IN, BY AN ANIMAL?
WHAT THE HELL ARE YOU SAYING, THERE'S A FUCKING WEREWOLF OUT THERE?
CORONER IS WAITING FOR A CONSULT, BUT HIS BEST FIRST GUESS IS THAT IT MAY HAVE BEEN A PACK OF STRAY DOGS.
WITH THE ECONOMY MELTING DOWN, ASSHOLES WHO CAN'T AFFORD THEIR PIT BULLS ANYMORE ARE JUST... CUTTING THEM LOOSE.
I WANT EVERY MAN, WOMAN AND RETIREE WHO'S EVER BEEN ON THE ANIMAL CONTROL PAYROLL OUT THERE DOING SWEEPS YESTERDAY.
AND ANY AND ALL HOMELESS IN A TEN-BLOCK RADIUS NEED TO BE INSIDE A SHELTER BY NIGHTFALL.
WE'RE ALREADY MOVING THAT POPULATION OFF THE STREETS IN PREPARATION FOR THE CAMERAS TOMORROW, MR. MAYOR.
IF THESE POOR FUCKS HAD LASTED ONE MORE DAY, THEY'D BE SPENDING THE NIGHT ON A WARM COT INSTEAD OF A SLAB IN THE M.E.'S OFFICE.
KINDA MAKES YOU FEEL GUILTY ABOUT THE PISSY LITTLE PROBLEMS WE WORRY ABOUT, HUH?

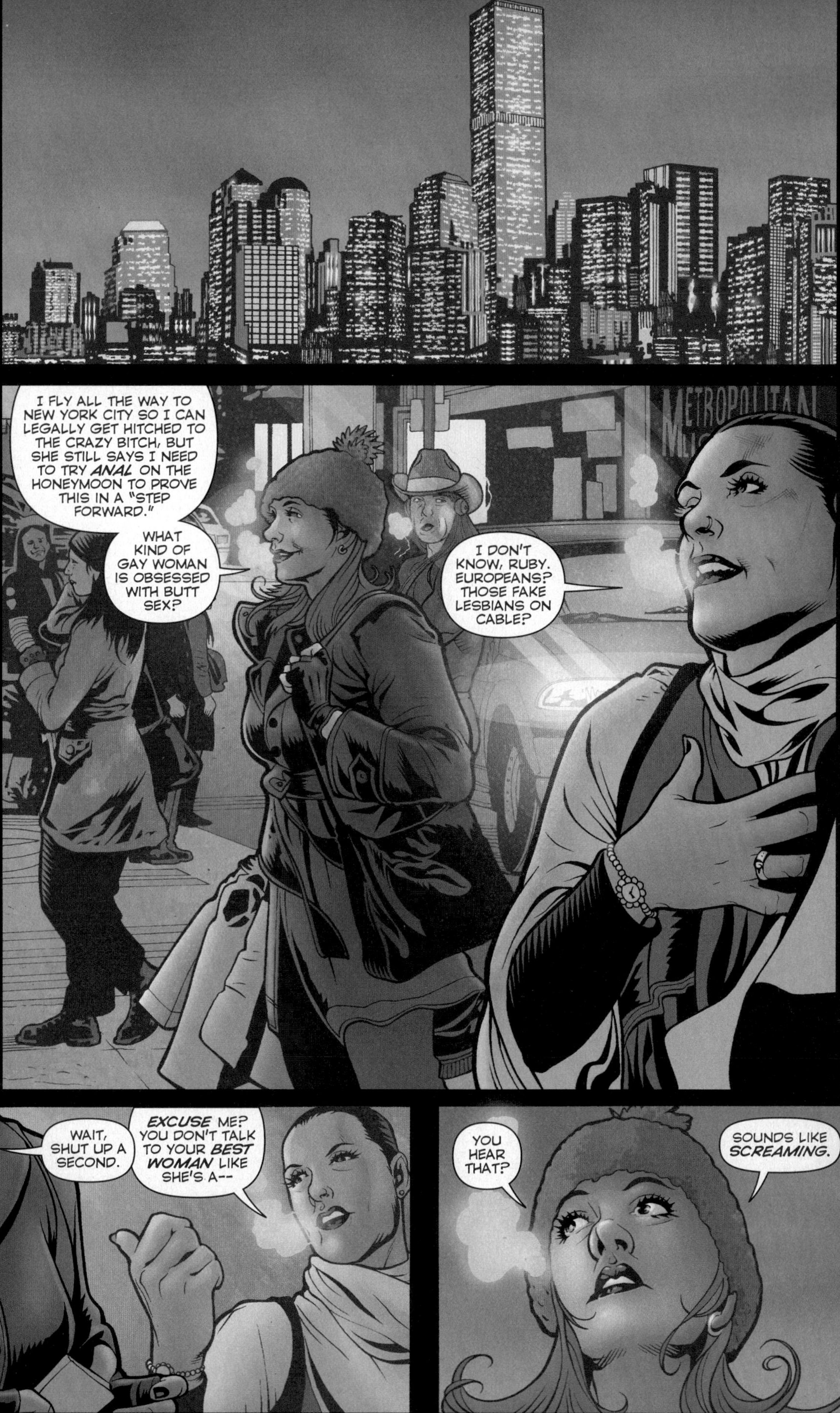

I FLY ALL THE WAY TO NEW YORK CITY SO I CAN LEGALLY GET HITCHED TO THE CRAZY BITCH, BUT SHE STILL SAYS I NEED TO TRY ANAL ON THE HONEYMOON TO PROVE THIS IN A "STEP FORWARD."
WHAT KIND OF GAY WOMAN IS OBSESSED WITH BUTT SEX?
I DON'T KNOW, RUBY. EUROPEANS? THOSE FAKE LESBIANS ON CABLE?
METROPOLITAN
WAIT, SHUT UP A SECOND.
EXCUSE ME? YOU DON'T TALK TO YOUR BEST WOMAN LIKE SHE'S A--
YOU HEAR THAT?
SOUNDS LIKE SCREAMING.

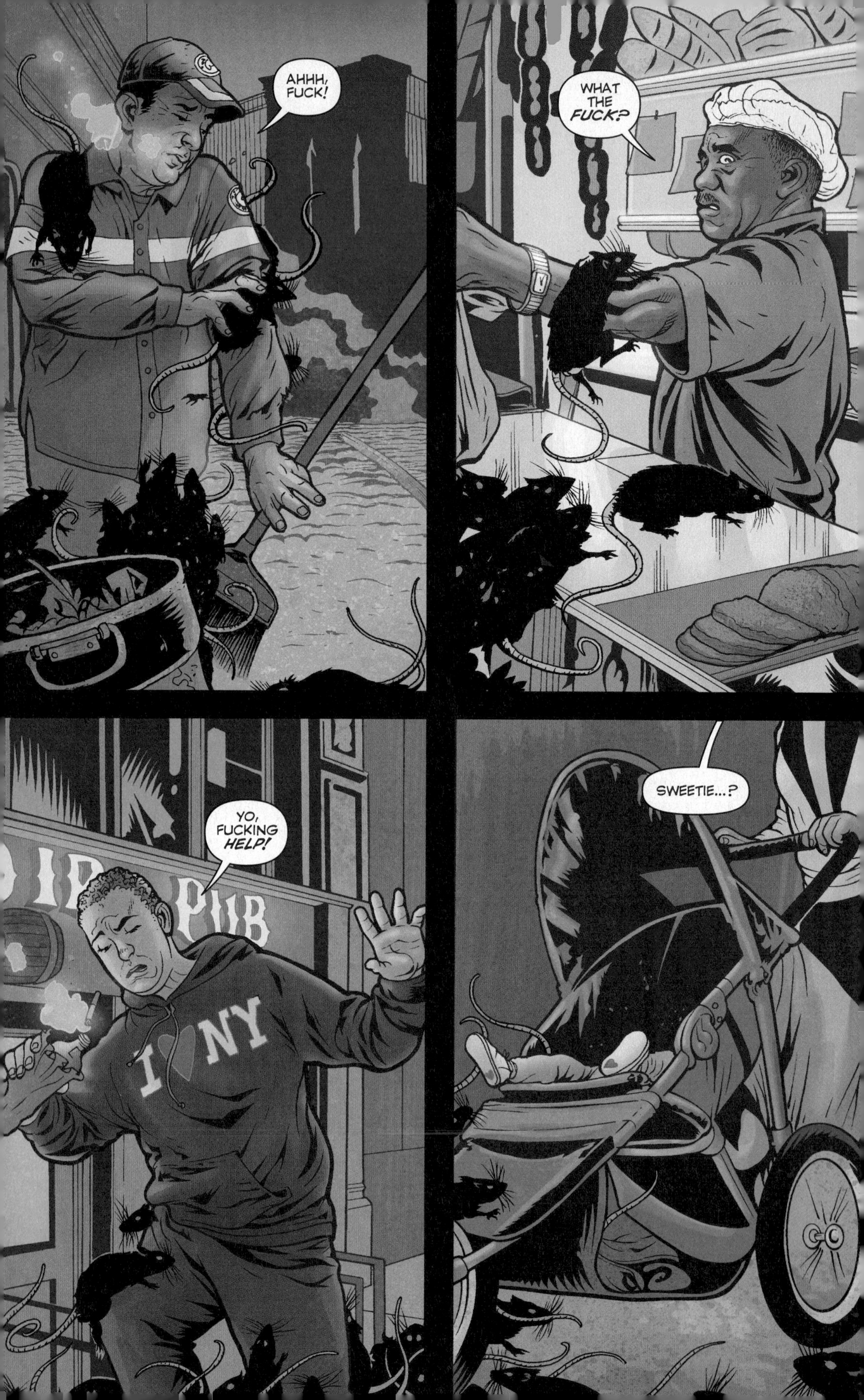
AHHH, FUCK!
WHAT THE *FUCK?*
YO, FUCKING *HELP!*
PUB
I ♥ NY
SWEETIE...?

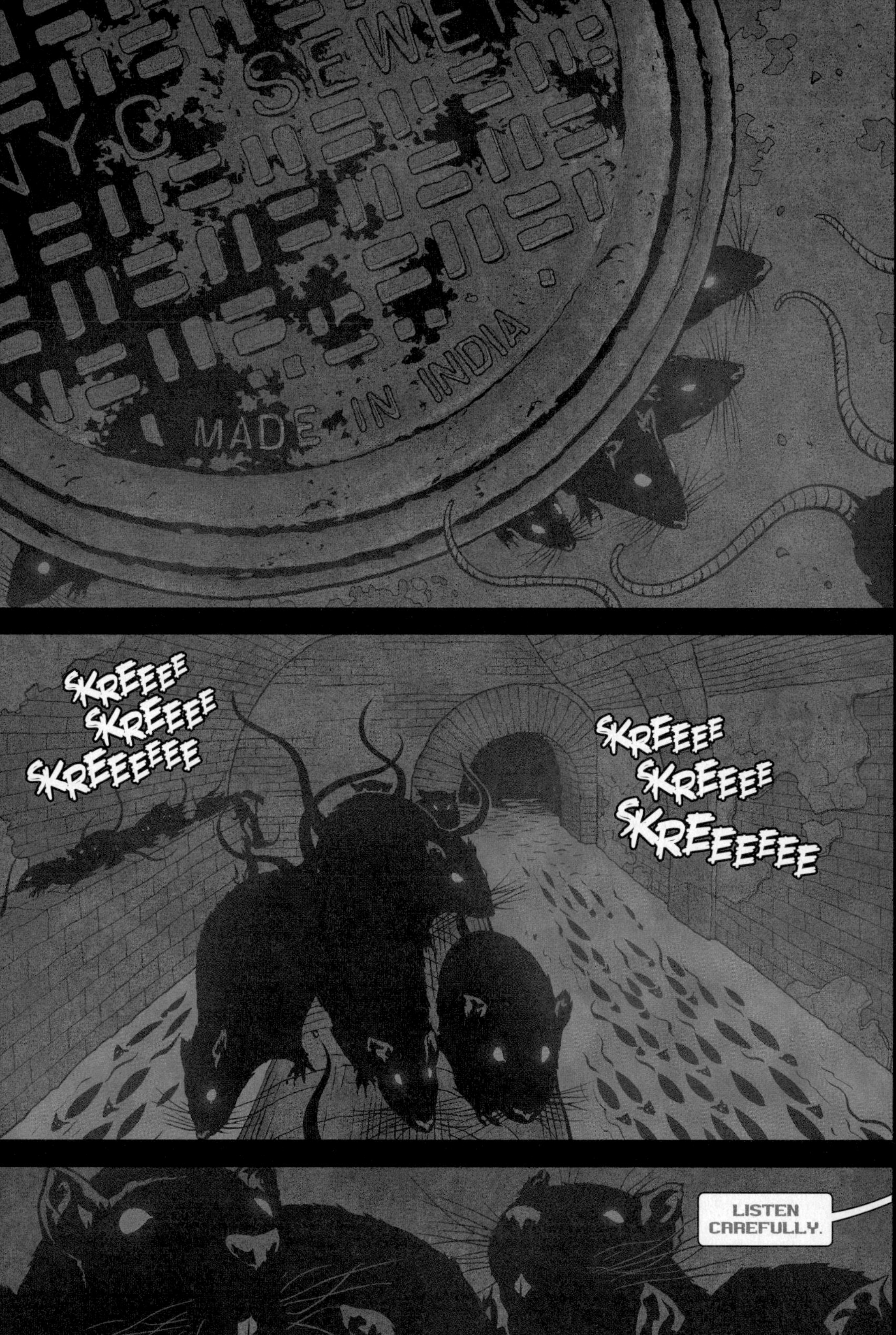
MADE IN INDIA
SKREEEE
SKREEEE
SKREEEEEE
SKREEEE
SKREEEE
SKREEEEEE
LISTEN CAREFULLY.

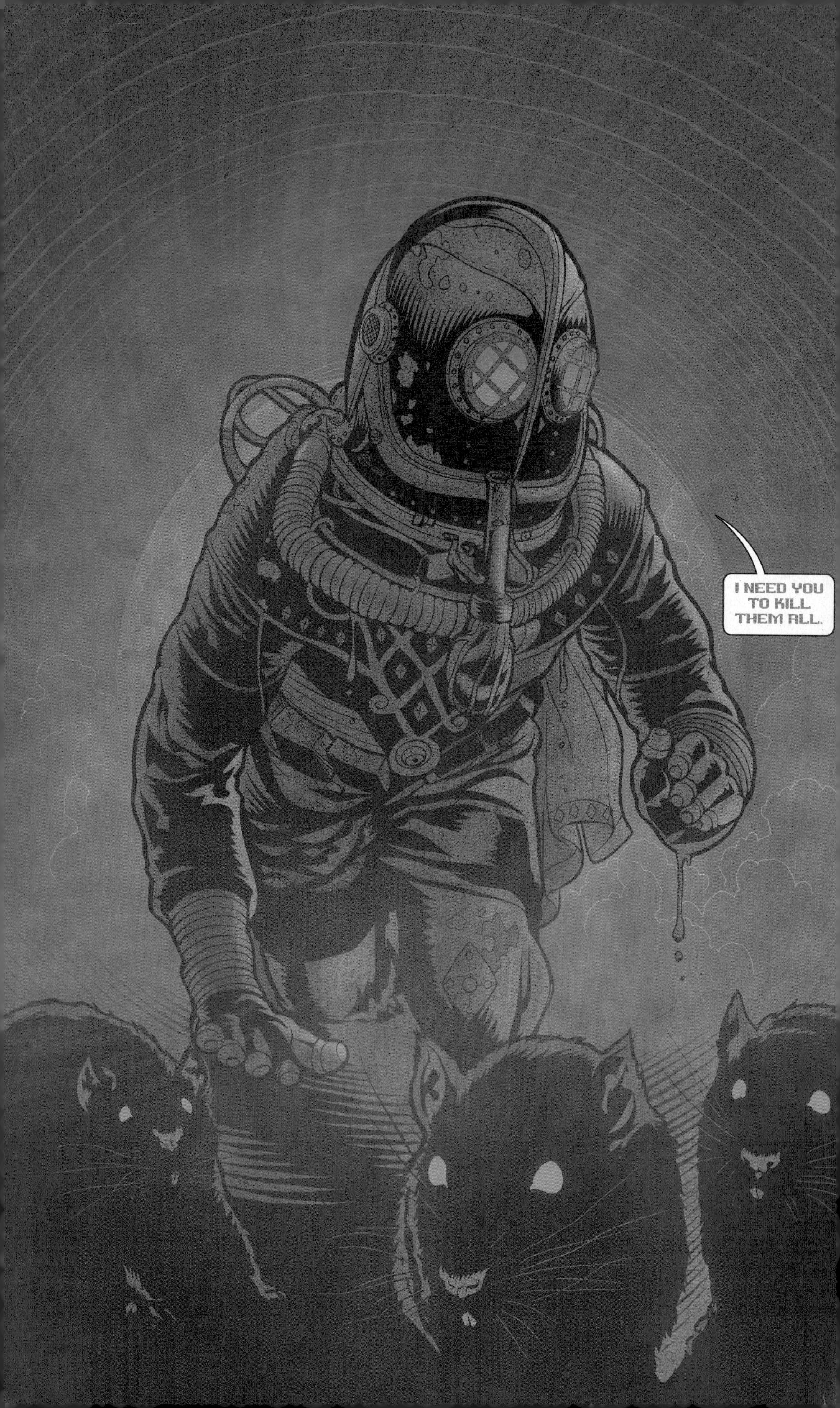
I NEED YOU TO KILL THEM ALL.

Ring Out the Old
part 3

Chapter 5

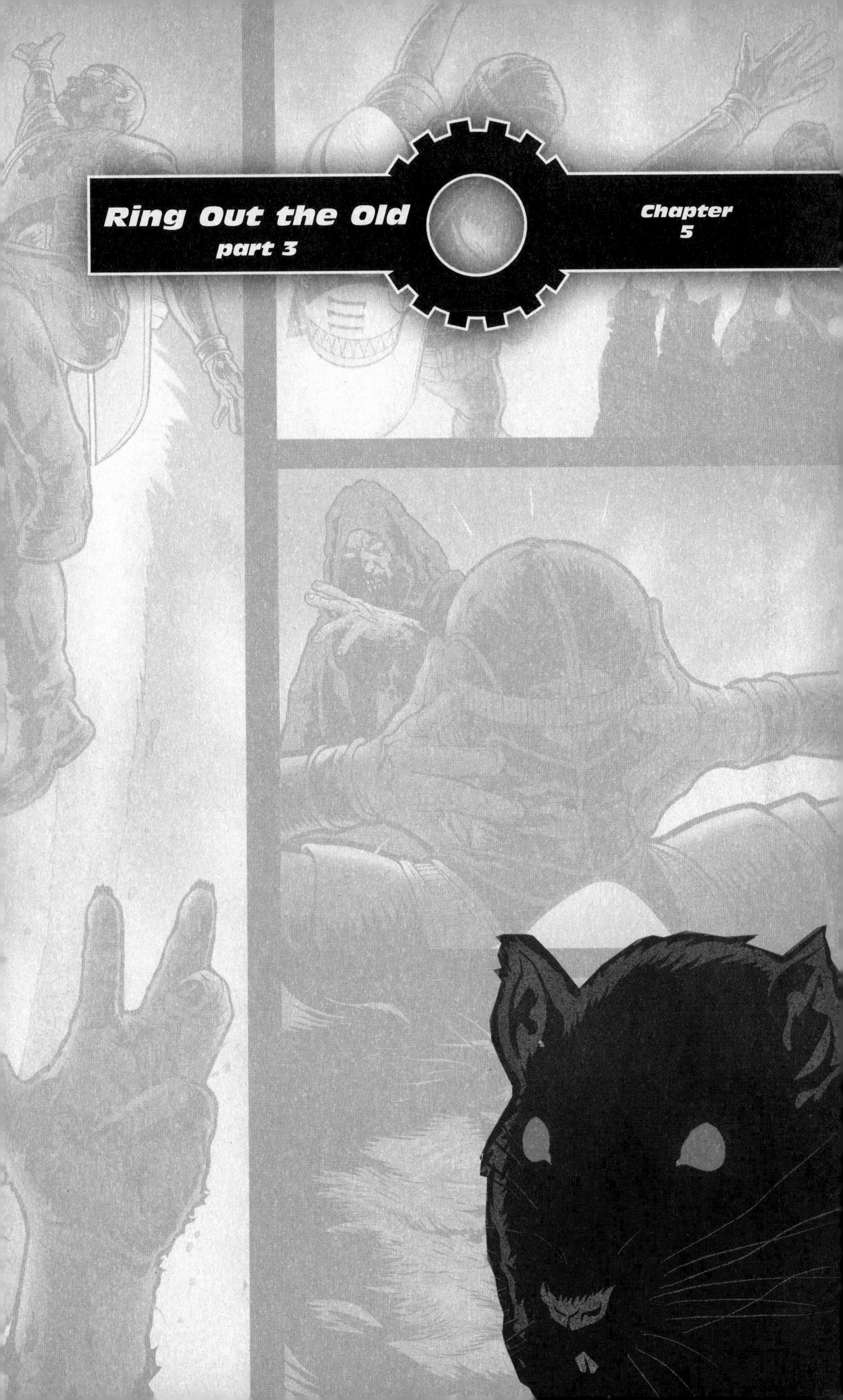

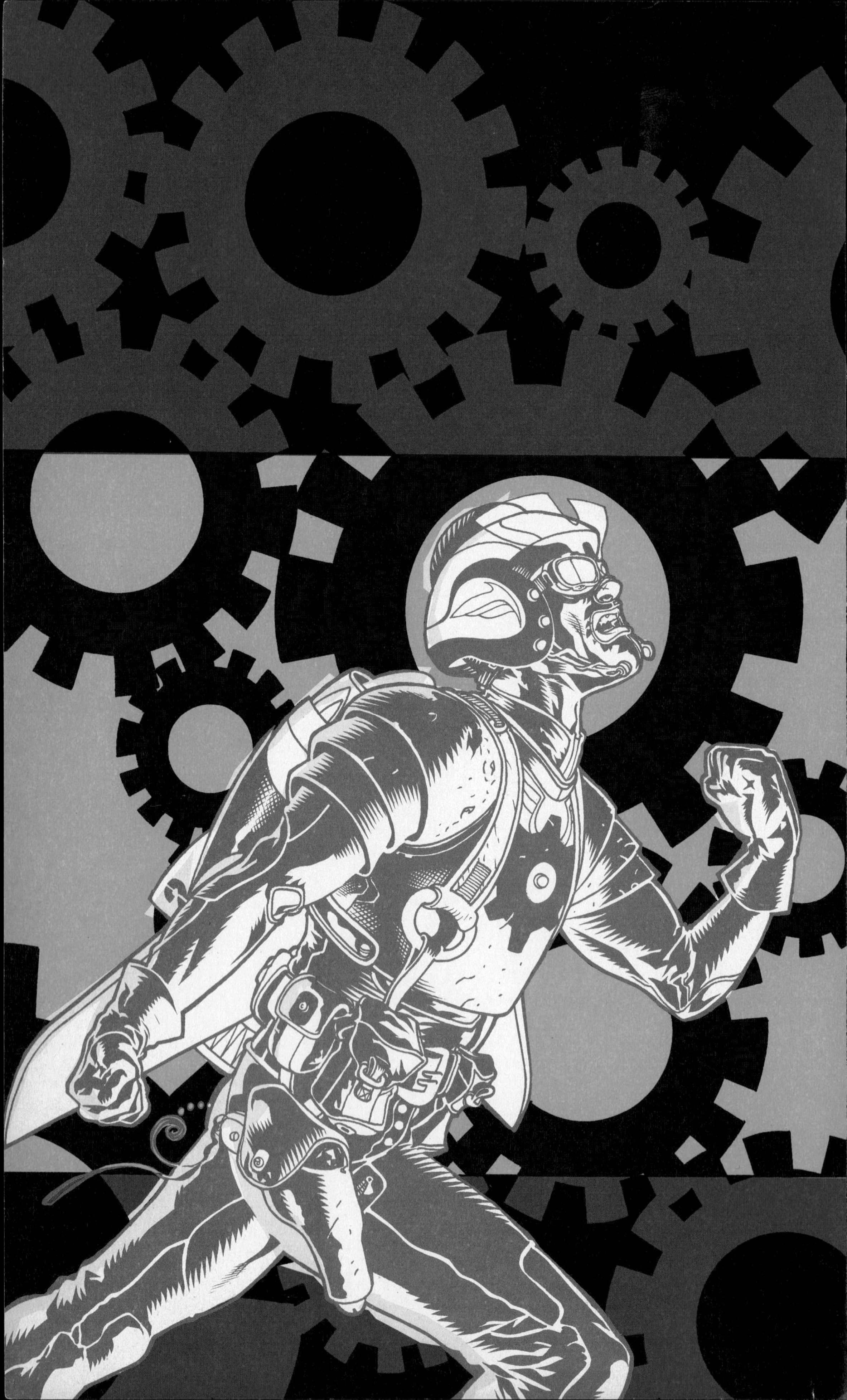

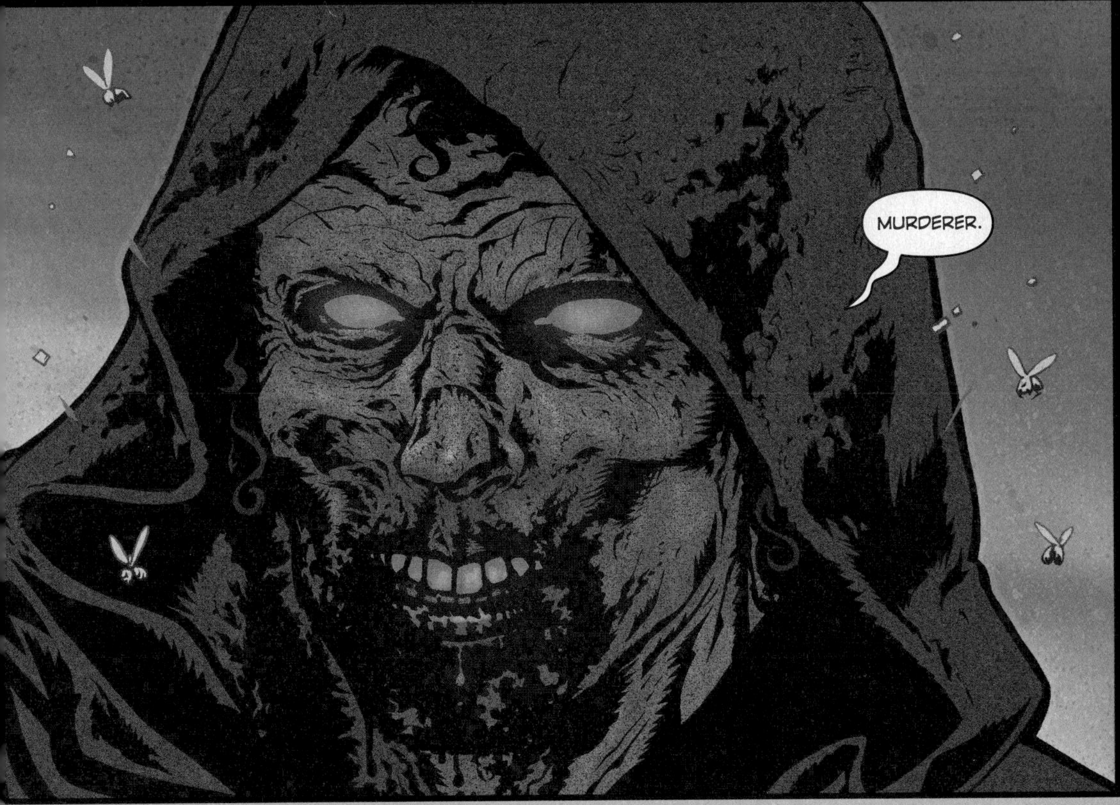
MURDERER.

FRIDAY, JUNE 1, 2001

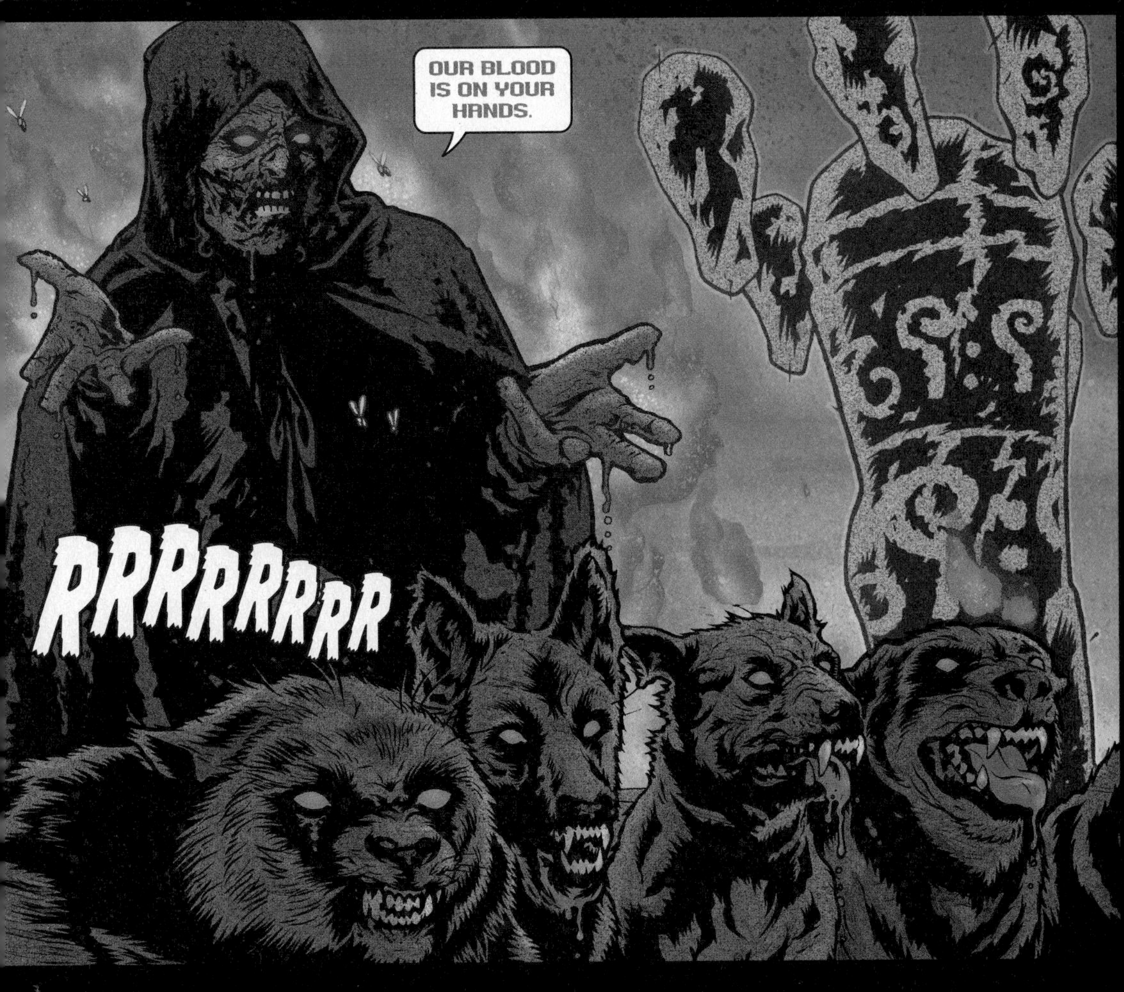
OUR BLOOD IS ON YOUR HANDS.
RRRRRRRR

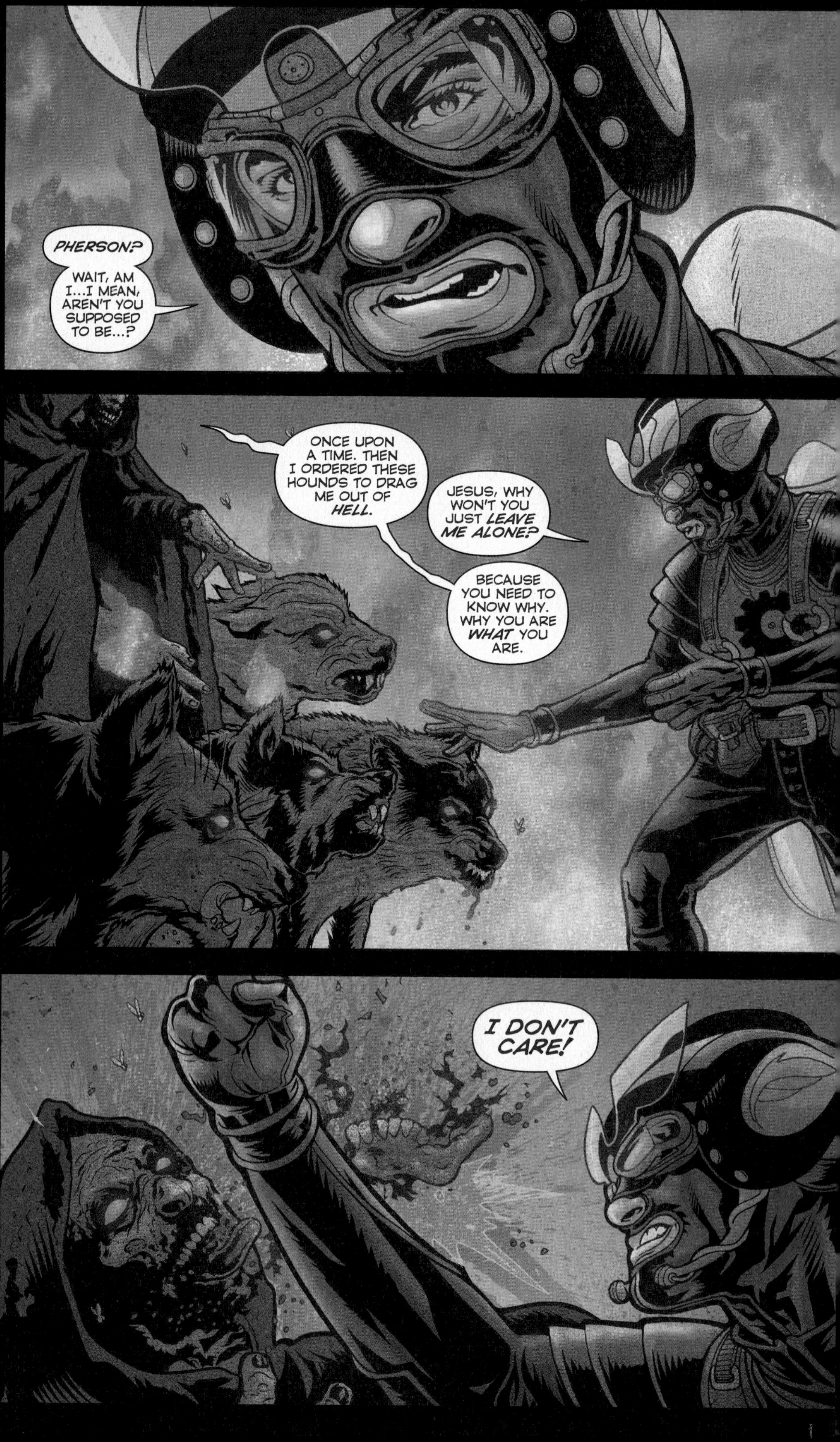
PHERSON?
WAIT, AM I...I MEAN, AREN'T YOU SUPPOSED TO BE...?
ONCE UPON A TIME. THEN I ORDERED THESE HOUNDS TO DRAG ME OUT OF HELL.
JESUS, WHY WON'T YOU JUST LEAVE ME ALONE?
BECAUSE YOU NEED TO KNOW WHY. WHY YOU ARE WHAT YOU ARE.
I DON'T CARE!

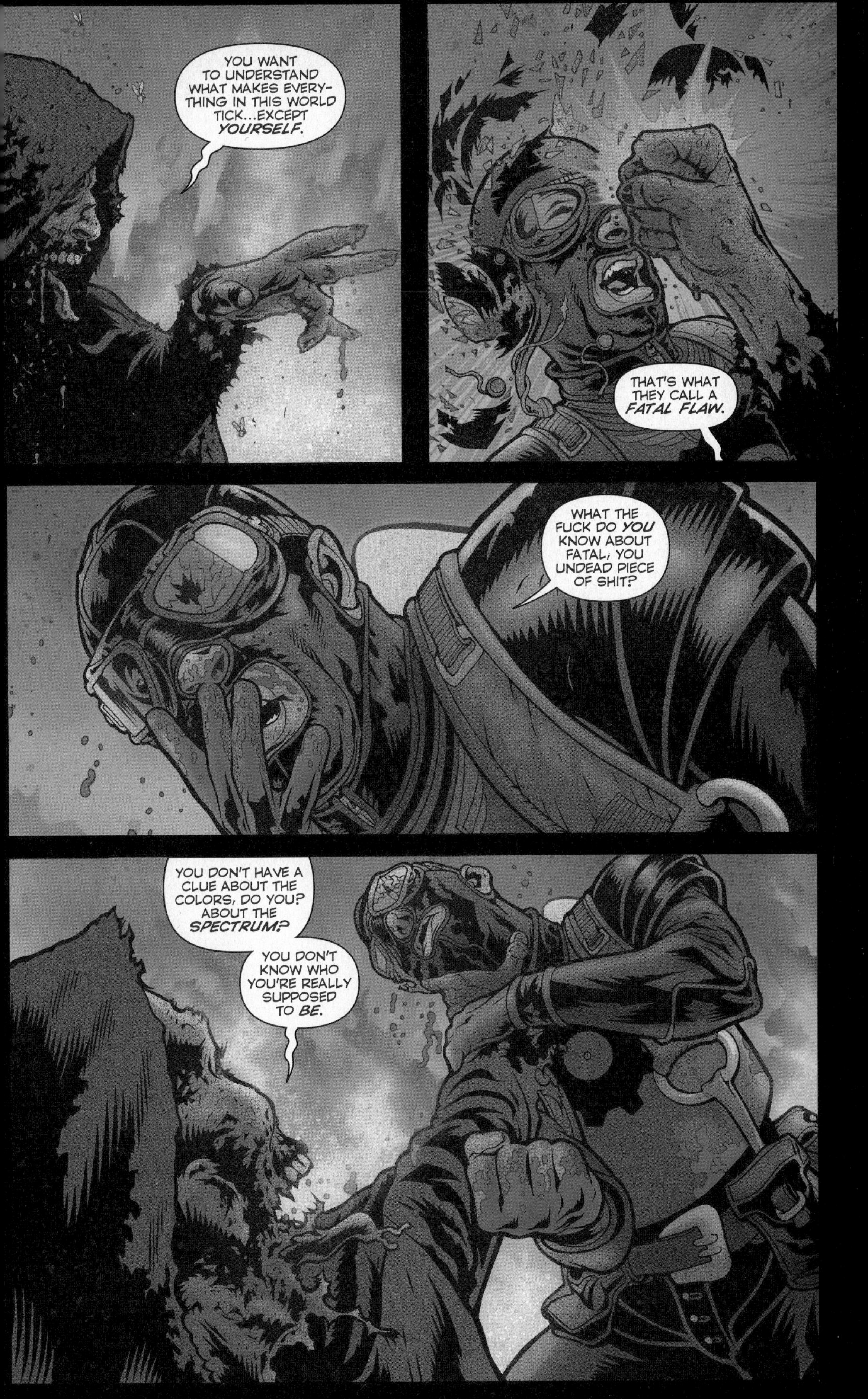
YOU WANT TO UNDERSTAND WHAT MAKES EVERY-THING IN THIS WORLD TICK...EXCEPT YOURSELF.
THAT'S WHAT THEY CALL A FATAL FLAW.
WHAT THE FUCK DO YOU KNOW ABOUT FATAL, YOU UNDEAD PIECE OF SHIT?
YOU DON'T HAVE A CLUE ABOUT THE COLORS, DO YOU? ABOUT THE SPECTRUM?
YOU DON'T KNOW WHO YOU'RE REALLY SUPPOSED TO BE.

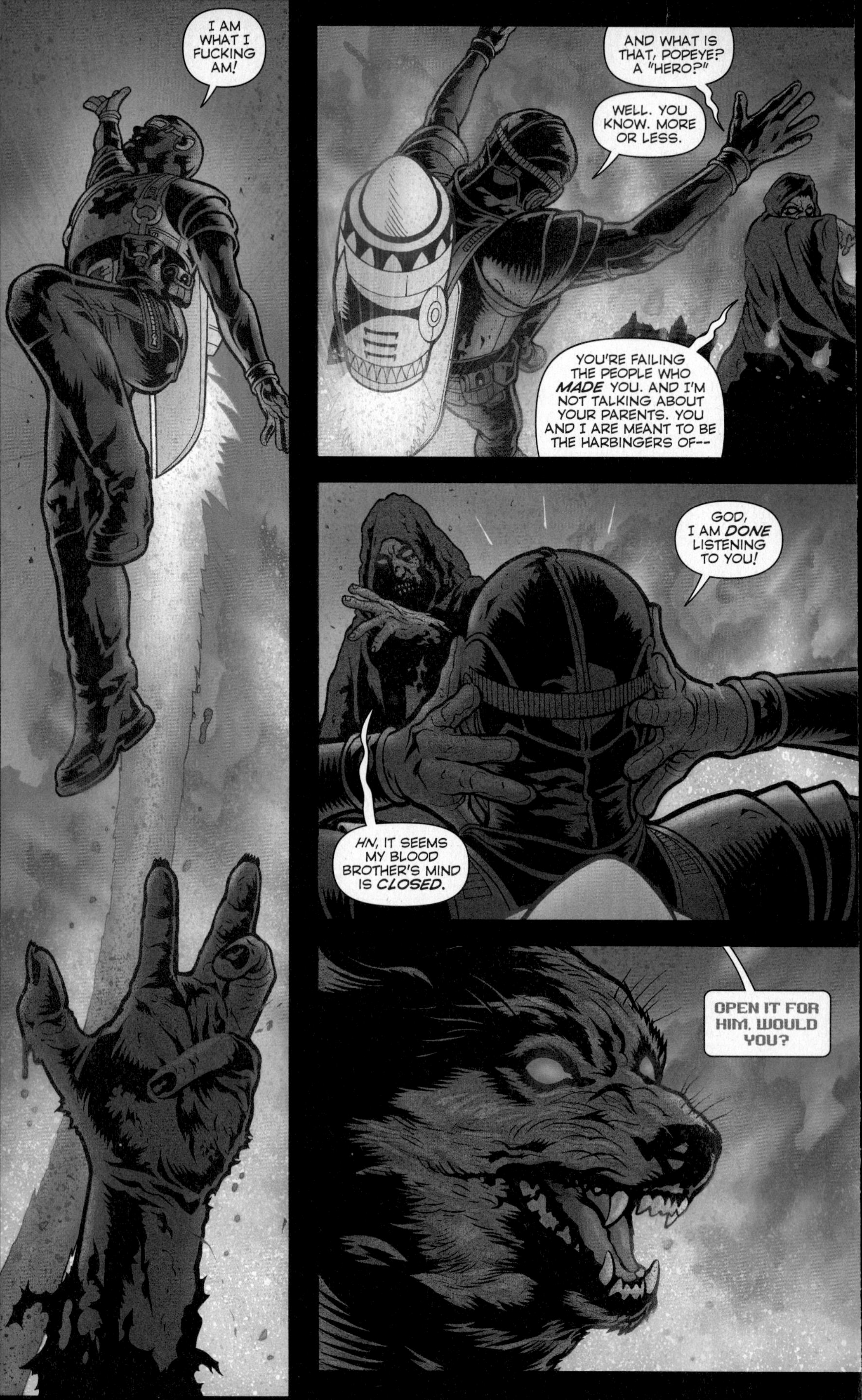
I AM WHAT I FUCKING AM!
AND WHAT IS THAT, POPEYE? A "HERO?"
WELL. YOU KNOW. MORE OR LESS.
YOU'RE FAILING THE PEOPLE WHO MADE YOU. AND I'M NOT TALKING ABOUT YOUR PARENTS. YOU AND I ARE MEANT TO BE THE HARBINGERS OF--
GOD, I AM DONE LISTENING TO YOU!
HN, IT SEEMS MY BLOOD BROTHER'S MIND IS CLOSED.
OPEN IT FOR HIM, WOULD YOU?

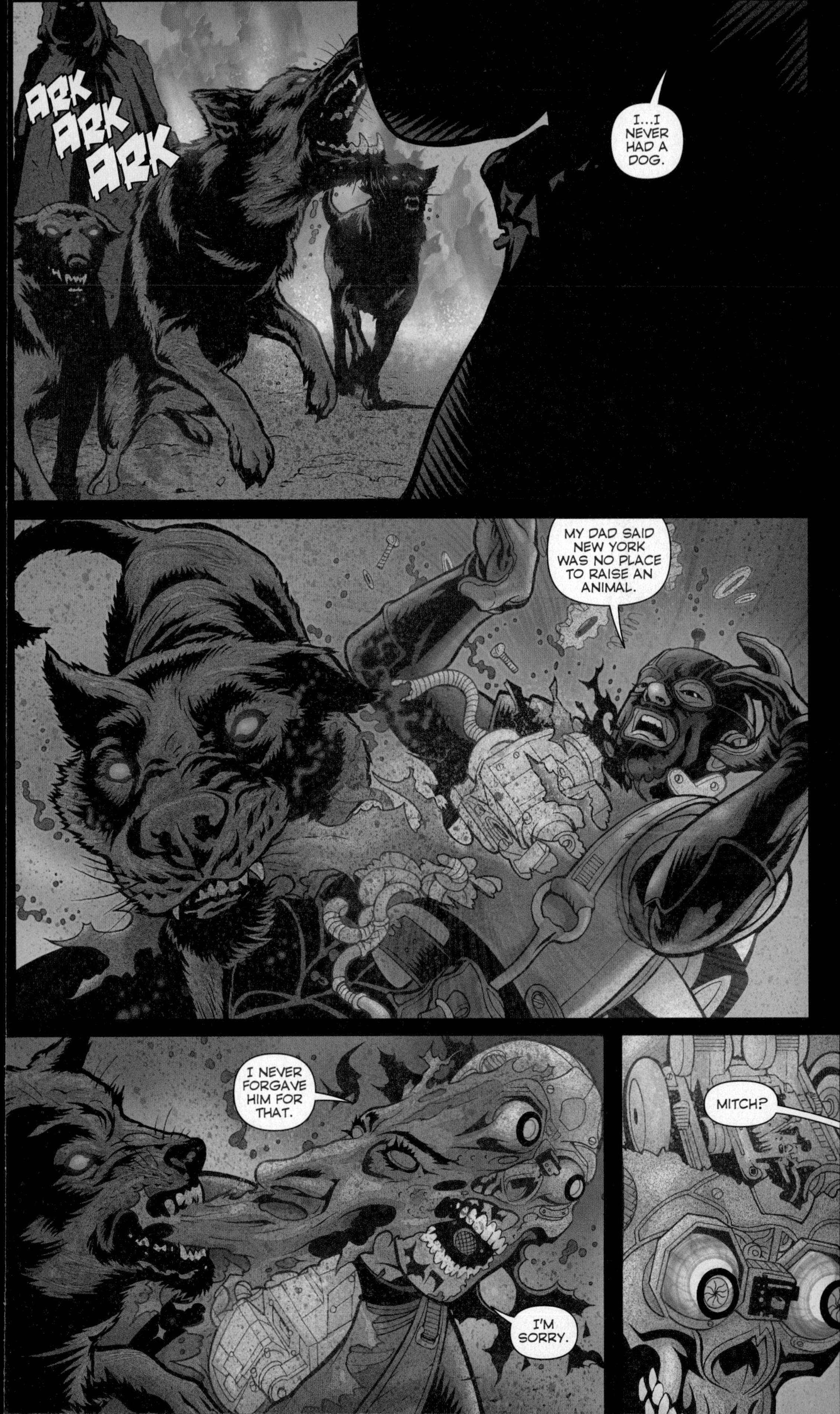
ARK ARK ARK
I...I NEVER HAD A DOG.
MY DAD SAID NEW YORK WAS NO PLACE TO RAISE AN ANIMAL.
I NEVER FORGAVE HIM FOR THAT.
I'M SORRY.
MITCH?

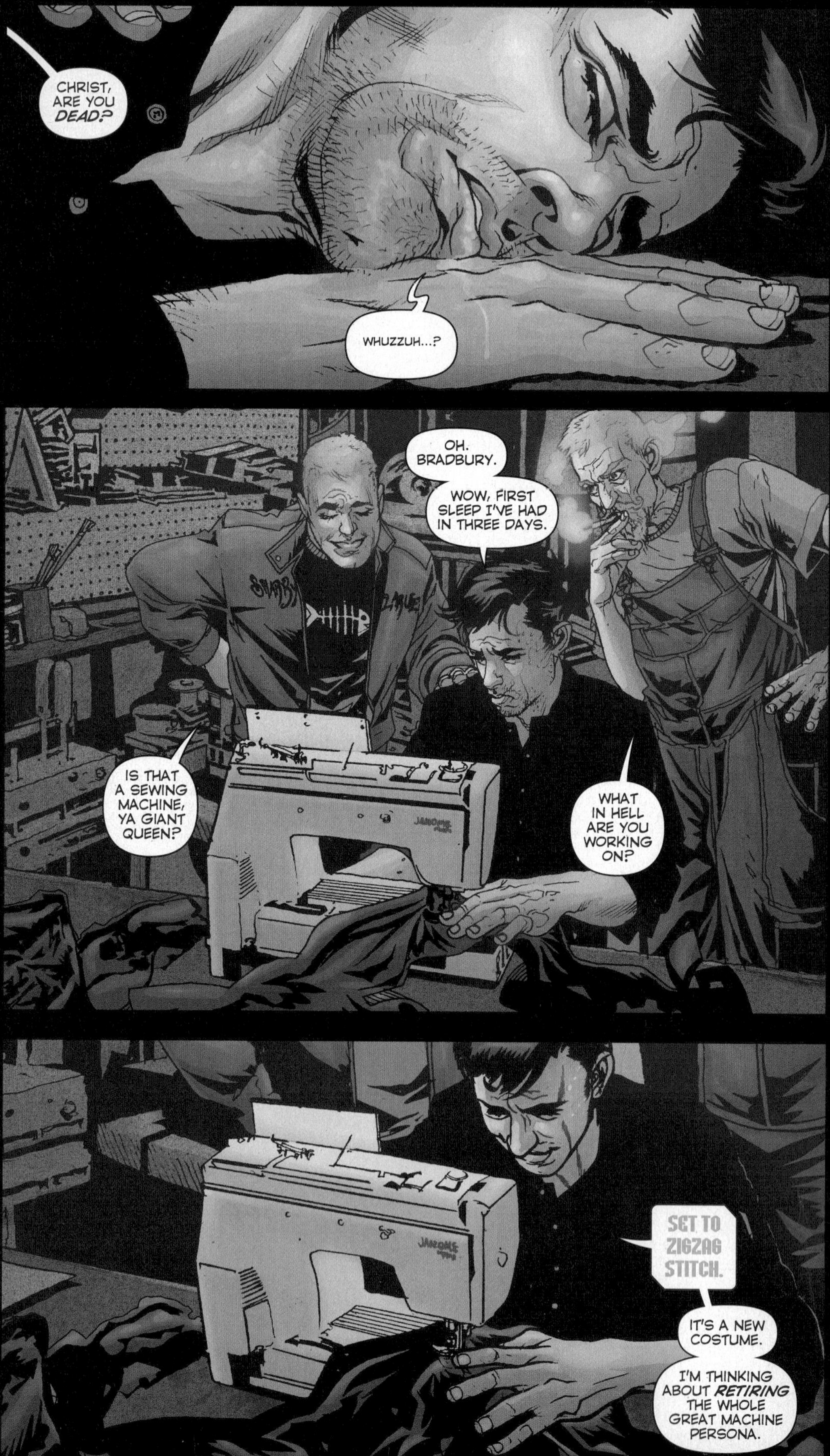
CHRIST, ARE YOU *DEAD?*
WHUZZUH...?
OH. BRADBURY.
WOW, FIRST SLEEP I'VE HAD IN THREE DAYS.
IS THAT A SEWING MACHINE, YA GIANT QUEEN?
WHAT IN HELL ARE YOU WORKING ON?
SET TO ZIGZAG STITCH.
IT'S A NEW COSTUME.
I'M THINKING ABOUT *RETIRING* THE WHOLE GREAT MACHINE PERSONA.

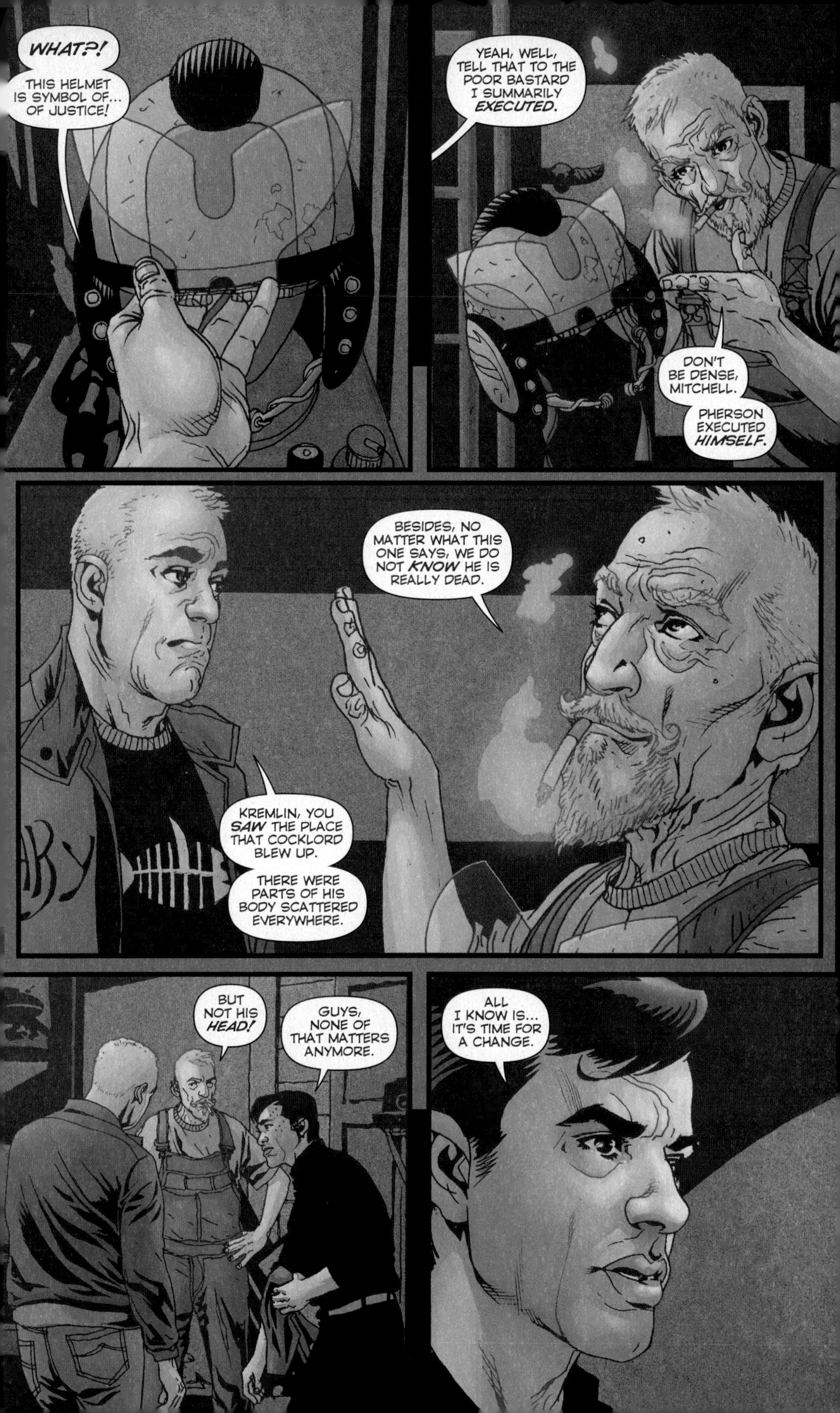
WHAT?!
THIS HELMET IS SYMBOL OF... OF JUSTICE!
YEAH, WELL, TELL THAT TO THE POOR BASTARD I SUMMARILY EXECUTED.
DON'T BE DENSE, MITCHELL.
PHERSON EXECUTED HIMSELF.
BESIDES, NO MATTER WHAT THIS ONE SAYS, WE DO NOT KNOW HE IS REALLY DEAD.
KREMLIN, YOU SAW THE PLACE THAT COCKLORD BLEW UP.
THERE WERE PARTS OF HIS BODY SCATTERED EVERYWHERE.
BUT NOT HIS HEAD!
GUYS, NONE OF THAT MATTERS ANYMORE.
ALL I KNOW IS... IT'S TIME FOR A CHANGE.

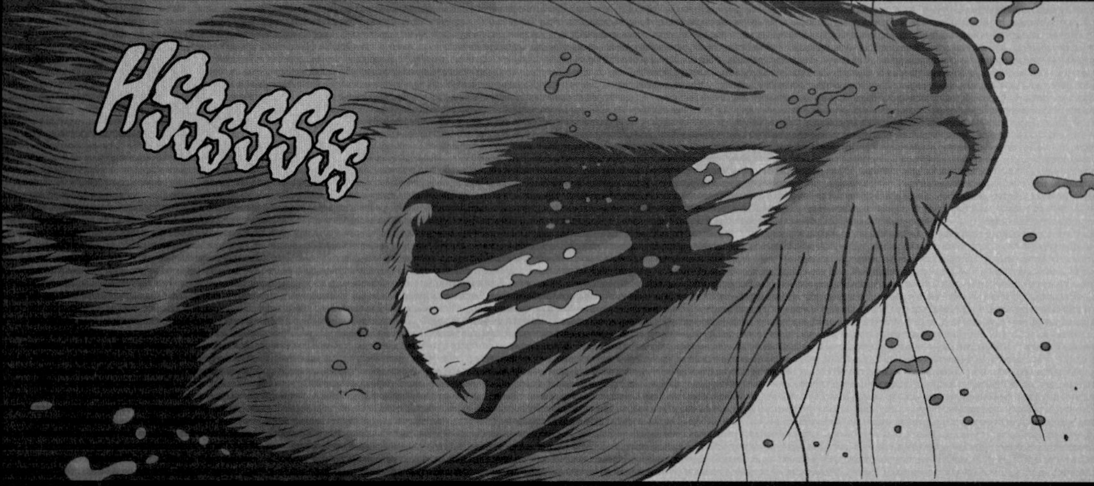
HSSSSSSS

THURSDAY, DECEMBER 30, 2004

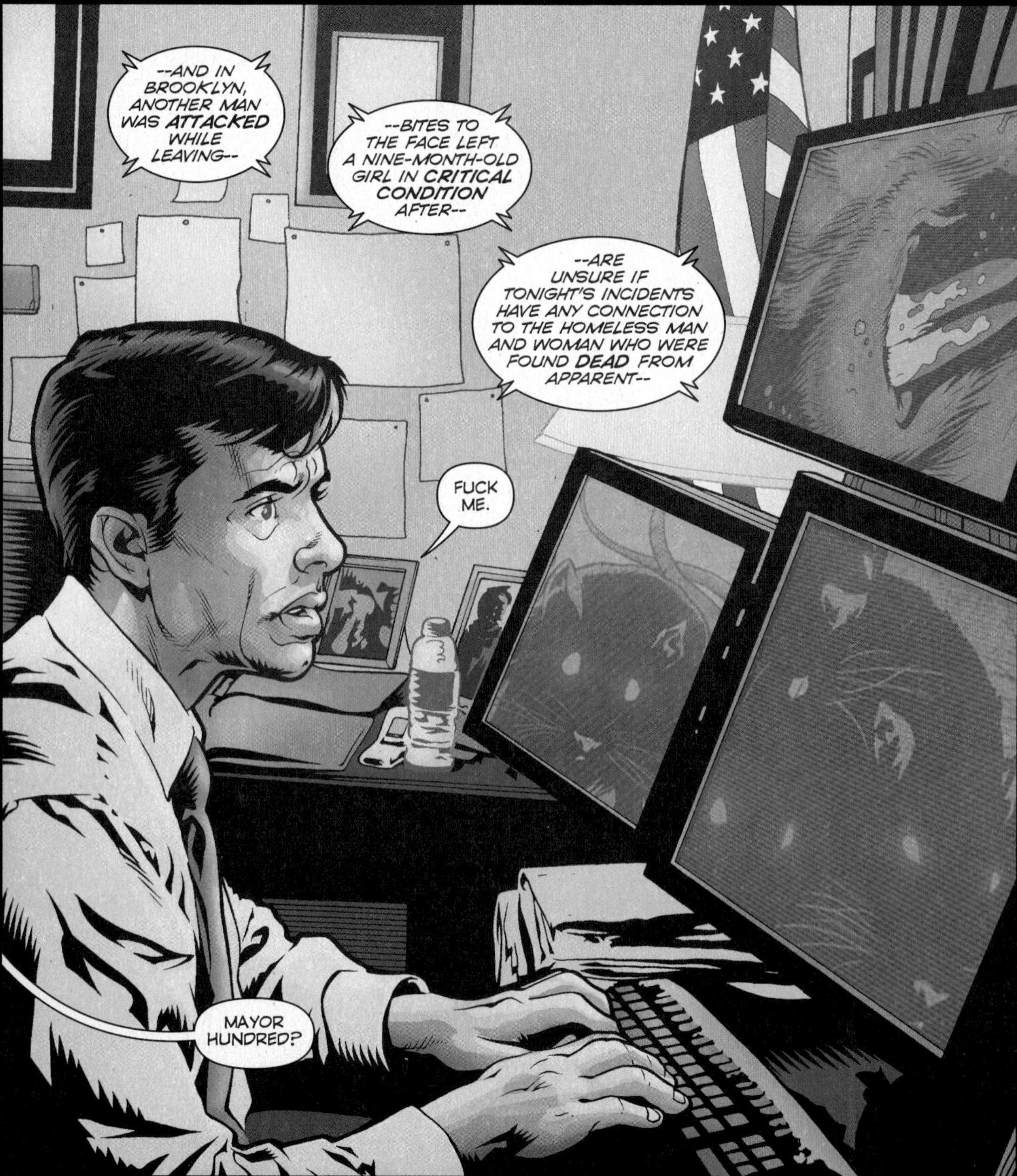
--AND IN BROOKLYN, ANOTHER MAN WAS ATTACKED WHILE LEAVING--
--BITES TO THE FACE LEFT A NINE-MONTH-OLD GIRL IN CRITICAL CONDITION AFTER--
--ARE UNSURE IF TONIGHT'S INCIDENTS HAVE ANY CONNECTION TO THE HOMELESS MAN AND WOMAN WHO WERE FOUND DEAD FROM APPARENT--
FUCK ME.
MAYOR HUNDRED?

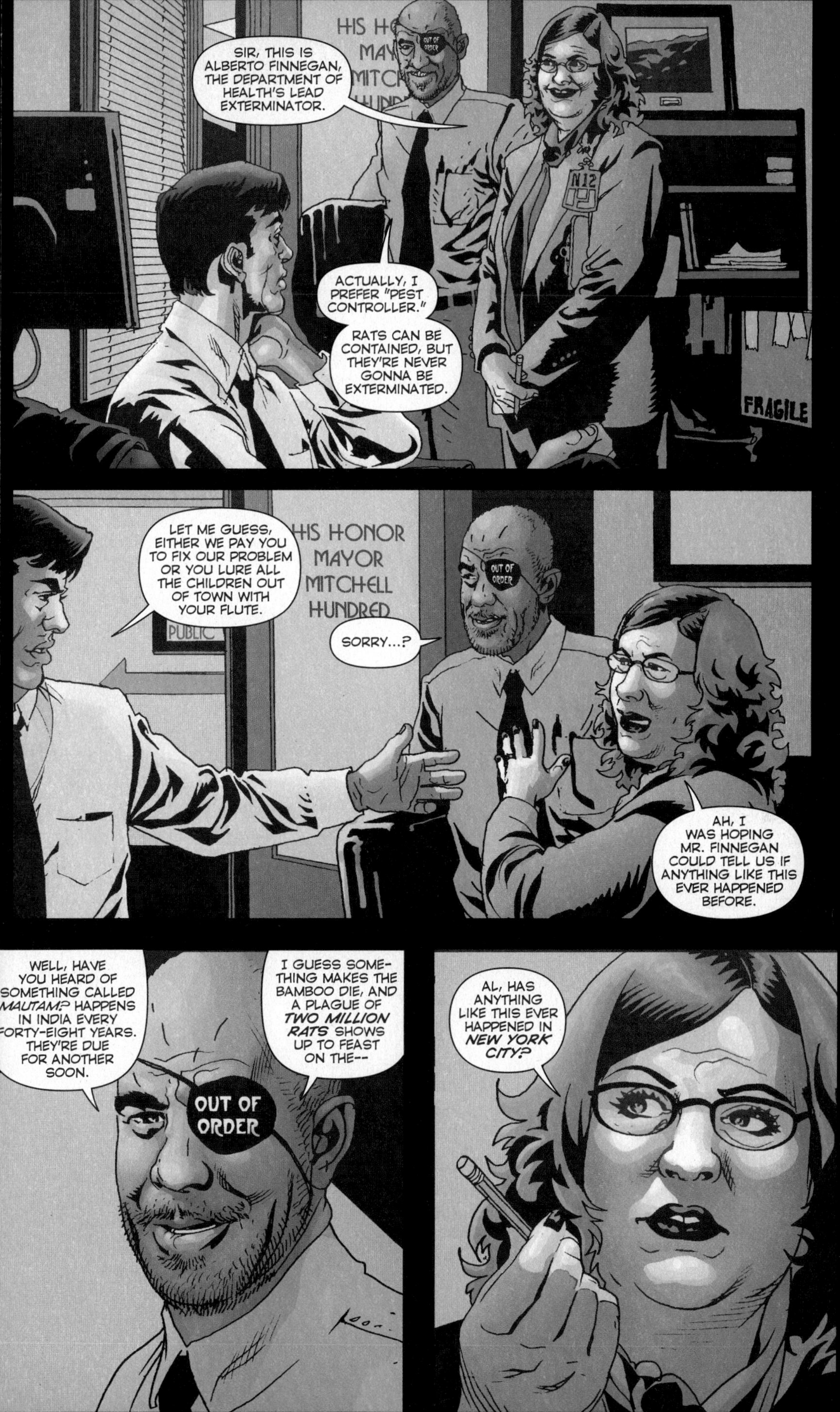
HIS HONOR MAYOR MITCHELL HUNDRED
SIR, THIS IS ALBERTO FINNEGAN, THE DEPARTMENT OF HEALTH'S LEAD EXTERMINATOR.
ACTUALLY, I PREFER "PEST CONTROLLER."
RATS CAN BE CONTAINED, BUT THEY'RE NEVER GONNA BE EXTERMINATED.
FRAGILE
LET ME GUESS, EITHER WE PAY YOU TO FIX OUR PROBLEM OR YOU LURE ALL THE CHILDREN OUT OF TOWN WITH YOUR FLUTE.
PUBLIC
SORRY...?
AH, I WAS HOPING MR. FINNEGAN COULD TELL US IF ANYTHING LIKE THIS EVER HAPPENED BEFORE.
WELL, HAVE YOU HEARD OF SOMETHING CALLED *MAUTAM?* HAPPENS IN INDIA EVERY FORTY-EIGHT YEARS. THEY'RE DUE FOR ANOTHER SOON.
I GUESS SOMETHING MAKES THE BAMBOO DIE, AND A PLAGUE OF ***TWO MILLION RATS*** SHOWS UP TO FEAST ON THE--
OUT OF ORDER
AL, HAS ANYTHING LIKE THIS EVER HAPPENED IN ***NEW YORK CITY?***

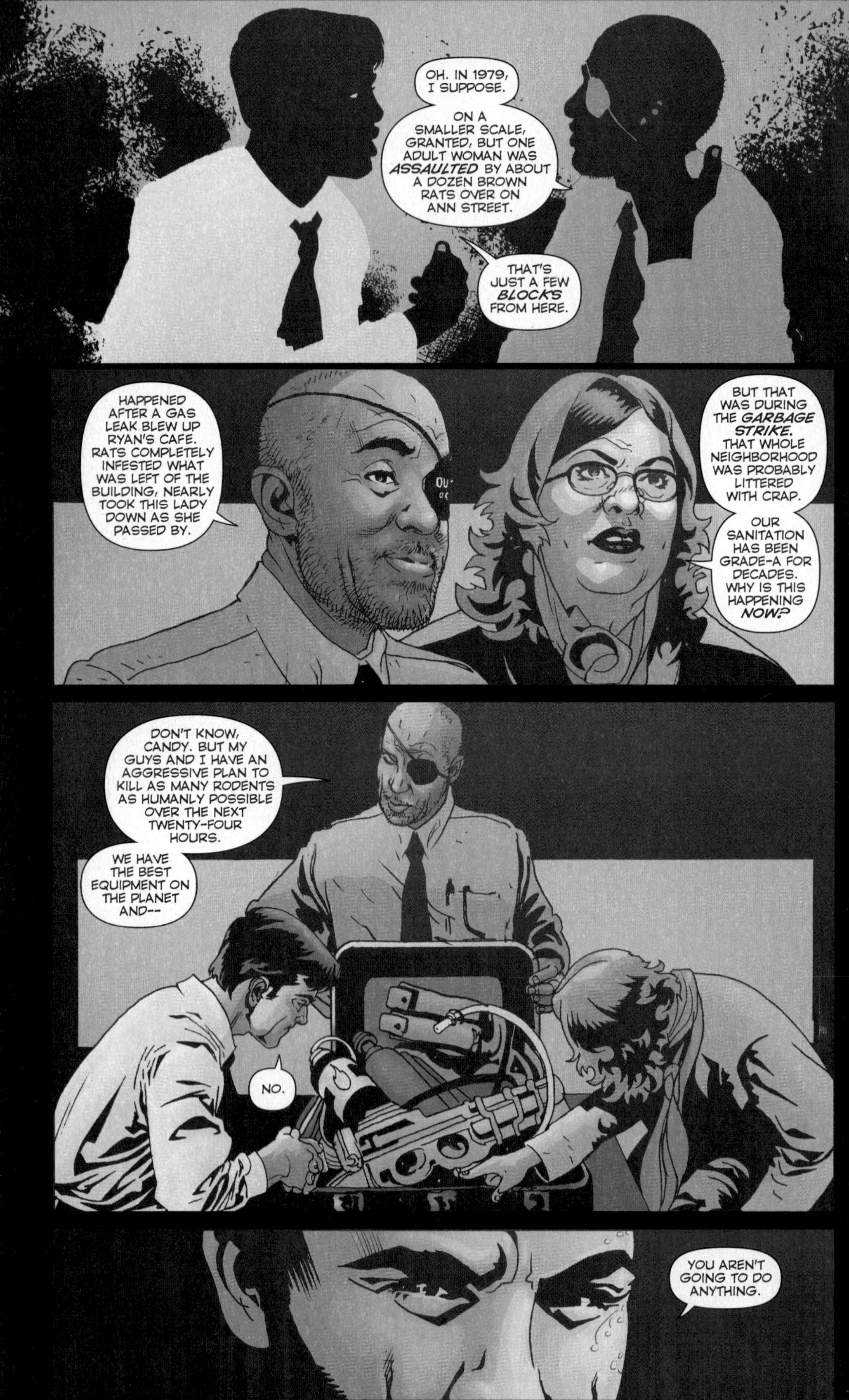
OH. IN 1979, I SUPPOSE.
ON A SMALLER SCALE, GRANTED, BUT ONE ADULT WOMAN WAS ASSAULTED BY ABOUT A DOZEN BROWN RATS OVER ON ANN STREET.
THAT'S JUST A FEW BLOCKS FROM HERE.
HAPPENED AFTER A GAS LEAK BLEW UP RYAN'S CAFE. RATS COMPLETELY INFESTED WHAT WAS LEFT OF THE BUILDING, NEARLY TOOK THIS LADY DOWN AS SHE PASSED BY.
BUT THAT WAS DURING THE GARBAGE STRIKE. THAT WHOLE NEIGHBORHOOD WAS PROBABLY LITTERED WITH CRAP.
OUR SANITATION HAS BEEN GRADE-A FOR DECADES. WHY IS THIS HAPPENING NOW?
DON'T KNOW, CANDY. BUT MY GUYS AND I HAVE AN AGGRESSIVE PLAN TO KILL AS MANY RODENTS AS HUMANLY POSSIBLE OVER THE NEXT TWENTY-FOUR HOURS.
WE HAVE THE BEST EQUIPMENT ON THE PLANET AND--
NO.
YOU AREN'T GOING TO DO ANYTHING.

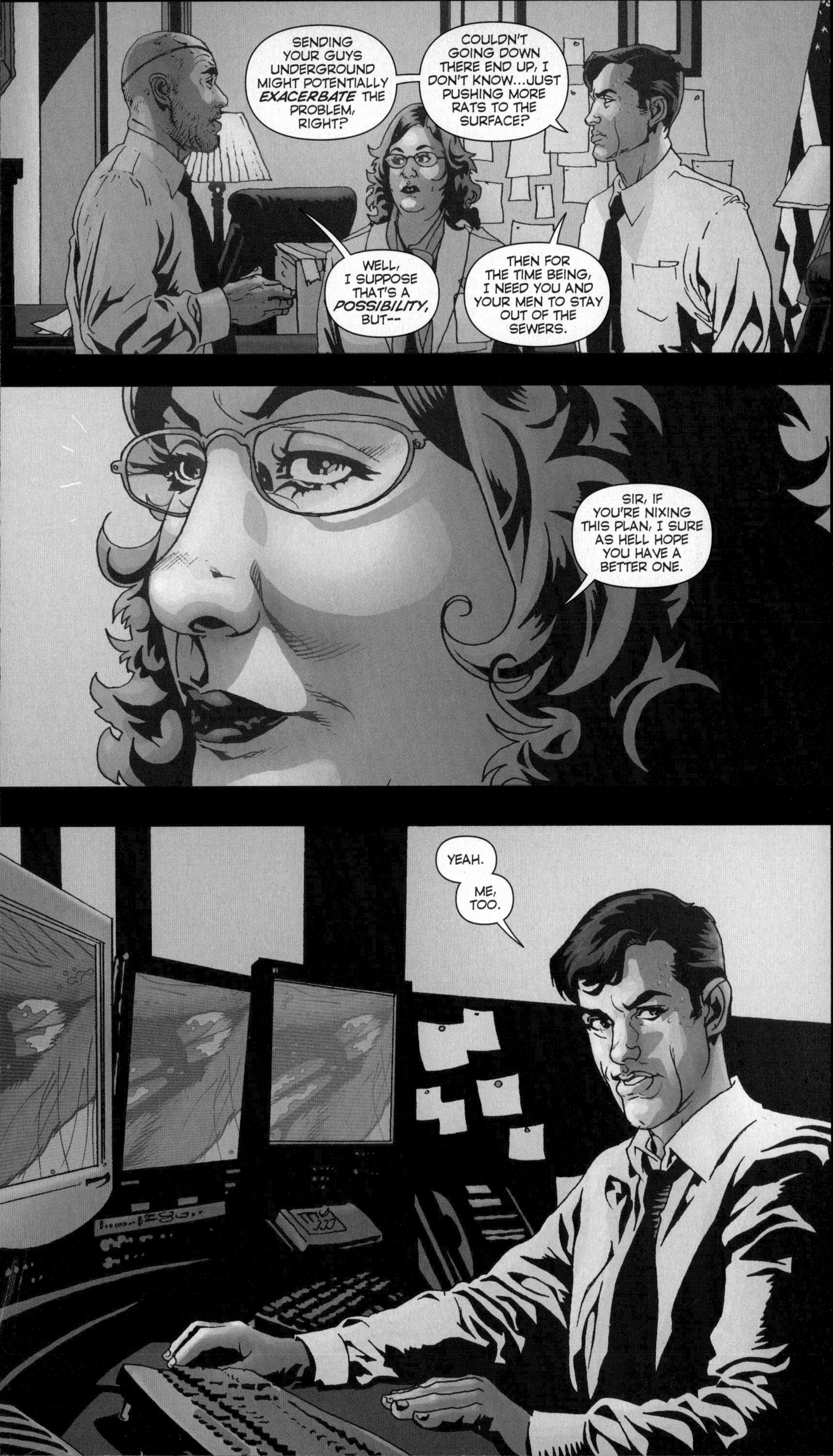
SENDING YOUR GUYS UNDERGROUND MIGHT POTENTIALLY *EXACERBATE* THE PROBLEM, RIGHT?
COULDN'T GOING DOWN THERE END UP, I DON'T KNOW...JUST PUSHING MORE RATS TO THE SURFACE?
WELL, I SUPPOSE THAT'S A *POSSIBILITY,* BUT--
THEN FOR THE TIME BEING, I NEED YOU AND YOUR MEN TO STAY OUT OF THE SEWERS.
SIR, IF YOU'RE NIXING THIS PLAN, I SURE AS HELL HOPE YOU HAVE A BETTER ONE.
YEAH.
ME, TOO.

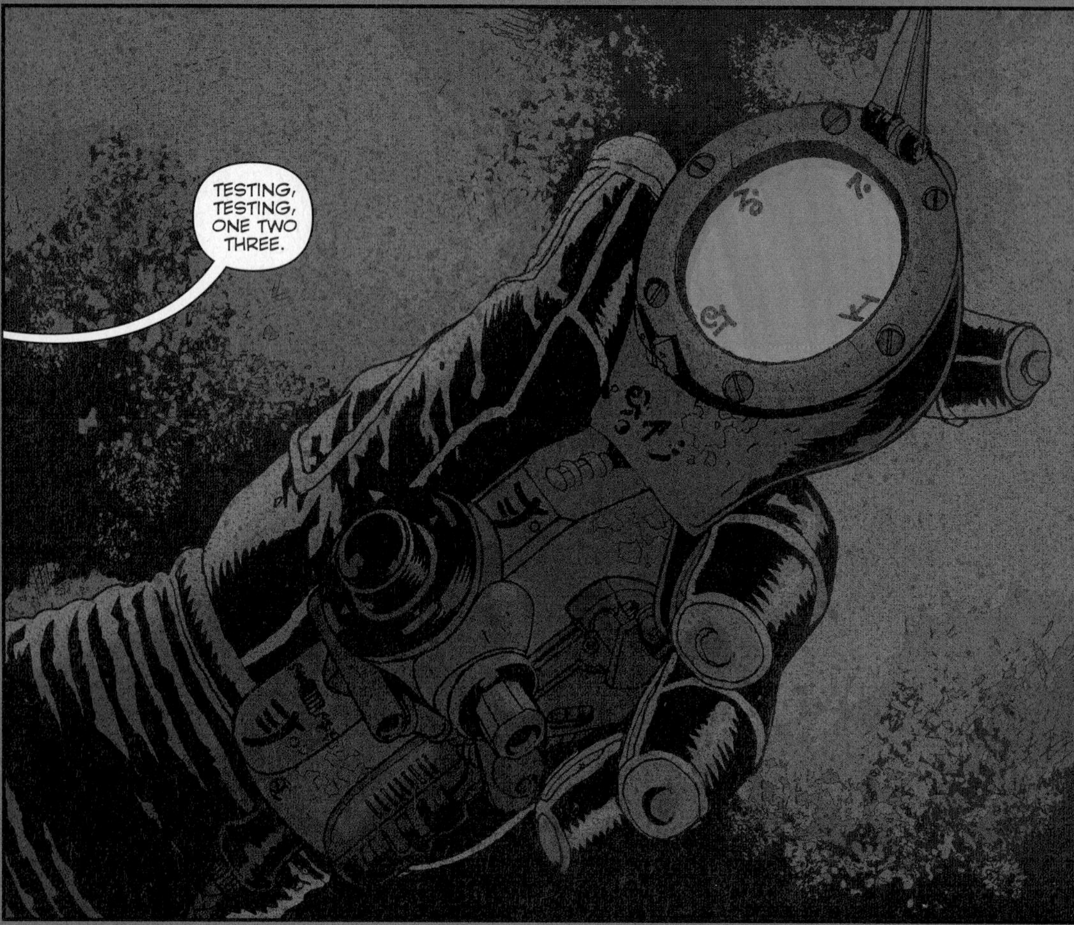
TESTING, TESTING, ONE TWO THREE.

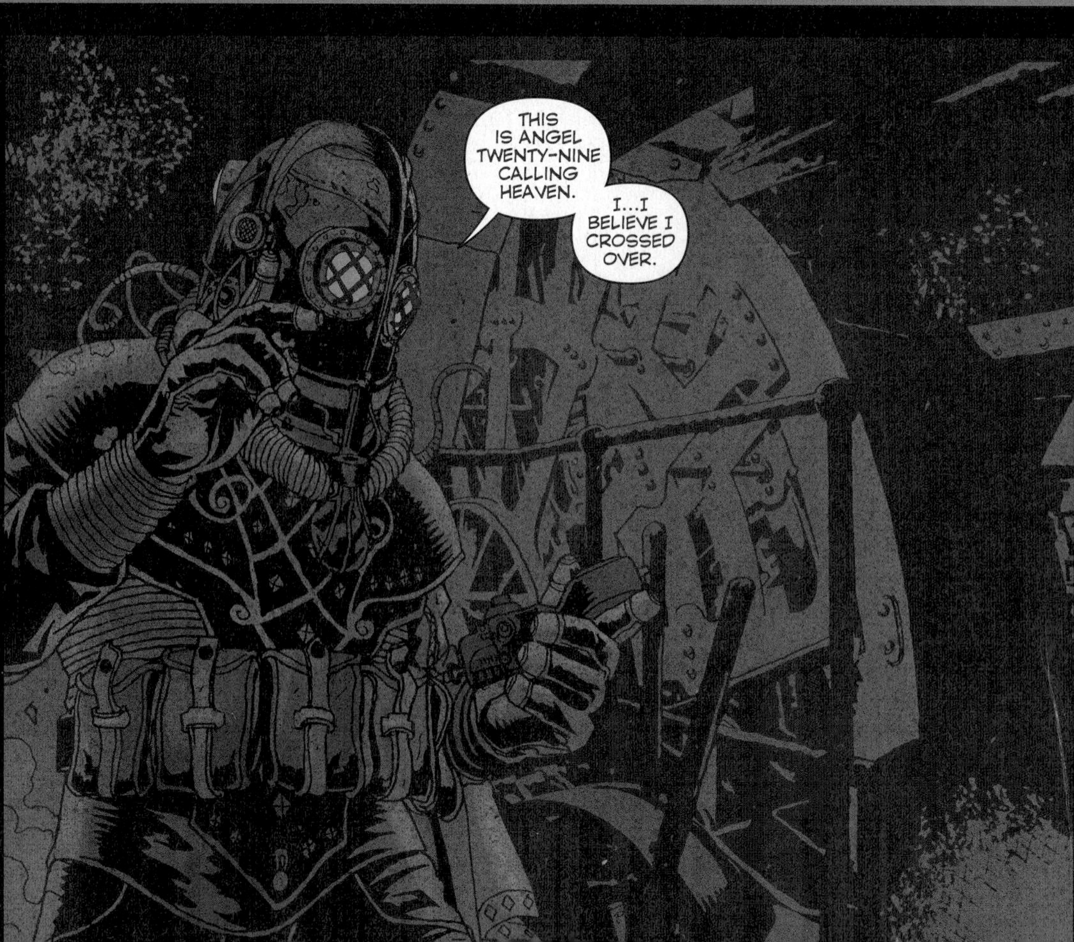
THIS IS ANGEL TWENTY-NINE CALLING HEAVEN.
I...I BELIEVE I CROSSED OVER.

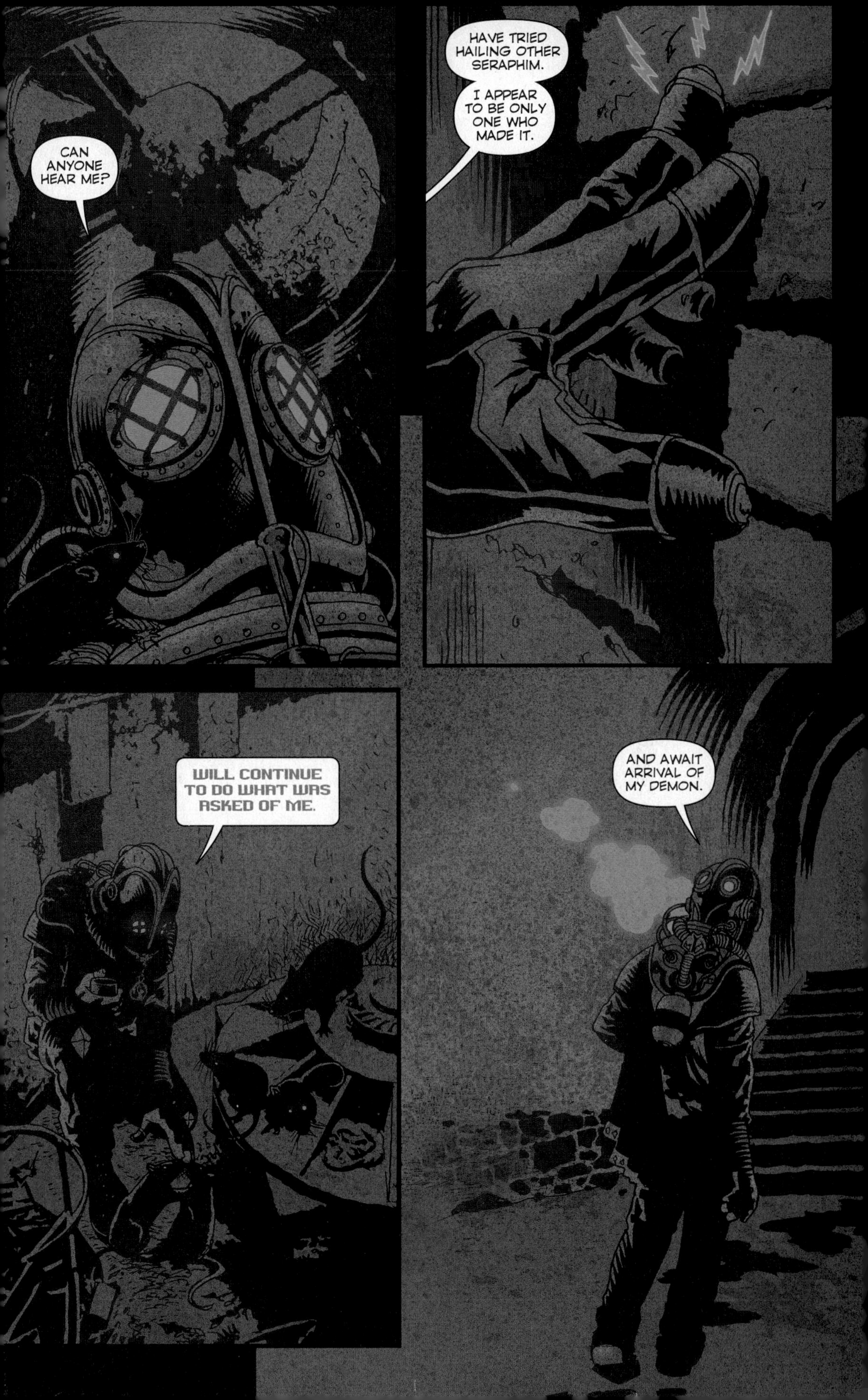
CAN ANYONE HEAR ME?
HAVE TRIED HAILING OTHER SERAPHIM.
I APPEAR TO BE ONLY ONE WHO MADE IT.
WILL CONTINUE TO DO WHAT WAS ASKED OF ME.
AND AWAIT ARRIVAL OF MY DEMON.

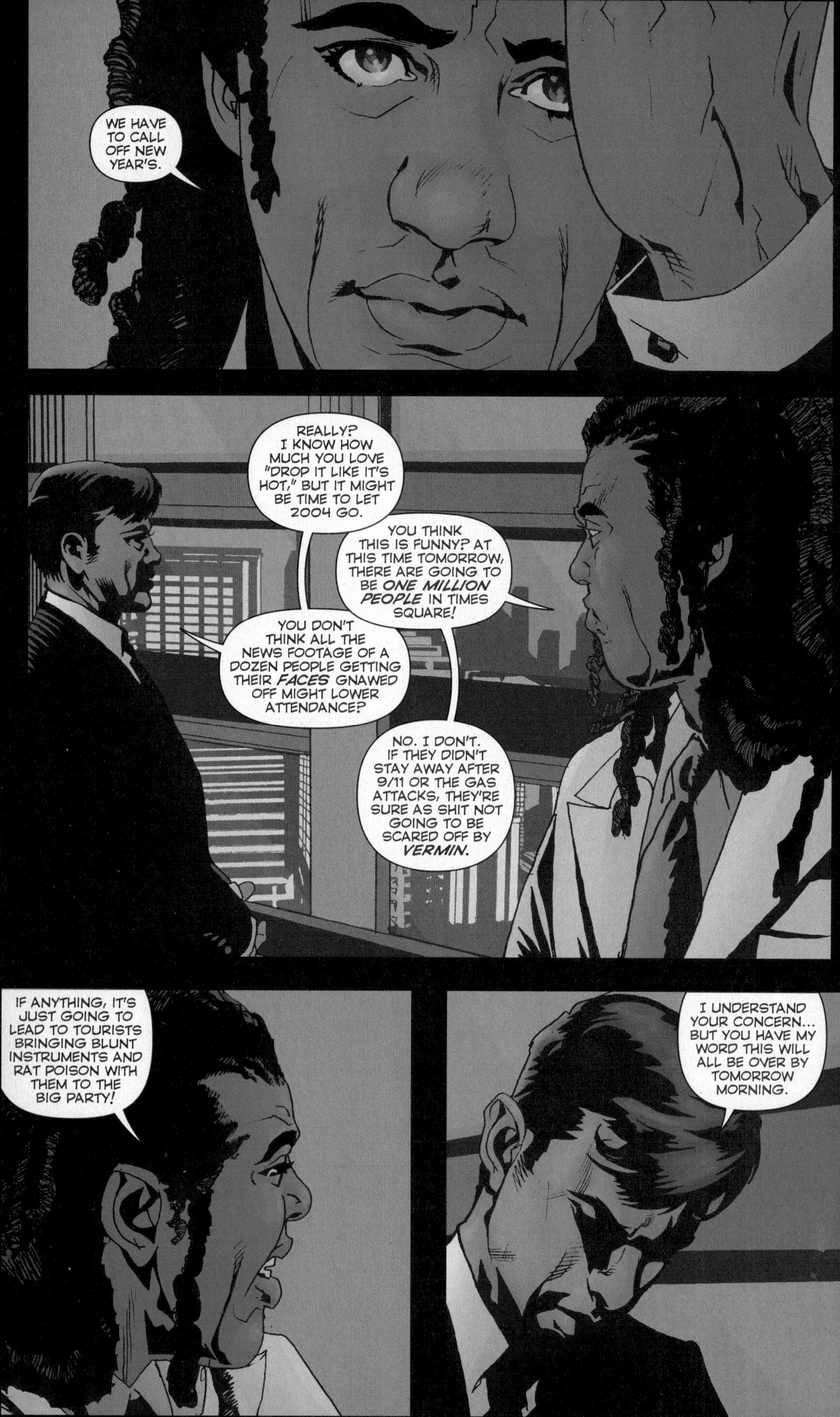
WE HAVE TO CALL OFF NEW YEAR'S.
REALLY? I KNOW HOW MUCH YOU LOVE "DROP IT LIKE IT'S HOT," BUT IT MIGHT BE TIME TO LET 2004 GO.
YOU THINK THIS IS FUNNY? AT THIS TIME TOMORROW, THERE ARE GOING TO BE *ONE MILLION PEOPLE* IN TIMES SQUARE!
YOU DON'T THINK ALL THE NEWS FOOTAGE OF A DOZEN PEOPLE GETTING THEIR *FACES* GNAWED OFF MIGHT LOWER ATTENDANCE?
NO. I DON'T. IF THEY DIDN'T STAY AWAY AFTER 9/11 OR THE GAS ATTACKS, THEY'RE SURE AS SHIT NOT GOING TO BE SCARED OFF BY ***VERMIN.***
IF ANYTHING, IT'S JUST GOING TO LEAD TO TOURISTS BRINGING BLUNT INSTRUMENTS AND RAT POISON WITH THEM TO THE BIG PARTY!
I UNDERSTAND YOUR CONCERN... BUT YOU HAVE MY WORD THIS WILL ALL BE OVER BY TOMORROW MORNING.

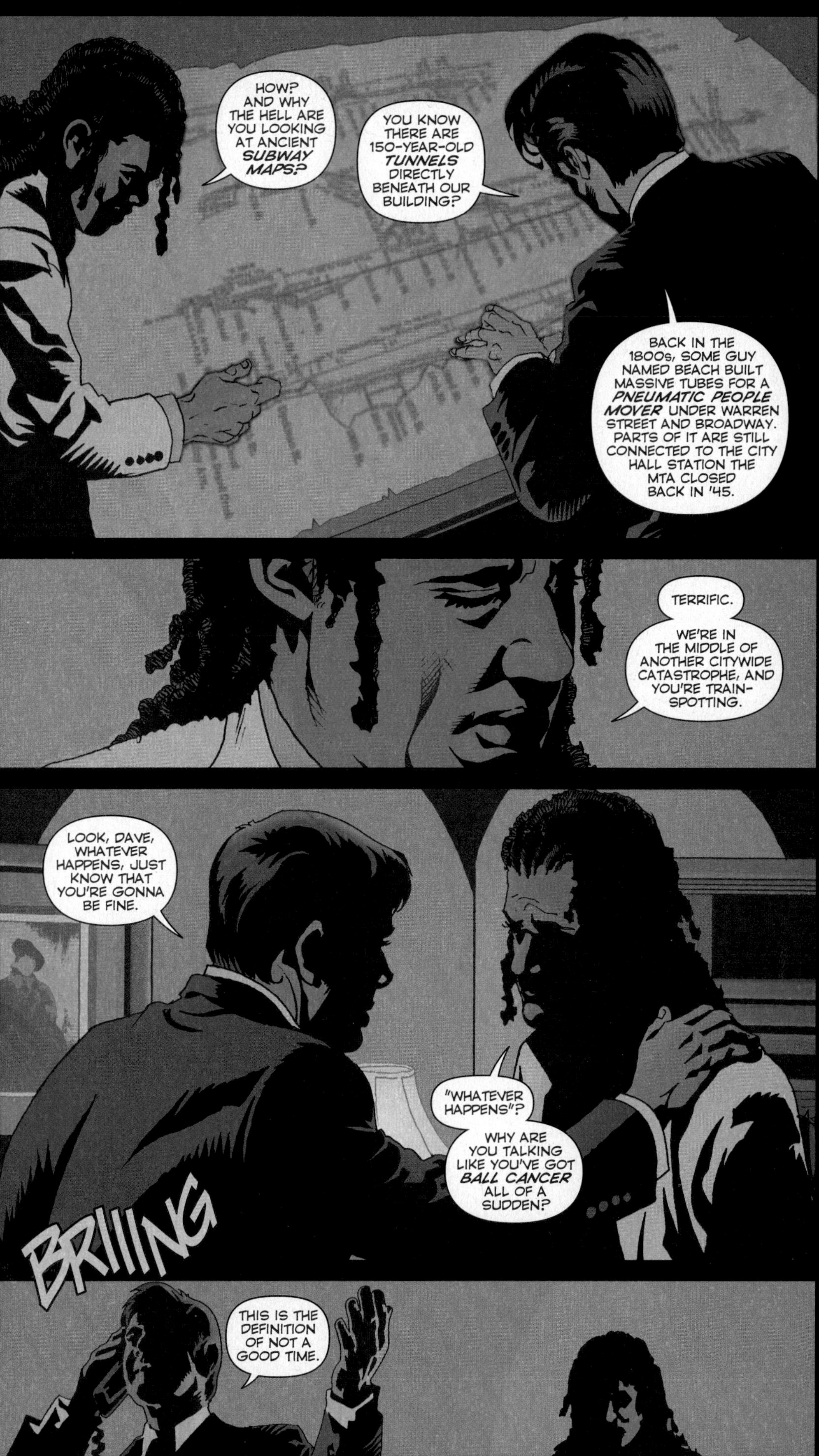
HOW? AND WHY THE HELL ARE YOU LOOKING AT ANCIENT SUBWAY MAPS?
YOU KNOW THERE ARE 150-YEAR-OLD TUNNELS DIRECTLY BENEATH OUR BUILDING?
BACK IN THE 1800s, SOME GUY NAMED BEACH BUILT MASSIVE TUBES FOR A PNEUMATIC PEOPLE MOVER UNDER WARREN STREET AND BROADWAY. PARTS OF IT ARE STILL CONNECTED TO THE CITY HALL STATION THE MTA CLOSED BACK IN '45.
TERRIFIC.
WE'RE IN THE MIDDLE OF ANOTHER CITYWIDE CATASTROPHE, AND YOU'RE TRAIN-SPOTTING.
LOOK, DAVE, WHATEVER HAPPENS, JUST KNOW THAT YOU'RE GONNA BE FINE.
"WHATEVER HAPPENS"?
WHY ARE YOU TALKING LIKE YOU'VE GOT BALL CANCER ALL OF A SUDDEN?
BRIIING
THIS IS THE DEFINITION OF NOT A GOOD TIME.

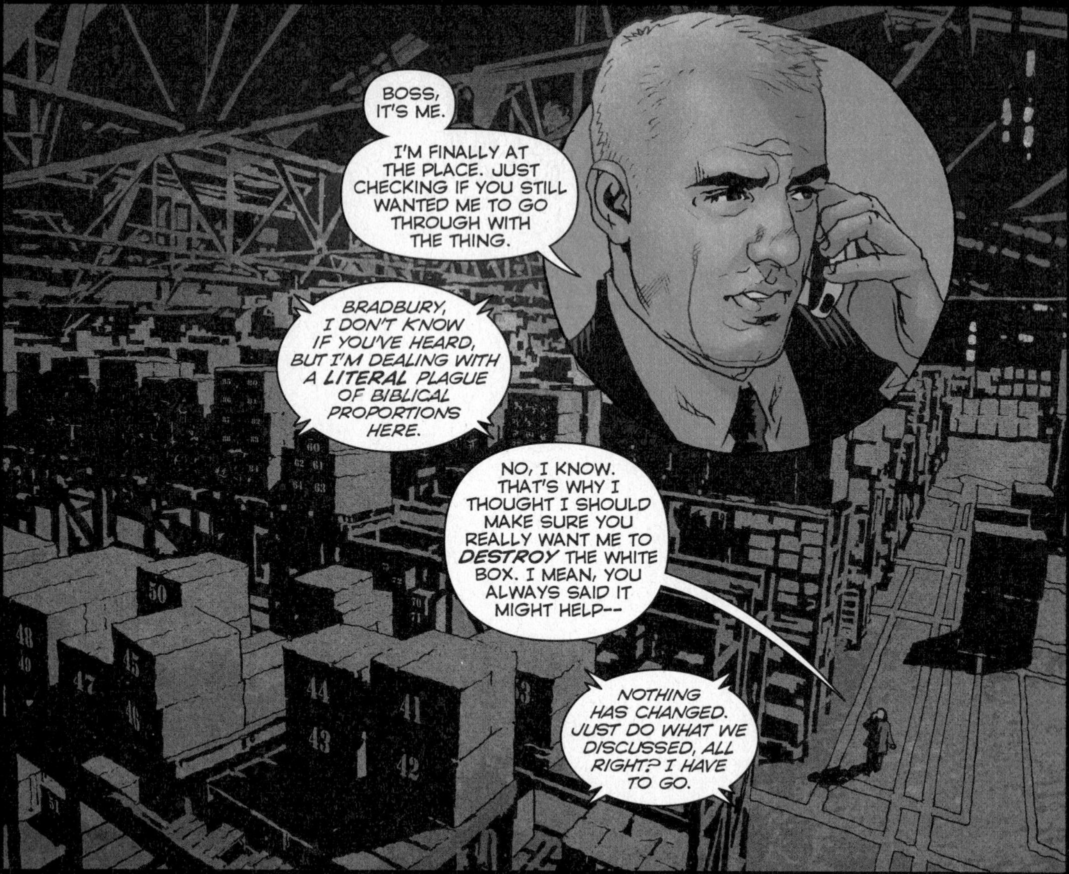
BOSS, IT'S ME.
I'M FINALLY AT THE PLACE. JUST CHECKING IF YOU STILL WANTED ME TO GO THROUGH WITH THE THING.
BRADBURY, I DON'T KNOW IF YOU'VE HEARD, BUT I'M DEALING WITH A LITERAL PLAGUE OF BIBLICAL PROPORTIONS HERE.
NO, I KNOW. THAT'S WHY I THOUGHT I SHOULD MAKE SURE YOU REALLY WANT ME TO DESTROY THE WHITE BOX. I MEAN, YOU ALWAYS SAID IT MIGHT HELP--
NOTHING HAS CHANGED. JUST DO WHAT WE DISCUSSED, ALL RIGHT? I HAVE TO GO.

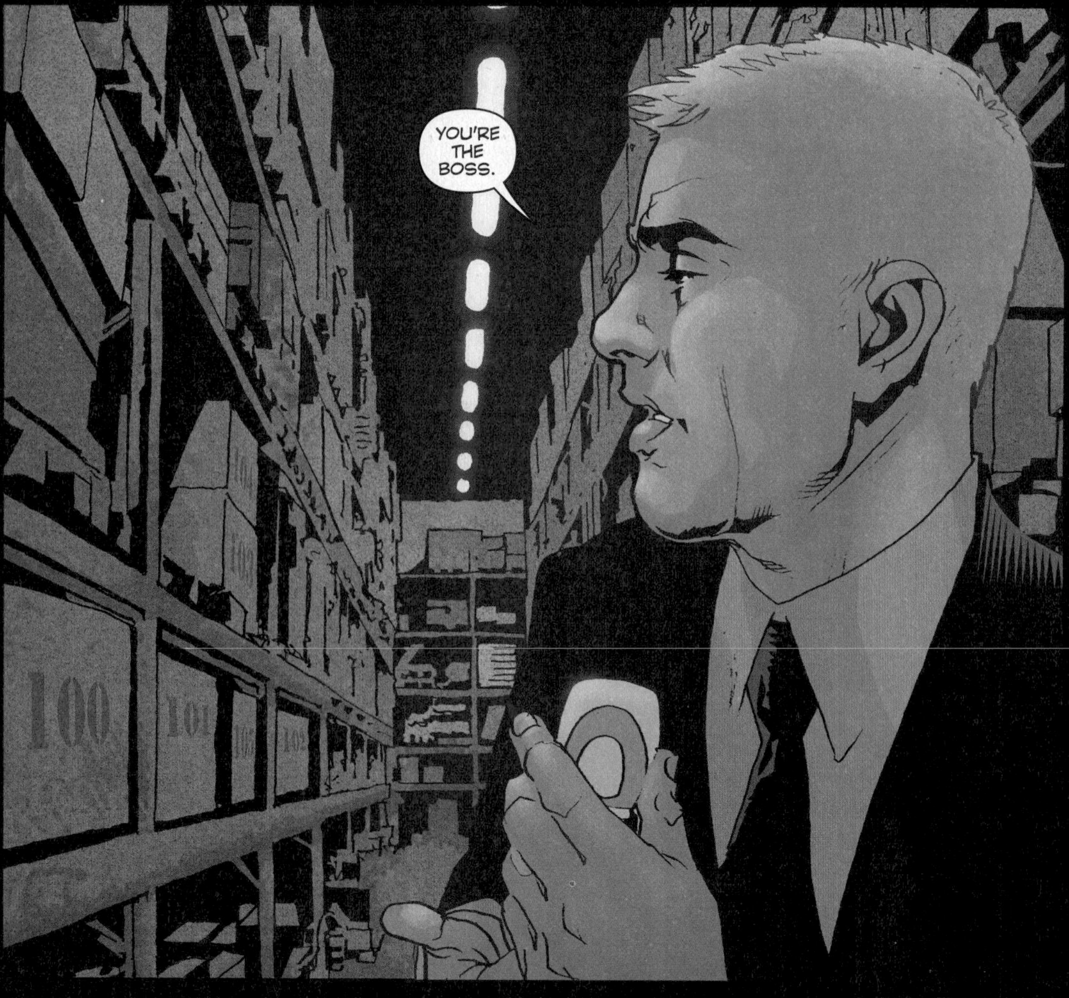
YOU'RE THE BOSS.

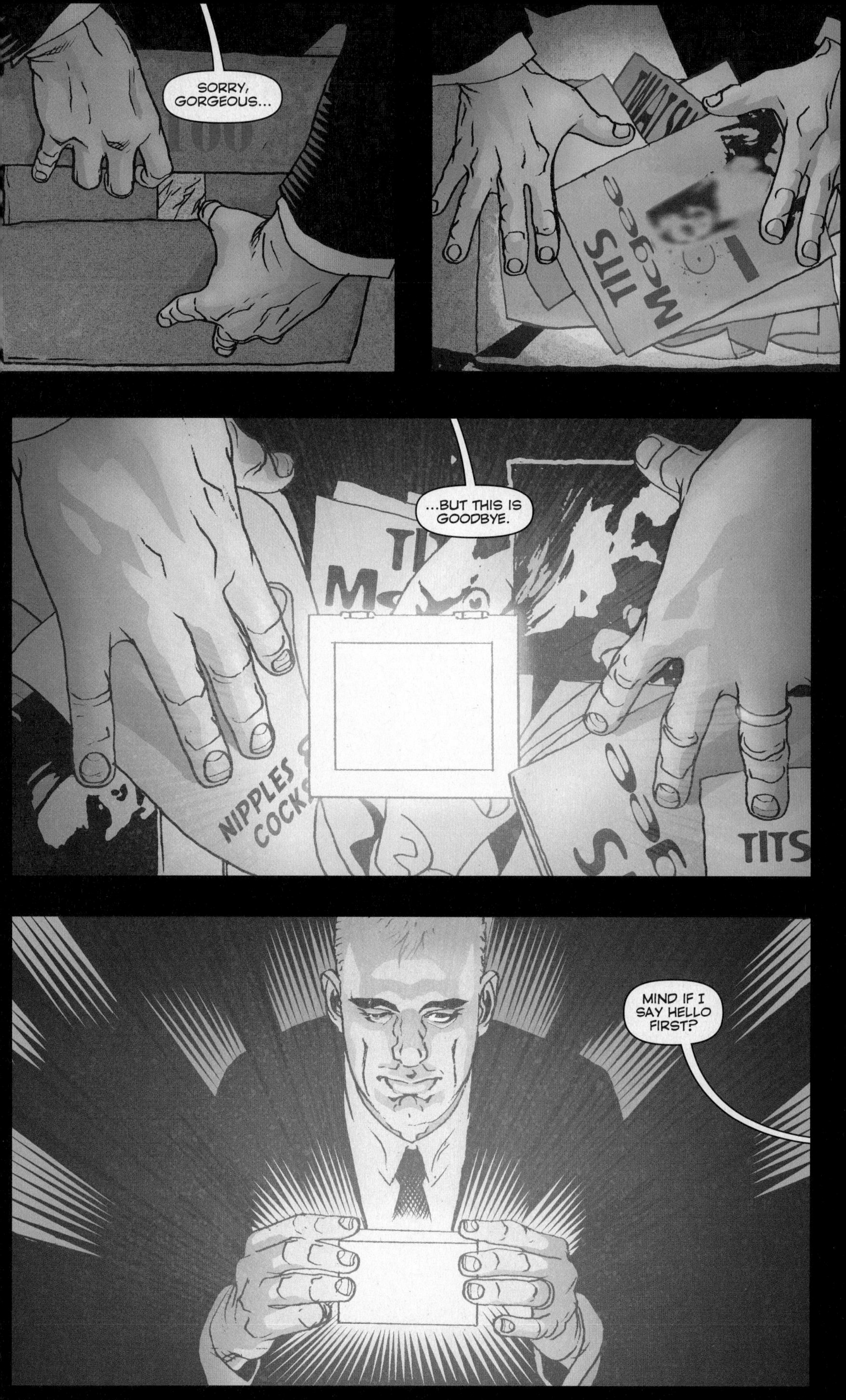
SORRY, GORGEOUS...
TITS
...BUT THIS IS GOODBYE.
NIPPLES
TITS
MIND IF I SAY HELLO FIRST?

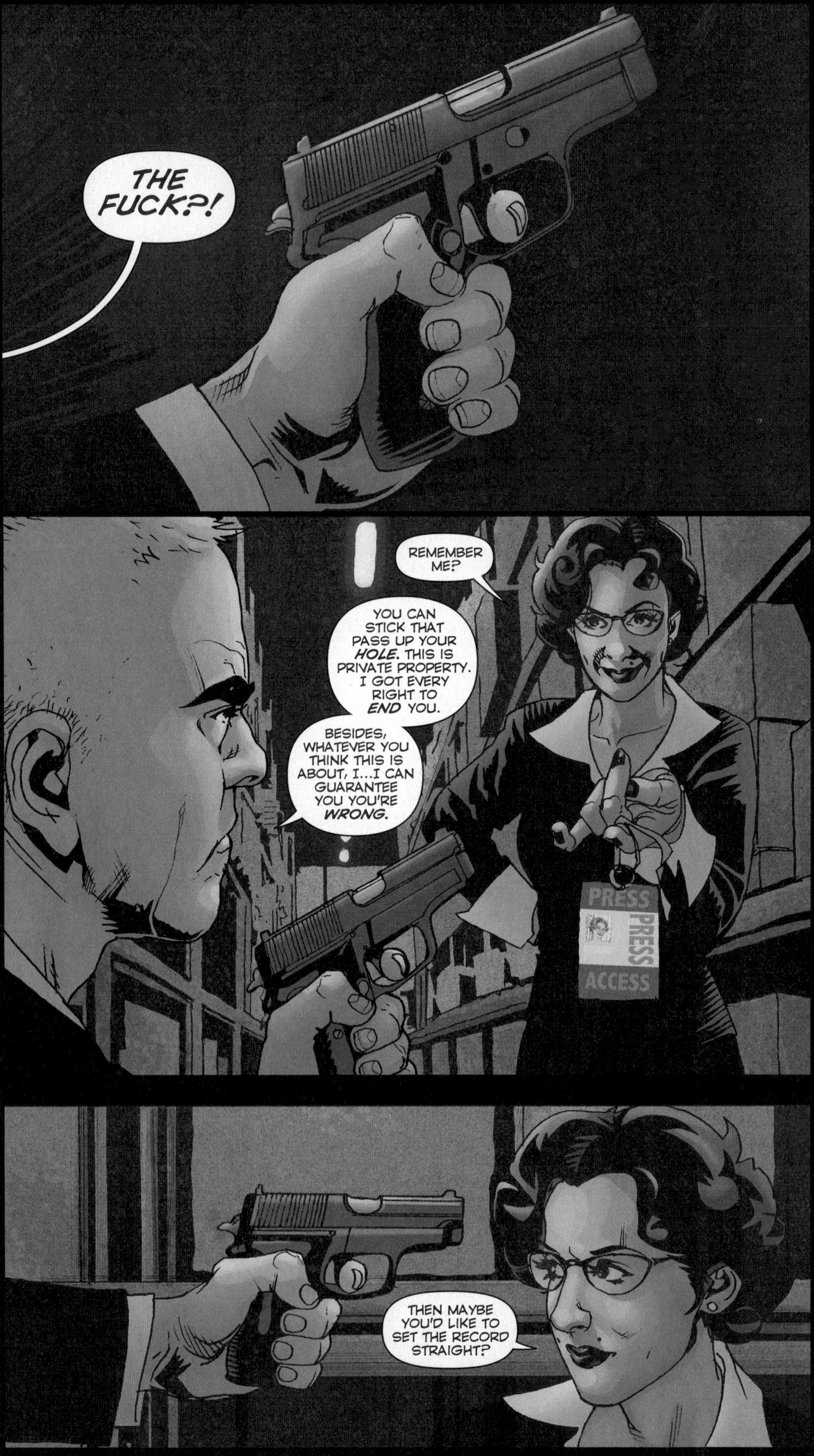
THE FUCK?!
REMEMBER ME?
YOU CAN STICK THAT PASS UP YOUR HOLE. THIS IS PRIVATE PROPERTY. I GOT EVERY RIGHT TO END YOU.
BESIDES, WHATEVER YOU THINK THIS IS ABOUT, I...I CAN GUARANTEE YOU YOU'RE WRONG.
PRESS
PRESS
ACCESS
THEN MAYBE YOU'D LIKE TO SET THE RECORD STRAIGHT?

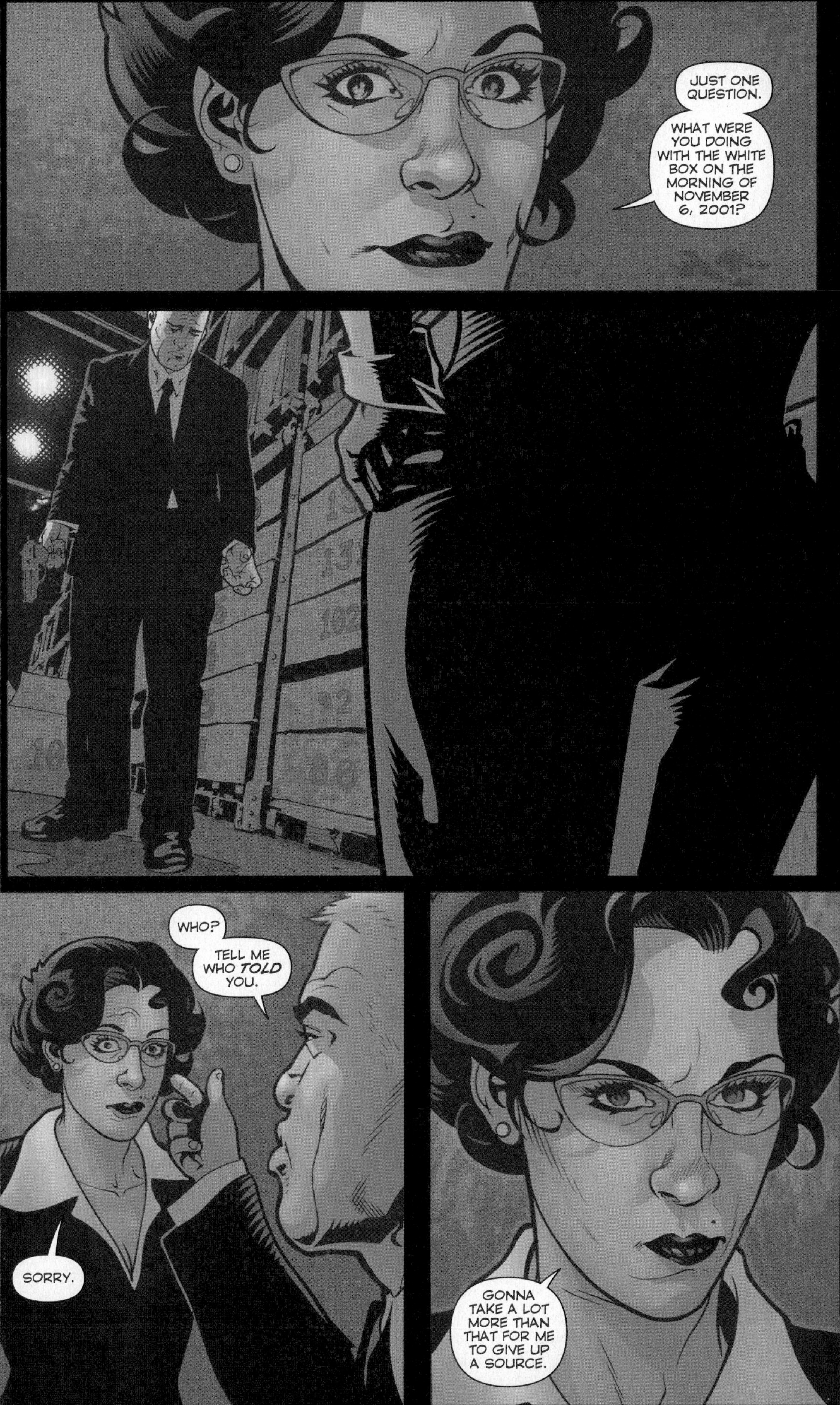
JUST ONE QUESTION.
WHAT WERE YOU DOING WITH THE WHITE BOX ON THE MORNING OF NOVEMBER 6, 2001?
WHO?
TELL ME WHO *TOLD* YOU.
SORRY.
GONNA TAKE A LOT MORE THAN THAT FOR ME TO GIVE UP A SOURCE.

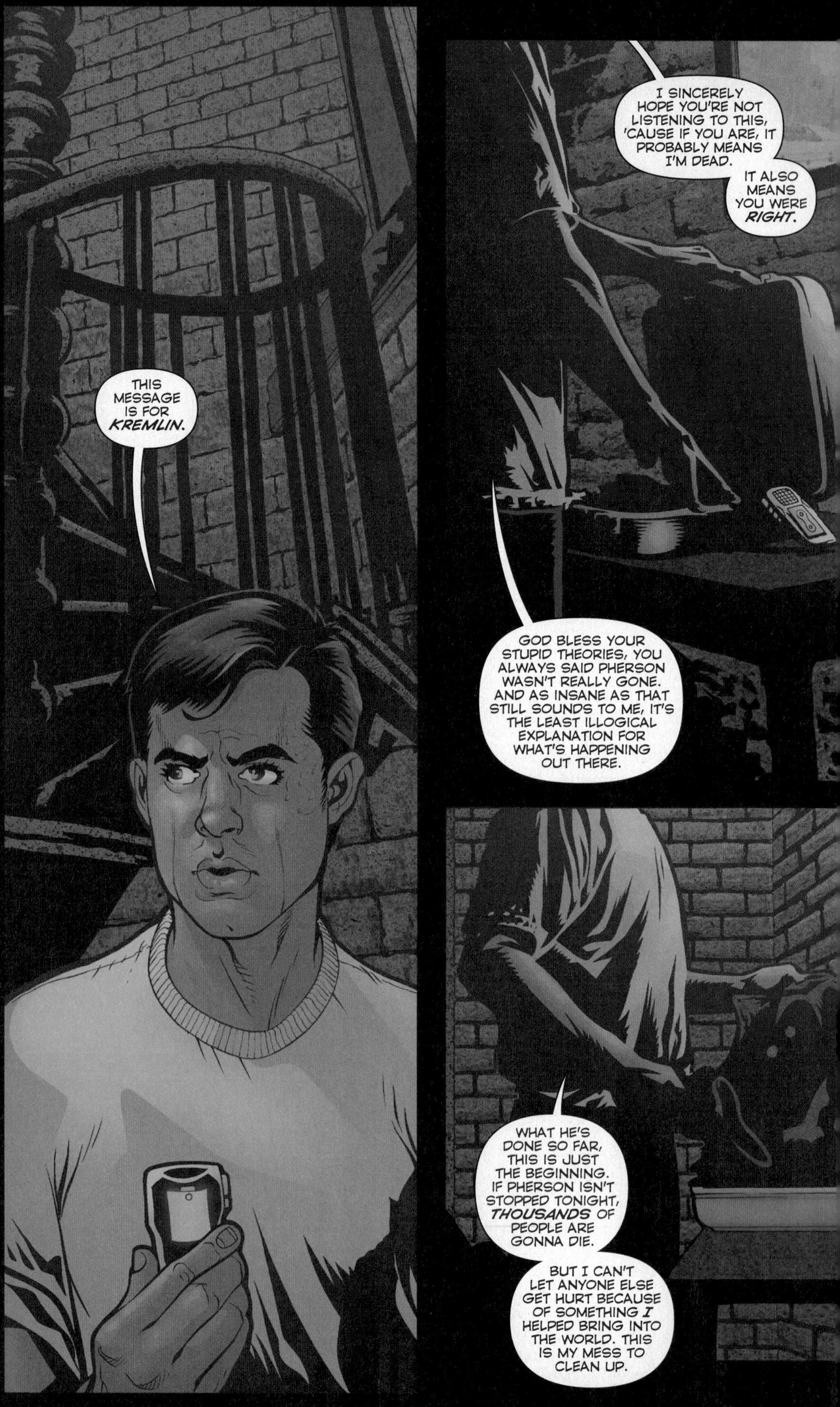
THIS MESSAGE IS FOR KREMLIN.
I SINCERELY HOPE YOU'RE NOT LISTENING TO THIS, 'CAUSE IF YOU ARE, IT PROBABLY MEANS I'M DEAD.
IT ALSO MEANS YOU WERE RIGHT.
GOD BLESS YOUR STUPID THEORIES, YOU ALWAYS SAID PHERSON WASN'T REALLY GONE. AND AS INSANE AS THAT STILL SOUNDS TO ME, IT'S THE LEAST ILLOGICAL EXPLANATION FOR WHAT'S HAPPENING OUT THERE.
WHAT HE'S DONE SO FAR, THIS IS JUST THE BEGINNING. IF PHERSON ISN'T STOPPED TONIGHT, THOUSANDS OF PEOPLE ARE GONNA DIE.
BUT I CAN'T LET ANYONE ELSE GET HURT BECAUSE OF SOMETHING I HELPED BRING INTO THE WORLD. THIS IS MY MESS TO CLEAN UP.

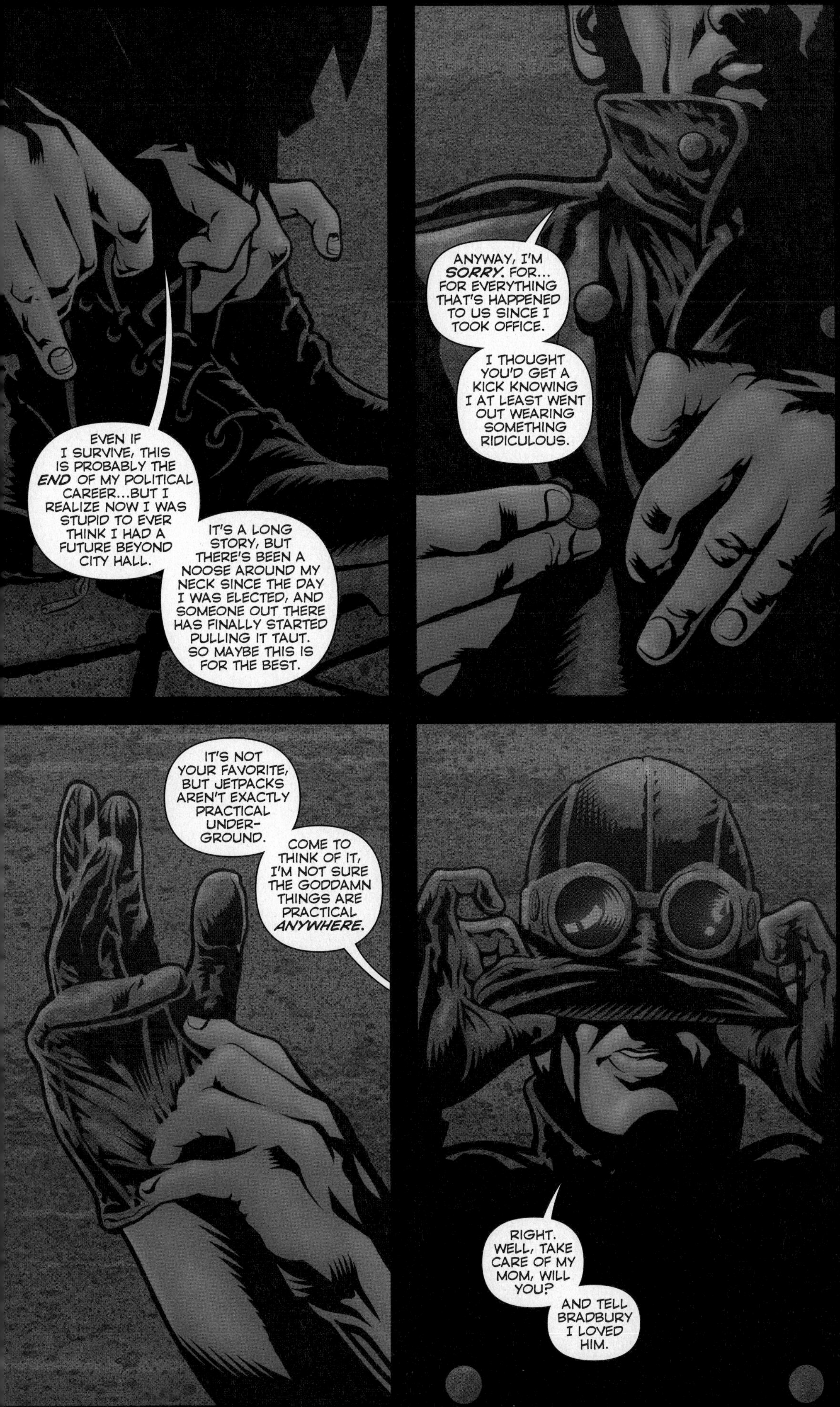

EVEN IF I SURVIVE, THIS IS PROBABLY THE END OF MY POLITICAL CAREER...BUT I REALIZE NOW I WAS STUPID TO EVER THINK I HAD A FUTURE BEYOND CITY HALL.
IT'S A LONG STORY, BUT THERE'S BEEN A NOOSE AROUND MY NECK SINCE THE DAY I WAS ELECTED, AND SOMEONE OUT THERE HAS FINALLY STARTED PULLING IT TAUT. SO MAYBE THIS IS FOR THE BEST.
ANYWAY, I'M SORRY. FOR... FOR EVERYTHING THAT'S HAPPENED TO US SINCE I TOOK OFFICE.
I THOUGHT YOU'D GET A KICK KNOWING I AT LEAST WENT OUT WEARING SOMETHING RIDICULOUS.
IT'S NOT YOUR FAVORITE, BUT JETPACKS AREN'T EXACTLY PRACTICAL UNDER-GROUND.
COME TO THINK OF IT, I'M NOT SURE THE GODDAMN THINGS ARE PRACTICAL ANYWHERE.
RIGHT. WELL, TAKE CARE OF MY MOM, WILL YOU?
AND TELL BRADBURY I LOVED HIM.

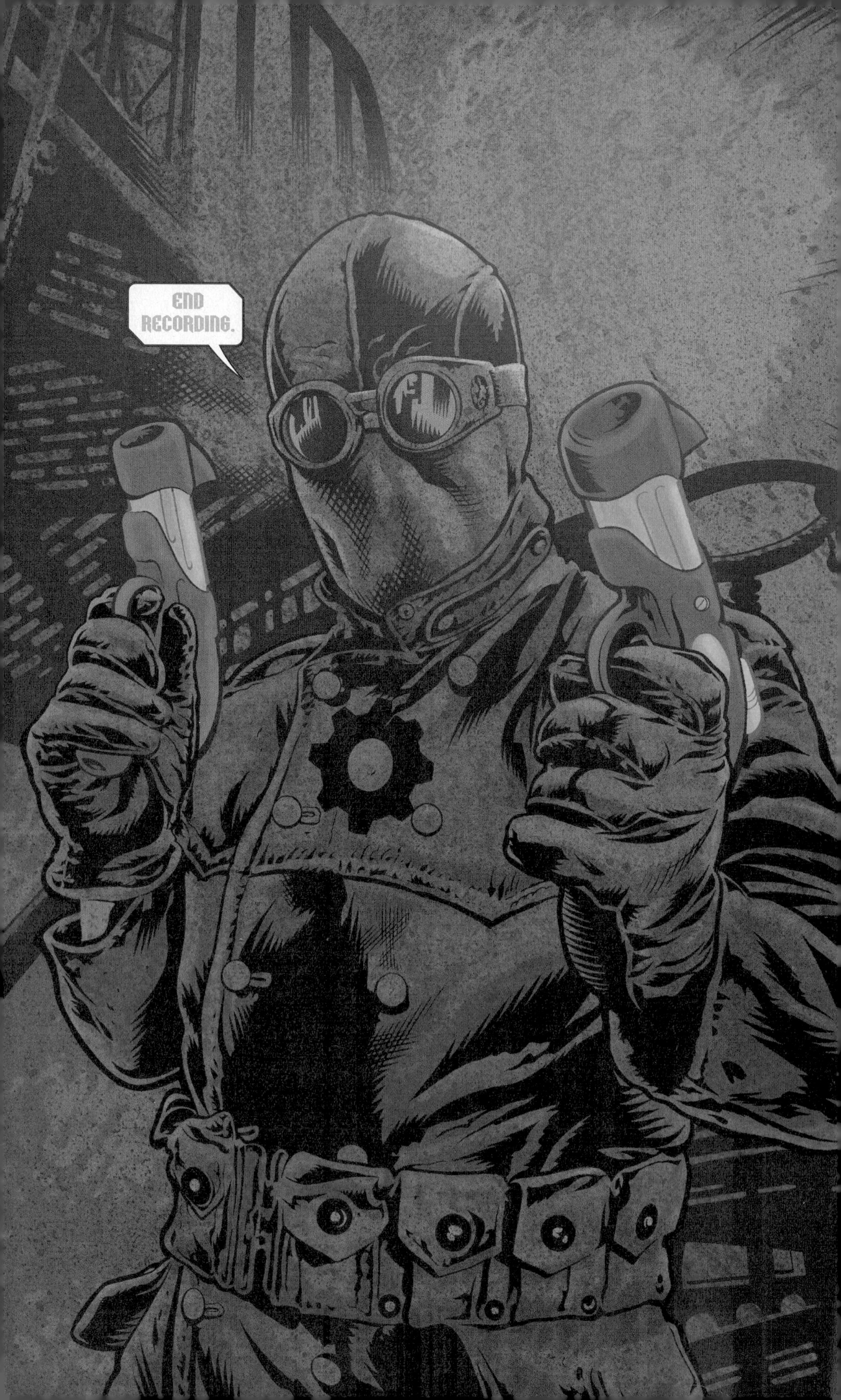
END RECORDING.

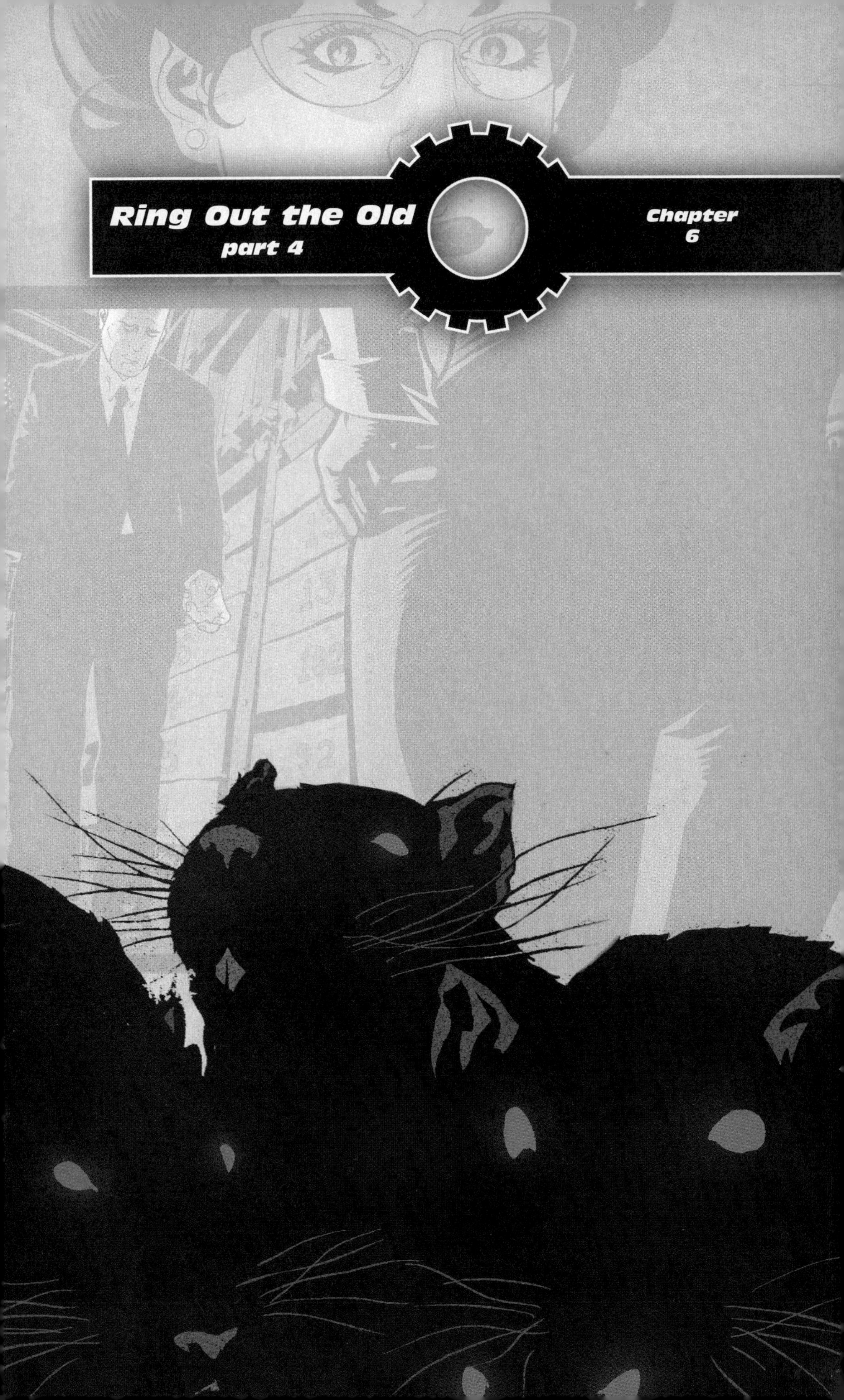
Ring Out the Old
part 4
Chapter
6

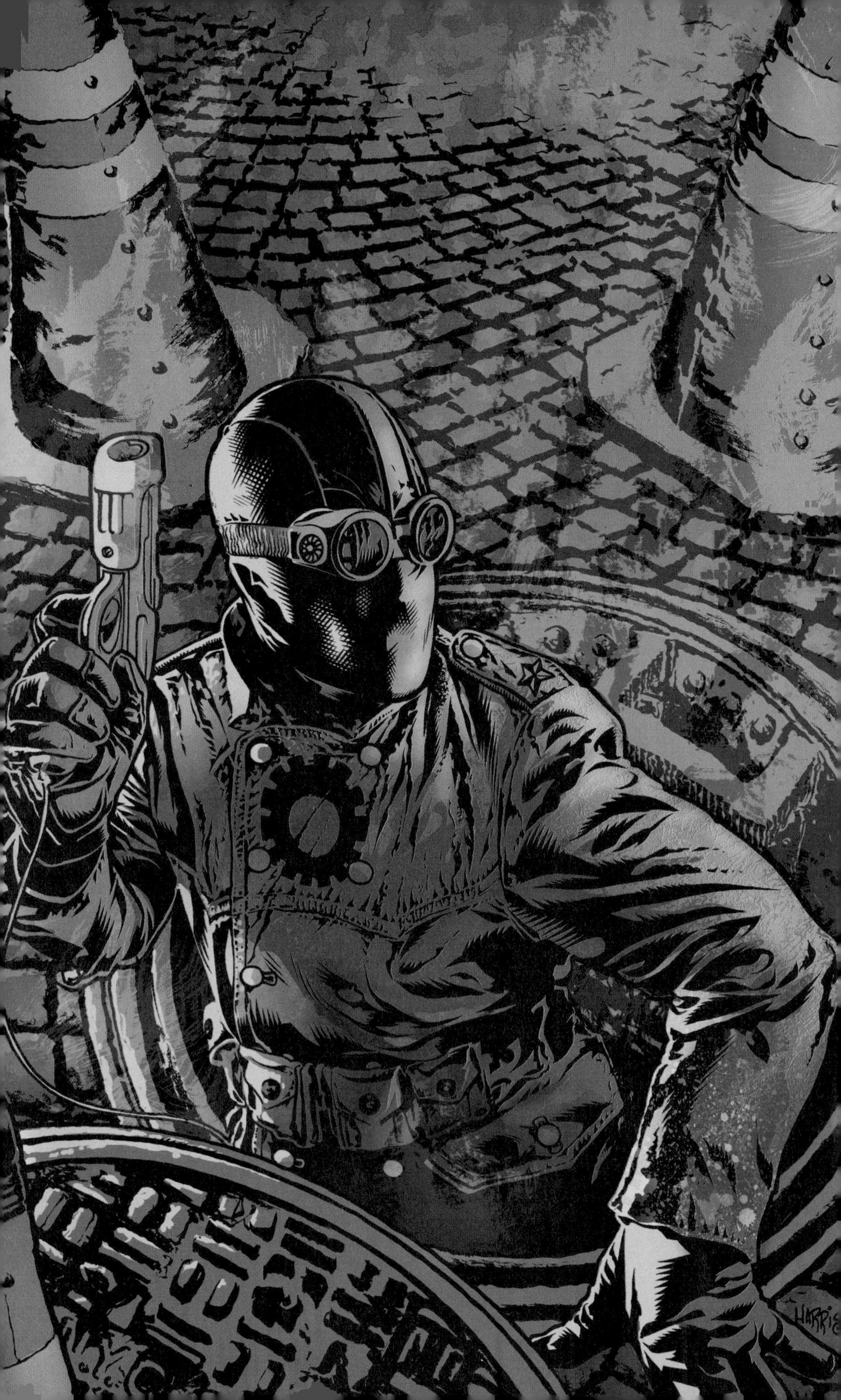

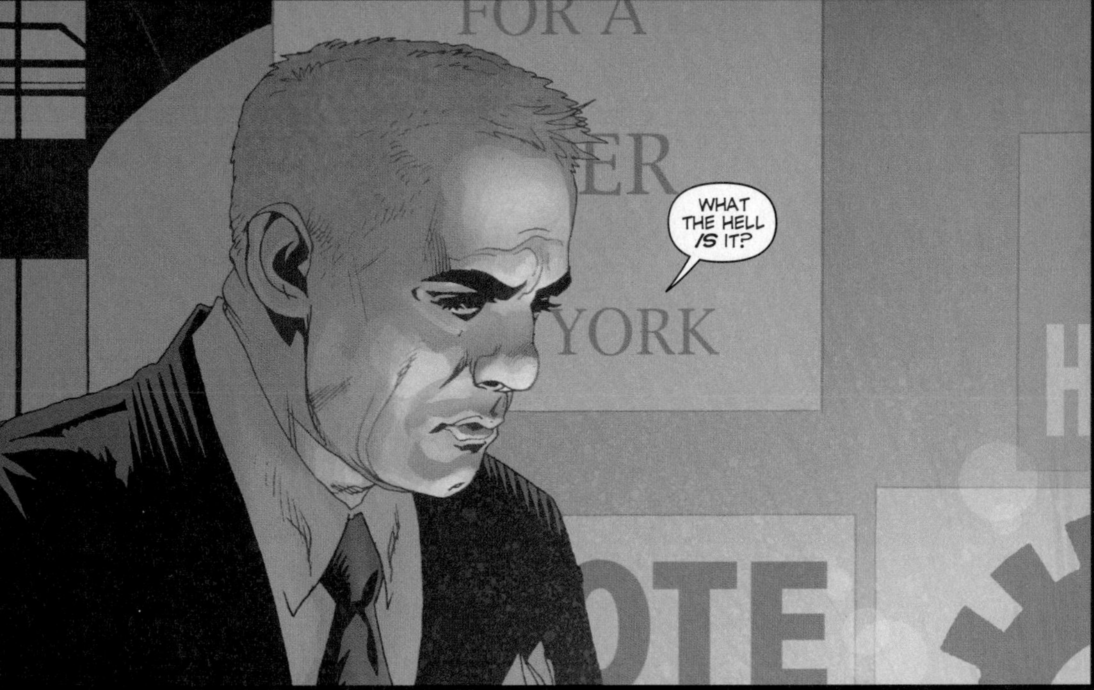
WHAT THE HELL *IS* IT?

MONDAY, NOVEMBER 5, 2001

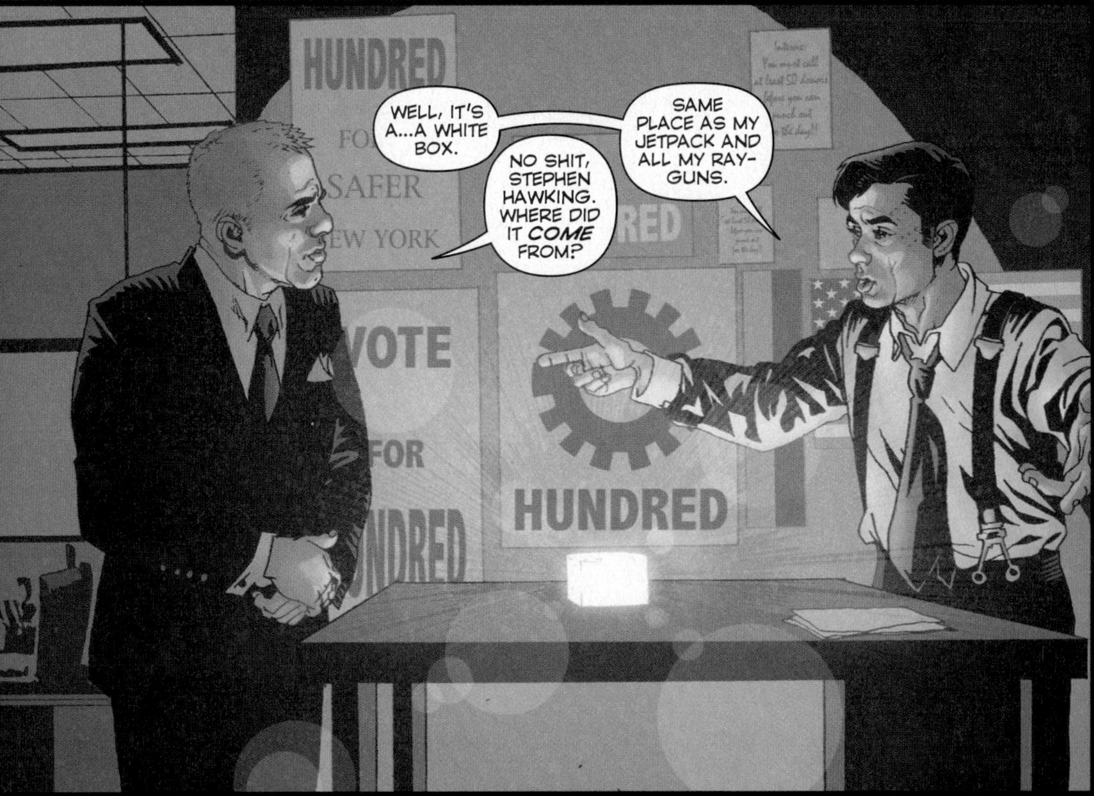
WELL, IT'S A...A WHITE BOX.
NO SHIT, STEPHEN HAWKING. WHERE DID IT *COME* FROM?
SAME PLACE AS MY JETPACK AND ALL MY RAY-GUNS.
HUNDRED

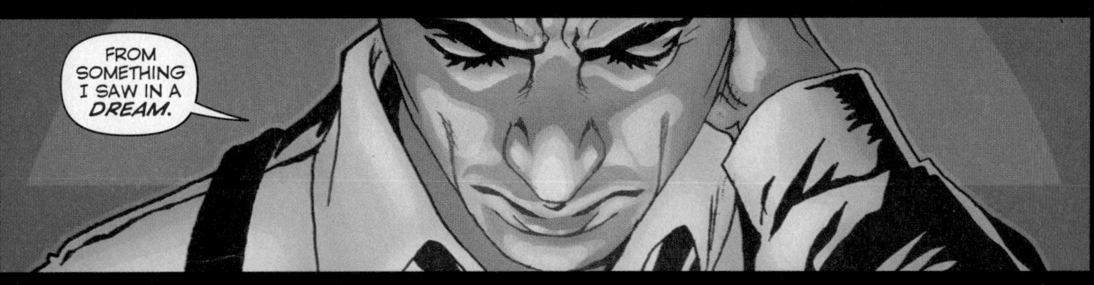
FROM SOMETHING I SAW IN A *DREAM*.

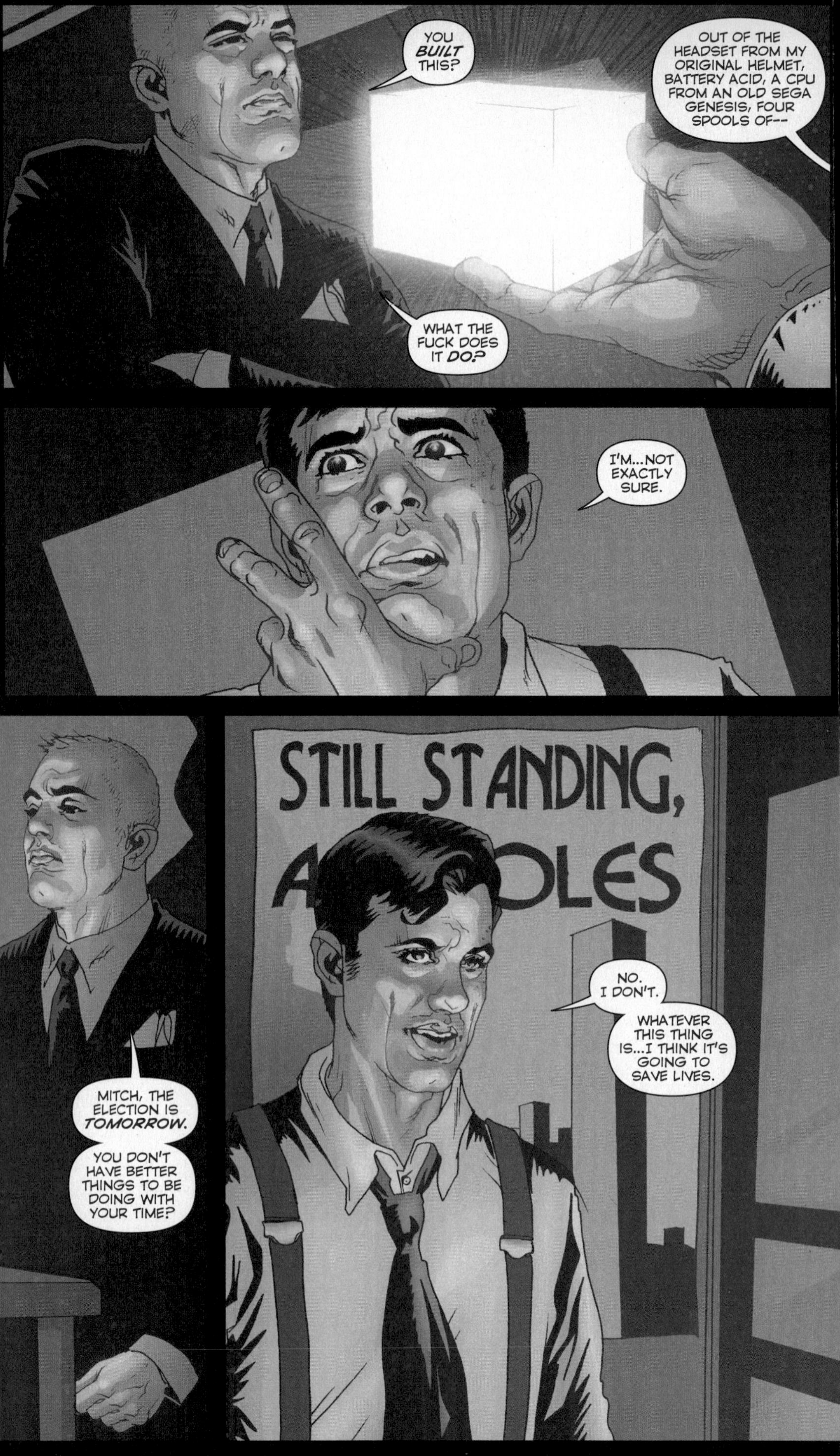
YOU *BUILT* THIS?
OUT OF THE HEADSET FROM MY ORIGINAL HELMET, BATTERY ACID, A CPU FROM AN OLD SEGA GENESIS, FOUR SPOOLS OF--
WHAT THE FUCK DOES IT *DO?*
I'M...NOT EXACTLY SURE.
STILL STANDING,
OLES
MITCH, THE ELECTION IS *TOMORROW*.
YOU DON'T HAVE BETTER THINGS TO BE DOING WITH YOUR TIME?
NO. I DON'T.
WHATEVER THIS THING IS...I THINK IT'S GOING TO SAVE LIVES.

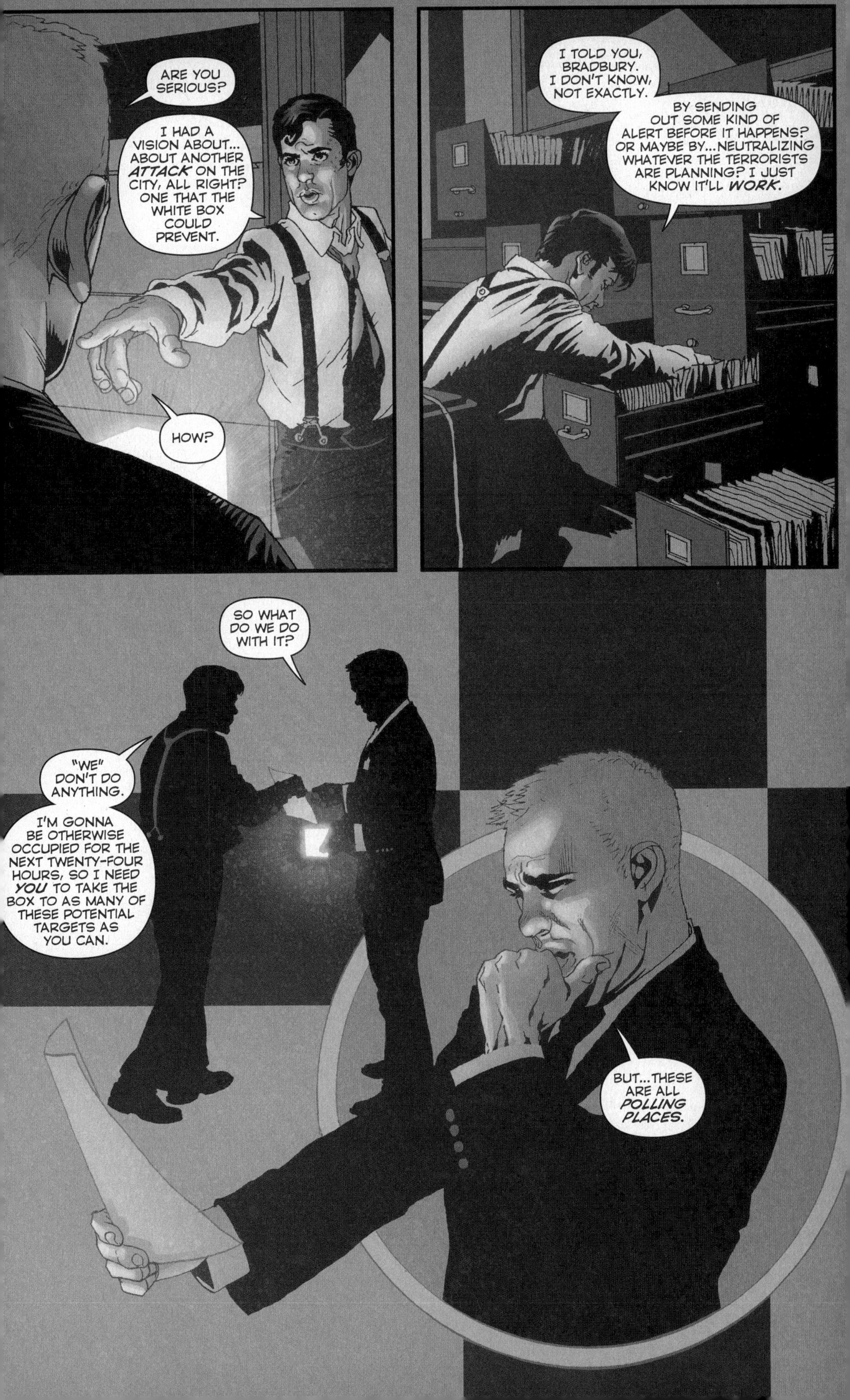

ARE YOU SERIOUS?
I HAD A VISION ABOUT... ABOUT ANOTHER *ATTACK* ON THE CITY, ALL RIGHT? ONE THAT THE WHITE BOX COULD PREVENT.
HOW?
I TOLD YOU, BRADBURY. I DON'T KNOW, NOT EXACTLY.
BY SENDING OUT SOME KIND OF ALERT BEFORE IT HAPPENS? OR MAYBE BY...NEUTRALIZING WHATEVER THE TERRORISTS ARE PLANNING? I JUST KNOW IT'LL *WORK*.
SO WHAT DO WE DO WITH IT?
"WE" DON'T DO ANYTHING.
I'M GONNA BE OTHERWISE OCCUPIED FOR THE NEXT TWENTY-FOUR HOURS, SO I NEED *YOU* TO TAKE THE BOX TO AS MANY OF THESE POTENTIAL TARGETS AS YOU CAN.
BUT...THESE ARE ALL *POLLING PLACES*.

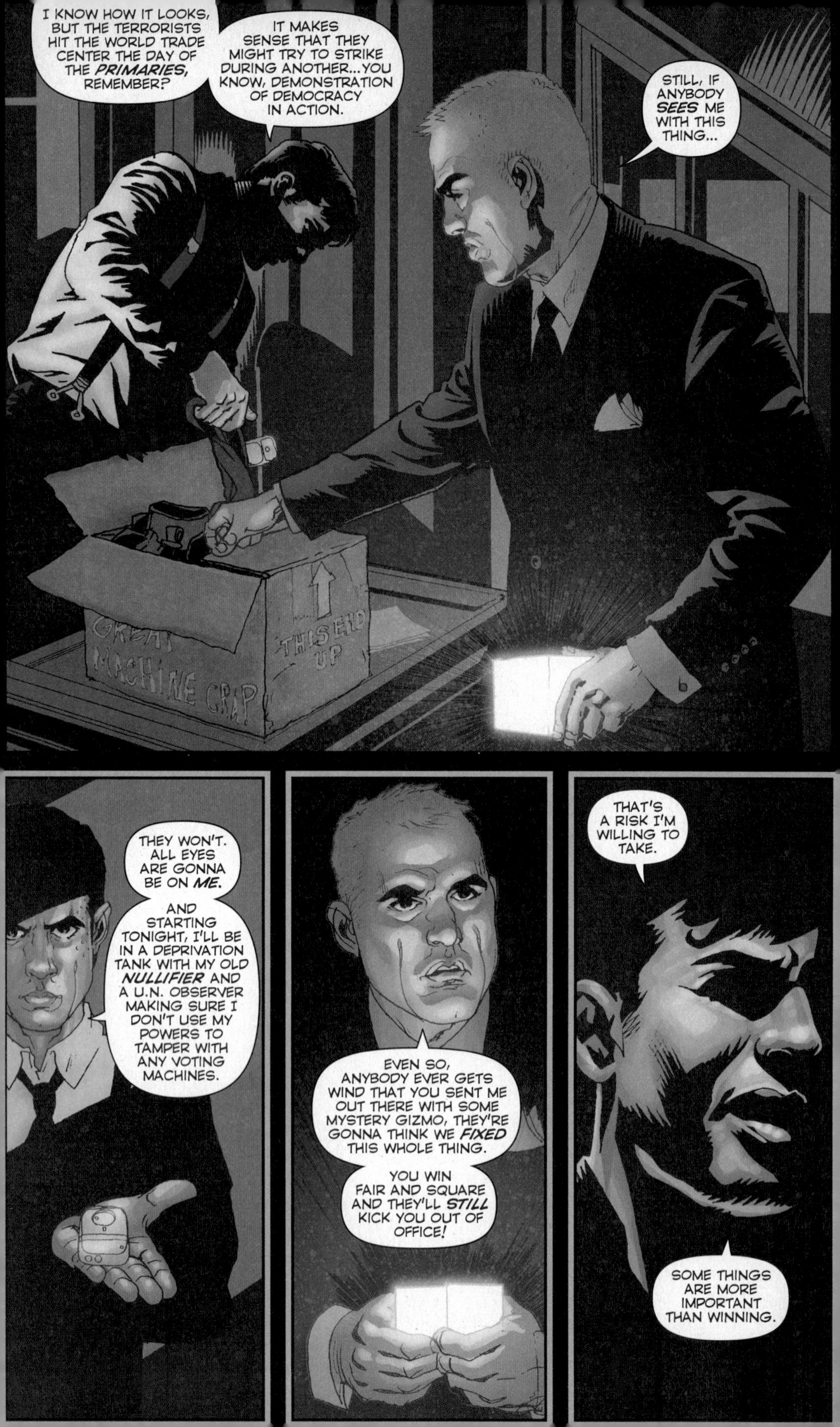
I KNOW HOW IT LOOKS, BUT THE TERRORISTS HIT THE WORLD TRADE CENTER THE DAY OF THE *PRIMARIES*, REMEMBER?
IT MAKES SENSE THAT THEY MIGHT TRY TO STRIKE DURING ANOTHER...YOU KNOW, DEMONSTRATION OF DEMOCRACY IN ACTION.
STILL, IF ANYBODY *SEES* ME WITH THIS THING...
MACHINE CRAP
THIS END UP
THEY WON'T. ALL EYES ARE GONNA BE ON *ME*.
AND STARTING TONIGHT, I'LL BE IN A DEPRIVATION TANK WITH MY OLD *NULLIFIER* AND A U.N. OBSERVER MAKING SURE I DON'T USE MY POWERS TO TAMPER WITH ANY VOTING MACHINES.
EVEN SO, ANYBODY EVER GETS WIND THAT YOU SENT ME OUT THERE WITH SOME MYSTERY GIZMO, THEY'RE GONNA THINK WE *FIXED* THIS WHOLE THING.
YOU WIN FAIR AND SQUARE AND THEY'LL *STILL* KICK YOU OUT OF OFFICE!
THAT'S A RISK I'M WILLING TO TAKE.
SOME THINGS ARE MORE IMPORTANT THAN WINNING.

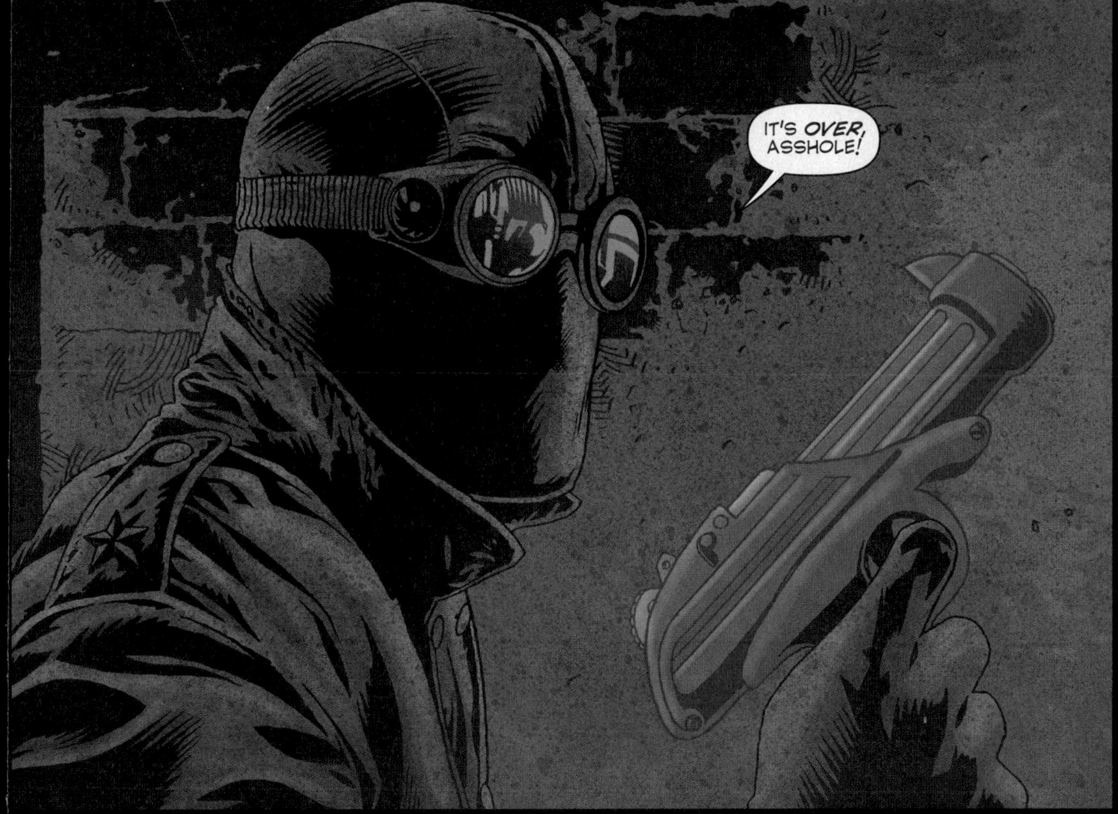
IT'S OVER, ASSHOLE!

THURSDAY, DECEMBER 30, 2004

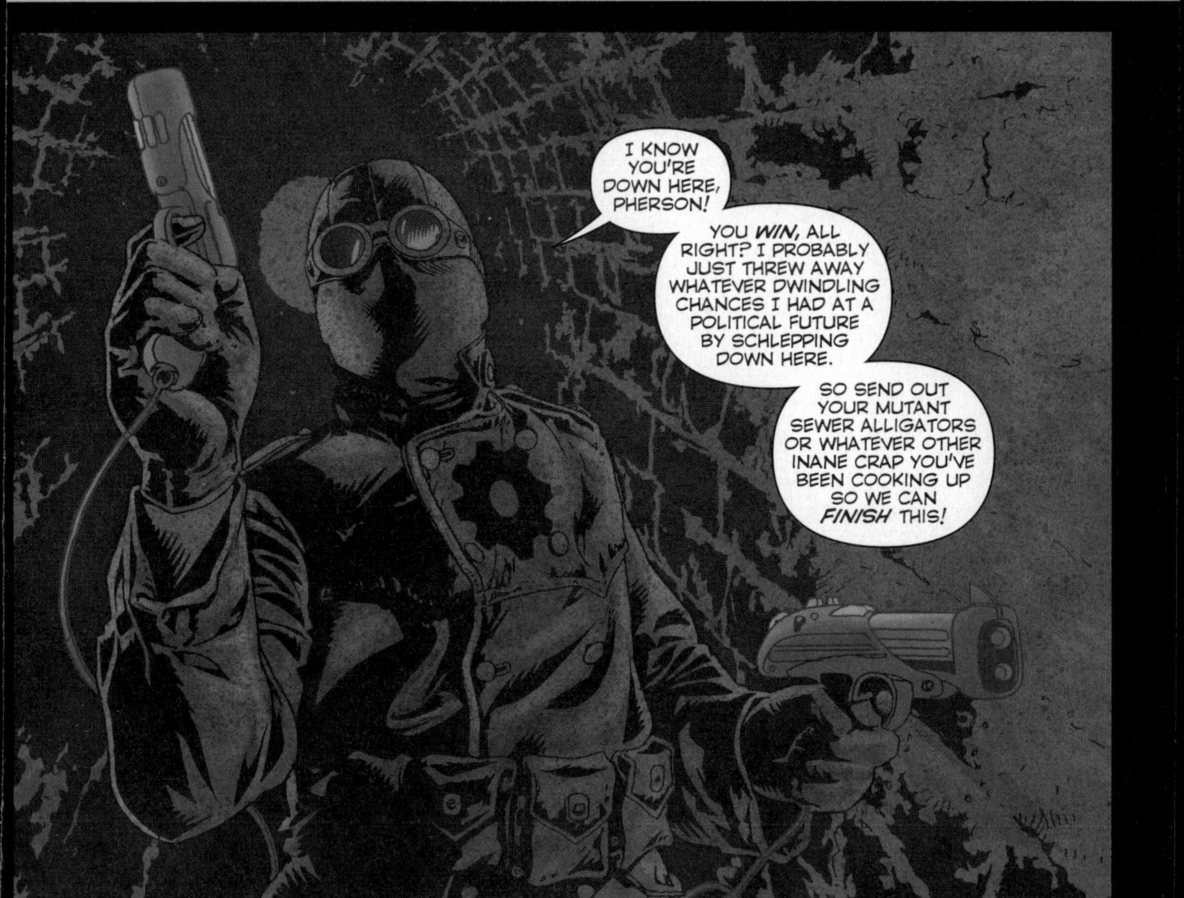
I KNOW YOU'RE DOWN HERE, PHERSON!
YOU WIN, ALL RIGHT? I PROBABLY JUST THREW AWAY WHATEVER DWINDLING CHANCES I HAD AT A POLITICAL FUTURE BY SCHLEPPING DOWN HERE.
SO SEND OUT YOUR MUTANT SEWER ALLIGATORS OR WHATEVER OTHER INANE CRAP YOU'VE BEEN COOKING UP SO WE CAN FINISH THIS!

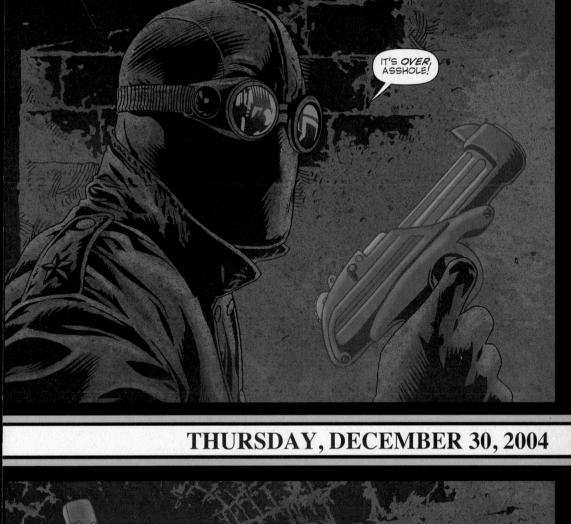

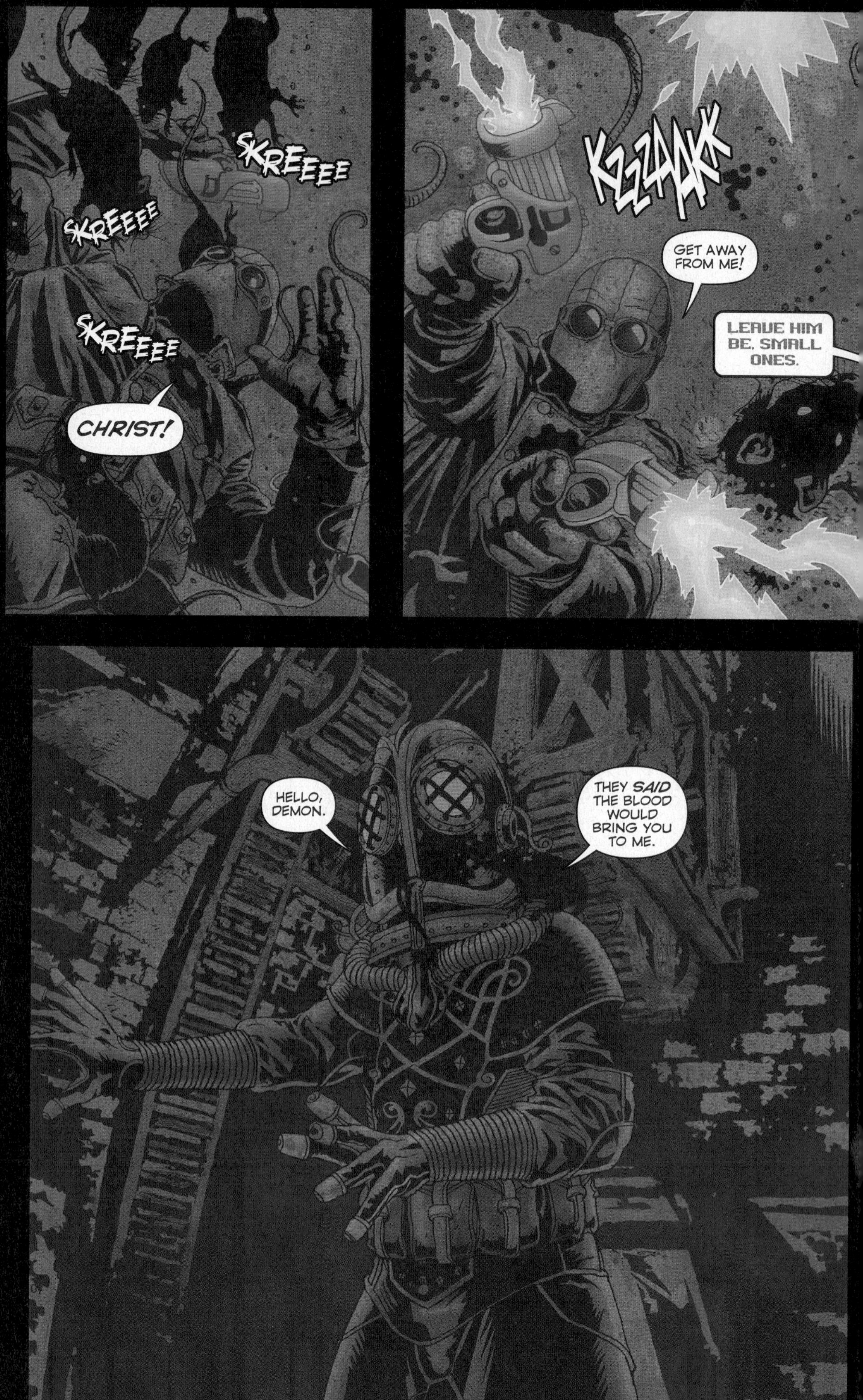
SKREEEEE
SKREEEE
SKREEEEE
CHRIST!
KZZZAKK
GET AWAY FROM ME!
LEAVE HIM BE, SMALL ONES.
HELLO, DEMON.
THEY *SAID* THE BLOOD WOULD BRING YOU TO ME.

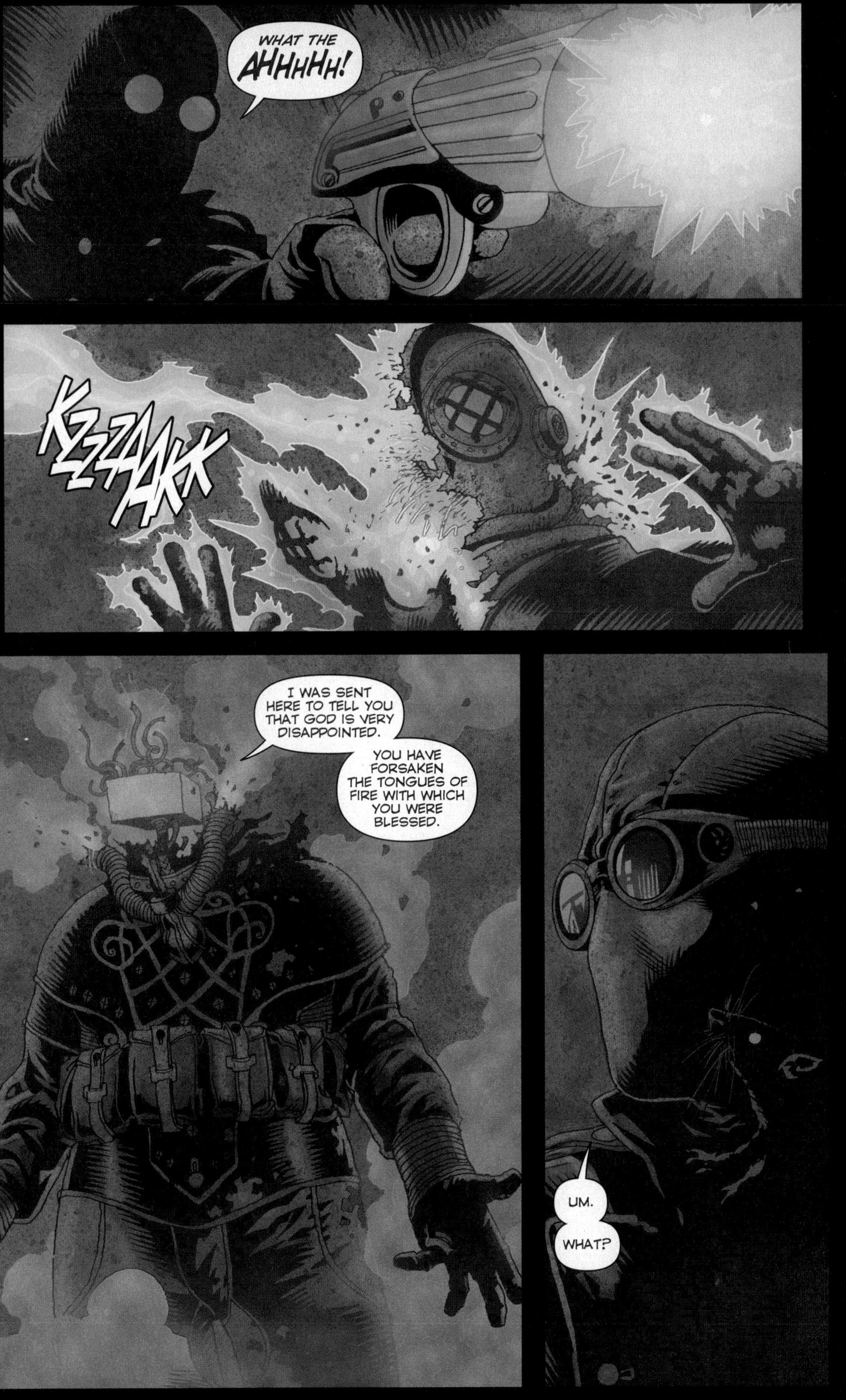

WHAT THE AHHHHH!
KZZZAAKK
I WAS SENT HERE TO TELL YOU THAT GOD IS VERY DISAPPOINTED.
YOU HAVE FORSAKEN THE TONGUES OF FIRE WITH WHICH YOU WERE BLESSED.
UM.
WHAT?

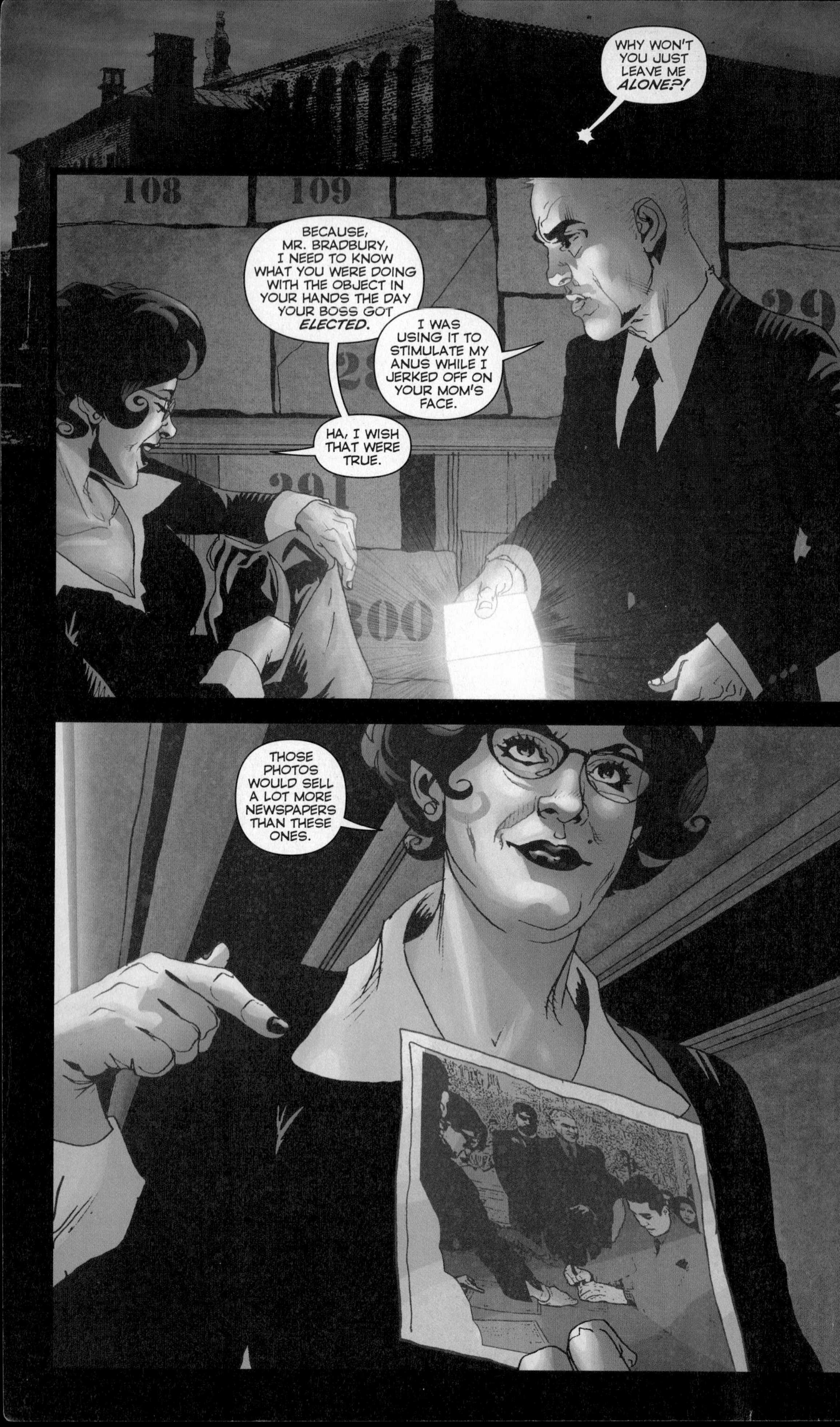
WHY WON'T YOU JUST LEAVE ME ALONE?!
BECAUSE, MR. BRADBURY, I NEED TO KNOW WHAT YOU WERE DOING WITH THE OBJECT IN YOUR HANDS THE DAY YOUR BOSS GOT ELECTED.
I WAS USING IT TO STIMULATE MY ANUS WHILE I JERKED OFF ON YOUR MOM'S FACE.
HA, I WISH THAT WERE TRUE.
THOSE PHOTOS WOULD SELL A LOT MORE NEWSPAPERS THAN THESE ONES.

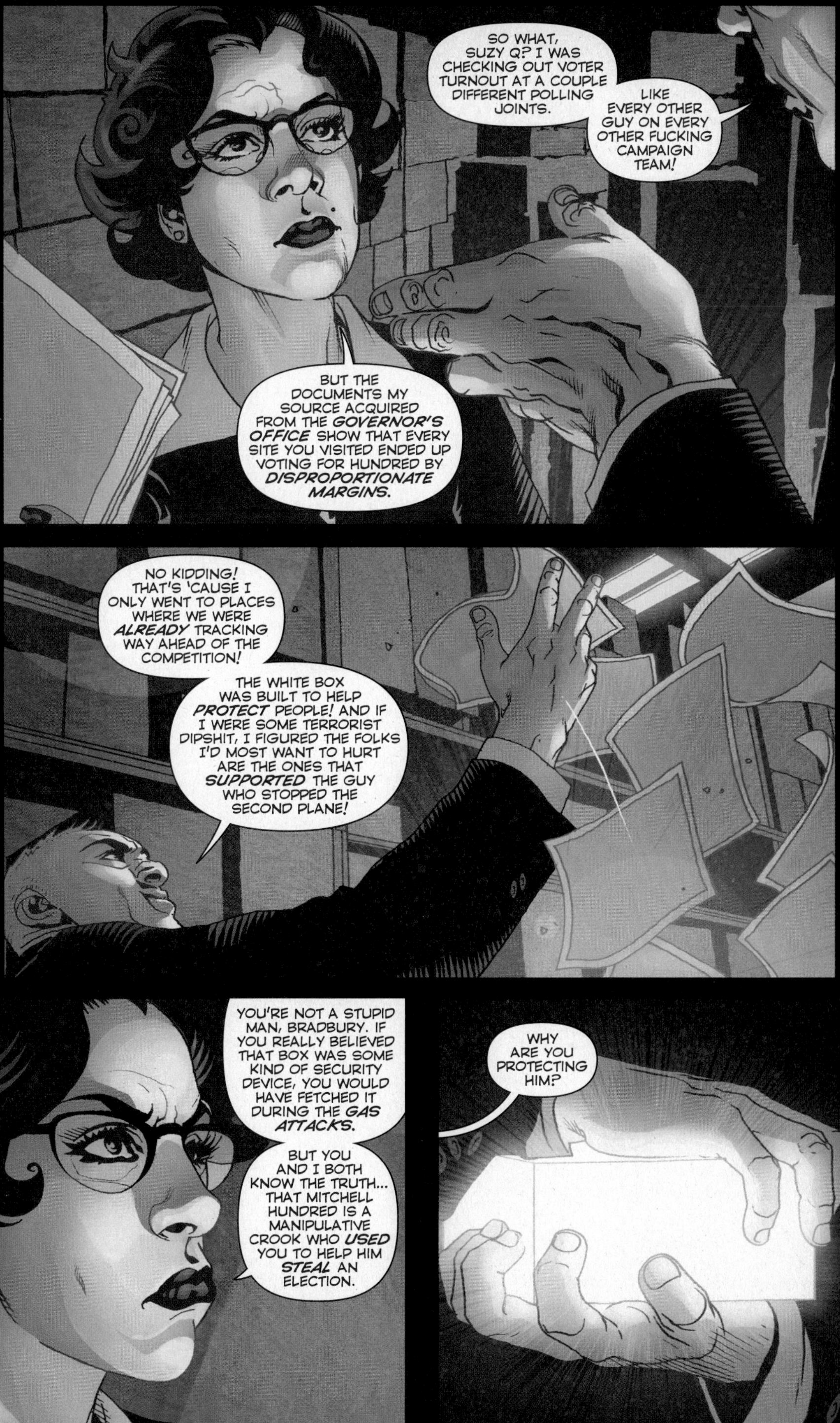
SO WHAT, SUZY Q? I WAS CHECKING OUT VOTER TURNOUT AT A COUPLE DIFFERENT POLLING JOINTS.
LIKE EVERY OTHER GUY ON EVERY OTHER FUCKING CAMPAIGN TEAM!
BUT THE DOCUMENTS MY SOURCE ACQUIRED FROM THE GOVERNOR'S OFFICE SHOW THAT EVERY SITE YOU VISITED ENDED UP VOTING FOR HUNDRED BY DISPROPORTIONATE MARGINS.
NO KIDDING! THAT'S 'CAUSE I ONLY WENT TO PLACES WHERE WE WERE ALREADY TRACKING WAY AHEAD OF THE COMPETITION!
THE WHITE BOX WAS BUILT TO HELP PROTECT PEOPLE! AND IF I WERE SOME TERRORIST DIPSHIT, I FIGURED THE FOLKS I'D MOST WANT TO HURT ARE THE ONES THAT SUPPORTED THE GUY WHO STOPPED THE SECOND PLANE!
YOU'RE NOT A STUPID MAN, BRADBURY. IF YOU REALLY BELIEVED THAT BOX WAS SOME KIND OF SECURITY DEVICE, YOU WOULD HAVE FETCHED IT DURING THE GAS ATTACKS.
BUT YOU AND I BOTH KNOW THE TRUTH... THAT MITCHELL HUNDRED IS A MANIPULATIVE CROOK WHO USED YOU TO HELP HIM STEAL AN ELECTION.
WHY ARE YOU PROTECTING HIM?

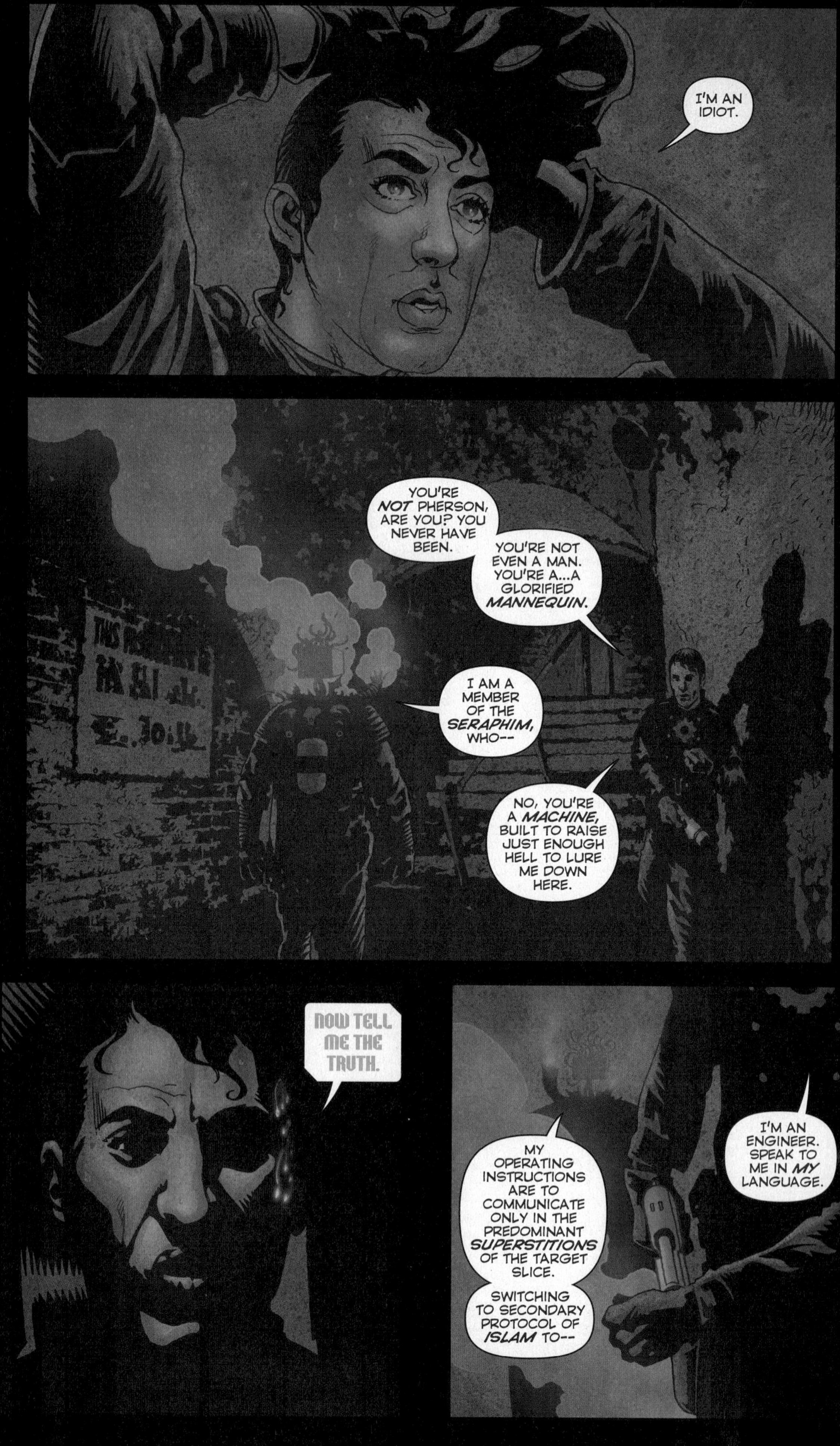

I'M AN IDIOT.
YOU'RE *NOT* PHERSON, ARE YOU? YOU NEVER HAVE BEEN.
YOU'RE NOT EVEN A MAN. YOU'RE A...A GLORIFIED *MANNEQUIN.*
I AM A MEMBER OF THE *SERAPHIM,* WHO--
NO, YOU'RE A *MACHINE,* BUILT TO RAISE JUST ENOUGH HELL TO LURE ME DOWN HERE.
NOW TELL ME THE TRUTH.
MY OPERATING INSTRUCTIONS ARE TO COMMUNICATE ONLY IN THE PREDOMINANT *SUPERSTITIONS* OF THE TARGET SLICE.
SWITCHING TO SECONDARY PROTOCOL OF *ISLAM* TO--
I'M AN ENGINEER. SPEAK TO ME IN *MY* LANGUAGE.

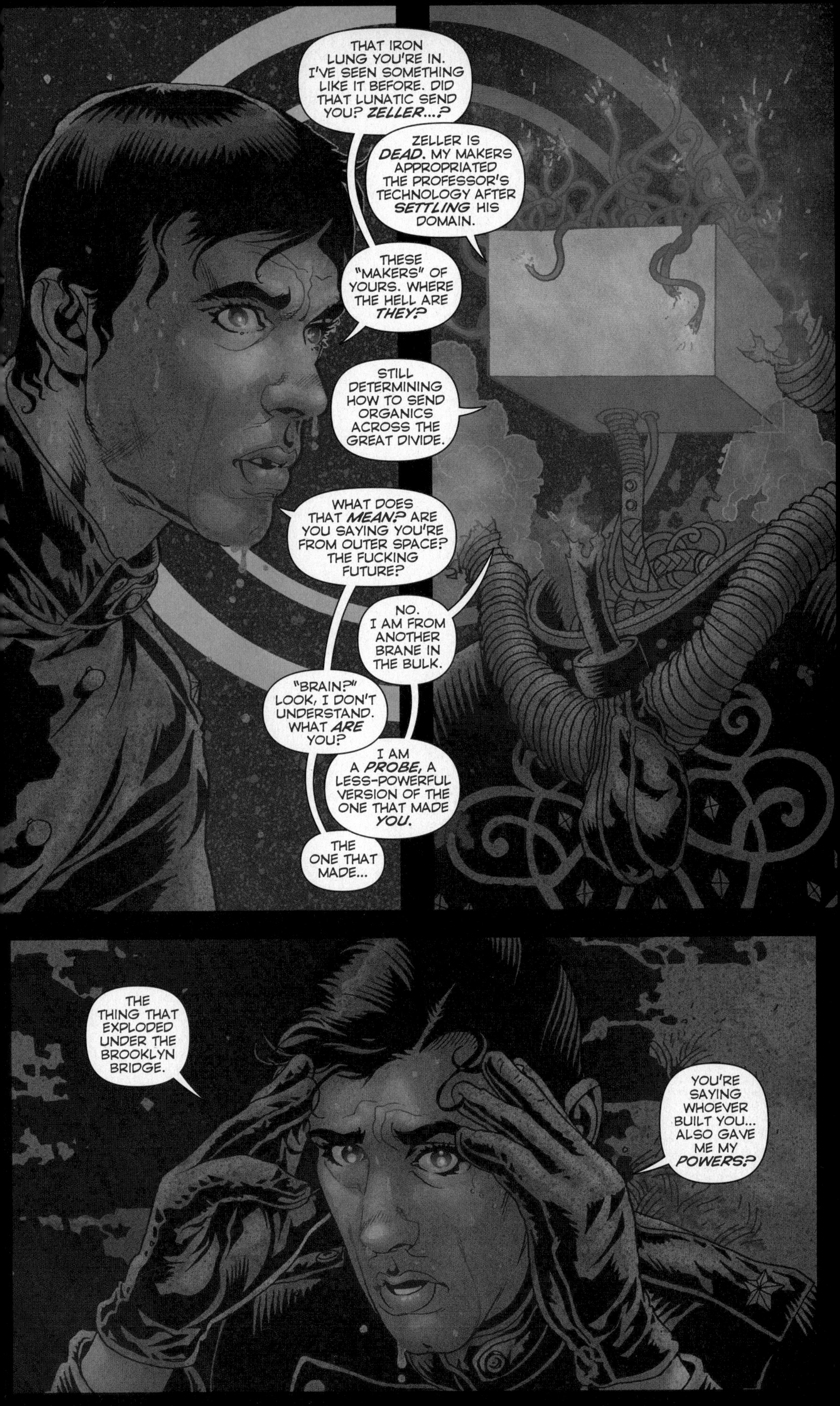
THAT IRON LUNG YOU'RE IN. I'VE SEEN SOMETHING LIKE IT BEFORE. DID THAT LUNATIC SEND YOU? ZELLER...?
ZELLER IS DEAD. MY MAKERS APPROPRIATED THE PROFESSOR'S TECHNOLOGY AFTER SETTLING HIS DOMAIN.
THESE "MAKERS" OF YOURS. WHERE THE HELL ARE THEY?
STILL DETERMINING HOW TO SEND ORGANICS ACROSS THE GREAT DIVIDE.
WHAT DOES THAT MEAN? ARE YOU SAYING YOU'RE FROM OUTER SPACE? THE FUCKING FUTURE?
NO. I AM FROM ANOTHER BRANE IN THE BULK.
"BRAIN?" LOOK, I DON'T UNDERSTAND. WHAT ARE YOU?
I AM A PROBE, A LESS-POWERFUL VERSION OF THE ONE THAT MADE YOU.
THE ONE THAT MADE...
THE THING THAT EXPLODED UNDER THE BROOKLYN BRIDGE.
YOU'RE SAYING WHOEVER BUILT YOU... ALSO GAVE ME MY POWERS?

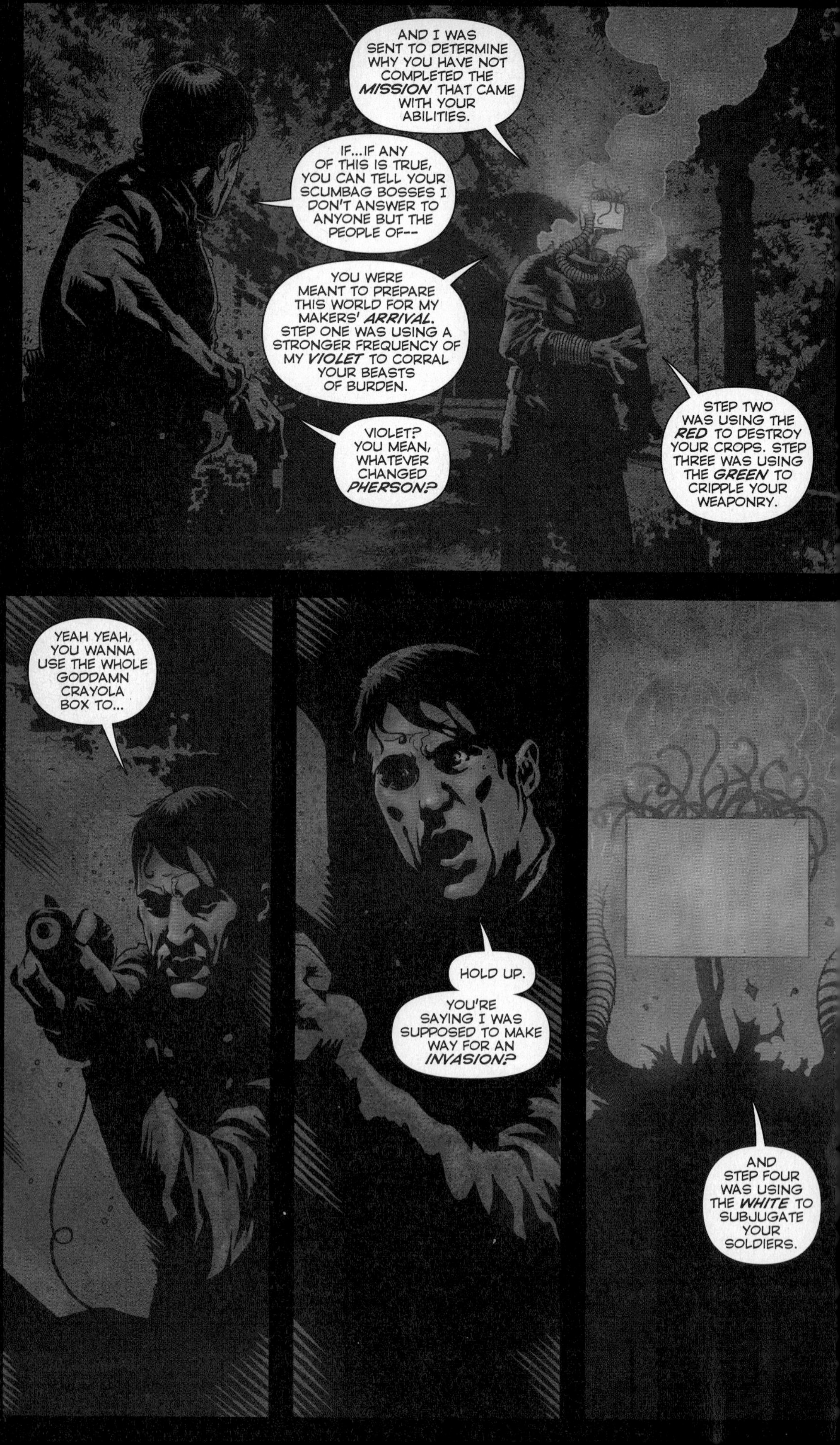
AND I WAS SENT TO DETERMINE WHY YOU HAVE NOT COMPLETED THE *MISSION* THAT CAME WITH YOUR ABILITIES.
IF...IF ANY OF THIS IS TRUE, YOU CAN TELL YOUR SCUMBAG BOSSES I DON'T ANSWER TO ANYONE BUT THE PEOPLE OF--
YOU WERE MEANT TO PREPARE THIS WORLD FOR MY MAKERS' *ARRIVAL.* STEP ONE WAS USING A STRONGER FREQUENCY OF MY *VIOLET* TO CORRAL YOUR BEASTS OF BURDEN.
VIOLET? YOU MEAN, WHATEVER CHANGED *PHERSON?*
STEP TWO WAS USING THE *RED* TO DESTROY YOUR CROPS. STEP THREE WAS USING THE *GREEN* TO CRIPPLE YOUR WEAPONRY.
YEAH YEAH, YOU WANNA USE THE WHOLE GODDAMN CRAYOLA BOX TO...
HOLD UP.
YOU'RE SAYING I WAS SUPPOSED TO MAKE WAY FOR AN *INVASION?*
AND STEP FOUR WAS USING THE *WHITE* TO SUBJUGATE YOUR SOLDIERS.

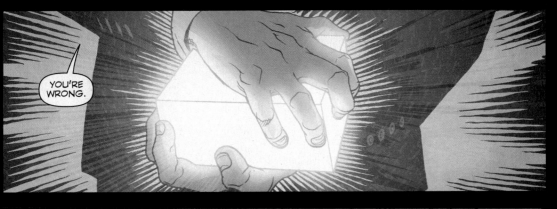

YOU'RE WRONG.

HUNDRED DIDN'T STEAL NOTHING. HE WON BY A GODDAMN LANDSLIDE!

HE WON BY 20,000 VOTES.

IT WAS ONLY CONSIDERED A LANDSLIDE BECAUSE OF HOW FAR BEHIND HE WAS IN THE POLLS AGAINST BOTH GREEN *AND* BLOOMBERG JUST THE DAY BEFORE.

WHATEVER, I GOT NOTHING TO SAY ON THE RECORD.

AND OFF THE RECORD?

I DON'T GIVE A SHIT IF HE RIGGED EVERY VOTE HE GOT.

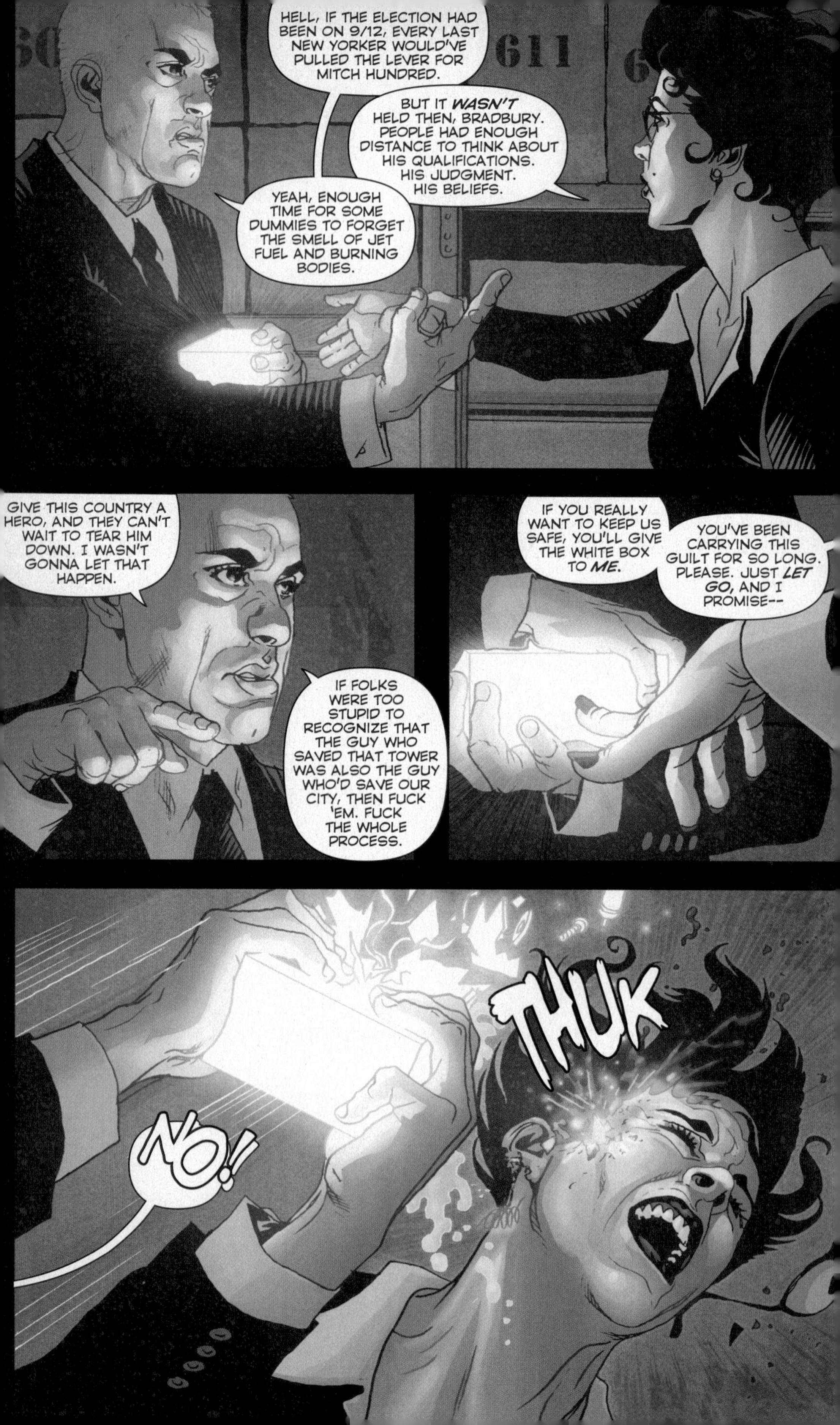

HELL, IF THE ELECTION HAD BEEN ON 9/12, EVERY LAST NEW YORKER WOULD'VE PULLED THE LEVER FOR MITCH HUNDRED.
BUT IT *WASN'T* HELD THEN, BRADBURY. PEOPLE HAD ENOUGH DISTANCE TO THINK ABOUT HIS QUALIFICATIONS. HIS JUDGMENT. HIS BELIEFS.
YEAH, ENOUGH TIME FOR SOME DUMMIES TO FORGET THE SMELL OF JET FUEL AND BURNING BODIES.
GIVE THIS COUNTRY A HERO, AND THEY CAN'T WAIT TO TEAR HIM DOWN. I WASN'T GONNA LET THAT HAPPEN.
IF FOLKS WERE TOO STUPID TO RECOGNIZE THAT THE GUY WHO SAVED THAT TOWER WAS ALSO THE GUY WHO'D SAVE OUR CITY, THEN FUCK 'EM. FUCK THE WHOLE PROCESS.
IF YOU REALLY WANT TO KEEP US SAFE, YOU'LL GIVE THE WHITE BOX TO *ME.*
YOU'VE BEEN CARRYING THIS GUILT FOR SO LONG. PLEASE. JUST *LET GO,* AND I PROMISE--
THUK
NO!!

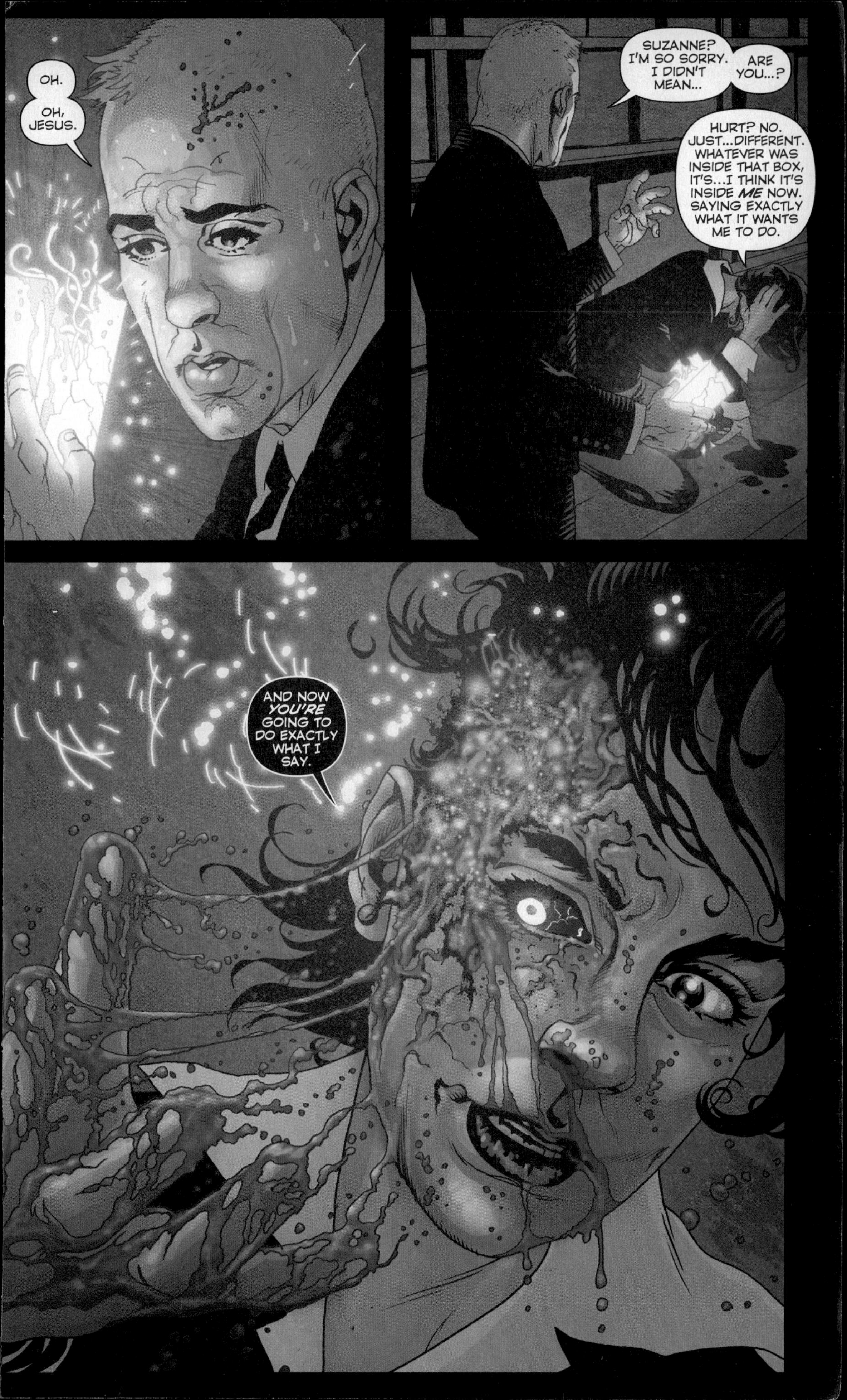
OH.
OH, JESUS.
SUZANNE? I'M SO SORRY. I DIDN'T MEAN...
ARE YOU...?
HURT? NO. JUST...DIFFERENT. WHATEVER WAS INSIDE THAT BOX, IT'S...I THINK IT'S INSIDE ME NOW. SAYING EXACTLY WHAT IT WANTS ME TO DO.
AND NOW YOU'RE GOING TO DO EXACTLY WHAT I SAY.

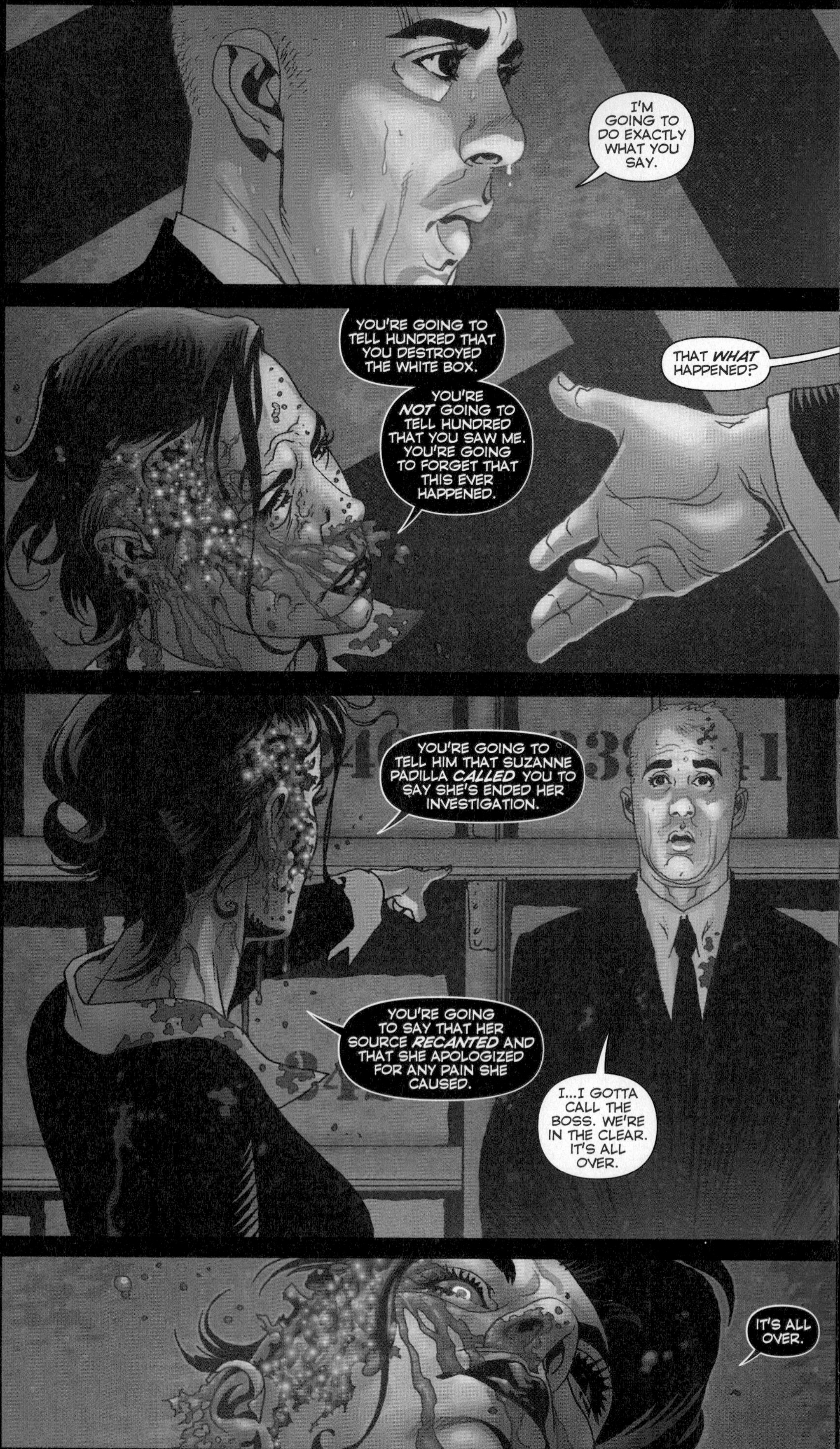
I'M GOING TO DO EXACTLY WHAT YOU SAY.
YOU'RE GOING TO TELL HUNDRED THAT YOU DESTROYED THE WHITE BOX.
YOU'RE *NOT* GOING TO TELL HUNDRED THAT YOU SAW ME. YOU'RE GOING TO FORGET THAT THIS EVER HAPPENED.
THAT *WHAT* HAPPENED?
YOU'RE GOING TO TELL HIM THAT SUZANNE PADILLA *CALLED* YOU TO SAY SHE'S ENDED HER INVESTIGATION.
YOU'RE GOING TO SAY THAT HER SOURCE *RECANTED* AND THAT SHE APOLOGIZED FOR ANY PAIN SHE CAUSED.
I...I GOTTA CALL THE BOSS. WE'RE IN THE CLEAR. IT'S ALL OVER.
IT'S ALL OVER.

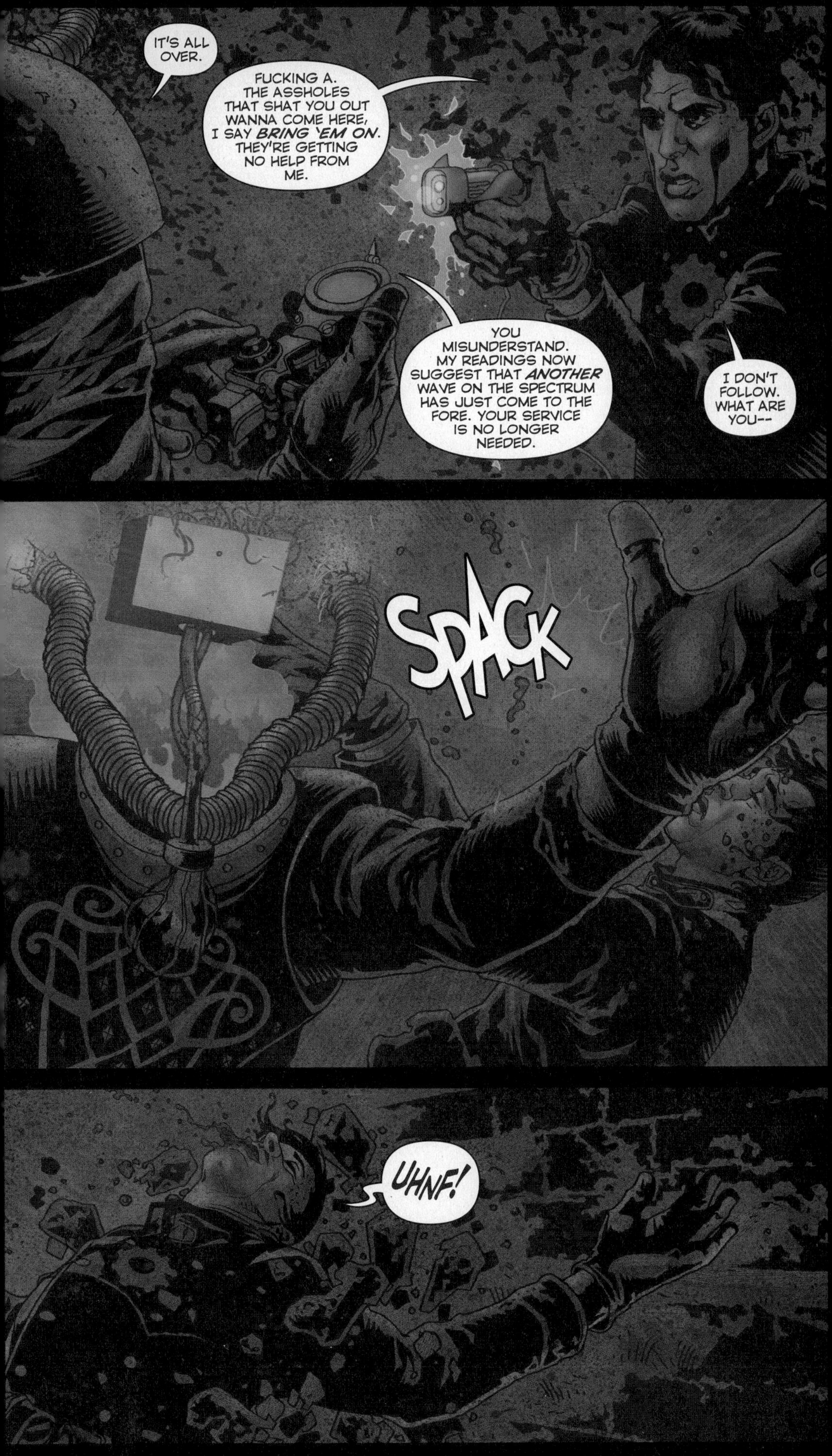
IT'S ALL OVER.
FUCKING A. THE ASSHOLES THAT SHAT YOU OUT WANNA COME HERE, I SAY BRING 'EM ON. THEY'RE GETTING NO HELP FROM ME.
YOU MISUNDERSTAND. MY READINGS NOW SUGGEST THAT ANOTHER WAVE ON THE SPECTRUM HAS JUST COME TO THE FORE. YOUR SERVICE IS NO LONGER NEEDED.
I DON'T FOLLOW. WHAT ARE YOU--
SPACK
UHNF!

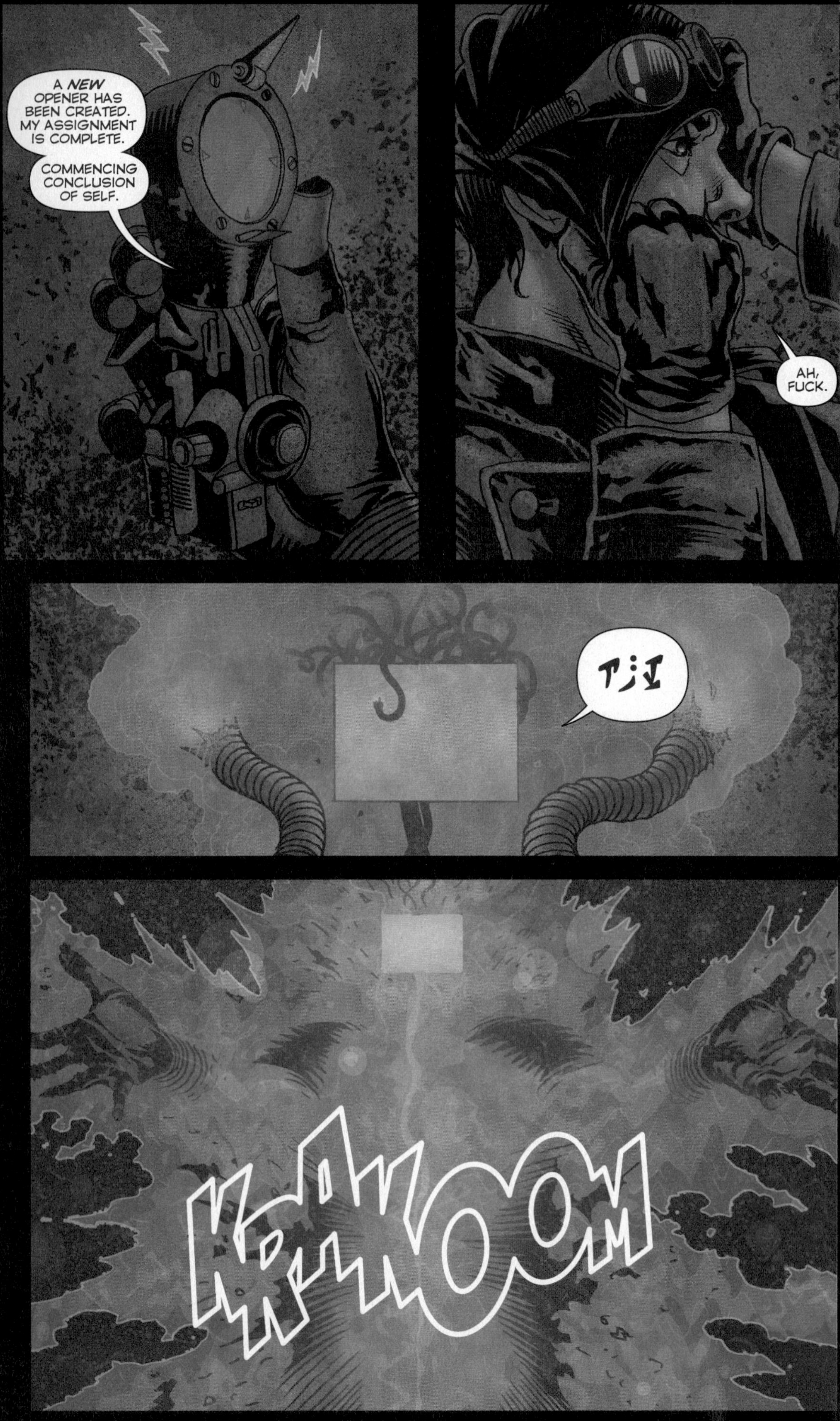
A NEW OPENER HAS BEEN CREATED. MY ASSIGNMENT IS COMPLETE.
COMMENCING CONCLUSION OF SELF.
AH, FUCK.
KRAKOOM

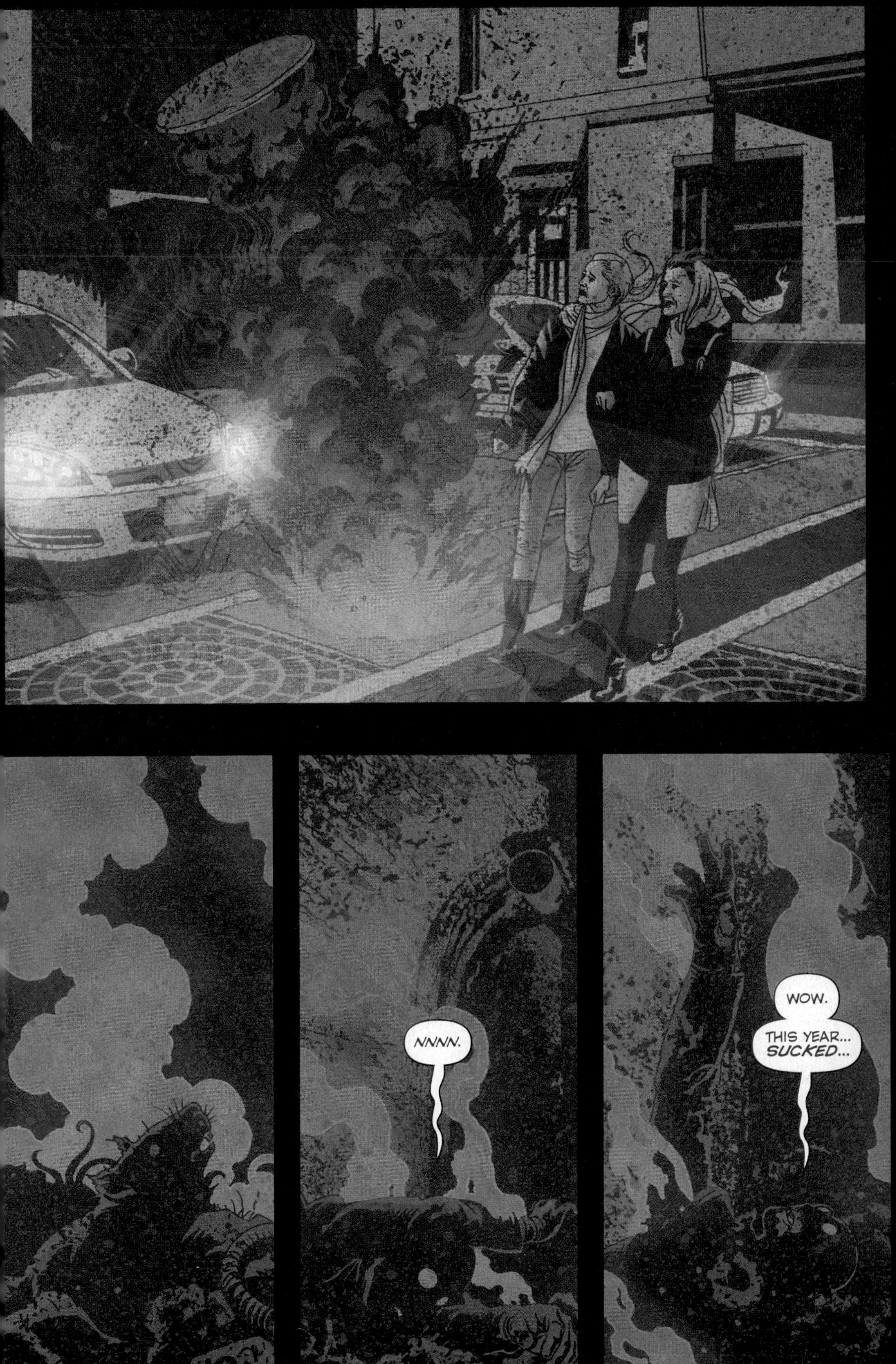
NNNN.
WOW.
THIS YEAR... SUCKED...

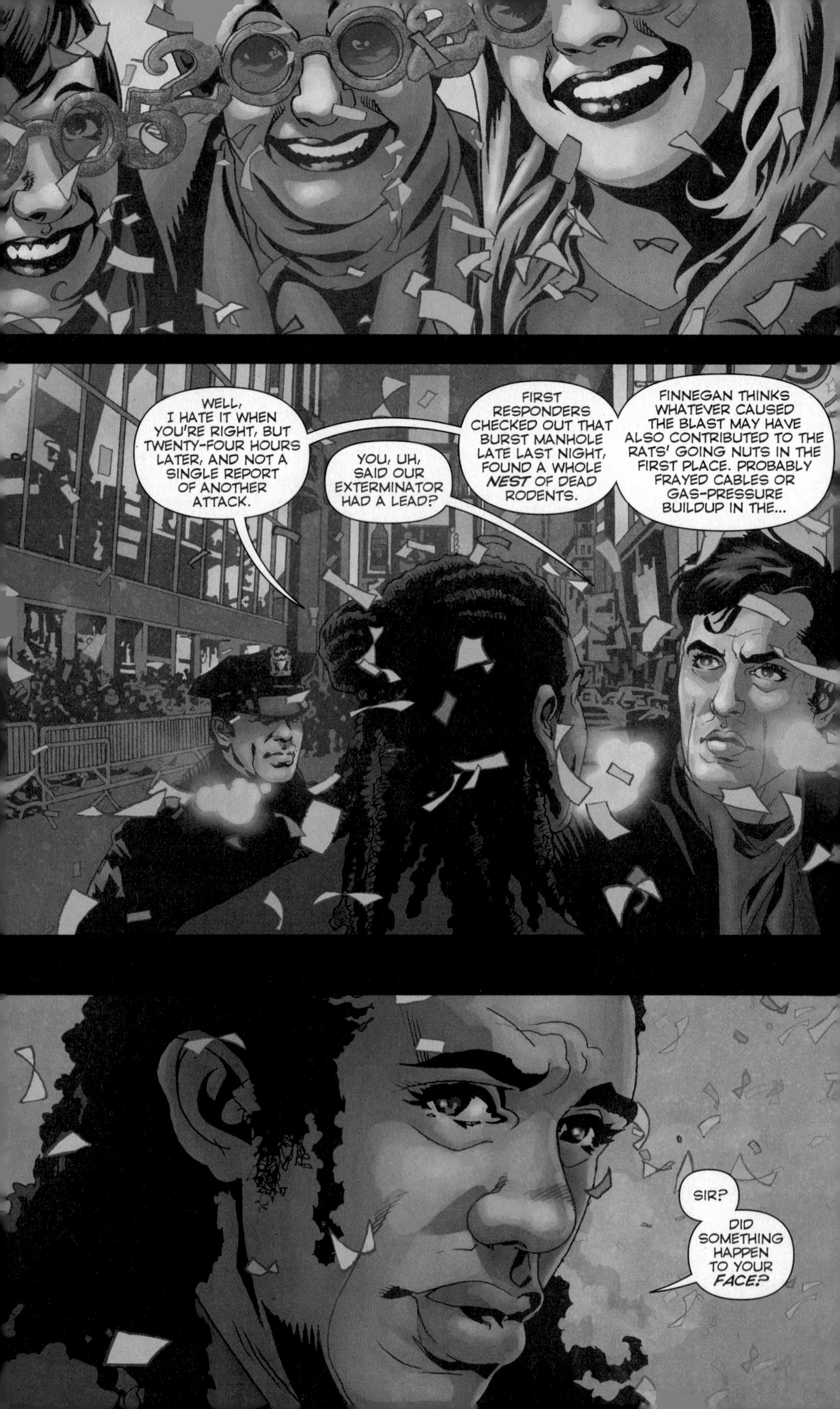
WELL, I HATE IT WHEN YOU'RE RIGHT, BUT TWENTY-FOUR HOURS LATER, AND NOT A SINGLE REPORT OF ANOTHER ATTACK.
FIRST RESPONDERS CHECKED OUT THAT BURST MANHOLE LATE LAST NIGHT, FOUND A WHOLE *NEST* OF DEAD RODENTS.
YOU, UH, SAID OUR EXTERMINATOR HAD A LEAD?
FINNEGAN THINKS WHATEVER CAUSED THE BLAST MAY HAVE ALSO CONTRIBUTED TO THE RATS' GOING NUTS IN THE FIRST PLACE. PROBABLY FRAYED CABLES OR GAS-PRESSURE BUILDUP IN THE...
SIR?
DID SOMETHING HAPPEN TO YOUR *FACE?*

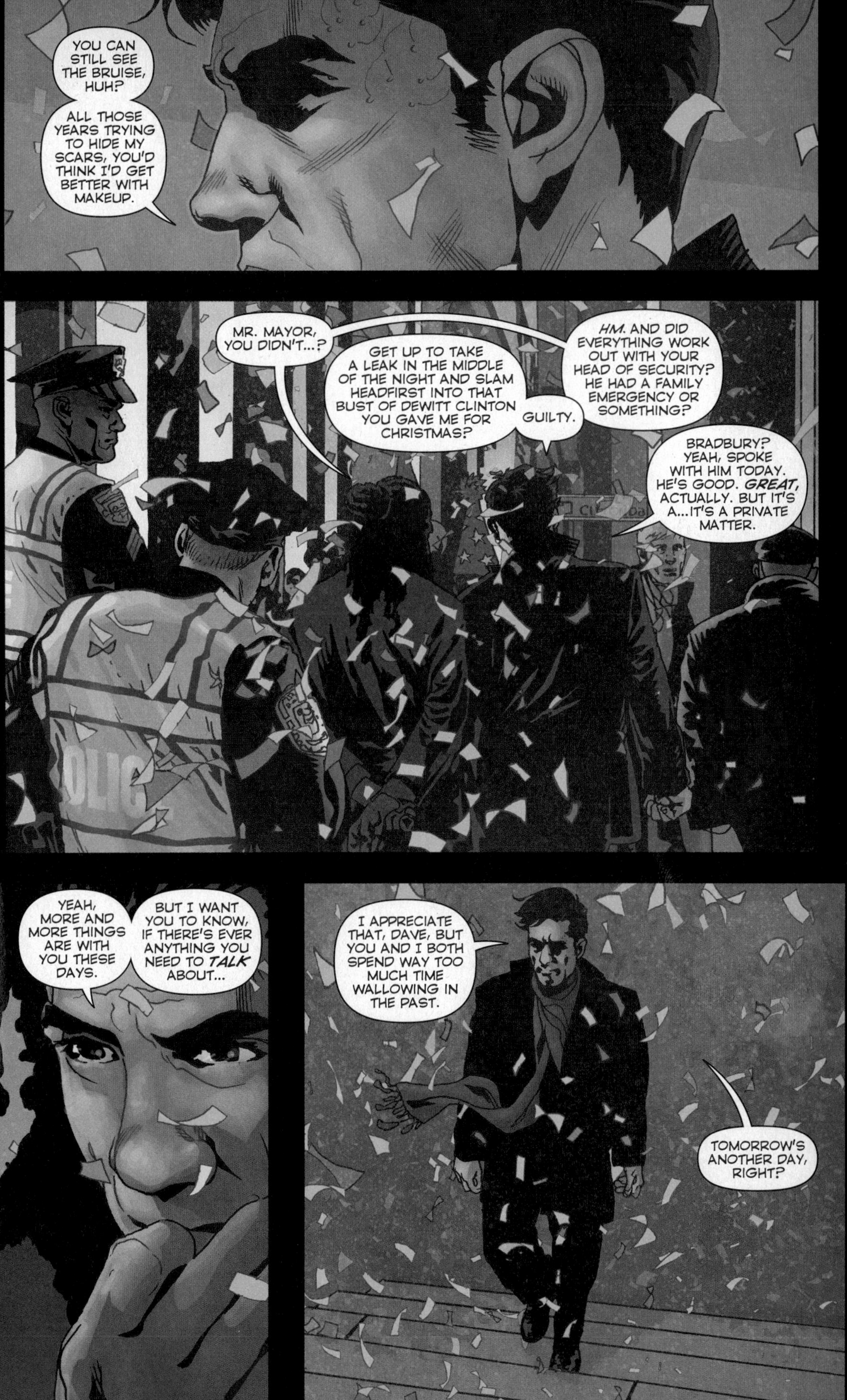
YOU CAN STILL SEE THE BRUISE, HUH?
ALL THOSE YEARS TRYING TO HIDE MY SCARS, YOU'D THINK I'D GET BETTER WITH MAKEUP.
MR. MAYOR, YOU DIDN'T...?
GET UP TO TAKE A LEAK IN THE MIDDLE OF THE NIGHT AND SLAM HEADFIRST INTO THAT BUST OF DEWITT CLINTON YOU GAVE ME FOR CHRISTMAS?
GUILTY.
HM. AND DID EVERYTHING WORK OUT WITH YOUR HEAD OF SECURITY? HE HAD A FAMILY EMERGENCY OR SOMETHING?
BRADBURY? YEAH, SPOKE WITH HIM TODAY. HE'S GOOD. ***GREAT,*** ACTUALLY. BUT IT'S A...IT'S A PRIVATE MATTER.
YEAH, MORE AND MORE THINGS ARE WITH YOU THESE DAYS.
BUT I WANT YOU TO KNOW, IF THERE'S EVER ANYTHING YOU NEED TO ***TALK*** ABOUT...
I APPRECIATE THAT, DAVE, BUT YOU AND I BOTH SPEND WAY TOO MUCH TIME WALLOWING IN THE PAST.
TOMORROW'S ANOTHER DAY, RIGHT?

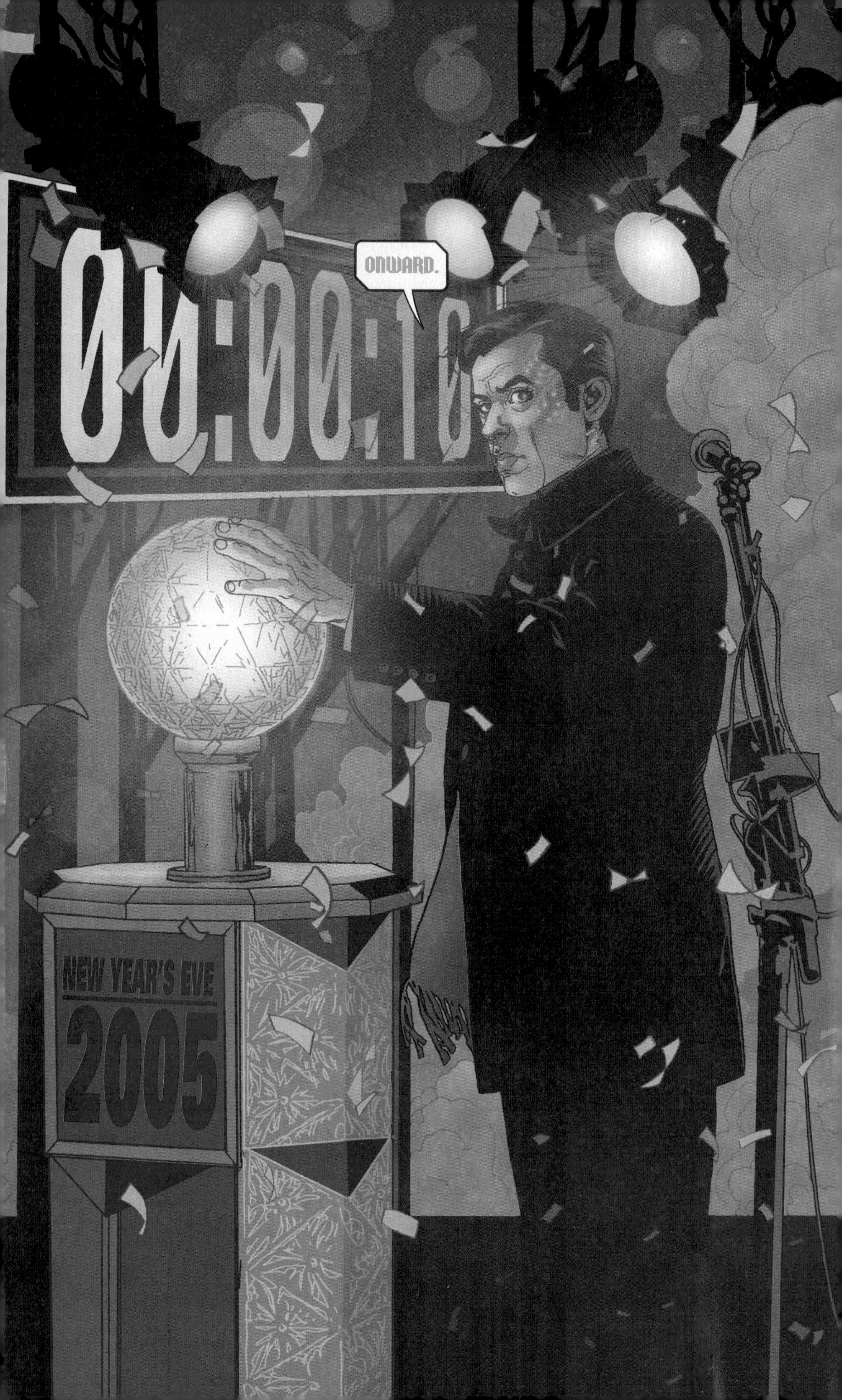
ONWARD.
NEW YEAR'S EVE
2005

Easily one of the most entertaining stories I've read in 2008." -IGN

EX MACHINA

BRIAN K. VAUGHAN with TONY HARRIS

EX MACHINA is half *X-Files*, half *West Wing* and 100% genius." – PUBLISHERS WEEKLY (STARRED REVIEW)

"Nominated for multiple Eisners and for the Harvey Award for Best New Series, this is a genuine hit."– LIBRARY JOURNAL

EX MACHINA Book 1: THE FIRST HUNDRED DAYS
EX MACHINA Book 2: TAG
EX MACHINA Book 3: FACT V. FICTION
EX MACHINA Book 4: MARCH TO WAR
EX MACHINA Book 5: SMOKE SMOKE
EX MACHINA Book 6: POWER DOWN
EX MACHINA Book 7: EX CATHEDRA
EX MACHINA Book 8: DIRTY TRICKS
EX MACHINA Book 9: RING OUT THE OLD
EX MACHINA Book 10: TERM LIMITS -November 2010

EX MACHINA
THE FIRST HUNDRED DAYS
BRIAN K. VAUGHAN
TONY HARRIS
TOM FEISTER

SUGGESTED FOR MATURE READERS

BATMAN:
FALSE FACES

Author of Y: THE LAST MAN and PRIDE OF BAGHDAD
BRIAN K. VAUGHAN
SCOTT McDANIEL RICK BURCHETT SCOTT KOLINS
BATMAN
FALSE FACES

Vaughan • McDaniel
Burchett • Kolins

STARMAN OMNIBUS
Books 1-3

STARMAN
OMNIBUS
JAMES ROBINSON TONY HARRIS WADE VON GRAWBADGER

Robinson • Harris

Y: THE LAST MAN
Books 1-10

Y
"The year's best movie is a comic book."
Brian K. Vaughan
Pia Guerra
THE LAST MAN
Kimono Dragons

Vaughan • Guerra
Various

SEARCH THE GRAPHIC NOVELS SECTION OF
WILDSTORM.COM
FOR ART AND INFORMATION ON ALL OF OUR BOOKS!

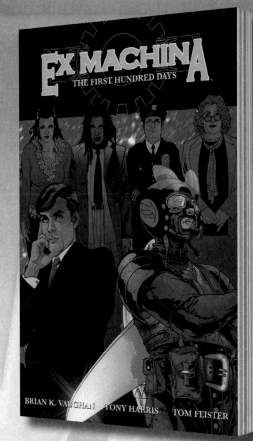

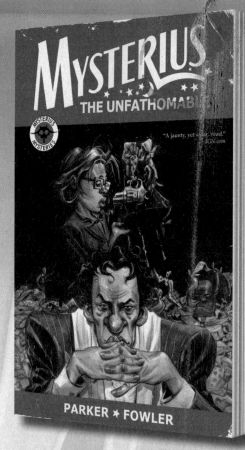